Unique features and highlights:

- Easy-to-follow *pronunciation keys* and complete phonetic transcriptions for all words and phrases in the book.
- Useful phrases for the *tourist*, grouped together by subject matter in a logical way so that the appropriate phrase is easy to locate when you need it.
- Thorough section on *food and drink*, with comprehensive food terms you will find on menus; these terms are often difficult or impossible to locate in dictionaries, but our section gives you a description of the preparation as well as a definition of what it is.
- *Emergency phrases* and terms you hope you won't need: legal complications, medical problems, theft or loss of valuables, replacement or repair of watches, camera, and the like.
- *Sightseeing itineraries*, shopping tips, practical travel tips, and regional food specialties to help you get off the beaten path and into the countryside, to the small towns and cities, and to the neighboring areas.

Enjoy your vacation and travel with confidence. You have a friend by your side.

THE TRAVELER'S PHRASE BOOK

A COMPENDIUM OF COMMONLY USED PHRASES IN FRENCH, GERMAN, ITALIAN AND SPANISH

BY

MARIO COSTANTINO, M.A.

GAIL STEIN, M.A.

HENRY STRUTZ, M.A.

HEYWOOD WALD, Ph.D.

Coordinating Editor (French and Italian)
HEYWOOD WALD, Ph.D.

BARRON'S EDUCATIONAL SERIES, INC.
New York ■ London ■ Toronto ■ Sydney

Cover and Book Design   Milton Glaser, Inc.

© Copyright 1985 by Barron's Educational Series, Inc.

Portions of this book from:
French At a Glance
German At a Glance
Italian At a Glance
Spanish At a Glance

All inquiries should be addressed to:
Barron's Educational Series, Inc.
250 Wireless Boulevard
Hauppauge, New York 11788

Library of Congress Catalog Card No. 84-28219

International Standard Book No. 0-8120-3558-5

Library of Congress Cataloging in Publication Data
Main entry under title:

The Traveler's phrase book.

    1. Languages, Modern—Conversation and phrase books.
I. Costantino, Mario.
PB73.T7   1985   418   84-28219
ISBN 0-8120-3558-5 (pbk.)

PRINTED IN THE UNITED STATES OF AMERICA
9012   900   98

CONTENTS

FRENCH

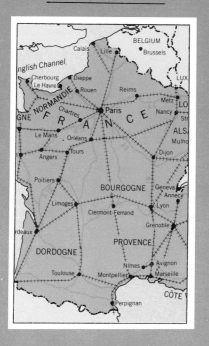

QUICK PRONUNCIATION GUIDE

CONSONANTS

In French, final consonants are usually silent, except for final C, R, F, and L (as in CaReFuL), which are usually pronounced.

FRENCH LETTER	ENGLISH SOUND	SYMBOL	EXAMPLE
b, d, f, k, l, m, n,	same as English		
p, s, t, v, z	same as English		
c (before e, i, y)	SS (S at beginning of word)	S	cigare *see-gahr*
ç (before a, o, u)	SS (S at beginning of word)	S	garçon *gahr-ssohn*
c (before a, o, u)	K	K	comme *kohm*
g (before e, i, y)	S as in plea<u>s</u>ure	ZH	rouge *roozh*
ge (before a, o)	S as in plea<u>s</u>ure	ZH	mangeons *mahn-zhohn*
g (before a, o, u)	G	G	gant *gahn*
gn	nuyh as in o<u>ni</u>on	NY	oignon *oh-nyohn*
h	always silent		hôtel *oh-tehl*
j	S as in plea<u>s</u>ure	ZH	je *zhuh*
qu, final q	K	K	cinq *sank*
r	Roll the R at the top back of the mouth as if you were gargling or spitting.	R	rue *rew*
ss	S	SS	poisson *pwah-ssohn*
s	beginning of word	S	six *sees*

FRENCH LETTER	ENGLISH SOUND	SYMBOL	EXAMPLE
s	next to consonant	SS	disque *deessk*
s	between vowels	Z	poison *pwah-zohn*
th	T	T	thé *tay*
x	S in these words only	SS	six *seess*, dix *deess*, soixante *swah-ssahnt*
x	X	KSS	excellent *ehkss-eh-lahn*

VOWELS

FRENCH LETTER	ENGLISH SOUND	SYMBOL	EXAMPLE
a, à, â	A as in yacht or A in after	AH	la *lah*
é, final er, final ez, et	A as in day	AY	musée *mew-zay*
e+2 consonants e+final pronounced consonant e, ê, è	E as in ever	EH	sept *seht*
e	sometimes like E of early with no R sound	UH	le *luh*
i (î), y	EE as in meet	EE	île *eel*
i+ vowel or ll	Y as in yes	EE	famille *fah-mee*
o+final pronounced consonant	O as in for	OH	homme *ohm*
o, o before se, o last sound in word, au, eau	O as in open	OH	au *oh*
ou	OO as in tooth	OO	où *oo*

FRENCH LETTER	ENGLISH SOUND	SYMBOL	EXAMPLE
oy, oi	WA as in watch	WAH	trois *trwah*
U	There is none. Round lips and say E and U at same time.	EW	du *dew*
U + vowel	WEE as in wee	WEE	huit *weet*

NASAL SOUNDS

Nasal sounds are produced through the mouth and the nose at the same time. Nasal sounds occur when N or M follow a vowel in the same syllable. There is NO nasal sound for VOWEL + NN, VOWEL + MM, VOWEL + N + VOWEL, VOWEL + M + VOWEL. NOTE: n̲ means there is a nasalized pronunciation of the "N" sound. The tip of the tongue does not touch the roof of the mouth.

FRENCH LETTER	ENGLISH SOUND	SYMBOL	EXAMPLE
AN, AM, EN, EM	similar to on	AH̲N	France *Frahn̲ss*
IN, IM, AIN, AIM	similar to an	AN̲	pain *pan̲*
IEN	similar to yan of Yankee	YAN̲	bien *byan̲*
ON, OM	similar to on of long.	OH̲N	bon *bohn̲*
UN, UM	similar to un of under.	UH̲N	un *uhn̲*

LIAISON

Liaison means linking. In French, the final consonant of a word is usually not pronounced. Sometimes, however, when the final consonant of one word is followed by a beginning vowel or "H" of the next word, liaison occurs.

EXAMPLE:

Nous arrivons. *noo zah-ree-vohn̲*

THE BASICS FOR GETTING BY

MOST FREQUENTLY USED EXPRESSIONS

yes	**oui**	*wee*
no	**non**	*nohn*
maybe	**peut-être**	*puh-teh-truh*
please	**s'il vous plaît**	*seel voo pleh*
thank you very much	**merci beaucoup**	*mehr-ssee boh-koo*
you're welcome	**de rien**	*duh ryan*
	Je vous en prie	*zhuh voo zahn pree*
Excuse me.	**Excusez-moi.**	*ehkss-kew-zay mwah*
	Pardon	*pahr-dohn*
I'm sorry.	**Je suis désolé(e).**	*zhuh swee day-zoh-lay*
Just a second.	**Un moment.**	*uhn moh-mahn*
That's all right, O.K.	**Ça va.**	*sah-vah*
	D'accord.	*dah-kohr*
	Bien entendu.	*byan nahn-tahn-dew*
It doesn't matter.	**Ça ne fait rien.**	*sah nuh feh ryan*
Good morning (afternoon).	**Bonjour.**	*bohn-zhoor*
Good evening (night).	**Bonsoir.**	*bohn-swahr*
	Bonne nuit.	*bohn nwee*
Sir	**Monsieur**	*muh-ssyuh*
Madame	**Madame**	*mah-dahm*
Miss	**Mademoiselle**	*mahd-mwah-zehl*
Good-bye.	**Au revoir.**	*oh ruh-vwahr.*

See you later (so long).	**À tout à l'heure.** *ah toot ah luhr.*
See you tomorrow.	**À demain.** *ah duh-man*
Do you speak English?	**Parlez-vous anglais?** *pahr-lay voo ahn-gleh*
I speak a little French.	**Je parle un peu le français.** *zhuh pahrl uhn puh luh frahn-sseh*
Do you understand?	**Comprenez-vous? (Vous comprenez?)** *voo kohn-pruh-nay (voo kohn-pruh-nay)*
I understand.	**Je comprends.** *zhuh kohn-prahn*
I don't understand.	**Je ne comprends pas.** *zhuh nuh kohn-prahn pah*
What did you say?	**Qu'est-ce que vous avez dit?** *kehss kuh voo zah-vay dee*
How do you say ____ in French?	**Comment dit-on ____ en français?** *koh-mahn dee tohn ____ ahn frahn-sseh*
What does this (that) mean?	**Que veut dire ceci (cela)?** *kuh vuh deer suh-see (suh-lah)*
Please repeat.	**Répétez, s'il vous plaît.** *Ray-pay-tay, seel voo pleh*
My name is ____.	**Je m'appelle ____.** *zhuh mah-pehl*
What's your name?	**Comment vous appelez-vous?** *koh-mahn voo zah-play voo*
How are you?	**Comment allez-vous?** *koh-mahn tah-lay voo*
How's everything?	**Comment ça va?** *koh-mahn sah vah*
Very well, thanks. And you?	**Très bien, merci. Et vous?** *treh byan mehr-ssee. ay voo*
Where is ____?	**Où est ____?** *oo eh*
the bathroom	**la salle de bains** *lah sahl duh ban*

■ the dining room	**la salle à manger**	*lah sahl ah mah<u>n</u>-zhay*
■ the entrance	**l'entrée**	*lah<u>n</u>-tray*
■ the exit	**la sortie**	*lah sohr-tee*
■ the taxi	**le taxi**	*luh tak-ssee*
■ the telephone	**le téléphone**	*luh tay-lay-fohn*
I'm lost.	**Je suis perdu(e).**	*zhuh swee pehr-dew*
Where are my friends?	**Où sont mes amis?**	*oo soh<u>n</u> may zah-mee*
Which way did they go?	**Par où sont-ils allés?**	*Pahr oo soh<u>n</u> teel zah-lay*
■ to the left	**à gauche**	*ah gohsh*
■ to the right	**à droite**	*ah drwaht*
■ straight ahead	**tout droit**	*too drwah*
How much is it?	**C'est combien?**	*Seh koh<u>n</u>-bya<u>n</u>*
I'd like ____.	**Je voudrais ____.**	*zhuh voo-dreh*
Please bring me ____.	**Apportez-moi, s'il vous plaît ____.**	*ah-pohr-tay mwah seel voo pleh*
I'm hungry.	**J'ai faim.**	*zhay fa<u>n</u>*
I'm thirsty.	**J'ai soif.**	*zhay swahf*
I'm tired.	**Je suis fatigué(e)**	*zhuh swee fah-tee-gay*
What's that?	**Qu'est-ce que c'est?**	*kehss-kuh-seh*
I (don't) know.	**Je (ne) sais (pas).**	*zhuh (nuh) seh (pah)*

QUESTIONS

Where is ____?	**Où est ____?**	*oo eh*
When?	**Quand?**	*kah<u>n</u>*

How much?	**Combien?**	*kohn-byan*
Who?	**Qui?**	*kee*
Why?	**Pourquoi?**	*poor-kwah*
How?	**Comment?**	*koh-mahn*
What?	**Quoi?**	*kwah*

PROBLEMS, PROBLEMS, PROBLEMS

Hurry up!	**Dépêchez-vous!**	*day-peh-shay voo!*
Look!	**Regardez!**	*ruh-gahr-day*
Watch out! Be careful!	**Faites attention!**	*feht zah-tahn-ssyohn*
	Soyez prudent(e)!	*swah-yay prew-dahn (t)*
Listen!	**Écoutez!**	*ay-koo-tay*
Wait!	**Attendez!**	*ah-tahn-day*
I have lost ____.	**J'ai perdu ____.**	*zheh pehr-dew*
Stop bothering me!	**Laissez-moi tranquille!**	*leh-ssay mwah trahn-keel*
Go away!	**Allez-vous-en!**	*ah-lay voo zahn*
Help, police!	**Au secours, police!**	*oh suh-koor, poh-leess*
I'm going to call a cop!	**Ja vais appeler la police!**	*zhuh veh zah-play ʃah poh-leess*
He has stolen ____.	**Il a volé ____.**	*eel ah voh-lay*
▪ my car	**ma voiture**	*mah vwah-tewr*
▪ my passport	**mon passeport**	*mohn pahss-pohr*
▪ my purse	**mon sac**	*mohn sahk*
▪ my suitcase	**ma valise**	*mah vah-leez*

■ my wallet	**mon portefeuille**	*mohn pohr-tuh-fuhy*
■ my watch	**ma montre**	*mah mohn-truh*
I want to go _____.	**Je voudrais aller _____.**	*zhuh voo-dreh zah-lay*
■ to the American consulate	**au consulat américain**	*oh kohn-sew-lah ah-may-ree-kan*
■ to the police station	**au commissariat de police**	*oh kah-mee-ssah-ryah duh poh-leess*
Can you help me, please?	**Pouvez-vous m'aider, s'il vous plaît?**	*poo-vay voo meh-day seel voo pleh*
Does anyone here speak English?	**Y a-t-il quelqu'un ici qui parle anglais?**	*ee ah teel kehl-kuhn ee-ssee kee pahrl ahn-gleh*

NUMBERS

CARDINAL NUMBERS

0	**zéro**	*zay-roh*
1	**un**	*uhn*
2	**deux**	*duh*
3	**trois**	*trwah*
4	**quatre**	*kah-truh*
5	**cinq**	*sank*
6	**six**	*seess*
7	**sept**	*seht*
8	**huit**	*weet*
9	**neuf**	*nuhf*
10	**dix**	*deess*
11	**onze**	*ohnz*

12	**douze**	*dooz*
13	**treize**	*trehz*
14	**quatorze**	*kah-tohrz*
15	**quinze**	*kanz*
16	**seize**	*sehz*
17	**dix-sept**	*dee-seht*
18	**dix-huit**	*dee-zweet*
19	**dix-neuf**	*deez-nuhf*
20	**vingt**	*van*
21	**vingt et un**	*van-tay-uhn*
22	**vingt-deux**	*van-duh*
23	**vingt-trois**	*van-trwah*
24	**vingt-quatre**	*van-kah-truh*
25	**vingt-cinq**	*van-sank*
26	**vingt-six**	*van-seess*
27	**vingt-sept**	*van-seht*
28	**vingt-huit**	*van-tweet*
29	**vingt-neuf**	*van-nuhf*
30	**trente**	*trahnt*
40	**quarante**	*kah-rahnt*
50	**cinquante**	*san-kahnt*
60	**soixante**	*swah-ssahnt*
70	**soixante-dix**	*swah-ssahnt-deess*
71	**soixante et onze**	*swah-ssahn-tay-ohnz*
72	**soixante-douze**	*swah-ssahnt-dooz*
80	**quatre-vingts**	*kah-truh-van*
81	**quatre-vingt-un**	*kah-truh-van-uhn*

90	**quatre-vingt-dix**	*kah-truh-va<u>n</u>-deess*
91	**quatre-vingt-onze**	*kah-truh-va<u>n</u>-ohnz*
100	**cent**	*sah<u>n</u>*
101	**cent un**	*sah<u>n</u>-uh<u>n</u>*
102	**cent deux**	*sah<u>n</u>-duh*
110	**cent dix**	*sah<u>n</u>-deess*
200	**deux cents**	*duh-sah<u>n</u>*
201	**deux cent un**	*duh-sah<u>n</u>-uh<u>n</u>*
330	**trois cent trente**	*trwah-sah<u>n</u>-trah<u>n</u>t*
1000	**mille**	*meel*
1001	**mille un**	*meel-uh<u>n</u>*
1100	**mille cent** / **onze cents**	*meel-sah<u>n</u>* / *ohnz-sah<u>n</u>*

ORDINAL NUMBERS

first	**premier/première (1er)**	*pruh-myay/pruh-myehr*
second	**deuxième (2e)**	*duh-zyehm*
third	**troisième**	*trwah-zyehm*
fourth	**quatrième**	*kah-tree-yehm*
fifth	**cinquième**	*sa<u>n</u>-kyehm*
sixth	**sixième**	*see-zyehm*
seventh	**septième**	*seh-tyehm*
eighth	**huitième**	*wee-tyehm*
ninth	**neuvième**	*nuh-vyehm*
tenth	**dixième**	*dee-zyehm*

WHEN YOU ARRIVE

PASSPORT AND CUSTOMS

My name is ____	**Je m'appelle** ____ *zhuh mah-pehl*
I'm American Canadian, British, Australian.	**Je suis américain(e) canadien(ne), anglais(e), australien(ne).** *zhuh swee zah-may-ree-kahn (kehn) kah-nah-dyan (dyehn), ahn-gleh (glehz), ohs-trah-lyan (yehn)*
My address is ____	**Mon adresse est** ____ *mohn nah-drehss eh*
I'm staying at ____	**Je loge à** ____ *zhuh lohzh ah*
Here is (are) ____.	**Voici** ____. *vwah-ssee*
■ my documents	**mes papiers** *may pah-pyay*
■ my passport	**mon passeport** *mohn pahss-pohr*
■ my identification card	**ma carte d'identité** *mah kahrt dee-dahn-tee-tay*
I'm ____.	**Je suis** ____. *zhuh swee*
■ on a business trip	**en voyage d'affaires** *zahn vwah-yahzh dah-fehr*
■ on vacation	**en vacances** *zahn vah-kahnss*
■ on a visit	**en visite** *zahn vee-zeet*
I'll be staying here ____.	**Je resterai ici** ____. *zhuh rehss-tray ee-ssee*
■ a few days	**quelques jours** *kehl-kuh zhoor*
■ a few weeks	**quelques semaines** *kehl-kuh suh-mehn*
■ a week	**huit jours** *wee zhoor*
■ two weeks	**quinze jours** *kanz zhoor*
■ a month	**un mois** *uhn mwah*

I have nothing to declare.	**Je n'ai rien à déclarer.** *zhuh nay ryan ah day-klah-ray*
I only have a carton of cigarettes.	**J'ai seulement une cartouche de cigarettes.** *zhay suhl-mahn ewn kahr-toosh duh see-gah-reht*
■ a bottle of whisky	**une bouteille de whisky** *ewn boo-tehy duh wheess-kee*
They're gifts.	**Ce sont des cadeaux.** *suh sohn day kah-doh*
They're for my personal use.	**Ils sont pour usage personnel.** *eel sohn poor ew-zazh pehr-soh-nehl*
Do I have to pay duty?	**Dois-je payer des droits de douane?** *dwahzh peh-yay day drwah duh dwahn*

BAGGAGE AND PORTERS

Where can I find a baggage cart?	**Où puis-je trouver un chariot à bagages?** *oo pweezh troo-vay uhn shah-ryoh ah bah-gahzh*
(I need a) porter.	**(Il me faut un) porteur.** *(eel muh foh tuhn) pohr-tuhr*
These are our (my) bags.	**Voici nos (mes) valises.** *vwah-ssee noh (may) vah-leez*

MONEY MATTERS

EXCHANGING MONEY

Where can I (change) _____?	**Où puis-je (changer) _____?** *oo pweezh (shahn-zhay)*
money	**de l'argent** *duh lahr-zhahn*
dollars	**des dollars** *day doh-lahr*

■ travelers' checks	**des chèques de voyage**	*day shehk duh vwah-yahzh*
■ cash a personal check	**toucher un chèque personnel**	*too-shay uhn shehk pehr-soh-nehl*
Where is there a bank?	**Où se trouve une banque?**	*Oo suh troov ewn bahnk*
■ money exchange	**un bureau de change**	*uhn bew-roh duh shahnzh*
At what time do they open (close)?	**À quelle heure ouvre (ferme) -t-on?**	*ah kehl uhr oo-vruh (fehrm) tohn*
Where is the cashier's window?	**Où est la caisse?**	*oo eh la kehss*
What's the current exchange rate?	**Quel est le cours (du change) le plus récent?**	*kehl eh luh koor (dew shahnzh) luh plew ray-sahn*
I'd like to cash this check.	**Je voudrais toucher ce chèque.**	*zhuh voo-dreh too-shay suh shehk*
Where do I sign?	**Où dois-je signer?**	*oo dwahzh see-nyay*
Where do I endorse it?	**Où est-ce que je l'endosse?**	*oo ehss kuh zhuh lahn-dohss*

AT THE HOTEL

CHECKING IN

I'd like a single (double) room for tonight ——.	**Je voudrais une chambre à un lit (à deux lits) pour ce soir ——.**	*zhuh voo-dreh zewn shahn-bruh ah uhn lee (ah duh lee) poor suh swahr*
■ with a shower	**avec douche**	*ah-vehk doosh*
■ with a bath	**avec salle de bains**	*ah-vehk sahl duh ban*

■ with a balcony **avec balcon** *ah-vehk bahl-kohn*

■ facing the ocean **qui donne sur l'océan** *kee dohn sewr loh-ssay-ahn*

■ facing the street **qui donne sur la rue** *kee dohn sewr lah rew*

■ facing the court- **qui donne sur la cour** *kee dohn yard* *sewr lah koor*

Does it have _____? **Y a-t-il _____?** *ee ah teel*

■ air conditioning **la climatisation** *lah klee-mah-tee-zah-ssyohn*

■ hot water **l'eau chaude** *loh shohd*

■ television **une télévision** *ewn tay-lay-vee-zyohn*

■ a private bathroom **une salle de bain privée** *ewn sahl duh ban pree-vay*

■ shower **une douche** *ewn doosh*

I (don't) have a res- **J'ai (Je n'ai pas) retenu une (de) ervation.** **chambre.** *zhay (zhuh nay pah) ruh-tuh-new ewn (duh) shahn-bruh*

Could you call an- **Pourriez-vous appeler un autre other hotel to see if** **hôtel pour voir s'ils ont une cham-they have some-** **bre de libre?** *poo-ree-yay voo zah-play thing?* *uhn noh-truh oh-tehl poor vwahr seel zohn tewn shahn-bruh duh lee-bruh*

May I see the room? **Puis-je voir la chambre?** *pweezh vwahr lah shahn-bruh*

I (don't) like it. **Elle me plaît.** *ehl muh pleh*

Elle ne me plaît pas. *ehl nuh muh pleh pah*

Do you have some- **Avez-vous quelque chose _____?** thing _____? *ah-vay voo kehl-kuh shohz*

■ better **de meilleur** *duh meh-yuhr*

■ larger **de plus grand** *duh plew grahn*

■ smaller	**de plus petit** *duh plew puh-tee*
■ cheaper	**de meilleur marché** *duh meh-yuhr mahr-shay*
On what floor is it?	**C'est à quel étage?** *seht ah kehl ay-tahzh*
Is there an elevator?	**Y a-t-il un ascenseur?** *ee ah teel uhn nah-sahn-suhr*
How much do you charge for ____?	**Quel est le tarif ____?** *kehl eh luh tah-reef*
■ the American plan	**pension complète** *pahn-ssyohn kohn-pleht*
■ bed and breakfast	**petit déjeuner compris** *puh-tee day-zhuh-nay kohn-pree*
■ breakfast and dinner	**en demi-pension** *ahn duh-mee pahn-ssyohn*
■ the room without meals	**pour la chambre sans repas** *poor lah shahn-bruh sahn ruh-pah*
Is everything included?	**Est-ce que tout est compris?** *ehss kuh too teh kohn-pree*
The room is very nice. I'll take it.	**Cette chambre me plaît. Je la prends.** *seht shahn-bruh muh pleh. Zhuh lah prahn*
I prefer a room in the back.	**Je préfère une chambre sur la cour.** *zhuh pray-fehr ewn shahn-bruh sewr lah koor*
Is there a reduction for children?	**Accordez-vous des réductions aux enfants?** *ah-kohr-day voo day ray-dewk-ssyohn oh zahn-fahn*
Could you put another bed in the room?	**Pourriez-vous mettre un autre lit dans la chambre?** *poo-ree-yay voo meh-truh uhn noh-truh lee dahn lah shahn-bruh*
Is there a charge? How much?	**Faut-il payer pour cela? Combien?** *foh teel peh-yay poor suhlah? kohn-byan*

OTHER ACCOMMODATIONS

I'm looking for ____.	**Je cherche** ____. *zhuh shehrsh*
■ a boarding house	**une pension** *ewn pahn-ssyohn*
■ a private house	**une maison particulière** *ewn meh-zohn pahr-tee-kew-lyehr*
I want to rent an apartment.	**Je voudrais louer un appartement.** *zhuh voo-dreh loo-ay uhn nah-pahr-tuh-mahn*
I need a living room, bedroom and kitchen.	**Il me faut un salon, une chambre à coucher et une cuisine.** *eel muh foh uhn sah-lohn, ewn shahn-bruh ah koo-shay ay ewn kwee-zeen*
Do you have a furnished room?	**Avez-vous une chambre meublée? (garnie?)** *ah-vay voo zewn shahn-bruh muh-blay (gahr-nee)*
How much is the rent?	**C'est combien le loyer?** *seh kohn-byan luh lwah-yay*
I'll be staying here for ____.	**Je resterai ici** ____. *zhuh rehss-tray ee-ssee*
■ two weeks	**quinze jours** *kahnz zhoor*
■ one month	**un mois** *uhn mwah*
■ the whole summer	**tout l'été** *too lay-tay*
I want a place that's centrally located near public transportation.	**Je voudrais (avoir) une résidence située au centre de la ville près des transports publics.** *zhuh voo-dreh zah-vwahr ewn ray-zee-dahnss see-tew-ay oh sahn-truh duh lah veel preh deh trahnss-pohr pew-bleek*
Is there a youth hostel around here?	**Y a-t-il une auberge de jeunesse par ici?** *ee ah teel ewn oh-behrzh duh zhuh-nehss preh dee-ssee*

ORDERING BREAKFAST

We'll have breakfast in the room.	**Nous prendrons le petit déjeuner à la chambre.** *noo prahn-drohn luh puh-tee day-zhuh-nay ah lah shahn-bruh*
Please send up ____	**Faites monter ____ s'il vous plaît** *feht mohn-tay seel voo pleh*
■ One (two) coffee(s)	**Un (deux) café(s)** *uhn (duh) kah-fay*
■ Tea	**Un thé** *uhn tay*
■ Chocolate	**Un chocolat** *uhn shoh-koh-lah*
■ A (some) croissant(s)	**Un (des) croissant(s)** *uhn (day) krwah-ssahn*
■ Fruit	**Des fruits** *day frwee*
■ Fruit juice	**Du jus de fruit** *dew zhew duh frwee*
I'll (we'll) eat breakfast in the dining room.	**Je (nous) prendrai (prendrons) le petit déjeuner à la salle à manger.** *zhuh (noo) prahn-dray (prahn-drohn) luh puh-tee day-zhuh-nay ah lah sahl ah mahn-zhay*
We'd like ____	**Nous voudrions ____** *noo voo-dree-yohn*
■ Scrambled (fried) (boiled) eggs	**Des oeufs brouillés (au plat) (à la coque)** *day zuh broo-yay (oh plah) (ah lah kohk)*
■ Toast	**Du pain grillé** *dew pan gree-yay*
■ Jam	**De la confiture** *duh lah kohn-fee-tewr*

HOTEL SERVICE

Where is ____?	**Où est ____?** *oo eh*
■ the dining room	**la salle à manger** *lah sahl ah mahn-zhay*
■ the bathroom	**la salle de bains** *lah sahl duh ban*

■the elevator	**l'ascenseur** *lah-ssah<u>n</u>-ssuhr*
■the phone	**le téléphone** *luh tay-lay-fohn*
What is my room number?	**Quel est le numéro de ma chambre?** *kehl eh luh new-may-roh duh mah shah<u>n</u>-bruh*
May I please have my key?	**Pourrais-je avoir la clef?** *poo-rehzh ah-vwahr lah klay*
I need ____.	**Il me faut ____.** *eel muh foh*
■a bellboy	**un chasseur** *tuh<u>n</u> shah-ssuhr*
■a chambermaid	**une femme de chambre** *tewn fahm duh shah<u>n</u>-bruh*
Please send ____ to my room	**Veuillez envoyer ____ à ma chambre** *vuh-yay ah<u>n</u>-vwah-yay ah mah shah<u>n</u>-bruh*
■breakfast	**le petit déjeuner** *luh puh-tee day-zhuh-nay*
■a towel	**une serviette** *ewn sehr-vyeht*
■a bar of soap	**une savonnette** *ewn sah-voh-neht*
■some hangers	**des cintres** *day sa<u>n</u>-truh*
■a pillow	**un oreiller** *uh<u>n</u> noh-reh-yay*
■a blanket	**une couverture** *ewn koo-vehr-tewr*
■some ice	**de la glace** *duh lah glahss*
■ice cubes	**des glaçons** *day glah-ssoh<u>n</u>*
■some ice water	**de l'eau glacée** *duh loh glah-ssay*
■an ashtray	**un cendrier** *uh<u>n</u> sah<u>n</u>-dree-yay*
■toilet paper	**un rouleau de papier hygiénique** *uh<u>n</u> roo-loh duh pah-pyay ee-zhyay-neek*
■a bottle of mineral water	**une bouteille d'eau minérale** *ewn boo-tehy doh mee-nay-rahl*

■ a reading lamp
une lumière pour lire *ewn lew-myehr poor leer*

■ an electric adaptor
un transformateur *uh<u>n</u> trah<u>n</u>ss-fohr-mah-tuhr*

NOTE: Electrical current is usually 220 volts. A European-style adaptor plug or an adaptable appliance is necessary for electric hair dryers or clocks. Large international hotels may have an adaptor plug at the reception desk, but smaller hotels or pensions are unlikely to be able to provide one.

Just a minute.
Un moment. *uh<u>n</u> moh-mah<u>n</u>*

Come in.
Entrez. *ah<u>n</u>-tray*

Put it on the table.
Mettez-ça sur la table. *meh-tay sah sewr lah tah-bluh*

Will you wake me?
Voulez-vous bien me réveiller? *voo-lay voo bya<u>n</u> muh ray-veh-yay*

Please wake me tomorrow at ____.
Réveillez-moi demain matin à ____, s'il vous plaît. *ray-veh-yay mwah duh-ma<u>n</u> mah-ta<u>n</u> ah seel voo pleh*

There is no ____.
Il n'y a pas ____. *eel nyah pah*

■ running water
d'eau courante *doh koo-rah<u>n</u>t*

■ hot water
d'eau chaude *doh shohd*

■ electricity
d'électricité *day-lehk-tree-ssee-tay*

The ____ doesn't work.
____ ne fonctionne pas. *nuh foh<u>n</u>k-ssyohn pah*

■ air conditioning
le climatiseur *luh klee-mah-tee-zuhr*

■ fan
le ventilateur *luh vah<u>n</u>-tee-lah-tuhr*

■ faucet
le robinet *luh roh-bee-neh*

■ lamp
la lampe *lah lah<u>n</u>p*

■ light
la lumière *lah lew-myehr*

■ radio
la radio *lah rah-dyoh*

■ socket   **la prise de courant** *lah preez duh koo-rahn*

■ switch   **le commutateur** *luh koh-mew-tah-tuhr*

■ television   **la télévision** *lah tay-lay-vee-zyohn*

Can you fix it?   **Pouvez-vous la réparer** *poo-vay voo lah ray-pah-ray*

■ now   **maintenent** *mant-nahn*

■ as soon as possible   **aussitôt que possible** *oh-ssee-toh kuh poh-ssee-bluh*

The room is dirty.   **La chambre est sale.** *lah shahn-bruh eh sahl*

Are there any ____ for me?   **Y a-t-il ____ pour moi.** *ee ah teel poor mwah*

■ letters   **des lettres** *day leh-truh*

■ messages   **des messages** *day meh-ssahzh*

■ packages   **des colis** *day koh-lee*

■ post cards   **des cartes postales** *day kahrt pohss-tahl*

Did anyone call for me?   **Est-ce que quelqu'un m'a téléphoné?** *ehss kuh kehl kuhn mah tay-lay-foh-nay*

Who is it?   **Qui est-ce?** *kee ehss*

Can you make a phone call for me?   **Pouvez-vous faire un appel téléphonique pour moi?** *poo-vay voo fehr uhn ah-pehl tay-lay-foh-neek poor mwah*

I'd like to put this in the hotel safe.   **Je voudrais mettre ceci dans le coffre-fort de l'hôtel.** *zhuh voo-dreh meh-truh ssuh-ssee dahn luh koh-fruh-fohr duh loh-tehl*

CHECKING OUT

I'd like the bill, please.	**Je voudrais l'addition, s'il vous plaît.** *zhuh voo-dreh lah-dee-ssyoh<u>n</u> seel voo pleh*
I'm leaving today (tomorrow).	**Je pars aujourd'hui (demain).** *zhuh pahr oh-zhoor-dwee (duh-ma<u>n</u>)*
Please send someone up for the baggage.	**Faites monter quelqu'un pour les valises, s'il vous plaît.** *feht moh<u>n</u>-tay kehl-kuh<u>n</u> poor lay vah-leez seel voo pleh*

GETTING AROUND TOWN

THE SUBWAY

Where is there a subway station?	**Où se trouve une station de métro?** *oo suh troov ewn stah-ssyoh<u>n</u> duh may-troh*
How much is the fare?	**Quel est le prix du trajet?** *kehl eh luh pree dew trah-zheh*
Where can I buy a ticket?	**Où puis-je acheter un billet?** *oo pweezh ahsh-tay uh<u>n</u> bee-yeh*
Which line goes to ____?	**Quelle ligne va à ____?** *kehl lee-nyuh vah ah*
What's the next station?	**Quelle est la prochaine station?** *kehl eh lah proh-shehn stah-ssyoh<u>n</u>*
Where should I get off to go to ____?	**Où dois-je descendre pour aller à ____?** *oo dwahzh day-sah<u>n</u>-druh poor ah-lay ah*
Do I have to change?	**Faut-il prendre une correspondance?** *foh teel prah<u>n</u>-druh ewn koh-rehss-poh<u>n</u>-dah<u>n</u>ss*

Please tell me when we get there.	**S'il vous plaît, dites-moi quand nous y arriverons.** *seel voo pleh, deet mwah kahn noo zee ah-ree-vrohn*

Défense de cracher	No spitting

THE BUS (STREETCAR, TRAM)

Défense de parler au conducteur	Do not speak to the driver

Where is the bus stop? (bus terminal)?	**Où est l'arrêt de bus?/le terminus?** *oo eh lah-reh dew bewss/luh tehr-mee-newss*
In which direction do I have to go?	**Dans quel sens dois-je aller?** *dahn kehl sahnss dwahzh ah-lay*
How often do the buses run?	**Quelle est la fréquence des bus?** *kehl eh lah fray-kahnss day bewss*
Do you go to ____?	**Est-ce que vous allez à ____?** *ehss kuh voo zah-lay ah*
I want to go to ____.	**Je voudrais aller à ____.** *zhuh voo-dreh zah-lay ah*
Is it far from here?	**C'est loin d'ici?** *seh lwan dee-ssee*
How many stops are there?	**Il y a combien d'arrêts?** *eel yah kohn-byan dah-reh*
Do I have to change?	**Faut-il changer de bus?** *foh teel shahn-zhay duh bewss*
How much is the fare?	**Quel est le prix du trajet?** *kehl eh luh pree dew trah-zheh*
Where do I get off?	**Où dois-je descendre?** *oo dwahzh day-sahn-druh*

TAXIS

Is there a taxi stand around here?	**Y a-t-il une station de taxis près d'ici?** *ee ah teel ewn stah-ssyohn duh tahk-see preh dee-ssee*
Where can I get a taxi?	**Où puis-je trouver un taxi?** *oo pweezh troo-vay uhn tahk-ssee*
Taxi! Are you available?	**Taxi! Êtes-vous libre?** *tahk-ssee eht voo lee-bruh*
Take me (I want to go) _____.	**Conduisez-moi (Je voudrais aller) _____.** *kohn-dwee-zay mwah (zhuh voo-dreh zah-lay)*
▪ to the airport	**à l'aéroport** *ah lahy-roh-pohr*
▪ to this address	**à cette adresse** *ah seht ah-drehss*
▪ to the hotel	**à l'hôtel** *ah loh-tehl*
▪ to the station	**à la gare** *ah lah gahr*
▪ to street _____	**à la rue _____** *ah lah rew*
Do you know where it is?	**Savez-vous où ça se trouve?** *sah-vay voo oo sah suh troov*
How much is it to _____?	**C'est combien pour aller à _____?** *seh kohn-byan poor ah-lay ah*
Faster! I'm in a hurry.	**Allez plus vite! Je suis pressé(e)!** *ah-lay plew veet zhuh swee preh-ssay*
Please drive slower.	**Conduisez plus lentement, s'il vous plaît.** *kohn-dwee-zay plew lahnt-mahn seel voo pleh*
Don't go so fast.	**Ne conduisez pas si vite, s'il vous plaît.** *Nuh kohn-dwee-zay pah see veet seel voo pleh*
Stop here at the corner.	**Arrêtez-vous ici, au coin.** *ah-reh-tay voo zee-ssee, oh kwan*

Stop at the next block.	**Arrêtez-vous à la prochaine rue.** *ah-reh-tay voo ah lah proh-sshehn rew*
Wait for me. I'll be right back.	**Attendez-mois, s'il vous plaît. Je reviens tout de suite** *ah-tahn-day mwah seel voo pleh zhuh ruh-vyan toot sweet*
How much do I owe you?	**Combien est-ce que je vous dois?** *kohn-byan ehss kuh zhuh voo dwah*
This is for you.	**Voilà pour vous.** *vwah-lah poor voo*
Where is the Tourist Office?	**Où est le Syndicat d'Initiative?** *oo eh luh san-dee-kah dee-nee-ssyah-teev*
I need an (English speaking) guide.	**J'ai besoin d'un guide (qui parle anglais).** *zhay buh-zwan duhn geed (kee pahrl ahn-gleh)*
How much does he charge ____?	**Quel est le prix ____?** *kehl eh luh pree* **C'est combien ____?** *seh kohn-byan*
■ per hour	**à l'heure** *ah luhr*
■ per day	**à la journée** *ah lah zhoor-nay*
There are two (four, six) of us.	**Nous sommes deux (quatre, six).** *noo sohm duh (kah-truh, seess)*
Where can I buy a guide book? (a map)	**Où puis-je acheter un guide touristique? (une carte)** *oo pweezh ahsh-tay uhn geed too-reess-teek (ewn kahrt)*
What are the main attractions?	**Qu'est-ce qu'il y a de plus intéressant?** *kehss keel yah duh plew zan-tay-reh-ssahn*
What are things of interest here?	**Qu'est-ce qu'il y a d'intéressant à voir par ici?** *kehss keel yah dan-tay-reh-ssahn ah vwahr pahr ee-ssee*
Are there trips through the city?	**Y a-t-il des visites guidées à travers la ville?** *ee ah teel day vee-zeet gee-day ah trah-vehr lah veel*

Where do they leave from?	**D'où partent-elles?** *doo pahr tehl*
We want to see ____.	**Nous voudrions voir ____.** *noo vood-ree-yohn vwahr*
■ the botanical garden	**le jardin botanique** *luh zhahr-dan boh-tah-neek*
■ the business center	**le quartier des affaires** *luh kahr-tyay day zah-fehr*
■ the castle	**le château** *luh shah-toh*
■ the cathedral	**la cathédrale** *lah kah-tay-drahl*
■ the church	**l'église** *lay-gleez*
■ the concert hall	**la salle de concert** *lah sahl duh kohn-ssehr*
■ the downtown area	**le centre de la ville** *luh sahn-truh duh la veel*
■ the fountains	**les fontaines** *lay fohn-tehn*
■ the library	**la bibliothèque** *lah bee-blee-oh-tehk*
■ the main park	**le parc principal** *luh pahrk pran-ssee-pahl*
■ the main square	**la place principale** *lah plahss pran-ssee-pahl*
■ the market	**le marché** *luh mahr-shay*
■ the mosque	**la mosquée** *lah mohss-kay*
■ the museum (of fine arts)	**le musée des beaux arts** *luh mew-zay day boh zahr*
■ a nightclub	**une boîte de nuit** *ewn bwaht duh nwee*
■ the old part of town	**la vieille ville** *lah vyehy veel*
■ the opera	**l'opéra** *loh-pay-rah*

■the palace	**le palais**	*luh pah-leh*
■the stadium	**le stade**	*luh stahd*
■the synagogue	**la synagogue**	*lah see-nah-gohg*
■the university	**l'université**	*lew-nee-vehr-see-tay*
■the zoo	**le zoo**	*luh zoh*

Is it all right to go in now? **Peut-on entrer maintenant?** *puh tohn ahn-tray mant-nahn*

Is it open? **C'est ouvert?** *seh too-vehr*

Is it closed? **C'est fermé?** *seh fehr-may*

At what time does it open? **À quelle heure ouvre -t-il / elle?** *ah kehl uhr oo-vruh teel/ tehl*

At what time does it close? **À quelle heure ferme-t-il/elle?** *ah kehl uhr fehrm teel/tehl*

What are the visiting hours? **Quelles sont les heures de visite?** *kehl sohn lay zuhr duh vee-zeet*

What's the admission price? **Combien coûte un billet d'entrée?** *kohn-byan koot uhn bee-yeh dahn-tray*

How much do children pay? **C'est combien pour les enfants?** *seh kohn-byan poor lay zahn-fahn*

Can they go in free? Until what age? **Est-ce gratuit pour les enfants? Jusqu'à quel âge?** *ehss grah-twee poor lay zahn-fahn. zhewss-kah kehl ahzh*

Is it all right to take pictures? **Peut-on prendre des photos?** *puh tohn prahn-druh day foh-toh*

PLANNING A TRIP

AIR SERVICE

When is there a flight to ____?	**Quand y a-t-il un vol pour ____?** *kahn tee ah teel uhn vohl poor*
I would like a round trip (one way) ticket in tourist class (first class).	**Je voudrais un aller et retour (un aller) en seconde classe (première classe).** *zhuh voo-dreh zuhn ah-lay ay ruh-toor (uhn nah-lay) ahn suh-gohnd klahss (pruh-myehr klahss)*
A seat ____.	**Une place ____.** *ewn plahss*
■ in the smoking section	**dans la section fumeurs.** *dahn lah sehk-ssyohn few-muhr*
■ in the non-smoking section	**dans la section non-fumeurs** *dahn lah sehk-ssyohn nohn few-muhr*
■ next to the window	**à côté de la fenêtre** *ah koh-tay duh lah fuh-neh-truh*
■ on the aisle	**côté couloir** *koh-tay koo-lwah*
What is the fare?	**Quel est le tarif?** *kehl eh luh tah-reef*
Are meals served?	**Sert-on des repas?** *sehr tohn day ruh-pah*
At what time does the plane leave?	**À quelle heure part l'avion?** *ah kehl uhr pahr lah vyohn*
At what time do we arrive?	**À quelle heure arrivons-nous?** *ah kehl uhr ah-reev-ohn noo*
When do we land in ____?	**Quand est-ce que l'avion atterrit en ____?** *kahn tehss kuh lah-vyohn ah-teh-ree ahn*
What is my flight number?	**Quel est le numéro de mon vol?** *kehl eh luh new-may-roh duh mohn vohl*

What gate do we leave from?	**De quelle porte partons-nous?** *duh kehl pohrt pahr-tohn noo*
I want to confirm (cancel) my reservation for flight ____.	**Je voudrais confirmer (annuler) ma réservation pour le vol numéro ____.** *zhuh voo-dreh kohn-feer-may (ah-new-lay) mah ray-zehr-vah-ssyohn poor luh vohl new-may-roh*
I'd like to check my bags.	**Je voudrais enregistrer mes bagages.** *zhuh voo-dreh zahn-ruh-zheess-tray may bah-gahzh*
I have only carry-on baggage.	**J'ai seulement des bagages à main.** *zhay suhl-mahn day bah-gazh ah man*
Please pass my film (camera) through by hand.	**Passez mon film (appareil) à la main, s'il vous plaît.** *pah-ssay mohn film (ah-pah-rehy) ah lah man seel voo pleh*

SHIPBOARD TRAVEL

Where is the dock?	**Où est le dock?** *oo eh luh dohk*
When does the next boat leave for ____?	**Quand part le prochain bateau pour ____?** *kahn pahr luh proh-shan bah-toh poor*
How long does the crossing take?	**La traversée dure combien de temps?** *lah trah-vehr-ssay dewr kohn-byan duh tahn*
Do we stop at any ports?	**Dans quels ports est-ce qu'on fait escale?** *dahn kehl pohr ehss kohn feh ehss-kahl*
How long will we remain in the port?	**L'escale dure combien de temps?** *lehss-kahl dewr kohn-byan duh tahn*
When do we land?	**Quand est-ce qu'on y arrive?** *kahn tehss kohn nee ah-reev*

At what time do we have to be back on board?	**À quelle heure faut-il retourner au bateau?** *ah kehl uhr foh teel ruh-toor-nay oh bah-toh*
I'd like a _____ ticket.	**Je voudrais un billet _____.** *zhuh voo-dreh zuhn bee-yeh*
■ first class	**de première classe** *duh pruh-myehr klahss*
■ tourist class	**de deuxième classe** *duh duh-zyehm klahss*
■ cabin	**de cabine** *duh kah-been*
I don't feel well.	**Je ne me sens pas bien.** *zhuh nuh muh sahn pah byan*
Can you give me something for sea sickness?	**Pouvez-vous me donner quelque chose contre le mal de mer?** *poo-vay voo muh doh-nay kehl-kuh shohz kohn-truh luh mahl duh mehr*

TRAIN SERVICE

Where is the train station? (the ticket office)	**Où est la gare? (le guichet)** *oo eh lah gahr (luh gee-sheh)*
I'd like to see the schedule.	**Je voudrais voir l'horaire.** *zhuh voo-dreh vwahr loh-rehr*
A first class (second class) ticket to _____, please.	**Un billet de première classe (seconde classe) pour _____, s'il vous plaît.** *uhn bee-yeh duh pruh-myehr klahss (suh-gohnd klahss) poor _____ seel voo pleh*
■ half-price ticket	**un billet de demi-tarif** *uhn bee-yeh duh duh-mee tah-reef*
■ one-way (round-trip) ticket	**un aller simple (aller et retour)** *uhn nah-lay san-pluh (nah-lay ay ruh-toor)*

I would like a (no) smoking compartment.	**Je voudrais un compartiment (non-) fumeurs.** *zhuh voo-dreh zuhn kohn-pahr-tee-mahn (nohn) few-muhr*
When does the train arrive (leave)?	**À quelle heure est-ce que le train arrive (part)?** *ah kehl uhr ehss kuh luh tran ah-reev (pahr)*
From what platform does it leave (arrive)?	**De (À) quel quai (De quelle voie) part (arrive) -t-il?** *duh (ah) kehl kay (duh kehl vwah) pahr (ah-reev) teel*
Does this train stop at ____?	**Est-ce que ce train s'arrête à ____?** *ehss kuh suh tran sah-reht ah*
Is the train late?	**Est-ce que le train a du retard?** *ehss kuh luh tran ah dew ruh-tahr*
How long does it stop?	**Il s'arrête pendant combien de temps?** *eel sah-reht pan-dan kohn-byan duh tahn*
Is there time to get a bite?	**A-t-on le temps de prendre quelque chose?** *ah tohn luh tahn duh prahn-druh kehl-kuh shohz*
Do we have to stand in line?	**Faut-il faire la queue?** *foh teel fehr lah kuh*
All aboard!	**En voiture, s'il vous plaît!** *ahn vwah-tewr seel voo pleh*
Is there a dining car (sleeping car)?	**Y a-t-il un wagon restaurant (un wagon-lit)?** *ee ah teel uhn vah-gohn rehss-toh-rahn (uhn vah-gohn lee)*
Is it a ____?	**Est-ce ____?** *ehss*
▪ a through train	**un rapide** *uhn rah-peed*
▪ a local	**un omnibus** *uhn nohm-nee-bewss*
▪ an express	**un express** *uhn nehkss-prehss*
Do I have to change trains?	**Dois-je changer de train?** *dwahzh shahn-zhay duh tran*

Is this seat taken?	**Est-ce que cette place est oc-cupée?** *ehss kuh seht plahss eh toh-kew-pay*
Where are we now?	**Où sommes-nous maintenant?** *oo sohm noo mant-nahn*
Will we arrive on time? (late)?	**Arriverons-nous à l'heure? (en re-tard?)** *ah-reev-rohn noo ah luhr? (ahn ruh-tahr)*

ENTERTAINMENT AND DIVERSIONS

MOVIES

What are they showing today?	**Qu'est-ce qu'on joue aujourd'hui?** *kehss kohn zhoo oh-zhoor-dwee*
It's a ___.	**C'est ___.** *seh*
■ mystery	**un mystère** *tuhn mee-sstehr*
■ comedy	**une comédie** *tewn koh-may-dee*
■ drama	**un drame** *tuhn drahm*
■ musical	**une comédie musicale** *tewn koh-may-dee mew-zee-kahl*
■ romance	**une histoire d'amour** *tewn eess-twahr dah-moor*
■ Western	**un western** *tuhn wehss-tehrn*
■ war film	**un film de guerre** *tuhn feelm duh gehr*
■ science fiction film	**une histoire de science fiction** *tewn eess-twahr duh see-yahnss feek-ssyohn*
Is it in English?	**Est-ce en anglais?** *ehss ahn nahn-gleh*

Are there English subtitles?	**Y-t-il des sous-titres en anglais?** *ee ah teel day soo-tee-truh ahn nahn-gleh*
Where is the box office (time schedule)?	**Où est le bureau de location (l'horaire)?** *oo eh luh bew-roh duh loh-kah-ssyohn (loh-rehr)*
What time does the (first) show begin?	**À quelle heure commence le (premier) spectacle?** *ah kehl uhr koh-mahnss luh (pruh-myay) spehk-tah-kluh*
What time does the (last) show end?	**À quelle heure se termine le (dernier) spectacle?** *ah kehl uhr suh tehr-meen luh (dehr-nyay) spehk-tah-kluh*
I'd like to speak to an usher.	**Je voudrais parler à une ouvreuse.** *zhuh voo-dreh pahr-lay ah ewn oo-vruhz*

THEATER

I need tickets for tonight.	**Il me faut des billets pour ce soir.** *eel muh foh day bee-yeh poor suh swahr*
Two _____ seats	**Deux places _____** *duh plahss*
■ orchestra	**à l'orchestre** *ah lohr-kehss-truh*
■ balcony	**au balcon** *oh bahl-kohn*
■ first balcony	**au premier balcon** *oh pruh-myay bahl-kohn*
■ mezzanine	**au parterre** *oh pahr-tehr*

OPERA-BALLET-CONCERT

We would like to attend _____.	**Nous voudrions assister à _____.** *noo voo-dree-yohn ah-sseess-tay ah*
■ a ballet	**un ballet** *uhn bah-leh*
■ a concert	**un concert** *uhn kohn-sehr*

■ an opera **un opéra** *uhn noh-pay-rah*

Is there a ___ nearby? **Y a-t-il par ici ___?** *ee ah teel pahr ee-ssee*

■ concert hall **une salle de concert** *ewn sahl duh kohn-ssehr*

■ opera house **un opéra** *uhn noh-pay-rah*

■ ballet **un ballet** *uhn bah-leh*

What are they playing? **Que joue-t-on?** *kuh zhoo tohn*

Who is the conductor? **Qui est le chef d'orchestre?** *kee eh luh shehf dohr-kehss-truh*

I prefer ___. **Je préfère ___.** *zhuh pray-fehr*

■ classical music **la musique classique** *lah mew-zeek klah-sseek*

■ modern music **la musique moderne** *lah mew-zeek moh-dehrn*

■ folk dances **les danses folkloriques** *lay dahnss fohl-kloh-reek*

Are there any seats for tonight's performance? **Y a-t-il des places pour ce soir?** *ee ah teel day plahss poor suh swahr*

When does the season end? **Quand se termine la saison théâtrale?** *kahn suh tehr-meen lah seh-zohn tay-ah-trahl*

Should I get the tickets in advance? **Faut-il acheter les billets d'avance?** *foh teel ahsh-tay lay bee-yeh dah-vahnss*

Do I have to dress formally? **La tenue de soirée est-elle de rigueur?** *lah tuh-new duh swah-ray eh tehl duh ree-guhr*

How much are the front row seats? **Combien coûtent les places au premier rang?** *kohn-byan koot lay plahss oh pruh-myay rahn*

What are the least expensive seats?	**Quelles sont les places les moins chères?** *kehl sohn lay plahss lay mwan shehr*
May I have a program?	**Un programme, s'il vous plaît.** *uhn proh-grahm seel voo pleh*
What opera are they putting on?	**Quel opéra jouent-ils?** *kehl oh-pay-rah zhoo teel*

NIGHT CLUBS

Let's go to a nightclub!	**Allons dans une boîte de nuit!** *ah-lohn dahn zewn bwaht duh nwee*
Is a reservation necessary?	**Faut-il réserver?** *foh teel ray-zehr-vay*
I feel like dancing.	**J'ai envie de danser.** *zhay ahn-vee duh dahn-ssay*
Is there a discotheque here?	**Y a-t-il une discothèque par ici?** *ee ah teel ewn deess-koh-tehk pahr ee-ssee*
Is there a dance at the hotel?	**Y a-t-il un bal à l'hôtel?** *ee ah teel uhn bahl ah loh-tehl*
I'd like a table near the dance floor.	**Je voudrais avoir une table près de la piste (de danse).** *zhuh voo-dreh zah-vwahr ewn tah-bluh preh duh lah peesst (duh dahnss)*
Is there a minimum (cover charge)?	**Y a-t-il un prix d'entrée?** *ee ah teel uhn pree dahn-tray*
Where is the checkroom?	**Où est le vestiaire?** *oo eh luh vehss-tyehr*
At what time does the floor show go on?	**À quelle heure commence le spectacle?** *ah kehl uhr koh-mahnss luh spehk-tah-kluh*

DANCING

May I have this dance?	**M'accordez-vous cette danse?** *mah-kohr-day voo seht dahnss*

Yes, all right. With pleasure.	**Oui, d'accord. Avec plaisir.** *wee dah-kohr. ah-vehk pleh-zeer*
Would you like a cigarette (a drink)?	**Voudriez-vous une cigarette (une boisson)?** *voo-dree-yay voo zewn see-gah-reht (ewn bwah-ssohn)*
Do you have a light?	**Avez-vous du feu?** *ah-vay voo dew fuh*
Do you mind if I smoke?	**Ça vous dérange si je fume?** *sah voo day-rahnzh see zhuh fewm*
May I take you home?	**Puis-je vous raccompagner chez vous?** *pweezh voo rah-kohn-pah-nyay shay voo*

SPECTATOR SPORTS

SOCCER

I'd like to see a soccer match.	**Je voudrais voir un match de football.** *zhuh voo-dreh vwahr uhn mahtch duh foot-bohl*
Where's the stadium?	**Où est le stade?** *oo eh luh stahd*
When does the first half begin?	**Quand commence la première mi-temps?** *kahn koh-mahnss lah pruh-myehr mee-tahn*
When are they going to kick off?	**Quand vont-ils donner le coup d'envoi?** *kahn vohn teel doh-nay luh koo dahn-vwah*
What teams are going to play?	**Quelles équipes vont jouer?** *kehl zay-keep vohn zhoo-ay*
What was the score?	**Quel a été le score?** *kehl ah ay-tay luh skohr*

JAI ALAI

I'd like to see a jai alai match.	**Je voudrais voir un match de pelote.** *zhuh voo-dreh vwahr uhn mahtch duh puh-loht*

Where can I get tickets?	**Où puis-je me procurer des billets?** *oo pweezh muh proh-kew-ray day bee-yeh*
Where is the jai alai court?	**Où est le fronton?** *oo eh luh frohn-tohn*
Where do I place my bet?	**Où fait-on les paris?** *oo feh-tohn lay pah-ree*
At that window.	**À ce guichet.** *ah suh gee-sheh*

HORSE RACING

Is there a racetrack here?	**Y a-t-il un champ de courses par ici?** *ee ah teel uhn shahn duh koorss pahr ee-ssee*
I want to see the horse races.	**Je voudrais voir les courses de chevaux.** *zhuh voo-dreh vwahr lay koorss duh shuh-voh*

ACTIVE SPORTS

TENNIS

Do you play tennis?	**Jouez-vous au tennis?** *zhoo-ay voo oh teh-neess*
I like the game.	**J'aime bien ce sport.** *zhehm byan suh spohr*
I (don't) play very well.	**Je (ne) joue (pas) bien.** *zhuh (nuh) zhoo (pah) byan*
I need practice.	**Je dois m'entraîner.** *zhuh dwah mahn-treh-nay*
Do you know where there is a (good) court?	**Savez-vous où se trouve un bon court de tennis?** *sah-vay voo oo suh troov uhn bohn koohr duh teh-neess*
Can I rent rackets and balls?	**Puis-je louer des raquettes et des balles?** *pweezh loo-ay day rah-keht ay day bahl*

| How much do they charge per hour (per day)? | **Quel est le tarif à l'heure/à la journée?** *kehl eh luh tah-reef ah luhr/ ah lah zhoor-nay* |

BEACH OR POOL

| Let's go to the beach (to the pool). | **Allons à la plage (à la piscine).** *ah-lohn zah lah plahzh (ah lah pee-sseen)* |

| Is it a sand beach? | **Est-ce une plage de sable?** *ehss ewn plahzh duh sah-bluh* |

| How do you get there? | **Comment y va-t-on?** *koh-mahn tee vah tohn* |

| Which bus will take us to the beach? | **Quel bus faut-il prendre pour aller à la plage?** *kehl bewss foh teel prahn-druh poor ah-lay ah lah plahzh* |

| Is there a pool in the hotel? | **Y a-t-il une piscine à l'hôtel?** *ee ah teel ewn pee-sseen ah loh-tehl* |

| Is it an indoor (outdoor) pool? | **Est-ce une piscine couverte (en plein air)?** *ehss ewn pee-sseen koo-vehrt (ahn pleh nehr)* |

| Is it safe to swim here? | **Peut-on nager ici sans danger?** *puh-tohn nah-zhay ee-ssee sahn dahn-zhay* |

| Is there any danger for children? | **Y a-t-il du danger pour les en-fants?** *ee ah teel dew dahn-zhay poor lay zahn-fahn* |

| Is there a lifeguard? | **Y a-t-il un maître- nageur?** *ee ah teel uhn meh-truh nah- zhuhr* |

| Where can I get ____? | **Où puis-je obtenir ____?** *oo pweezh ohb-tuh-neer* |

| ▦ an air mattress | **un matelas pneumatique** *uhn maht-lah pnuh-mah-teek* |

| ▦ a bathing suit | **un maillot de bain** *uhn mah-yoh duh ban* |

■ a beach chair

une chaise longue pour la plage
ewn shehz lohng poor lah plahzh

■ a surfboard

une planche de surf *ewn plahnsh
duh sewrf*

■ water skis

des skis nautiques *day skee noh-
teek*

ON THE SLOPES

Which ski area do
you recommend?

**Quelle station de ski recomman-
dez-vous?** *kehl stah-ssyohn duh skee
ruh-koh-mahn-day voo*

I am a novice (inter-
mediate, expert) ski-
er.

**Je suis un(e) débutant(e) (un
skieur moyen; un expert).** *zhuh
swee zuhn (zewn) day-bew-tahn(t) (zuhn
skee-uhr mwah-yan/zuhn ehkss-pehr)*

What kind of lifts are
there?

Quel type de téléski y a-t-il? *kehl
teep duh tay-lay-sskee ee-yah-teel*

How much does the
lift cost?

Combien coûte le trajet? *kohn-
byan koot luh trah-zheh*

Do they give les-
sons?

Donne-t-on des leçons? *dohn-tohn
day luh-ssohn*

Where can I stay at
the summit?

Où puis-je loger au sommet? *oo
pweezh loh-zhay oh soh-meh*

Is there any cross
country skiing?

**Est-ce qu'on fait du ski de prome-
nade?** *ehss-kohn feh dew skee duh
proh-muh-nahd*

Is there enough
snow this time of
year?

**Y a-t-il assez de neige en ce mo-
ment?** *ee ah teel ah-ssay duh nehzh
ahn suh moh-mahn*

How would I get to
that place?

Comment aller à cet endroit-là?
*koh-mahn tah-lay ah seht ahn-drwah
lah*

Can I rent ____ there?	**Peut-on y louer ____?** *puh-tohn nee loo-ay*
■ equipment	**un équipement de ski** *uhn nay-keep-mahn duh skee*
■ poles	**des bâtons** *day bah-tohn*
■ skis	**des skis** *day skee*
■ ski boots	**des chaussures de ski** *day shoh-ssewr duh skee*

ON THE LINKS

Is there a golf course here?	**Y a-t-il un terrain de golf par ici?** *ee ah teel uhn teh-ran duh gohlf pahr ee-ssee*
Can one rent clubs?	**Peut-on louer des clubs?** *puh tohn loo-ay day kluhb*

CAMPING

Is there a camping site near here?	**Y a-t-il un terrain de camping par ici?** *ee ah teel uhn teh-ran duh kahn-peeng pahr ee-ssee*
Can you show me how to get there?	**Pouvez-vous m'indiquer comment y aller?** *poo-vay voo man-dee-kay koh-mahn tee ah-lay*
Where is it on the map?	**Où se trouve-t-il sur la carte?** *oo suh troov teel sewr lah kahrt*
Where can we park our trailer?	**Où pouvons-nous installer notre caravane?** *oo poo-vohn noo an-stah-lay noh-truh kah-rah-vahn*
Can we camp for the night?	**Pouvons-nous camper cette nuit?** *poo-vohn noo kahn-pay seht nwee*
Where can we spend the night?	**Où pouvons-nous passer la nuit?** *oo poo-vohn noo pah- ssay lah nwee*

Is there ____?	**Y a-t-il ____?** *ee ah teel*
◼ drinking water	**de l'eau potable** *duh loh poh-tah-bluh*
◼ running water	**de l'eau courante** *duh loh koo-rah<u>n</u>t*
◼ gas	**du gaz** *dew gahz*
◼ electricity	**de l'électricité** *duh lay-lehk-tree-ssee-tay*
◼ a children's playground	**un terrain de jeu pour enfants** *uh<u>n</u> teh-ra<u>n</u> duh zhuh poor ah<u>n</u>-fah<u>n</u>*
◼ a grocery store	**une épicerie** *ewn ay-peess-ree*
Are there ____?	**Y a-t-il ____?** *ee ah teel*
◼ toilets	**des toilettes** *day twah-leht*
◼ showers	**des douches** *day doosh*
◼ washrooms	**des lavabos** *day lah-vah-boh*
◼ tents	**des tentes** *day tah<u>n</u>t*
◼ cooking facilities	**des installations pour faire la cuisine** *day za<u>n</u>-stah-lah-ssyoh<u>n</u> poor fehr lah kwee-zeen*
How much do they charge per person? (per car)?	**Quel est le tarif par personne/pour une caravane?** *kehl eh luh tah-reef pahr pehr-ssoh<u>n</u>/poor ewn kah-rah-vah<u>n</u>*
We intend staying ____ days/weeks.	**Nous pensons rester ____ jours/semaines.** *noo pah<u>n</u>-ssoh<u>n</u> rehss-tay zhoor/suh-mehn*

IN THE COUNTRYSIDE

I'd like to drive through the countryside.	**Je voudrais conduire dans la campagne.** *zhuh voo-dreh koh<u>n</u>-dweer dah<u>n</u> lah kah<u>n</u>-pah-nyuh*

Where can I rent a car for the day?	**Où puis-je louer une voiture à la journée?** *oo pweezh loo-ay ewn vwah-tewr ah lah zhoor-nay*
Are there tours to the country?	**Y a-t-il des excursions à la campagne?** *ee ah teel day zehkss-kewr-zyohn ah lah kahn-pah-nyuh*
When do they leave?	**Quand sont les départs?** *kahn ssohn lay day-pahr*
From where do they leave?	**D'où partent-elles?** *doo pahrt-ehl*
Is there anyone who can take me?	**Y a-t-il quelqu'un qui puisse me conduire?** *ee ah teel kehl kuhn kee pweess muh kohn-dweer*
What a beautiful landscape!	**Quel beau paysage!** *kehl boh pay-zahzh*
Where does this _____ lead to?	**Où mène _____?** *oo mehn*
■ road	**ce chemin** *suh shuh-man*
■ path	**ce sentier** *suh sahn-tyay*
■ highway	**cette grande route** *seht grahnd root*
How far away is _____?	**À quelle distance est _____?** *ah kehl deess-tahnss eh*
■ the city	**la ville** *lah veel*
■ the crossroads	**le carrefour** *luh kahr-foor*
■ the inn	**l'auberge (f.)** *loh-behrzh*
How long does it take to get to _____?	**Combien de temps faut-il pour aller à _____?** *kohn-byan duh tahn foh teel poor ah-lay ah*
I'm lost.	**J'ai perdu mon chemin.** *zhay pehr-dew mohn shuh-man*
Can you show me the way to _____?	**Pouvez-vous m'indiquer le chemin pour _____?** *poo-vay voo man-dee-kay luh shuh-man poor*

FOOD AND DRINK

Auberge, Relais, Hostellerie	a country inn.
Bistro	a small neighborhood restaurant in town, similar to a pub or tavern and usually very informal.
Brasserie	a large café which serves quick meals throughout the day or evening; most meals involve only the entrée, such as a steak or chop.
Cabaret	a nightclub where you may also eat a meal.
Café	a neighborhood spot to socialize, either indoors or out, where you can linger over a coffee or glass of wine or beer and perhaps have a little snack. Cafés also serve breakfast (usually a **croissant** and **café au lait**) and later in the day serve soft drinks and ice cream.
Casse-croûte	a restaurant specializing in sandwiches.
Crêperie	a small stand specializing in the preparation of crêpes—thin pancakes dusted with sugar or covered with jam and rolled up.
Fast-food place	a small place to eat an American-style snack, mostly hamburgers and French fries; most are in Paris along the Champs-Elysée and many are American chains such as McDonald's and Burger King.

Restaurant	can range from a small, family-owned inn, where mom seats you, dad cooks the meal, and the children serve you, to a formal, three-star palace where you receive the most elegant service and most beautifully garnished foods.
Self	a cafeteria, popular with students and mostly located near a university.
Troquet	a wine shop where you can also have a snack.

EATING OUT

Do you know a good restaurant?
Connaissez-vous un bon restaurant? *koh-neh-ssay voo uhn bohn rehss-toh-rahn?*

It is very expensive?
C'est très cher? *seh treh shehr*

Do you know a restaurant that serves regional dishes?
Connaissez-vous un restaurant de cuisine régionale? *koh-neh-ssay voo uhn rehss-toh-rahn duh kwee-zeen ray-zhyoh-nahl*

I'd like to make a reservation ____.
Je voudrais retenir une table ____. *zhuh voo-dreh ruh-tuh-neer ewn tah-bluh*

■ for tonight
pour ce soir *poor suh swahr*

■ for tomorrow evening
pour demain soir *poor duh-man swahr*

■ for two (four) persons
pour deux (quatre) personnes *poor duh (kah-truh) pehr-ssohn*

■ at 8 (8:30 P.M.)
à vingt heures (vingt heures trente) *ah van-tuhr (van-tuhr trahnt)*

Waiter!
Garçon! *gahr-ssohn!*

Miss!	**Mademoiselle** *mahd-mwah-zehl*
A table for two in the corner (near the window).	**Une table pour deux dans un petit coin (près de la fenêtre).** *ewn tah-bluh poor duh dahn zuhn puh-tee kwan (preh duh lah fuh-neh-truh)*
We'd like to have lunch (dinner) now.	**Nous voudrions déjeuner (dîner) maintenant.** *noo voo-dree-yohn day-zhuh-nay (dee-nay) mant-nahn*
The menu, please.	**La carte (Le menu), s'il vous plaît.** *lah kahrt (luh muh-new) seel voo pleh*
I'd like the fifty-franc menu.	**Je voudrais le menu à cinquante francs.** *zhuh voo-dreh luh muh-new ah san-kahnt frahn*
What's today's special?	**Quel est le plat du jour?** *kehl eh luh plah dew zhoor*
What do you recommend?	**Qu'est-ce que vous me recommandez?** *kehss kuh voo muh ruh-koh-mahn-day*
What's the house specialty?	**Quelle est la spécialité de la maison?** *kehl eh lah spay-ssyah-lee-tay duh lah meh-zohn*
Do you serve children's portions?	**Servez-vous des demi-portions pour les enfants?** *sehr-vay voo day duh-mee pohr-ssyohn poor lay zahn-fahn*
Do you have a house wine?	**Avez-vous du vin ordinaire?** *ah-vay-voo dew van ohr-dee-nehr*
Is it dry (mellow, sweet)?	**Est-ce sec (moelleux, doux)?** *ehss sehk (mwah-luh, doo)*
Please also bring us ____.	**Apportez-nous aussi, s'il vous plaît ____.** *ah-pohr-tay noo oh-ssee seel voo pleh*
a roll	**un petit pain** *uhn puh-tee pan*
bread	**du pain** *dew pan*

■ butter	**du beurre** *dew buhr*
Waiter, we need ____.	**Garçon, apportez-nous ____, s'il vous plaît.** *gahr-ssoh<u>n</u> ah-pohr-tay noo seel voo pleh*
■ a knife	**un couteau** *uh<u>n</u> koo-toh*
■ a fork	**une fourchette** *ewn foor-sheht*
■ a spoon	**une cuiller** *ewn kwee-yehr*
■ a teaspoon	**une cuiller à café** *ewn kwee-yehr ah kah-fay*
■ a glass	**un verre** *uh<u>n</u> vehr*
■ a goblet	**un gobelet** *uh<u>n</u> gohb-leh*
■ a cup	**une tasse** *ewn tahss*
■ a saucer	**une soucoupe** *ewn soo-koop*
■ a plate	**une assiette** *ewn ah-ssyeht*
■ a napkin	**une serviette** *ewn sehr-vyeht*
■ a toothpick	**un cure-dent** *uh<u>n</u> kewr-dah<u>n</u>*

APPETIZERS (STARTERS)

1. ARTICHAUTS À LA VINAIGRETTE   artichokes in a vinaigrette dressing.

2. CRUDITÉS VARIÉES   assorted vegetables—sliced tomatoes, shredded carrots, sliced cooked beets—in a vinaigrette dressing.

3. ESCARGOTS À LA BOURGUIGNONNE   snails cooked and served in the shell, seasoned with a garlic, shallot, and parsley butter.

4. FOIE GRAS   fresh, often uncooked liver of a force-fed goose; sliced and served with toasted French bread slices.

5. PÂTÉ   any of a number of meat loaves, made from puréed liver and usually also with meat—pork, veal, or chicken. **Pâté de foie gras** is made with goose liver; **pâté de campagne** is "of the country" and is a coarser mixed meat paté; **pâté en croute** is a liver pâté encased in pastry.

6. QUICHE LORRAINE   an egg custard tart, sometimes with bacon strips or bits; some versions now also made with Gruyère cheese.
7. QUENELLES   light dumplings, usually made from **brochet** (pike) but also from shellfish; served in a white sauce.
8. RILLETTES   a pork mixture that has been potted, then served as a spread, usually with French bread.
9. TERRINE   A type of pâté, usually served from a deep pot rather than sliced as pâté would be. Terrines can be made from pork, poultry, game, or fish.

SOUPS

1. BISQUE D'ÉCREVISSES   a creamy soup made with crawfish; other bisques are made with lobster, shrimp, or oysters.
2. BOUILLABAISSE   a seafood stew, made with a variety of fish and shellfish depending on the region, seasoned with saffron and fennel or pernod.
3. CONSOMMÉ   a clear broth, made usually from chicken or beef and flavored with herbs; **en gelée** is consommé that has been jelled and sliced; **madrilène** is with tomatoes; **printanier** has a variety of vegetables.
4. CRÈME   A creamy soup, made from any of a number of vegetables and usually enriched with egg yolks. **D'Argenteuil** is cream of asparagus soup; **de volaille** is a creamy chicken soup.
5. PETITE MARMITE   a rich consommé served with the meat and vegetables.
6. POTAGE   a coarser soup, usually made with a purée of vegetables; some varieties of potage are **parmentier** (leeks and potatoes), **au cresson** (watercress), **julienne** (shredded vegetables).
7. SOUPE À L'OIGNON   famous French onion soup, served over French bread and covered with cheese.
8. VELOUTÉ   a creamy soup, most common of which is **de volaille** (cream of chicken) and **de tomate** (tomato).

EGG DISHES

1. OEUFS BERCY   eggs baked with sausages in a tomato sauce.

2. OEUFS EN COCOTTE   eggs gently baked in individual cups until softly cooked, sometimes with cream, then eaten with a spoon.

3. OEUFS EN GELÉE   poached eggs that are set into jelled consommé and served chilled as a salad.

4. OMELETTE   a French omelette is puffy and contains a variety of fillings—**aux fines herbes** is with a mixture of parsley, chives, and tarragon.

5. PIPERADE   scrambled eggs mixed with tomatoes, onions, and sweet peppers.

6. SOUFFLÉ   soufflés can be made with almost any ingredients—vegetables, chicken livers, cheese, ham, and so on; they are always light and puffy.

FISH COURSE

les anchois	*lay zah<u>n</u>-shwah*	anchovies
les anguilles	*lay zah<u>n</u>-gee*	eel
le bar	*luh bahr*	bass (hake)
la barbue	*lah bahr-bew*	brill
la baudroie	*lah boh-drwah*	anglerfish, monkfish
le brochet	*luh broh-sheh*	pike
le cabillaud	*luh kah-bee-yoh*	cod
le calmar	*luh kahl-mahr*	squid
la carpe	*lah kahrp*	carp
le carrelet	*luh kahr-leh*	flounder
le congre	*luh koh<u>n</u>-gruh*	conger eel
les crevettes	*lay kruh-veht*	shrimp
la daurade	*lah doh-rahd*	porgy
les écrevisses	*lay zay-kruh-veess*	crawfish
les escargots	*lay zehss-kahr-goh*	snails

les harengs (fumés)	*lay ah-rahn (few-may)*	herring (smoked)
le homard	*luh oh-mahr*	lobster
les huîtres	*lay zwee-truh*	oysters
la lamproie	*lah lahn-prwah*	lamprey
la langouste	*lah lahn-goosst*	spiny lobster
les langoustines	*lay lahn-goo-ssteen*	large shrimp
la lotte	*lah loht*	monkfish
le loup de mer	*luh loo duh mehr*	sea bass
le maquereau	*luh mah-kroh*	mackerel
le merlan	*luh mehr-lahn*	whiting
la morue	*lah moh-rew*	cod
les moules	*lay mool*	mussels
les palourdes	*lay pah-loord*	clams
la perche	*lah pehrsh*	perch
les poulpes	*lay poolp*	octopus
la rascasse	*lah rahss-kahss*	scorpionfish
les sardines	*lay sahr-deen*	sardines
le saumon	*luh soh-mohn*	salmon
les scampi	*lay skahn-pee*	large shrimp
le thon	*luh tohn*	tuna
la truite	*lah trweet*	trout
le turbot	*luh tewr-boh*	European turbot

POULTRY AND GAME

la caille	*lah kahy*	quail
le cerf	*luh sehr*	venison
la canard, caneton	*luh kah-nahr, kahn-tohn*	duckling

le chapon	*luh shah-pohn*	capon
le chevreuil	*luh shuh-vruhy*	venison
le cochon de lait	*luh koh-shohn duh leh*	suckling pig
la dinde	*lah dand*	turkey
le faisan	*luh feh-zahn*	pheasant
le lapin	*luh lah-pan*	rabbit
le lièvre	*luh lyeh-vruh*	hare
l'oie *(f.)*	*lwah*	goose
le perdreau, la perdrix	*luh pehr-droh, lah pehr-dree*	partridge
le pigeon, le pigeonneau	*luh pee-zhohn, luh pee-zhoh-noh*	squab
la pintade, le pintadeau	*lah pan-tahd, luh pan-tah-doh*	guinea fowl
la poule	*lah pool*	stewing fowl
le poulet, poussin, la volaille	*luh poo-leh, poo-ssan, lah voh-lahy*	chicken

MEATS

l'agneau *(m.)*	*lah-nyoh*	lamb
le bœuf	*luh buhf*	beef
la chèvre	*lah sheh-vruh*	goat
le jambon	*luh zhahn-bohn*	ham
le mouton	*luh moo-tohn*	mutton
le porc	*luh pohr*	pork
le veau	*luh voh*	veal
les andouilles	*lay zahn-dooy*	pork sausages

le bifteck	*luh beef-tehk*	steak
le boudin	*luh boo-da<u>n</u>*	blood sausage
le carré d'ag-neau	*luh kah-ray dah-nyoh*	rack of lamb
le cervelas	*luh sehr-vuh-lah*	garlicky pork sausage
la cervelle	*lah sehr-vehl*	brains
la charcuterie	*lah shahr-kew-tree*	assorted sausages, pâtés, and terrines
le chateaubriand	*luh shah-toh-bree-ah<u>n</u>*	porterhouse steak
la côte de boeuf	*lah koht duh buhf*	ribs of beef
les côtelettes	*lay koht-leht*	cutlets
les côtes de porc, de veau	*lay koht duh pohr, duh voh*	chops, pork or veal
les crépinettes	*lay kray-pee-neht*	small sausages
l'entrecôte *(f.)*	*lah<u>n</u>-truh-koht*	sirloin steak
l'escalope *(f.)*	*lehss-kah-lohp*	cutlet
le filet de bœuf	*luh fee-leh duh buhf*	fillet of beef
le foie	*luh fwah*	liver
le gigot d'agneau	*luh zhee-goh dah-nyoh*	leg of lamb
la langue	*lah lah<u>ng</u>*	tongue
le lard	*luh lahr*	bacon
les médaillons de veau	*lay may-dah-yoh<u>n</u> duh voh*	small rounds of veal
les noisettes	*lay nwah-zeht*	small fillets
les pieds de porc	*lay pyay duh pohr*	pig's feet
le ris de veau	*luh ree duh voh*	veal sweetbreads

les rognons d'agneau	*lay roh-nyohn dah-nyoh*	lamb kidneys
le rosbif	*luh rohss-beef*	roast beef
les saucisses	*lay soh-sseess*	sausages
la selle d'agneau	*lah sehl dah-nyoh*	saddle of lamb
le steak	*luh stehk*	steak
le tournedos	*luh toor-nuh-doh*	small fillets of beef
les tripes	*lay treep*	tripe
Is it ____?	**C'est ____?**	*seh*
■ baked	**au four**	*oh foor*
■ boiled	**bouilli(e)**	*boo-yee*
■ braised (stewed)	**braisé(e)**	*breh-zay*
■ broiled (grilled)	**grillé(e)**	*gree-yay*
■ roasted	**rôti(e)**	*roh-tee*
■ poached	**poché(e)**	*poh-shay*
I like the steak ____.	**Je préfère le steak ____.**	*zhuh pray-fehr luh stehk*
■ well-done	**bien cuit (e)**	*byan kwee*
■ medium	**à point**	*ah pwan*
■ rare	**saignant (e)**	*seh-nyahn*
■ tender	**tendre**	*tahn-druh*

VEGETABLES

l'artichaut *(m.)*	*lahr-tee-shoh*	artichoke
les asperges	*lay zahss-pehrzh*	asparagus
l'aubergine *(f.)*	*loh-behr-zheen*	eggplant
la betterave	*lah beh-trahv*	beet
les carottes	*lay kah-roht*	carrots

le céleri	*luh sayl -ree*	celery
le céleri rave	*luh sahl-ree-rahv*	knob celery
les champignons	*lay shaẖn-pee-nyoẖn*	mushrooms
le chou	*luh shoo*	cabbage (green)
le chou-fleur	*luh shoo-fluhr*	cauliflower
la courgette	*lah koor-zheht*	zucchini
le cresson	*luh kreh-ssoẖn*	watercress
les épinards	*lay zay-pee-nahr*	spinach
les flageolets	*lay flah-zhoh-leh*	green shell beans
les haricots verts	*lay ah-ree-koh vehr*	green beans
les oignons	*lay zoh-nyoẖn*	onions
l'oseille *(f.)*	*loh-zehy*	sorrel
le piment	*luh pee-maẖn*	green pepper
les pois	*lay pwah*	peas
le poireau	*luh pwah-roh*	leek
les pommes de terre	*lay pohm duh tehr*	potatoes
la tomate	*lah toh-maht*	tomato

CHEESE COURSE

What is that cheese?	**Quel est ce fromage?**	*kehl eh suh froh-mahzh*
Is it ____?	**Est-il ____?**	*eh-teel*
■ mild	**maigre**	*meh-gruh*
■ sharp	**piquant**	*pee-kaẖn*
■ hard	**fermenté**	*fehr-maẖn-tay*
■ soft	**à pâte molle**	*ah paht mohl*

Among the more popular cheeses are the following.

1. BANON   Made from sheep's or goat's milk, a soft cheese with a natural rind; a mild cheese with a mild nutty flavor.

2. BLEU D'AUVERGNE   Made from cow's milk, this soft cheese has an internal mold and when cut, the veins are visible. With a very sharp flavor.

3. BOURSIN   A soft cow's milk cheese, with a mild flavor, sometimes enhanced with herbs.

4. BRIE   A variety of cheeses made from cow's milk and with a bloomy rind. Varieties range in flavor from mild to very pronounced, some with a fruity flavor.

5. CAMEMBERT   Less delicate than brie, but also a cow's milk cheese with a bloomy rind. Should be eaten firm.

6. CANTAL   A cow's milk cheese that varies with length of aging. Some varieties are softer and milder, while more aged ones are hard and with a more pronounced flavor.

7. CHÈVRE   Any of an almost infinite variety of goat's milk cheeses, which vary from very soft to quite firm, and from mild and creamy to tart and crumbly. There will always be a few chèvres on the cheese tray.

8. COLOMBIÈRE   This cow's milk cheese is soft and supple, with a mild flavor.

9. MUNSTER   A cow's milk cheese that is soft and spicy, with a tangy flavor. In Alsace, where the cheese comes from, it is eaten young.

10. PONT-L'ÉVÊQUE   A cow's milk cheese that is very smooth and supple, with a pronounced flavor.

11. PORT-SALUT   The brand name for the Saint-Paulin from the monastery of Port-du-Salut.

12. REBLOCHON   A soft cow's milk cheese with a mild and creamy flavor.

13. ROQUEFORT   A sheep's milk cheese that is soft and pungent. The cheese is cured in caves, an ancient process with rigid standards for production. Texture is very buttery.

14. SAINT-PAULIN   Made from cow's milk, this is a velvety smooth cheese with a mild flavor.

15. TOMME DE SAVOIE   A mild cow's milk cheese with a nutty flavor.

FRUITS AND NUTS

Here are the names of some common fruits, followed by nuts.

l'abricot	*lah-bree-koh*	apricot
l'ananas	*lah-nah-nah*	pineapple
la banane	*lah bah-nahn*	banana
les cassis	*lay kah-sseess*	black currants
la cerise	*lah suh-reez*	cherry
le citron	*luh see-trohn*	lemon
la datte	*lah daht*	date
la figue	*lah feeg*	fig
les fraises	*lay frehz*	strawberries
les fraises des bois	*lay frehz duh bwah*	wild strawberries
les framboises	*lay frahn-bwahz*	raspberries
les groseilles	*lay groh-sehy*	red currants
la limette	*lah lee-meht*	lime
la mandarine	*lah mahn-dah-reen*	tangerine
le melon	*luh muh-lohn*	melon
les mûres	*lay mewr*	mulberries
les myrtilles	*lay meer-tee*	blueberries
l'orange	*loh-rahnzh*	orange
la noix de coco	*lah nwah duh koh-koh*	coconut
le pample-mousse	*luh pahn-pluh-mooss*	grapefruit
la pêche	*lah pehsh*	peach
la poire	*lah pwahr*	pear
la pomme	*lah pohm*	apple

la prune	*lah prewn*	plum
le pruneau	*luh prew-noh*	prune
le raisin	*luh reh-za<u>n</u>*	grape
l'amande *(f.)*	*lah-mah<u>n</u>d*	almond
le marron	*luh mah-roh<u>n</u>*	chestnut
la noisette	*lah nwah-zeht*	hazelnut
les noix	*lay nwah*	nuts

DESSERTS—SWEETS

1. BAVAROISE   A bavarian cream; mont-blanc is a bavarian cream made with chestnuts.

2. BEIGNETS   Fritters, often made from fruit such as apple.

3. BOMBE   An ice cream construction, often with different flavors and sometimes also with sherbet.

4. CHARLOTTE   An assemblage of sponge fingers and pudding; usually the sponge cake is used to line the dish and pudding is in the center.

5. CRÈME CARAMEL   An egg custard served with a caramel sauce.

6. CRÊPES   Dessert crêpes, the most famous of which are **Crêpes Suzette,** made with orange flavoring and served flaming with Grand Marnier.

7. GÂTEAU   An elaborate layer cake, made with thin layers of sponge cake and pastry cream, and decorated.

8. MOUSSE AU CHOCOLAT   An airy pudding made with chocolate, cream, eggs, and brandy, garnished with whipped cream.

9. MACÉDOINE DE FRUITS   A fresh fruit salad.

10. OEUFS À LA NEIGE   Soft meringue ovals served floating on a custard sauce.

11. OMELETTE NORVÉGIENNE   Baked Alaska.

12. PÂTISSERIE   Pastry selection of any variety, including éclairs, millefeuilles, savarin, Saint-Honoré (cream puff cake).

13. POIRES HÉLÈNE   A poached pear, served with vanilla ice cream and chocolate sauce.

14. PROFITEROLES   Cream puffs, served with chocolate
sauce.
15. SOUFFLÉ   An endless variety of sweet soufflés, the famous one being the Grand Marnier soufflé.
16. TARTE   Open-faced fruit pies, often made with apples or
plums.

In addition, ice cream is a French favorite, as is sherbet and
granité (fruit ice). Here's how to ask for these:

ice cream	**une glace**	*ewn glahss*
■chocolate	**au chocolat**	*oh shoh-koh-lah*
■vanilla	**à la vanille**	*ah lah vah-nee*
■strawberry	**aux fraises**	*oh frehz*
sundae	**une coupe**	*ewn koop*
sherbet	**un sorbet**	*uhn sohr-beh*
fruit ice	**un granité**	*uhn grah-nee-tay*

SPECIAL CIRCUMSTANCES

I don't want anything fried (salted).	**Je ne veux rien de frit (salé).** *zhuh nuh vuh ryan duh free (sah-lay)*
I cannot eat anything made with ____.	**Je ne peux rien manger de cuisiné au (à la) ____.** *zhuh nuh puh ryan mahn-zhay duh kwee-zee-nay oh (ah lah)*
Do you have any dishes without meats?	**Avez-vous des plats sans viande?** *ah-vay voo day plah sahn vyahnd*

BEVERAGES

Waiter, please bring me ____.	**Garçon, apportez-moi ____.** *gahr-ssohn ah-pohr-tay mwah*
coffee	**du café** *dew kah-fay*
■with milk (morning only)	**du café au lait** *dew kah-fay oh leh*

■ espresso   **du café-express** *dew kah-fay ehkss-prehss*

■ with cream   **du café-crème** *dew kah-fay krehm*

■ black coffee   **du café noir** *dew kah-fay nwahr*

■ iced coffee   **du café glacé** *dew kah-fay glah-ssay*

cider (alcoholic)   **du cidre** *dew see-druh*

juice   **du jus** *dew zhew*

lemonade   **de la citronnade** *duh lah see-troh-nahd*

milk   **du lait** *dew leh*

■ cold   **froid** *frwah*

■ hot   **chaud** *shoh*

■ milk shake   **un frappé** *uhn frah-pay*

orangeade   **une orangeade** *ewn oh-rahn-zhahd*

punch   **un punch** *uhn puhnsh*

soda   **un soda** *uhn soh-dah*

tea   **un thé** *uhn tay*

■ with milk   **au lait** *oh leh*

■ with lemon   **au citron** *oh see-trohn*

■ with sugar   **sucré** *sew-kray*

■ iced   **glacé** *glah-ssay*

water   **de l'eau** *(f.)* *duh loh*

■ cold   **de l'eau fraîche** *duh loh frehsh*

■ ice   **de l'eau glacée** *duh loh glah-ssay*

■ mineral   **de l'eau minérale** *duh loh mee-nay-rahl*

■ with gas   **gazeuse** *gah-zuhz*

■ without gas   **plate** *plaht*

SETTLING UP

The check, please.	**L'addition, s'il vous plaît.** *lah-dee-ssyohn seel voo pleh*
Separate checks.	**Des notes sépareés.** *day noht say-pah-ray*
Is the service (tip) included?	**Le service est compris?** *luh sehr-veess eh kohn-pree*
I haven't ordered this.	**Je n'ai pas commandé ceci.** *zhuh nay pah koh-mahn-day suh-ssee*
I don't think the bill is right.	**Je crois qu'il y a une erreur dans l'addition.** *zhuh krwah keel yah ewn ehr-ruhr dahn lah-dee-ssyohn*
We're in a hurry.	**Nous sommes pressés.** *noo sohm preh-ssay*
Is it ready?	**Est-elle prête?** *eh-tehl preht*
Will it take long?	**Il faudra longtemps?** *eel foh-drah lohn-tahn*
This is for you.	**Ceci est pour vous.** *suh-ssee eh poor voo*

APÉRITIFS AND WINES

APÉRITIFS

Byrrh **Dubonnet** **Saint-Raphaël**	wine-and-brandy–based, flavored with herbs and bitters
Pernod **Ricard**	anise-based, licorice-flavored
Vermouth	fortified wine made from red or white grapes
Cynar	bitter tasting, distilled from artichoke hearts

WINE

wine	**le vin**	*luh van*
■ red wine	**le vin rouge**	*luh van roozh*
■ rosé	**le vin rosé**	*luh van roh-zay*
■ sparkling wine	**le vin mous-seux**	*luh van moo-ssuh*
■ sherry	**un sherry**	*uhn sheh-ree*
■ white wine	**le vin blanc**	*luh van blahn*

GETTING TO KNOW PEOPLE

MEETING PEOPLE

Do you live here?	**Habitez-vous ici?**	*ah-bee-tay voo zee-ssee*
I am ____.	**Je suis ____.**	*zhuh swee*
■ from the United States	**des États-Unis**	*day zay-tah zew-nee*
■ from England	**de l'Angleterre**	*duh lahn-gluh-tehr*
■ from Canada	**du Canada**	*dew kah-nah-dah*
■ from Australia	**de l'Australie**	*duh lohss-trah-lee*
I like France (Paris) very much.	**La France (Paris) me plaît beaucoup.**	*lah frahnss (pah-ree) muh pleh boh-koo*
I would like to go there.	**Je voudrais y aller.**	*zhuh voo-dreh zee ah-lay*

How long will you be staying?	**Combien de temps resterez-vous ici?** *kohn-byan duh tahn rehss-tray voo zee-ssee*
I'll stay for a few days (a week).	**Je resterai quelques jours (une semaine).** *zhuh rehss-tray kehl-kuh zhoor (ewn suh-mehn)*
Where are you living now?	**Où habitez-vous en ce moment?** *oo ah-bee-tay voo zahn suh moh-mahn*
What hotel are you at?	**À quel hôtel êtes-vous?** *ah kehl oh-tehl eht voo*

GREETINGS AND INTRODUCTIONS

May I introduce _____.	**Puis-je vous présenter _____.** *pweezh voo pray-zahn-tay*
▪ my brother	**mon frère** *mohn frehr*
▪ my father	**mon père** *mohn pehr*
▪ my friend	**mon ami(e)** *mohn nah-mee*
▪ my husband	**mon mari** *mohn mah-ree*
▪ my mother	**ma mère** *mah mehr*
▪ my sister	**ma soeur** *mah suhr*
▪ my sweetheart	**mon(ma) fiancé(e)** *mohn (mah) fee-yahn-ssay*
▪ my wife	**ma femme** *mah fahm*
How do you do (Glad to meet you).	**Enchanté(e).** *ahn-shahn-tay*
How do you do (The pleasure is mine).	**Moi de même.** *mwah duh mehm*
Allow me to introduce myself.	**Permettez-moi de me présenter.** *pehr-meh-tay mwah duh muh pray-zahn-tay*

My name is ____.	**Je m'appelle ____.** *zhuh mah-pehl*
Mine is ____.	**Et moi, je m'appelle ____.** *ay mwah zhuh mah-pehl*
I am ____.	**Je suis ____.** *zhuh swee*
■ a teacher	**instituteur (institutrice)** *zan-sstee tew-tuhr (zan-sstee-tew-treess)*
■ a doctor	**médecin** *mayd-san*
■ a lawyer	**avocat(e)** *zah-voh-kah(t)*
■ a businessperson	**homme (femme) d'affaires** *zohm (fahm) dah-fehr*
■ a student	**étudiant(e)** *zay-tew-dyahn(t)*

DATING AND SOCIALIZING

May I have this dance?	**M'accordez-vous cette danse?** *mah-kohr-day voo seht dahnss*
Yes, all right. With pleasure.	**Oui, d'accord. Avec plaisir.** *wee, dah-kohr. ah-vehk pleh-zeer*
Would you like a cigarette (a drink)?	**Voudriez-vous une cigarette (une boisson)?** *voo-dree-yay voo ewn see-gah-reht (ewn bwah-ssohn)*
Do you have a light?	**Avez-vous du feu?** *ah-vay voo dew fuh*
Do you mind if I smoke?	**Ça vous dérange si je fume?** *sah voo day-rahnzh see zhuh fewm*
May I take you home?	**Puis-je vous raccompagner chez vous?** *pweezh voo rah-kohn-pah-nyay shay voo*
May I call you?	**Puis-je vous téléphoner?** *pweezh voo tay-lay-foh-nay*

What is your telephone number?	**Quel est votre numéro de téléphone?** *kehl eh voh-truh new-may-roh duh tay-lay-fohn*
Here's my telephone number (address).	**Voici mon numéro de téléphone (mon adresse).** *vwah ssee mohn new-may-roh duh tay-lay fohn (mohn nah-drehss)*
Will you write to me?	**Est-ce que vous m'écrirez?** *ehss kuh voo may-kree-ray*
Are you married?	**Êtes-vous marié(e)?** *eht voo mah-ree-ay*
Are you alone?	**Êtes-vous seul(e)?** *eht voo suhl*
Is your husband (wife) here?	**Êtes-vous ici avec votre mari (femme)?** *eht voo zee-ssee ah-vehk voh-truh mah-ree (fahm)*
I'm here with my family.	**Je suis ici avec ma famille.** *zhuh swee zee-ssee ah-vehk mah fah-mee*
Do you have any children?	**Avez-vous des enfants?** *ah-vay voo day zahn-fahn*
How many?	**Combien en avez-vous?** *kohn-byan-ahn nah-vay voo*
How old are they?	**Quel âge ont-ils?** *kehl ahzh ohn teel*
I'm single.	**Je suis célibataire.** *zhuh swee say-lee-bah-tehr*
You must come to visit us.	**Vous devez venir nous rendre visite.** *voo duh-vay vuh-neer noo rahn-druh vee-zeet*
Would you like me to take a picture (snapshot) of you?	**Voudriez-vous que je vous prenne en photo?** *voo-dree-yay voo kuh zhuh voo prehn ahn foh-toh*
Stand here.	**Restez ici.** *rehss-tay zee-ssee*
Don't move.	**Ne bougez pas.** *nuh boo-zhay pah*

Smile.	**Souriez.** *soo-ryay*
That's it.	**C'est ça.** *seh sah*
Will you take a picture of me (us)?	**Voudriez-vous me (nous) prendre en photo?** *voo-dree-yay voo muh (noo) prahn-druh-ahn foh-toh*
Are you doing anything tomorrow?	**Avez-vous quelque chose à faire demain?** *ah-vay voo kehl-kuh shohz ah fehr duh-man?*
Are you free this evening?	**Êtes-vous libre ce soir?** *eht voo lee-bruh suh swahr*
Would you like to go together?	**Voudriez-vous aller ensemble?** *voo-dree-yay voo zah-lay ahn-sahn-bluh*
I'll wait for you in front of the hotel.	**Je vous attendrai devant l'hôtel.** *zhuh voo zah-tahn-dray duh-vahn loh-tehl*
I'll pick you up at your house (hotel).	**Je viendrai vous prendre chez vous (à votre hôtel).** *zhuh vyan-dray voo prahn-druh shay voo (ah voh-truh oh-tehl*

SAYING GOOD-BYE

Nice to have met you.	**(Je suis) enchanté(e) d'avoir fait votre connaissance.** *(zhuh swee z)ahn-shahn-tay dah-vwahr feh voh-truh koh-neh-ssahnss*
The pleasure is mine.	**Le plaisir est partagé.** *luh pleh-zeer eh pahr-tah-zhay*
Regards to _____.	**Mon meilleur souvenir à _____.** *mohn meh-yuhr soo-vuh-neer ah*

SHOPPING

GOING SHOPPING

Where can I find _____?	**Où pourrais-je trouver _____?** *oo poo-rehzh troo-vay*
■ a bakery	**une boulangerie** *ewn boo-lahnzh-ree*
■ a barber shop	**un coiffeur** *uhn kwah-fuhr*
■ a beauty parlor	**un salon de beauté** *uhn sah-lohn duh boh-tay*
■ a bookstore	**une librairie** *ewn lee-breh-ree*
■ a butcher	**une boucherie** *ewn boosh-ree*
■ a camera shop	**un magasin d'appareils-photo** *uhn mah-gah-zan dah-pah-rehy foh-toh*
■ a candy store	**une confiserie** *ewn kohn-feess-ree*
■ a clothing store	**un magasin de vêtements** *uhn mah-gah-zan duh veht-mahn*
for children's clothes	**pour enfants** *poor ahn-fahn*
men's store	**pour hommes** *poor ohm*
women's boutique	**pour femmes** *poor fahm*
■ a delicatessen	**une charcuterie** *ewn shahr-kew-tree*
■ a department store	**un grand magasin** *uhn grahn mah-gah-zan*
■ a drugstore	**une pharmacie** *ewn fahr-mah-ssee*
■ a dry cleaner's	**une teinturerie** *ewn tan-tew-ruh-ree*

■ a florist   **un fleuriste** *uh<u>n</u> fluh-reesst*

■ a gift (souvenir) shop   **un magasin de souvenirs** *uh<u>n</u> mah-gah-za<u>n</u> duh soov-neer*

■ a grocery store   **une épicerie** *ewn ay-peess-ree*

■ a hardware store   **une quincaillerie** *ewn kah<u>n</u>-kahy-ree*

■ a jewelry store   **une bijouterie** *ewn bee-zhoo-tree*

■ a laundry   **une blanchisserie** *ewn blah<u>n</u>-sheess-ree*

■ a liquor store   **un magasin de vins et spiritueux** *uh<u>n</u> mah-gah-za<u>n</u> duh va<u>n</u> ay spee-ree-tew-uh*

■ a newsstand   **un kiosque à journaux** *uh<u>n</u> kee-ohsk ah zhoor-noh*

■ an optician   **un opticien** *uh<u>n</u> nohp-tee-ssya<u>n</u>*

■ a record store   **un magasin de disques** *uh<u>n</u> mah-gah-za<u>n</u> duh deessk*

■ a shoemaker   **un cordonnier** *uh<u>n</u> kohr-doh-nyay*

■ a shoe store   **un magasin de chaussures** *uh<u>n</u> mah-gah-za<u>n</u> duh shoh-ssewr*

■ a supermarket   **un supermarché** *uh<u>n</u> sew-pehr-mahr-shay*

■ a tailor   **un tailleur** *uh<u>n</u> tah-yuhr*

■ a tobacco shop   **un bureau de tabac** *uh<u>n</u> bew-roh duh tah-bah*

■ a toy store   **un magasin de jouets** *uh<u>n</u> mah-gah-za<u>n</u> duh zhoo-eh*

■ a travel agent   **une agence de voyages** *ewn ah-zhah<u>n</u>ss duh vwah-yahzh*

■ a watchmaker   **un horlogier** *uh<u>n</u> nohr-lohzh-yay*

■ a wine merchant   **un négociant en vins** *uh<u>n</u> nay-gohss-yah<u>n</u> ah<u>n</u> va<u>n</u>*

BOOKS

Where is the best (biggest) bookstore here?	**Où se trouve la meilleure (la plus grande) librairie par ici?** *oo suh troov lah meh-yuhr (lah plew grahnd) lee-breh-ree pahr ee-ssee*
What can I do for you?	**On vous sert?** *ohn voo sehr*
I'm looking for a copy of _____.	**Je cherche un exemplaire de _____.** *zhuh shehrsh uhn nehg-zahn-plehr duh*
Do you have books (novels) in English?	**Avez-vous des livres (des romans) en anglais?** *ah-vay voo day lee-vruh (day roh-mahn) ahn nahn-gleh*
I would like _____.	**Je voudrais _____.** *zhuh voo-dreh*
■ a guide book	**un guide touristique** *uhn geed too-reess-teek*
■ a map of this city	**un plan de la ville** *uhn plahn duh lah veel*
■ a pocket dictionary	**un dictionnaire de poche** *uhn deek-ssyoh-nehr duh pohsh*
■ a French-English dictionary	**un dictionnaire français-anglais** *uhn deek-ssyoh- nehr frahn-sseh ahn-gleh*
I'll take these books.	**Je vais prendre ces livres.** *zhuh veh prahn-druh say lee-vruh*
Will you wrap them, please?	**Voulez-vous bien les emballer?** *voo-lay voo byan lay zahn-bah-lay*

CLOTHING

Would you please show me _____?	**Veuillez me montrer _____?** *vuh-yay muh mohn-tray*
■ a belt	**une ceinture** *ewn san-tewr*

■ a blouse	**un chemisier** *uhn shuh-mee-zyay*
■ a bra	**un soutien-gorge** *uhn soo-tyan gohrzh*
■ a dress	**une robe** *ewn rohb*
■ an evening gown	**une robe du soir** *ewn rohb duh swahr*
■ leather (suede) gloves	**des gants en cuir (en daim)** *day gahn ahn kweer (ahn dan)*
■ handkerchiefs	**des mouchoirs** *day moo-shwahr*
■ a hat	**un chapeau** *uhn shah-poh*
■ a jacket	**un veston** *uhn vehss-tohn*
■ an overcoat	**un manteau/pardessus** *uhn mahn-toh/pahr-duh-ssew*
■ panties (women)	**un slip** *uhn sleep*
■ pants	**un pantalon** *uhn pahn-tah-lohn*
■ pantyhose	**des collants** *day koh-lahn*
■ a raincoat	**un imperméable** *uhn nan-pehr-may-ah-bluh*
■ a robe	**une robe de chambre** *ewn rohb duh shahn-bruh*
■ a shirt	**une chemise** *ewn shuh-meez*
■ (a pair of) shoes	**une paire de chaussures** *ewn pehr duh shoh-ssewr*
■ shorts (briefs)	**des caleçons** *day kahl-ssohn*
■ a skirt	**une jupe** *ewn zhewp*
■ a slip	**un jupon** *uhn zhew-pohn*
■ slippers	**des pantoufles** *day pahn-too-fluh*
■ socks	**des chaussettes** *day shoh-seht*
■ (nylon) stockings	**des bas (nylon)** *day bah (nee-lohn)*

■ a suit	**un complet/un tailleur** *uhn kohn-pleh/uhn tah-yuhr*
■ a sweater	**un chandail** *uhn shahn-dahy*
■ a tie	**une cravate** *ewn krah-vaht*
■ an undershirt (T-shirt)	**un sous-vêtement** *uhn soo veht-mahn*
■ a wallet	**un portefeuille** *uhn pohr-tuh-fuhy*

Is there a special sale today?
Y a-t-il des soldes aujourd'hui? *ee ah teel day sohld oh-zhoor-dwee*

I'd like the _____ with short (long) (no) sleeves.
Je voudrais le/la _____ à manches courtes (longues) (sans manches). *zhuh voo-dreh luh/lah _____ ah mahnsh koort (lohng) (sahn mahnsh)*

Do you have anything _____?
Avez-vous quelque chose _____? *ah-vay voo kehl-kuh shohz*

■ cheaper	**de moins cher** *duh mwan shehr*
■ else	**d'autre** *doh-truh*
■ larger	**de plus grand** *duh plew grahn*
■ more (less) expensive	**de plus (moins) cher** *duh plew (mwan) shehr*
■ longer	**de plus long** *duh plew lohn*
■ of better quality	**de meilleure qualité** *duh meh-yuhr kah-lee-tay*
■ shorter	**de plus court** *duh plew koor*
■ smaller	**de plus petit** *duh plew puh-tee*

I don't like the color.
Je n'aime pas la couleur. *zhuh nehm pah lah koo-luhr*

Do you have it in _____?
L'avez-vous en _____? *lah-vay voo zahn*

■ black	**noir** *nwahr*
■ blue	**bleu** *bluh*

■ brown	**brun/marron** *bruhn/mah-rohn*
■ gray	**gris** *gree*
■ green	**vert** *vehr*
■ pink	**rose** *rohze*
■ red	**rouge** *roozh*
■ white	**blanc** *blahn*
■ yellow	**jaune** *zhohn*
I want something in _____.	**Je voudrais quelque chose en _____.** *zhuh voo-dreh kehl-kuh shohz ahn*
■ chiffon	**mousseline de soie** *mooss-leen duh swah*
■ corduroy	**velours côtelé** *vuh-loor koht-lay*
■ cotton	**coton** *koh-tohn*
■ denim	**coutil** *koo-tee*
■ felt	**feutre** *fuh-truh*
■ flannel	**flanelle** *flah-nehl*
■ gabardine	**gabardine** *gah-bahr-deen*
■ lace	**dentelle** *dahn-tehl*
■ leather	**cuir** *kweer*
■ linen	**lin** *lan*
■ nylon	**nylon** *nee-lohn*
■ permanent press	**infroissable** *an-frwah-ssah-bluh*
■ polyester	**polyester** *poh-lee-ehss-tehr*
■ satin	**satin** *sah-tan*
■ silk	**soie** *swah*
■ suede	**daim** *dan*
■ terrycloth	**tissu-éponge** *tee-ssew-ay-pohnzh*

■ velvet	**velours** *vuh-loor*
■ wash and wear	**ne pas repasser** *nuh pah ruh-pah-ssay*
■ wool	**laine** *lehn*
It doesn't fit me.	**Cela ne me va pas.** *suh-lah nuh muh vah pah*
It fits very well.	**Ça va à la perfection.** *sah vah ah lah pehr-fehk-ssyohn*
I'll take it.	**Je le/la prends.** *zhuh luh/lah prahn*
Will you wrap it?	**Voulez-vous l'emballer, s'il vous plaît?** *voo-lay voo lahn-bah-lay, seel voo pleh*
That's all I want for now.	**C'est tout pour le moment.** *seh too poor luh moh-mahn*
Please take my measurements.	**Veuillez prendre mes mesures.** *vuh-yay prahn-druh may muh-zewr*
Can I try it on?	**Puis-je l'essayer?** *pweezh leh-sseh-yay*
Can you alter it?	**Pouvez-vous le/la retoucher?** *poo-vay voo luh/lah ruh-too-shay*
Can I return the article?	**Puis-je rendre cet article?** *pweezh rahn-druh seht ahr-tee-kluh*
Do you have something hand-made?	**Avez-vous quelque chose fait à la main?** *ah-vay voo kehl-kuh shohz feh-tah-lah-man*

FOOD AND HOUSEHOLD ITEMS

I'd like ____.	**Je voudrais ____.** *zhuh voo-dreh*
■ a bar of soap	**une savonnette** *ewn sah-voh-neht*

■ a bottle of juice   **une bouteille de jus** *ewn boo-tehy duh jew*

■ a box of cereal   **une boîte de céréale** *ewn bwaht duh say-ray-ahl*

■ a can of tomato sauce   **une boîte de sauce-tomate** *ewn bwaht duh sohss toh-maht*

■ a dozen eggs   **une douzaine d'oeufs** *ewn doo-zehn duh*

■ a jar of coffee   **un bocal de café** *uhn boh-kahl duh kah-fay*

■ a kilo (2.2 lbs.) of potatoes   **un kilo de pommes de terre** *uhn kee-loh duh pohm duh tehr*

■ a half-kilo (1.1 lbs.) of cherries   **un demi-kilo de cerises** *uhn duh-mee kee-loh duh suh-reez*

■ a liter (quart) of milk   **un litre de lait** *uhn lee-truh duh leh*

■ a package of candies   **un paquet de bonbons** *uhn pah-keh duh bohn-bohn*

■ a ¼ pound of cheese   **cent grammes de fromage** *sahn grahm duh froh-mahzh*

■ a roll of toilet paper   **un rouleau de papier hygiénique** *uhn roo-loh duh pah-pyay ee-zhyay-neek*

Can you give me 2 liters (half a gallon) of milk?   **Pouvez-vous me donner deux litres de lait?** *poo-vay voo muh doh-nay duh lee-truh duh leh*

I'd like a half liter of beer.   **Je voudrais un demi-litre de bière.** *zhuh voo-dreh zuhn duh-mee lee-truh duh byehr*

I'd like _____.   **Je voudrais _____.** *zhuh voo-dreh*

■ a kilo of oranges   **un kilo d'oranges** *zuhn kee-loh d'oh-rahnzh*

■ a half kilo of butter — **un demi-kilo de beurre** *zuhn duh-mee kee-loh duh buhr*

■ 200 grams (about ½ pound) of cookies — **deux cents grammes de biscuits** *duh sahn grahm duh beess-kwee*

■ a hundred grams of bologna. — **cent grammes de mortadelle** *sahn grahm duh mohr-tah-dehl*

What is this (that)? — **Qu'est-ce que c'est?** *kehss kuh seh*

Is it fresh? — **Est-ce frais?** *ehss freh*

JEWELER

I'd like to see ____. — **Je voudrais voir ____.** *zhuh voo-dreh vwahr*

■ a bracelet — **un bracelet** *uhn brahss-leh*

■ a brooch — **une broche** *ewn brohsh*

■ a chain — **une chaînette** *ewn sheh-neht*

■ a charm — **un porte-bonheur** *uhn pohrt boh-nuhr*

■ some earrings — **des boucles d'oreille** *day boo-kluh doh-rehy*

■ a necklace — **un collier** *uhn koh-lyay*

■ a pin — **une épingle** *ewn ay-pan-gluh*

■ a ring — **une bague** *ewn bahg*

　an engagement ring — **une bague de fiançailles** *ewn bahg duh fee-ahn-ssahy*

　a wedding ring — **une alliance** *ewn ah-lee-ahnss*

■ a watch — **une montre** *ewn mohn-truh*

■ a wristwatch (digital) — **une montre-bracelet (digitale)** *ewn mohn-truh brahss-leh (dee-zhee-tahl)*

Is this ____?	**Est-ce ____?** *ehss*
■ gold	**en or** *ahn nohr*
■ platinum	**en platine** *ahn plah-teen*
■ silver	**en argent** *ahn nahr-zhahn*
■ stainless steel	**en acier inoxydable** *ahn nah-ssyay ee-nohk-ssee-dah-bluh*

Is it solid gold or gold-plated?	**C'est en or massif ou en plaqué or?** *seh-tahn-nohr mah-sseef oo ahn plah-kay ohr*
How many carats is it?	**Combien de carats y a-t-il?** *kohn-byan duh kah-rah ee ah teel*
What is that stone?	**Quelle est cette pierre?** *kehl eh seht pyehr*

I would like ____.	**Je voudrais ____.** *zhuh voo-dreh*
■ an amethyst	**une améthyste** *zewn ah-may-teesst*
■ an aquamarine	**une aigue-marine** *zewn ehg mah-reen*
■ a diamond	**un diamant** *zuhn dee-ah-mahn*
■ an emerald	**une émeraude** *zewn aym-rohd*
■ ivory	**un ivoire** *zuhn nee-vwahr*
■ jade	**un jade** *zuhn zhahd*
■ onyx	**un onyx** *zuhn oh-neeks*
■ pearls	**des perles** *day pehrl*
■ a ruby	**un rubis** *uhn rew-bee*
■ a sapphire	**un saphir** *uhn sah-feer*
■ a topaz	**une topaze** *ewn toh-pahz*
■ turquoise	**une turquoise** *ewn tewr-kwahz*

I love this ring!	**J'adore cette bague.** *zhah-dohr seht bahg*
How much is it?	**Cela coûte combien?** *suh-lah koot kohn-byan*

MUSIC, RECORDS AND TAPES

Is there a record shop around here?	**Y a-t-il un magasin de disques par ici?** *ee ah teel uhn mah-gah-zan duh deessk pahr ee-ssee*
Where is the _____ section?	**Où est le rayon de/des _____?** *oo eh luh reh-yohn duh/day*
▪ American music	**la musique américaine** *lah mew-zeek ah-may-ree-kehn*
▪ classical music	**la musique classique** *lah mew-zeek klah-sseek*
▪ folk music	**la musique folklorique** *lah mew-zeek fohl-kloh-reek*
▪ latest hits	**derniers succès** *dehr-nyay sewk-sseh*
▪ French music	**la musique française** *lah mew-zeek frahn-ssehz*
▪ opera	**l'opéra** *loh-pay-rah*
▪ pop music	**la musique pop** *lah mew-zeek pohp*

NEWSSTAND

Do you carry newspapers (magazines) in English?	**Avez-vous des journaux (magazines) en anglais?** *ah-vay voo day zhoor-noh (mah-gah-zeen) ahn nahn-gleh*
I'd like to buy some (picture) postcards.	**Je voudrais acheter des cartes postales (illustrées).** *zhuh voo-dreh zahsh-tay day kahrt pohss-tahl (ee-lewss-tray)*
Do you have stamps?	**Avez-vous des timbres?** *ah-vay voo day tan-bruh*

How much is it?	**C'est combien?** *seh kohn-byan*
I'd like ____.	**Je voudrais ____.** *zhuh voo-dreh*
■ a daily	**un quotidien** *zuhn koh-tee-dyan*
■ a weekly	**un hebdomadaire** *zuhn ehb-doh-mah-dehr*
■ a monthly	**un mensuel** *zuhn mahn-ssew-ehl*

PHOTOGRAPHIC SUPPLIES

Where is there a camera shop?	**Où y a-t-il le magasin de photos?** *oo ee-ah-teel luh mah-gah-zan duh foh-toh*
Do you develop film here?	**Développez-vous les films ici?** *Day-vloh-pay voo lay feelm ee-ssee*
How much does it cost to develop a roll?	**Combien coûte le développement d'une pellicule?** *kohn-byan koot luh day-vlohp-mahn dewn peh-lee-kewl*
I have two rolls.	**J'ai deux pellicules.** *zhay duh peh-lee-kewl*
I want ____.	**Je voudrais ____.** *zhuh voo-dreh*
■ a print of each	**une épreuve de chacune** *zewn ay-pruhv duh shah-kewn*
■ an enlargement	**un agrandissement** *zuhn nah-grahn-deess-mahn*
■ with a glossy finish	**sur papier brillant** *sewr pah-pyay bree-yahn*
■ with a matte finish	**sur papier mat** *sewr pah-pyay maht*
I want a roll of 20 (36) exposures of color (black and white) film.	**Je voudrais une pellicule de vingt (trente-six) en couleur (noir et blanc).** *zhuh voo-dreh zewn peh-lee-kewl duh van (trahn-seess) ahn koo-luhr (nwahr ay blahn)*

for slides

pour diapositives *poor dee-ah-poh-zee-teev*

a film pack, number . . .

une cartouche, numéro . . . *ewn kahr-toosh, new-may-roh*

When can I pick up the pictures?

Quand puis-je venir chercher les photos? *kahn pweezh vuh-neer shehr-shay lay foh-toh*

Do you sell cameras?

Vendez-vous des appareils? *vahn-day voo day zah-pah-rehy*

I want an expensive (inexpensive) camera.

Je cherche un appareil cher (pas très cher). *zhuh shehrsh uhn nah-pah-rehy shehr (pah treh shehr)*

SOUVENIRS

I'd like ____.

Je voudrais ____. *zhuh voo-dreh*

a pretty gift

un joli cadeau *zuhn zhoh-lee kah-doh*

a small gift

un petit cadeau *zuhn puh-tee kah-doh*

a souvenir

un souvenir *zuhn soov-neer*

It's for . . .

C'est pour . . . *seh poor*

Could you suggest something?

Pourriez-vous me suggérer quelque chose? *poo-ree-yay voo muh sewg-zhay-ray kehl-kuh shohz*

Would you show me your selection of ____.

Voudriez-vous me montrer votre choix de ____. *voo-dree-yay voo muh mohn-tray voh-truh shwah duh*

blown glass

verre soufflé *vehr soo-flay*

carved objects

objets sculptés *ohb-zheh skewl-tay*

cut crystal

cristal taillé *kreess-tahl tah-yay*

dolls

poupées *poo-pay*

■ earthenware (pottery)	**poterie** *poh-tree*
■ fans	**éventails** *ay-vahn-tahy*
■ jewelry	**bijouterie** *bee-zhoo-tree*
■ lace	**dentelles** *dahn-tehl*
■ leather goods	**objets en cuir** *ohb-zheh ahn kweer*
■ liqueurs	**liqueurs** *lee-kuhr*
■ musical instruments	**instruments de musique** *an-strew-mahn duh mew-zeek*
■ perfumes	**parfums** *pahr-fuhn*
■ pictures	**tableaux** *tah-bloh*
■ posters	**affiches** *ah-feesh*
■ religious articles	**articles religieux** *ahr-tee-kluh ruh-lee-zhuh*
I don't want to spend more than ___ francs.	**Je ne voudrais pas dépenser plus de ___ francs.** *zhuh nuh voo-dreh pah day-pahn-ssay plew duh ___ frahn*

STATIONERY

I want to buy ___.	**Je voudrais acheter ___.** *zhuh voo-dreh zahsh-tay*
■ a ball-point pen	**un stylo à bille** *uhn stee-loh ah bee*
■ a deck of cards	**un paquet de cartes** *uhn pah-keh duh kahrt*
■ envelopes	**des enveloppes** *day zahn-vlohp*
■ an eraser	**une gomme** *ewn gohm*
■ glue	**de la colle** *duh lah kohl*

■a notebook	**un cahier** *uhn kah-yay*
■pencils	**des crayons** *day kreh-yohn*
■a pencil sharpener	**un taille-crayon** *uhn tahy kreh-yohn*
■a ruler	**une règle** *ewn reh-gluh*
■Scotch tape	**une bande adhésive (un scotch)** *ewn bahnd ahd-ay-zeev (uhn skohtsh)*
■some string	**de la ficelle** *duh lah fee-ssehl*
■typing paper	**du papier pour machine à écrire** *dew pah-pyay poor mah-sheen ah ay-kreer*
■wrapping paper	**du papier d'emballage** *dew pah-pyay dahn-bah-lahzh*
■a writing pad	**un bloc** *uhn blohk*
■writing paper	**du papier à lettres** *dew pah-pyay ah leh-truh*

TOBACCO SHOP

A pack (carton) of cigarettes, please.	**Un paquet (une cartouche) de cigarettes, s'il vous plaît.** *uhn pah-keh (ewn kahr-toosh) duh see-gah-reht, seel voo pleh*
■filtered	**avec filtre** *ah-vehk feel-truh*
■unfiltered	**sans filtre** *sahn feel-truh*
■menthol	**mentholées** *mahn-toh-lay*
■king-size	**long format** *lohn fohr-mah*
Are these cigarettes (very) strong (mild)?	**Ces cigarettes sont elles (très) fortes (douces)?** *say see-gah-reht sohn-tehl (treh) fohrt (dooss)*

Do you have American cigarettes?	**Avez-vous des cigarettes américaines?** *ah-vay voo day see-gah-reht ah-may-ree-kehn*
What brands?	**Quelles marques?** *kehl mahrk*
Please give me a pack of matches also.	**Donnez-moi aussi une boîte d'allumettes, s'il vous plaît.** *doh-nay mwah oh-see ewn bwaht dah-lew-meht, seel voo pleh*
Do you sell ____?	**Vendez-vous ____?** *vahn-day voo*
■ chewing tobacco	**du tabac à chiquer** *dew tah-bah ah shee-kay*
■ a cigarette holder	**un fume-cigarettes** *uhn fewm see-gah-reht*
■ cigars	**des cigares** *day see-gahr*
■ flints	**des pierres à briquet** *day pyehr ah bree-keh*
■ lighter fluid	**de l'essence à briquet** *duh leh-ssahnss ah bree-keh*
■ lighters	**des briquets** *day bree-keh*
■ pipes	**des pipes** *day peep*
■ pipe tobacco	**du tabac pour pipe** *dew tah-bah poor peep*

TOILETRIES

Do you have ____?	**Avez-vous ____?** *ah-vay voo*
■ bobby pins	**des épingles à cheveux** *day zay-pan-gluh ah shuh-vuh*
■ a brush	**une brosse** *ewn brohss*
■ cleansing cream	**une crème démaquillante** *ewn krehm day-mah-kee-yahnt*

■ a comb	**un peigne** *uhn peh-nyuh*
■ a deodorant	**du déodorant** *dew day-oh-doh-rahn*
■ (disposable) diapers	**des couches disponibles** *day koosh deess-poh-nee-bluh*
■ emery boards	**des limes à ongles** *day leem ah ohn-gluh*
■ eye liner	**du traceur à paupières** *dew trah-ssuhr ah poh-pyehr*
■ eyebrow pencil	**le crayon pour les yeux** *luh kreh-yohn poor lay zyuh*
■ eye shadow	**du fard à paupières** *dew fahr ah poh-pyehr*
■ hair spray	**la laque** *lah lahk*
■ lipstick	**le rouge à lèvres** *luh roozh ah leh-vruh*
■ makeup	**le maquillage** *luh mah-kee-yahzh*
■ mascara	**le cosmétique pour les cils** *luh kohz-may-teek poor lay seel*
■ a mirror	**un miroir** *uhn meer-wahr*
■ mouth wash	**le dentifrice** *luh dahn-tee-freess*
■ nail clippers	**un coupe-ongles** *uhn koop ohn-gluh*
■ a nail file	**une lime à ongles** *ewn leem ah ohn-gluh*
■ nail polish	**du vernis à ongles** *dew vehr-nee ah ohn-gluh*
■ nail polish remover	**du dissolvant** *dew dee-ssohl-vahn*
■ a prophylactic	**un prophylactique** *uhn proh-fee-lahk-teek*
■ a razor	**un rasoir** *uhn rah-zwahr*

■ razor blades	**une lame de rasoir**	*ewn lahm duh rah-zwahr*
■ rouge	**du fard**	*dew fahr*
■ sanitary napkins	**des serviettes hygiéniques**	*day sehr-vyeht ee-zhyay-neek*
■ (cuticle) scissors	**des ciseaux**	*day see-zoh*
■ shampoo	**le shampooing**	*luh shahn-pwan*
■ shaving lotion	**la lotion à raser**	*lah loh-ssyohn ah rah-zay*
■ soap	**du savon**	*dew sah-vohn*
■ a sponge	**une éponge**	*ewn ay-pohnzh*
■ talcum powder	**le talc**	*luh tahlk*
■ tampons	**des tampons périodiques**	*day tahn-pohn pay-ree-oh-deek*
■ tissues	**des mouchoirs en papier**	*day moo-shwahr ahn pah-pyay*
■ toilet paper	**du papier hygiénique**	*dew pah-pyay ee-zhyay-neek*
■ a toothbrush	**une brosse à dents**	*ewn brohss ah dahn*
■ toothpaste	**de la pâte dentifrice**	*duh lah paht dahn-tee-freess*
■ tweezers	**une pince à épiler**	*ewn panss ah ay-pee-lay*

PERSONAL CARE AND SERVICES

AT THE BARBER

Where is there a good barber shop? | **Où y a-t-il un bon coiffeur?** *oo ee-ah-teel uhn bohn kwah-fuhr*

I want a shave.	**Je voudrais me faire raser.** *zhuh voo-dreh muh fehr rah-zay*
I want a haircut.	**Je voudrais une coupe de cheveux.** *zhuh voo-dreh zewn koop duh shuh-vuh*
Short in back, long in front.	**Plus courts sur la nuque, plus longs sur le dessus.** *plew koor sewr lah newk plew lohn sewr luh duh-ssew*
Leave it long.	**Laissez-les longs.** *leh-ssay lay lohn*
I want it (very) short.	**Je les veux (très) courts.** *zhuh lay vuh treh koor*
You can cut a little _____.	**Vous pouvez dégager un peu _____.** *voo poo-vay day-gah-zhay uhn puh*
◾ in back	**derrière** *deh-ryehr*
◾ in front	**devant** *duh-vahn*
◾ off the top	**dessus** *duh-ssew*
◾ on the sides	**les côtés** *lay koh-tay*
That's enough.	**Ça suffit.** *sah sew-fee*
It's fine that way.	**C'est parfait comme ça.** *seh pahr-feh kohm sah*
I (don't) want _____.	**Je (ne) veux (pas de) _____.** *zhuh (nuh) vuh (pah duh)*
◾ shampoo	**un shampooing** *uhn shan-pwan*
◾ tonic	**une lotion** *ewn loh-ssyohn*
Use the scissors only.	**Employez seulement les ciseaux.** *ahn-plwah-yay suhl-mahn lay see-zoh*
I would like a razor cut.	**Je voudrais une coupe au rasoir.** *zhuh voo-dreh zewn koop oh rah-zwahr*
You can use the machine.	**Vous pouvez employer la machine.** *voo poo-vay zahn-plwah-yay lah mah-sheen*

Please trim my _____.	**Rafraîchissez moi** _____. *rah-freh-sshee-ssay mwah*
■ beard	**la barbe** *lah bahrb*
■ moustache	**la moustache** *lah mooss-tahsh*
■ sideburns	**les favoris** *lay fah-voh-ree*
Where's the mirror?	**Où est le miroir?** *oo eh luh meer-wahr*
How much do I owe you?	**Combien vous dois-je?** *kohn-byan voo dwahzh*

AT THE BEAUTY PARLOR

Is there a beauty parlor (hairdresser) near the hotel?	**Y a-t-il un salon de beauté près de l'hôtel?** *ee ah teel uhn sah-lohn duh boh-tay preh duh loh-tehl*
I'd like to make an appointment for this afternoon (tomorrow).	**Je voudrais prendre rendez-vous pour cet après-midi (demain).** *zhuh voo-dreh prahn-druh rahn-day voo poor seht ah-preh mee-dee (duh-man)*
Can you give me _____?	**Pouvez-vous me donner** _____? *poo-vay voo muh doh-nay*
■ a color rinse	**un shampooing colorant** *uhn shahn-pwan koh-loh-rahn*
■ a facial massage	**un massage facial** *uhn mah-ssahzh fah-ssyahl*
■ a haircut	**une coupe de cheveux** *ewn koop duh shuh-vuh*
■ a manicure	**une manucure** *ewn mah-new-kewr*
■ a permanent	**une permanente** *ewn pehr-mah-nahnt*
■ a shampoo	**un shampooing** *uhn shahn-pwan*
■ a tint	**des reflets** *day ruh-fleh*
■ a touch up	**une retouche** *ewn ruh-toosh*

| a wash and set | **un shampooing et une mise en plis** *uhn shahn-pwan ay ewn meez ahn plee* |

I'd like to see a color chart. | **Je voudrais voir une échelle de teintes.** *zhuh voo-dreh vwahr ewn ay-shehl duh tant* |

I want _____. | **Je voudrais _____.** *zhuh voo-dreh* |

| auburn | **auburn** *oh-buhrn* |

| (light) blond | **blond (clair)** *blohn (klehr)* |

| brunette | **brun** *bruhn* |

| a darker color | **une teinte plus foncée** *ewn tant plew fohn-ssay* |

| a lighter color | **une teinte plus claire** *ewn tant plew klehr* |

| the same color | **la même couleur** *lah mehm koo-luhr* |

Don't apply any hair-spray. | **Ne mettez pas de laque, s'il vous plaît.** *nuh meh-tay pah duh lahk seel voo pleh* |

Not too much hair-spray. | **Pas trop de laque.** *pah troh duh lahk* |

LAUNDRY AND DRY CLEANING

Where is the nearest laundry? | **Où est la blanchisserie la plus proche?** *oo eh lah blahn-sheess-ree lah plew prohsh* |

Where is the nearest laundromat? | **Où est la laverie automatique la plus proche?** *oo eh lah lah-vree oh-toh-mah-teek lah plew prohsh* |

Where is the nearest dry cleaner's?	**Où est la teinturerie la plus proche?** *oo eh lah tahn-tew-ruh-ree lah plew prohsh*
I have a lot of (dirty) clothes to be ____.	**J'ai beaucoup de vêtements (sales) à faire ____.** *zhay boh-koo duh veht-mahn sahl ah fehr*
■dry cleaned	**nettoyer à sec** *neh-twah-yay ah sehk*
■washed	**laver** *lah-vay*
■mended	**réparer** *ray-pah-ray*
■ironed	**repasser** *ruh-pah-ssay*
I need them for ____.	**J'en ai besoin pour ____.** *zhahn nay buh-zwan poor*
■tonight	**ce soir** *suh swahr*
■tomorrow	**demain** *duh-man*
■next week	**la semaine prochaine** *lah suh-mehn proh-shehn*
■the day after tomorrow	**après-demain** *ah-preh duh-man*
■at the latest	**au plus tard** *oh plew tahr*
I'm leaving ____.	**Je pars ____.** *zhuh pahr*
■soon	**bientôt** *byan-toh*
■tomorrow	**demain** *duh-man*
When will you bring it back?	**Quand est-ce que vous me le rendrez?** *kahn tehss kuh voo muh luh rahn-dray*
When will it be ready?	**Quand sera-t-il prêt?** *kahn suh-rah teel preh*
This isn't my laundry.	**Ce n'est pas ma lessive.** *suh neh pah mah lay-sseev*

SHOE REPAIRS

Can you fix these shoes (boots)?
Pouvez-vous réparer ces chaussures (bottes)? *poo-vay voo ray-pah-ray say shoh-ssewr (boht)*

Put on (half) soles and rubber heels.
Mettez les (demi-) semelles et les talons en caoutchouc. *meh-tay lay duh-mee suh-mehl ay lay tah-lohn ahn kah-oo-tshoo*

When will they be ready?
Quand seront-elles prêtes? *kahn suh-rohn tehl preht*

I need them by Saturday (without fail).
Il me les faut samedi (sans faute). *eel muh lay foh sahm-dee (sahn foht)*

WATCH REPAIRS

Can you fix this watch (alarm clock) for me?
Pouvez-vous me réparer cette montre (ce réveil)? *poo-vay voo muh ray-pah-ray seht mohn-truh (suh ray-vehy)*

When will it be ready?
Quand sera-t-elle prête? *kahn suh-rah tehl preht?*

May I have a receipt?
Puis-je avoir un reçu? *pweezh ah-vwahr uhn ruh-ssew?*

Can you look at it?
Pouvez-vous l'examiner? *poo-vay voo lehg-zah-mee-nay*

It doesn't run well.
Elle ne marche pas bien. *ehl nuh mahrsh pah byan*

It's fast (slow).
Cette montre avance (retarde). *seht mohn-truh ah-vahnss (ruh-tahrd)*

It's stopped.
Elle s'est arrêtée. *ehl seh tah-reh-tay*

CAMERA REPAIRS

Can you fix this camera?	**Pouvez-vous réparer cet appareil?** *poo-vay voo ray-pah-ray seht ah-pah-rehy*
How much will the repair cost?	**Combien coûtera la réparation?** *kohn-byan koo-trah lah ray-pah-rah-ssyohn*
When can I come and get it?	**Quand puis-je venir le chercher?** *kahn pweezh vuh-neer luh shehr-shay*
I need it as soon as possible.	**Il me le faut aussitôt que possible.** *Eel muh luh foh oh-see-toh kuh poh-ssee-bluh*

MEDICAL CARE

AT THE PHARMACY

Where is the nearest (all-night) pharmacy?	**Où se trouve la pharmacie de garde (de nuit) la plus proche?** *oo suh troov lah fahr-mah-ssee duh gahrd (duh nwee) lah plew prohsh*
At what time does the pharmacy open (close)?	**À quelle heure ouvre (ferme) la pharmacie?** *ah kehl uhr oo-vruh (fehrm) lah fahr-mah-ssee*
I need something for ____.	**Il me faut quelque chose pour ____.** *eel muh foh kehl-kuh shohz poor*
■ a cold	**un rhume** *uhn rewm*
■ constipation	**la constipation** *lah kohn-sstee-pah-ssyohn*
■ a cough	**une toux** *ewn too*
■ diarrhea	**la diarrhée** *lah dee-ah-ray*
■ a fever	**une fièvre** *ewn fyeh-vruh*

▪ hay fever	**le rhume des foins** *luh rewm day fwan*
▪ a headache	**un mal de tête** *uhn mahl duh teht*
▪ insomnia	**l'insomnie** *lan-sohm-nee*
▪ nausea	**la nausée** *lah noh-zay*
sunburn	**les coups de soleil** *lay koo duh soh-lehy*
▪ a toothache	**un mal de dents** *uhn mahl duh dahn*
▪ an upset stomach	**les indigestions** *lay-zan-dee-zhehss-tyohn*
Is a prescription needed for the medicine?	**Faut-il avoir une ordonnance pour ce médicament?** *foh-teel ah-vwahr ewn ohr-doh-nahnss poor suh may-dee-kah-mahn*
Can you fill this prescription for me now?	**Pourriez-vous me préparer cette ordonnance maintenant?** *poo-ree-yay voo muh pray-pah-ray seht ohr-doh-nahnss mant-nahn*
It's an emergency.	**C'est urgent.** *seh-tewr-zhahn*
Can I wait for it?	**Puis-je l'attendre?** *pweezh lah-tahn-druh*
How long will it take?	**Ça prendra combien de temps?** *sah prahn-drah kohn-byan duh tahn*
When can I come for it?	**Quand puis-je venir la chercher?** *kahn pweezh vuh-neer lah shehr-shay*
When can I come back?	**Quand puis-je revenir?** *kahn pweezh ruh-vuh-neer*
I would like _____.	**Je voudrais _____.** *zhuh voo-dreh*
▪ adhesive tape	**une bande adhésive** *zewn bahnd ahd-ay-zeev*
▪ alcohol	**l'alcool** *lahl-kohl*

■ an antacid	**un anti-acide** *zuhn nahn-tee ah-sseed*
■ an antiseptic	**un antiseptique** *zuhn nahn-tee-ssehp-teek*
■ aspirins	**des aspirines** *day-zahss-pee-reen*
■ bandages	**des bandes** *day bahnd*
■ Band-Aids	**des bandages** *day bahn-dazh*
■ corn plasters	**des emplâtres pour les cors** *day zahn-plah-truh poor lay kohr*
■ (absorbent) cotton	**de l'ouate** *duh lwaht*
■ cough drops	**des pastilles contre la toux** *day pahss-tee kohn-truh lah too*
■ cough syrup	**le sirop contre la toux** *luh see-roh kohn-truh lah too*
■ ear drops	**les gouttes pour les oreilles** *lay goot poor lay zoh-rehy*
■ eye drops	**les gouttes pour les yeux** *lay goot poor lay zyuh*
■ iodine	**de la teinture d'iode** *duh lah tan-tewr dyohd*
■ a (mild) laxative	**un laxatif (léger)** *zuhn lahk-ssah-teef (lay-zhay)*
■ milk of magnesia	**le lait de magnésie** *luh leh duh mah-nyay-zee*
■ suppositories	**les suppositoires** *lay sew-poh-zee-twahr*
■ a thermometer	**un thermomètre** *uhn tehr-moh-meh-truh*
■ tranquilizers	**des tranquillisants** *day trahn-kee-lee-zahn*
■ vitamins	**des vitamines** *day vee-tah-meen*

DOCTORS

I don't feel well.	**Je ne me sens pas bien.** *zhuh nuh muh sahn pah byan*
I feel sick.	**Je me sens mal.** *zhuh muh sahn mahl*
I need a doctor.	**Il me faut un docteur.** *eel muh foh tuhn dohk-tuhr*
Do you know a doctor who speaks English?	**Connaissez-vous un docteur qui parle anglais?** *koh-neh-ssay voo uhn dohk-tuhr kee pahrl ahn-gleh*
Where is his office?	**Où se trouve son cabinet?** *oo suh troov sohn kah-bee-neh*
I'm dizzy.	**J'ai des vertiges.** *zhay day vehr-teezh*
I have _____.	**J'ai _____.** *zhay*
■ an abscess	**un abcès** *uhn nahb-sseh*
■ a broken bone	**une fracture** *ewn frahk-tewr*
■ a bruise	**une contusion** *ewn kohn-tew-zyohn*
■ a burn	**une brûlure** *ewn brew-lewr*
■ something in my eye	**quelque chose dans l'oeil** *kehl-kuh shohz dahn luhy*
■ the chills	**des frissons** *day free-ssohn*
■ a cold	**un rhume** *uhn rewm*
a chest cold	**une bronchite** *ewn brohn-sheet*
a head cold	**un rhume de cerveau** *uhn rewm duh sehr voh*
■ cramps	**des crampes** *day krahnp*
■ a cut	**une coupure** *ewn koo-pewr*
■ diarrhea	**la diarrhée** *lah dee-ah-ray*

■dysentery — **la dysenterie** *lah dee-ssahn-tree*

■a fever — **de la fièvre** *duh lah fyeh-vruh*

■a fracture — **une fracture** *ewn frahk-tewr*

■a headache — **mal à la tête** *mahl ah lah teht*

■an infection — **une infection** *ewn an-fehk-ssyohn*

■a lump — **une grosseur** *ewn groh-ssuhr*

■a sore throat — **mal à la gorge** *mahl ah lah gohrzh*

■a stomach ache — **mal à l'estomac** *mahl ah lehss-toh-mah*

■swelling — **une enflure** *ewn ahn-flewr*

■a wound — **une blessure** *ewn bleh-ssewr*

I am constipated. — **Je suis constipé(e).** *zhuh swee kohn-sstee-pay*

It hurts me here. — **J'ai mal ici.** *zhay mahl ee-ssee*

My whole body hurts. — **Tout mon corps me fait mal.** *too mohn kohr muh feh mahl*

My ____ hurts. — **J'ai mal ____.** *zhay mahl*

■ankle — **à la cheville** *ah lah shuh-vee*

■arm — **au bras** *oh brah*

■back — **au dos** *oh doh*

■cheek — **à la joue** *ah lah zhoo*

■ear — **à l'oreille** *ah loh-rehy*

■eye — **aux yeux** *oh zyuh*

■face — **à la figure** *ah lah fee-gewr*

■finger — **au doigt** *oh dwah*

■foot — **au pied** *oh pyay*

■glands — **aux ganglions** *oh gahn-glee-yohn*

■head — **à la tête** *ah lah teht*

■ hand	**à la main**	*ah lah ma<u>n</u>*
■ hip	**à la hanche**	*ah lah ah<u>n</u>sh*
■ leg	**à la jambe**	*ah lah zhah<u>n</u>b*
■ lip	**à la lèvre**	*ah lah leh-vruh*
■ neck	**au cou**	*oh koo*
■ nose	**au nez**	*oh nay*
■ shoulder	**à l'épaule**	*ah lay-pohl*
■ throat	**à la gorge**	*ah lah gohrzh*
■ thumb	**au pouce**	*oh pooss*
■ toe	**à l'orteil**	*ah lohr-tehy*
■ wrist	**au poignet**	*oh pwah-nyeh*

I've had this pain since yesterday. **J'ai cette douleur depuis hier.** *zhay seht doo-luhr duh-pwee yehr*

There's a (no) history of asthma (diabetes) in my family. **Il y a (Il n'y a pas) d'asthme (de diabète) dans ma famille.** *eel yah (eel nyah pah) dahss-muh (duh dee-ah-beht) dah<u>n</u> mah fah-mee*

I'm (not) allergic to antibiotics (penicillin). **Je (ne) suis (pas) allergique aux antibiotiques.** *zhuh (nuh) swee (pah) zah-lehr-zheek oh zah<u>n</u>-tee-bee-oh-teek*

I have a pain in my chest around my heart. **J'ai une douleur à la poitrine près du coeur.** *zhay ewn doo-luhr ah lah pwah-treen preh dew kuhr*

I had a heart attack _____ year(s) ago. **J'ai eu une crise cardiaque il y a _____ ans.** *zhay ew ewn kreez kahr-dyahk eel yah _____ ah<u>n</u>*

I'm taking this medicine. **Je prends ce médicament.** *zhuh prah<u>n</u> suh may-dee-kah-mah<u>n</u>*

I'm pregnant. **J'attends un enfant.** *zah-tah<u>n</u> zuh<u>n</u> nah<u>n</u>-fah<u>n</u>*

I feel faint. **Je vais m'évanouir.** *zhuh veh may-vah-nweer*

I feel all right now.	**Je vais bien maintenant.** *zhuh veh byan mant-nahn*
I feel better.	**Je vais mieux.** *zhuh veh myuh*
I feel worse.	**Je me sens moins bien.** *zhuh muh sahn mwan byan*
Do I have ____?	**Est-ce que j'ai ____?** *ehss kuh zhay*
■ appendicitis	**l'appendicite** *lah-pahn-dee-sseet*
■ the flu	**la grippe** *lah greep*
■ tonsilitis	**une amygdalite** *ewn nah-meeg-dah-leet*
Is it serious (contagious)?	**C'est grave? (contagieux)?** *seh grahv (kohn-tah-zhyuh)*
Do I have to go to the hospital?	**Dois-je aller à l'hôpital?** *dwahzh ah-lay ah loh-pee-tahl*
When can I continue my trip?	**Quand pourrai-je poursuivre mon voyage?** *kahn poo-rayzh poor-sweevruh mohn vwah-yahzh*

DOCTOR'S INSTRUCTIONS

Open your mouth.	**Ouvrez la bouche.** *oo-vray lah boosh*
Stick out your tongue.	**Tirez la langue.** *tee-ray lah lahng*
Cough.	**Toussez.** *too-ssay*
Breathe deeply.	**Respirez profondément.** *rehss-peeray proh-fohn-day-mahn*
Take off your clothing (to the waist).	**Déshabillez-vous (jusqu'à la ceinture).** *day-zah-bee-yay voo (zhewss-kah lah san-tewr)*
Lie down.	**Étendez-vous.** *ay-tahn-day voo*
Stand up.	**Levez-vous.** *luh-vay voo*
Get dressed.	**Habillez-vous.** *ah-bee-yay voo*

PATIENT

| Are you going to give me a prescription? | **Allez-vous me donner une ordonnance?** *ah-lay voo muh doh-nay ewn ohr-doh-nahnss* |

| How often must I take this medicine (these pills)? | **Combien de fois par jour dois-je prendre ce médicament (ces pilules)?** *kohn-byan duh fwah pahr zhoor dwahzh prahn-druh suh may-dee-kah-mahn (seh pee-lewl)* |

| (How long) do I have to stay in bed? | **(Combien de temps) dois-je garder le lit?** *(kohn-byan duh tahn) dwahzh gahr-day luh lee* |

| Thank you (for everything), doctor. | **Merci bien (pour tout), monsieur le docteur.** *mehr-ssee byan (poor too), muh-ssyuh luh dohk-tuhr* |

| What is your fee? | **Quels sont vos honoraires?** *kehl sohn voh zoh-noh-rehr* |

| I have medical insurance. | **J'ai une assurance médicale.** *zhay ewn ah-ssew-rahnss may-dee-kahl* |

IN THE HOSPITAL (ACCIDENTS)

| Help! | **Au secours!** *oh suh-koor* |

| Help me, somebody! | **Que quelqu'un m'aide, je vous en prie!** *kuh kehl-kuhn mehd zhuh voo zahn pree* |

| Get a doctor, quick! | **Vite, appelez un docteur!** *veet, ah-play uhn dohk-tuhr* |

| Call an ambulance! | **Faites venir une ambulance!** *feht vuh-neer ewn ahn-bew-lahnss* |

| Take me (him, her) to the hospital. | **Emmenez-moi (le, la) à l'hôpital.** *ahn-muh-nay mwah (luh, lah) ah loh-pee-tahl* |

| I need first aid. | **J'ai besoin de premiers soins.** *zhay buh-zwan duh pruh-myay swan* |

I've fallen.	**Je suis tombé(e).** *zhuh swee tohn-bay*
I was knocked down (run over).	**On m'a renversé(e).** *ohn mah rahn-vehr-ssay*
I've had a heart attack.	**J'ai eu une crise cardiaque.** *zhay ew ewn kreez kahr-dyahk*
I burned myself.	**Je me suis brûlé(e).** *zhuh muh swee brew-lay*
I cut myself.	**Je me suis coupé(e).** *zhuh muh swee koo-pay*
I'm bleeding.	**Je saigne.** *zhuh seh-nyuh*
I've (He's) lost a lot of blood.	**J'ai (Il a) perdu beaucoup de sang.** *zhay (eel ah) pehr-dew boh-koo duh sahn*

AT THE DENTIST

I have to go to the dentist.	**Il me faut aller chez le dentiste.** *eel muh foh tah-lay shay luh dahn-teesst*
Can you recommend a dentist?	**Pouvez-vous me recommander un dentiste?** *poo-vay voo muh ruh-koh-mahn-day uhn dahn-teesst*
I have a toothache that's driving me crazy.	**J'ai un mal de dents à tout casser. (J'ai une rage de dents.)** *zhay uhn mahl duh dahn ah too kah-ssay (zhay ewn rahzh duh dahn)*
I have a rotten tooth that's giving me a lot of pain.	**J'ai une dent cariée qui me fait très mal.** *zhay ewn dahn kah-ree-yay kee muh feh treh mahl*
I've lost a filling.	**J'ai perdu un plombage.** *zhay pehr-dew uhn plohn-bahzh*
I've broken a tooth.	**Je me suis cassé une dent.** *zhuh muh swee kah-ssay ewn dahn*
I can't chew.	**Je ne peux pas mâcher.** *zhuh nuh puh pah mah-shay*

My gums hurt me.	**Les gencives me font mal.** *lay zhahn-sseev muh fohn mahl*
Is there an infection?	**Y a-t-il une infection?** *ee ah-teel ewn an-fehk-ssyohn*
Will you have to extract the tooth?	**Faut-il extraire la dent?** *foh teel ehkss-trehr lah dahn*
Can you fill it ____?	**Pouvez-vous l'obturer ____?** *poo-vay voo lohb-tew-ray*
Can you fix ____?	**Pouvez-vous réparer ____?** *poo-vay voo ray-pah-ray*
■ this bridge	**ce bridge** *suh breedzh*
■ this crown	**cette couronne** *seht koo-rohn*
■ this denture	**ce dentier** *suh dahn-tyay*
■ these false teeth	**ces fausses dents** *say fohss dahn*
When should I come back?	**Quand devrais-je revenir?** *kahn duh-vreh-zhuh ruh-vuh-neer*
What is your fee? . . . are your fees?	**Combien vous dois-je?** *kohn-byan voo dwahzh*

WITH THE OPTICIAN

Can you repair these glasses (for me)?	**Pouvez-vous (me) réparer ces lunettes?** *poo-vay voo (muh) ray-pah-ray say lew-neht*
I've broken a lens (the frame).	**J'ai cassé un verre (la monture).** *zhay kah-ssay uhn vehr (lah mohn-tewr)*
Can you put in a new lens?	**Pouvez-vous mettre un nouveau verre?** *poo-vay voo meh-truh uhn noo-voh vehr*
Can you tighten the screw?	**Pouvez-vous resserrer la vis?** *poo-vay voo ruh-ssay-ray lah veess*

I need the glasses as soon as possible.	**Il me faut ces lunettes aussitôt que possible.** *eel muh foh say lew-neht oh-ssee-toh kuh poh-ssee-bluh*
I don't have any others.	**Je n'ai pas d'autre paire.** *zhuh nay pah doh-truh pehr*
Do you sell contact lenses?	**Vendez-vous des verres de contact?** *vahn-day voo day vehr duh kohn-tahkt*
I've lost a lens.	**J'ai perdu un verre.** *zhay pehr-dew uhn vehr*
Can you replace it right away?	**Pouvez-vous le remplacer tout de suite?** *poo-vay voo luh rahn-plah-ssay toot sweet*
Do you sell sun glasses?	**Vendez-vous des lunettes de soleil?** *vahn-day voo day lew-neht duh soh-lehy*

COMMUNICATIONS

POST OFFICE

I want to mail a letter.	**Je voudrais mettre cette lettre à la poste.** *zhuh voo-dreh meh-truh seht leh-truh ah lah pohsst*
Where's the post office?	**Où se trouve le bureau de poste?** *oo suh troov luh bew-roh duh pohsst*
What is the postage on ____ to the United States?	**Quel est l'affranchissement ____ pour les États-Unis?** *kehl eh lah-frahn-sheess-mahn poor lay zay-tah zew-nee*
▪ a letter	**d'une lettre** *dewn leh-truh*
▪ an air-mail letter	**pour une lettre envoyée par avion** *poor ewn leh-truh ahn-vwah-yay pahr ah-vyohn*

■ an insured letter **pour une lettre recommandée** *poor ewn leh-truh ruh-koh-mah<u>n</u>-day*

■ a registered letter **pour une lettre recommandée** *poor ewn leh-truh ruh-koh-mah<u>n</u>-day*

■ a special delivery letter **pour une lettre par exprès** *poor ewn leh-truh pahr ehkss-prehss*

■ a package **un colis** *zuh<u>n</u> koh-lee*

■ a post card **une carte postale** *zewn kahrt pohss-tahl*

When will it arrive? **Quand arrivera-t-il (elle)?** *kah<u>n</u> tah-ree-vrah teel? (tehl)*

Which is the _____ window? **Quel est le guichet _____?** *kehl eh luh gee-sheh*

■ general delivery **pour la poste restante** *poor lah pohsst rehss-tah<u>n</u>t*

■ money order **pour les mandats-poste** *poor lay mah<u>n</u>-dah pohsst*

■ stamp **pour les timbres-poste** *poor lay ta<u>n</u>-bruh pohsst*

Are there any letters for me? **Y a-t-il des lettres pour moi?** *ee ah-teel day leh-truh poor mwah*

My name is _____. **Je m'appelle _____.** *zhuh mah-pehl*

I'd like _____. **Je voudrais _____.** *zhuh voo-dreh*

■ 10 post cards **dix cartes postales** *dee kahrt pohss-tahl*

■ 5 (air mail) stamps **cinq timbres (courrier aérien)** *sa<u>n</u>k tah<u>n</u>-bruh (koo-ree-yay ah-ay-rya<u>n</u>)*

TELEGRAMS

I'd like to send a telegram (night letter) to _____. **Je voudrais envoyer un télégramme (une lettretélégramme) à _____.** *zhuh voo-dreh zah<u>n</u>-vwah-yay uh<u>n</u> tay-lay-grahm (ewn leh-truh tay-lay-grahm) ah*

Where's the telegraph window?	**Où est le guichet pour les télégrammes?** *oo eh luh gee-sheh poor lay tay-lay-grahm*
How much is it per word?	**Quel est le tarif par mot?** *kehl eh luh tah-reef pahr moh*
Where are the forms?	**Où sont les formulaires (imprimés)?** *oo sohn lay fohr-mew-lehr (an-pree-may)*
I want to send it collect.	**Je voudrais l'envoyer en P.C.V.** *zhuh voo-dreh lahn-vwah-yay ahn pay say vay*

TELEPHONES

Where is _____?	**Où y a-t-il _____?** *oo ee ah-teel*
■ a public telephone	**un téléphone public** *uhn tay-lay-fohn pew-bleek*
■ a telephone booth	**une cabine téléphonique** *ewn kah-been tay-lay-foh-neek*
■ a telephone directory	**un annuaire téléphonique** *uhn nah-new-ehr tay-lay-foh-neek*
May I use your phone?	**Puis-je me servir de votre téléphone?** *pweezh muh sehr-veer duh voh-truh tay-lay-fohn*
I want to make a _____ to	**Je voudrais téléphoner _____** *zhuh voo-dreh tay-lay-foh-nay*
■ local call	**en ville** *ahn veel*
■ long distance call	**à l'extérieur** *ah lehkss-tay-ryuhr*
■ person to person call	**avec préavis** *ah-vehk pray-ah-vee*
Can I call direct?	**Puis-je téléphoner en direct?** *pweezh tay-lay-foh-nay ahn dee-rehkt*
Do I need tokens for the phone?	**Faut-il des jetons pour le téléphone?** *foh teel day zhuh-tohn poor luh tay-lay-fohn*

Can you give me a token, please?	**Pourriez-vous me donner un jeton, s'il vous plaît?** *poo-ree-yay voo muh doh-nay uhn zhuh-tohn seel voo pleh*
How do I get the _____.	**Que fait-on pour _____?** *kuh feh-tohn poor*
■ Operator?	**parler à la téléphoniste?** *pahr-lay ah lah tay-lay-foh-neesst*
■ area code	**obtenir le code régional** *ohp-tuh-neer luh kohd ray-zhyohn-nahl*
Operator, can you get me number 23.34.56?	**Mademoiselle, pourriez vous me donner le vingt-trois, trente-quatre, cinquante-six?** *mahd-mwah-zehl poo-ree-yay voo muh doh-nay luh van-trwah trahnt kah-truh san-kahnt seess*
My number is _____.	**Mon numéro est _____.** *mohn new-may-roh eh*
May I speak to _____?	**Est-ce que je pourrais parler à _____?** *ehss kuh zhuh poo-reh pahr-lay ah*
I'd like to speak to _____.	**Je voudrais parler à _____.** *zhuh voo-dreh pahr-lay ah*
Is Mr. _____ in?	**Monsieur _____, est-il là?** *Muh-ssyuh _____ eh-teel lah*
Speaking.	**C'est _____ à l'appareil.** *seh _____ ah lah-pah-rehy*
Hello.	**Allô.** *ah-loh*
Who is calling?	**Qui est à l'appareil?** *kee eh tah lah-pah-rehy*
I can't hear.	**Je ne peux pas vous entendre.** *zhuh nuh puh pah voo zahn-tahn-druh*
Speak louder.	**Parlez plus fort.** *pahr-lay plew fohr*
Don't hang up.	**Ne quittez pas.** *nuh kee-tay pah*

This is ____.	**Ici ____.** *ee-ssee*
Operator, there's no answer (They don't answer).	**Mademoiselle, ça ne répond pas.** *mahd-mwah-zehl, sah nuh ray-pohn pah*
The line is busy.	**La ligne est occupée.** *lah lee-nyuh eh toh-kew-pay*
You gave me (that was) a wrong number.	**Vous m'avez donné le mauvais numéro.** *voo mah-vay doh-nay luh moh-veh new-may-roh*
I was cut off.	**J'ai été coupé.** *zhay ay-tay koo-pay*
Please dial it again.	**Veuillez recomposez le numéro.** *vuh-yay ruh-kohn-poh-zay luh new-may-roh*
I want to leave a message.	**Je voudrais laisser un message.** *zhuh voo-dreh leh-ssay uhn meh-ssahzh*

DRIVING A CAR

ROAD SYSTEM

Autoroute	a high-speed super freeway for long distance trips. These are toll roads.
Route nationale	a main highway used by cars going from one small town to another.
Route départementale	minor highway
Chemin communal	a local road
Chemin rural	a scenic country road

SIGNS

Accotement non stabilisé	Soft shoulder
Allumez vos phares	Put on headlights
Arrêt interdit	No stopping
Attention	Caution
Céder le passage	Yield

No U-turn

No passing

Border crossing

Traffic signal ahead

Speed limit

Traffic circle (roundabout) ahead

Minimum speed limit

All traffic turns left

End of no passing zone

One-way street

Detour

Danger ahead

Entrance to expressway

Expressway ends

Guarded railroad crossing

Yield

Stop

Right of way

Dangerous intersection ahead

Gasoline (petrol) ahead

Parking

No vehicles allowed

Dangerous curve

Pedestrian crossing

Oncoming traffic has right of way

No bicycles allowed

No parking allowed

No entry

No left turn

Chaussée déformée	Poor roadway
Chute de pierres	Falling rocks
Circulation interdite	No thoroughfare
Descente (Pente) dangereuse	Steep slope (hill)
Déviation	Detour
Douane	Customs
École	School
Entrée interdite	No entrance
Fin d'interdiction de _____	End of _____ zone
Interdiction de doubler	No Passing
Interdiction de stationner	No Parking
Interdit aux piétons	No Pedestrians
Piste réservée aux transports publics	Lane for Public Transportation
Ralentir (Ralentissez)	Slow
Réservé aux piétons	Pedestrians only
Sens interdit	Wrong way
Sens unique	One Way
Serrez à gauche (à droite)	Keep left (right)
Sortie d'autoroute	Freeway (throughway) Exit
Sortie de véhicules	Vehicle Exit
Stationnement autorisé	Parking Permitted
Stationnement interdit	No Parking
Tenez la droite (gauche)	Keep to the right (left)
Verglas	Icy Road
Virage dangereux	Dangerous Curve
Voie de dégagement	Private Entrance
Zone Bleue	Blue Zone (parking)

CAR RENTALS

Where can I rent a car?	**Où puis-je louer une voiture?** *oo pweezh loo-ay ewn vwah-tewr*
■ a motorcycle	**une motocyclette** *ewn moh-toh-see-kleht*

■ a bicycle	**une bicyclette**	*ewn bee-ssee-kleht*
■ a scooter	**un scooter**	*uhn skoo-tehr*
■ a moped	**un mobilette**	*uhn moh-bee-leht*
I want a ____.	**Je voudrais ____.**	*zhuh voo-dreh*
■ a small car	**une petite voiture**	*zewn puh-teet vwah-tewr*
■ large car	**une grande voiture**	*zewn grahnd vwah-tewr*
■ sports car	**une voiture de sport**	*zewn vwah-tewr duh spohr*
I prefer automatic transmission.	**Je préfère la transmission automatique.**	*zhuh pray-fehr lah trahnz-mee-ssyohn oh-toh-mah-teek*
How much does it cost ____?	**Quel est le tarif ____?**	*kehl eh luh tah-reef*
■ per day	**à la journée**	*ah lah zhoor-nay*
■ per week	**à la semaine**	*ah lah suh-mehn*
■ per kilometer	**au kilomètre**	*oh kee-loh-meh-truh*
How much is the insurance?	**Quel est le montant de l'assurance?**	*kehl eh luh mohn-tahn duh lah-ssew-rahnss*
Is the gas included?	**Est-ce que l'essence est comprise?**	*ehss kuh leh-ssahnss eh kohn-preez*
Do you accept credit cards? Which ones?	**Acceptez vous des cartes de crédit? Lesquelles?**	*ahk-ssehp-tay voo day kahrt duh kray-dee? Lay-kehl*
Here's my driver's license.	**Voici mon permis de conduire.**	*vwah-ssee mohn pehr-mee duh kohn-dweer*
Do I have to leave a deposit?	**Dois-je verser des arrhes?**	*dwahzh vehr-ssay day zahr*

Is there a drop-off charge?	**Faut-il payer plus en cas de non-retour ici?** *foh-teel peh-yay plews ahn kah duh nohn-ruh-toor ee-ssee*
I want to rent the car here and leave it in _____ (name of city).	**Je veux louer la voiture ici et la laisser à _____.** *zhuh vuh loo-ay lah vwah-tewr ee-ssee ay lah leh-ssay ah*
What kind of gas does it take?	**Quelle essence emploie-t-elle?** *kehl eh-ssahnss ahn-plwah-tehl*

ON THE ROAD

Excuse me.	**Excusez-moi.** *ehkss-kew-zay mwah* **Pardon** *pahr-dohn*
Can you tell me _____?	**Pouvez-vous me dire _____?** *poo-vay voo muh deer*
Which way is it to _____?	**Comment aller à _____?** *koh-mahn ah-lay ah*
How do I get to _____?	**Comment puis-je aller à _____?** *koh-mahn pweezh ah-lay ah*
I think we're lost.	**Je crois que nous nous sommes égarés.** *zhuh krwah kuh noo noo sohm zay-gah-ray* **Nous sommes sur la mauvaise route.** *noo sohm sewr lah moh-vehz root*
Which is the road to _____?	**Quelle est la route pour _____?** *kehl eh lah root poor*
Is this the road (way) to _____?	**Est-ce la route de _____?** *ehss lah root duh*
Where does this road go?	**Où mène cette route?** *oo mehn seht root*
How far is it from here to the next town?	**À quelle distance sommes-nous du prochain village?** *ah kehl deess-tahnss sohm noo dew proh-shan vee-lahzh*

How far away is _____?	**À quelle distance est _____?** *ah kehl deess-tahnss eh*
Is the next town far?	**Le prochain village, est-il loin?** *luh proh-shan vee-lahzh eh-teel lwan*
What's the next town called?	**Comment s'appelle le prochain village?** *koh-mahn sah-pehl luh proh-shan vee-lahzh*
Do you have a road map?	**Avez-vous une carte routière?** *Ah-vay voo zewn kahrt roo-tyehr*
Can you show it to me on the map?	**Pourriez-vous me l'indiquer sur la carte?** *poo-ree-yay voo muh lan-dee-kay sewr lah kahrt*
Is the road in good condition?	**Est-ce que la route est en bon état?** *ehss kuh lah root eh tahn bohn nay-tah*
Is this the shortest way?	**Est-ce le chemin le plus court?** *ehss luh shuh-man luh plew koor*
Are there any detours?	**Y a-t-il des déviations?** *ee ah-teel day day-vee-ah-ssyohn*
Do I go straight?	**Est-ce que je vais tout droit?** *ehss kuh zhuh veh too drwah*
Do I turn to the right (to the left)?	**Est-ce que je tourne à droite (à gauche)?** *ehss kuh zhuh toorn ah drwaht (ah gohsh)*

AT THE SERVICE STATION

| Where is there a gas station? | **Où y a-t-il une station-service?** *oo ee ah-teel ewn stah-ssyohn sehr-veess* |
| I need gas. | **J'ai besoin d'essence.** *zhay buh-zwan deh-ssahnss* |

Fill'er up with _____.	**Faites-le plein, s'il vous plaît _____.** *feht-luh plan seel-voo pleh*	
diesel	**du gas-oil** *dew gahz-wahl*	
regular	**de l'ordinaire** *duh lohr-dee-nehr*	
super	**du super** *dew sew-pehr*	
Give me _____ liters.	**Donnez m'en _____ litres, s'il vous plaît.** *doh-nay mahn _____ lee-truh, seel voo pleh*	
I need 60 liters of gas.	**Je voudrais 60 (soixante) litres d'essence.** *zhuh voo-dreh swah-ssahnt lee-truh deh-ssahnss*	
Please check _____.	**Veuillez vérifier _____.** *vuh-yay vay-ree-fyay*	
the battery	**la batterie** *lah bah-tree*	
the brakes	**les freins** *lay fran*	
the carburetor	**le carburateur** *luh kahr-bew-rah-tuhr*	
the oil	**le niveau de l'huile** *luh nee-voh duh lweel*	
the spark plugs	**les bougies** *lay boo-zhee*	
the tires	**les pneus** *lay pnuh*	
the tire pressure	**la pression des pneus** *lah preh-ssyohn day pnuh*	
the water	**le niveau de l'eau** *luh nee-voh duh loh*	
Change the oil.	**Changez l'huile, s'il vous plaît.** *shahn-zhay lweel seel voo pleh*	
Grease the car.	**Faites un graissage complet de la voiture, s'il vous plaît.** *feht uhn greh-ssahzh kohn-pleh duh lah vwah-tewr seel voo pleh*	

ACCIDENTS, REPAIRS

It overheats.	**Elle chauffe.** *ehl shohf*
It doesn't start.	**Elle ne démarre pas.** *ehl nuh day-mahr pah*
It doesn't go.	**Elle ne marche pas.** *ehl nuh mahrsh pah*
I have a flat tire.	**J'ai un pneu crevé.** *zhay-uhn pnuh kruh-vay*
My car has broken down.	**Ma voiture est en panne.** *mah vwah-tewr eh tahn pahn*
The radiator is leaking.	**Le radiateur coule.** *luh rah-dee-ah-tuhr kool*
The battery is dead.	**La batterie ne fonctionne plus.** *lah bah-tree nuh fohnk-ssyohn plew*
The keys are locked inside the car.	**Les clés sont enfermées à l'intérieur de la voiture.** *lay klay sohn tahn-fehr-may ah lan-tay-ree-yuhr duh lah vwah-tewr*
Is there a garage near here?	**Y a-t-il un garage par ici?** *ee ah-teel uhn gah-rahzh pahr ee-ssee*
I need a mechanic (tow truck).	**Il me faut un mécanicien (une dépanneuse).** *eel muh foh tuhn may-kah-nee-ssyan (ewn day-pah-nuhz)*
Can you _____?	**Pouvez-vous _____?** *poo-vay voo*
▪ help me	**m'aider** *meh-day*
▪ push me	**me pousser** *muh poo-ssay*
▪ tow me	**me remorquer** *muh ruh-mohr-kay*
Can you lend me _____?	**Pouvez-vous me prêter _____?** *poo-vay voo muh preh-tay*
▪ a flashlight	**une lampe de poche** *ewn lahnp duh pohsh*

◼ a hammer	**un marteau** *uhn mahr-toh*
◼ a jack	**un cric** *uhn kree*
◼ a monkey wrench	**une clé anglaise** *ewn klay ahn-glehz*
◼ pliers	**des pinces** *day panss*
◼ a screwdriver	**un tournevis** *uhn toorn-veess*
I need ____.	**J'ai besoin ____.** *zhay buh-zwan*
◼ a bolt	**d'un boulon** *duhn boo-lohn*
◼ a bulb	**d'une ampoule** *dewn ahn-pool*
◼ a filter	**d'un filtre** *duhn feel-truh*
◼ a nut	**d'un écrou** *duhn nay-kroo*
Can you fix the car?	**Pouvez-vous réparer la voiture?** *Poo-vay voo ray-pah-ray lah vwah-tewr*
Can you repair it temporarily?	**Pouvez-vous la réparer provisoirement?** *poo-vay voo lah ray-pah-ray proh-vee-zwahr-mahn*
Do you have the part?	**Avez-vous la pièce de rechange?** *ah-vay voo lah pyehss duh ruh-shahnzh*
I think there's something wrong with ____.	**Je crois que ____ ne fonctionne pas.** *zhuh krwah kuh ____ nuh fohnk-ssyohn pas.*
◼ the directional signal	**le clignotant** *luh klee-nyoh-tahn*
◼ the door handle	**la poignée** *lah pwah-nyay*
◼ the electrical system	**l'installation électrique** *lan-stah-lah-ssyohn ay-lehk-treek*
◼ the fan	**le ventilateur** *luh vahn-tee-lah-tuhr*
◼ the fan belt	**la courroie de ventilateur** *lah koor-wah duh vahn-tee-lah-tuhr*
◼ the fuel pump	**la pompe à essence** *lah pohnp ah eh-ssahnss*

■ the gears	**l'engrenage** *lahn-gruh-nahzh*
■ the gear shift	**le changement de vitesses** *luh shahnzh-mahn duh vee-tehss*
■ the headlight	**le phare** *luh fahr*
■ the horn	**le klaxon** *luh klahk-ssohn*
■ the ignition	**l'allumage** *lah-lew-mahzh*
■ the radio	**la radio** *lah rah-dyoh*
■ the starter	**le démarreur** *luh day-mah-ruhr*
■ the steering wheel	**le volant** *luh voh-lahn*
■ the tail light	**le feu arrière** *luh fuh ah-ryehr*
■ the transmission	**la transmission** *lah trahnz-mee-ssyohn*
■ the water pump	**la pompe à eau** *lah pohnp ah oh*
■ the windshield wipers	**les essuie-glaces** *lay zeh-sswee glahss*
■ the brakes	**les freins** *lay fran*
What's the matter?	**Qu'est-ce qui ne va pas?** *kehss kee nuh vah pah*
Is it possible to (Can you) fix it today?	**Pouvez-vous la réparer aujourd'hui?** *poo-vay-voo lah ray-pah-ray oh-zhoor-dwee*
How long will it take?	**Combien de temps faudra-t-il?** *kohn-byan duh tahn foh-drah-teel*
Is everything O.K. now?	**Tout est arrangé (réparé) maintenant?** *too teh tah-rahn-zhay (ray-pah-ray) mant-nahn*
How much do I owe you?	**Combien vous dois-je?** *kohn-byan voo dwahzh*

GENERAL INFORMATION

TELLING TIME

What time is it?	**Quelle heure est-il?**	*kehl uhr eh teel*
It is ____.	**Il est ____.**	*eel eh*
■ noon	**midi**	*mee-dee*
■ 1:05	**une heure cinq**	*ewn-uhr sank*
■ 2:10	**deux heures dix**	*duh-zuhr deess*
■ 3:15	**trois heures et quart**	*trwah-zuhr ay kahr*
■ 4:20	**quatre heures vingt**	*kahtruh-uhr van*
■ 6:30	**six heures et demie**	*seez-uhr ay duh-mee*
■ 7:35	**sept heures trente-cinq**	*seht-uhr trahnt-sank*
■ 8:40	**neuf heures moins vingt**	*nuhv-uhr mwan van*
■ 9:45	**dix heures moins le quart**	*deez-uhr mwan luh kahr*

EXPRESSIONS OF TIME

At what time ____?	**À quelle heure ____?**	*ah kehl-uhr ____?*
When?	**Quand?**	*kahn?*
at ____ o'clock	**à ____ heures**	*ah ____ uhr*
in an hour	**dans une heure**	*dahn zewn-uhr*
until 5 o'clock	**jusqu'à cinq heures**	*zhewss-kah sank uhr*
since what time ____?	**depuis quelle heure ____?**	*duh-pwee kehl uhr*

three hours ago	**il y a trois heures**	*eel yah trwah-zuhr*
early	**tôt**	*toh*
	de bonne heure	*duh bohn-uhr*
late	**tard**	*tahr*
late (in arriving)	**en retard**	*ah<u>n</u> ruh-tahr*
on, in time	**à l'heure**	*ah luhr*
noon	**midi**	*mee-dee*
midnight	**minuit**	*mee-nwee*
in the morning	**le matin**	*luh mah-ta<u>n</u>*
in the afternoon	**l'après-midi**	*lah-preh mee-dee*
in the evening	**le soir**	*luh swahr*
at night	**la nuit**	*lah nwee*
minute	**une minute**	*ewn mee-newt*
a quarter of an hour	**un quart d'heure**	*uh<u>n</u> kahr duhr*
a half hour	**une demi-heure**	*ewn duh-mee uhr*

Official time is based on the 24-hour clock. You will find train schedules and other such times expressed in terms of a point within the 24-hour sequence.

The train leaves at 15:30.	**Le train part à 15:30.**	*luh tra<u>n</u> pahr ah ka<u>n</u>z-uhr trah<u>n</u>t*

DAYS OF THE WEEK

What day is today?	**Quel jour est-ce aujourd'hui?** *kehl zhoor ess oh-zhoor-dwee*
	Quel jour sommes-nous aujourd'hui? *kehl zhoor sohm noo oh-zhoor-dwee*
Today is ____.	**C'est aujourd'hui ____.** *seh toh-zhoor-dwee*
	Nous sommes ____ *noo sohm*

Monday	**lundi**	*luhn-dee*
Tuesday	**mardi**	*mahr-dee*
Wednesday	**mercredi**	*mehr-kruh-dee*
Thursday	**jeudi**	*zhuh-dee*
Friday	**vendredi**	*vahn-druh-dee*
Saturday	**samedi**	*sahm-dee*
Sunday	**dimanche**	*dee-mahnsh*

NOTE: In French, the names of the days and the months and seasons are written in small letters.

last Monday	**lundi dernier**	*luhn-dee dehr-nyay*
the day before	**la veille**	*lah vehy*
the day before yesterday	**avant-hier**	*ah-vahn-tyehr*
yesterday	**hier**	*yehr*
today	**aujourd'hui**	*oh-zhoor-dwee*
tomorrow	**demain**	*duh-man*
the day after tomorrow	**après-demain**	*ah-preh-duh-man*
the next day	**le lendemain**	*luh lahn-duh-man*
next Monday	**lundi prochain**	*luhn-dee proh-shan*
the day	**le jour**	*luh zhoor*
2 days ago	**il y a deux jours**	*eel-yah duh zhoor*
in 2 days	**dans deux jours**	*dahn duh zhoor*
every day	**tous les jours**	*too lay zhoor*
day off	**(le) jour de congé**	*(luh) zhoor duh kohn-zhay*
holiday	**(le) jour de fête**	*(luh) zhoor duh feht*
birthday	**l'anniversaire**	*lah-nee-vehr-ssehr*
per day	**par jour**	*pahr zhoor*

during the day	**pendant la journée**	*pahn-dahn lah zhoor-nay*
from this day on	**dès aujourd'hui**	*deh zoh-zhoor-dwee*
the week	**la semaine**	*lah suh-mehn*
a week day	**un jour de semaine**	*uhn zhoor duh suh-mehn*
the week end	**le week-end**	*luh week-ehnd*
last week	**la semaine passée**	*lah suh-mehn pah-ssay*
this week	**cette semaine**	*seht suh-mehn*
next week	**la semaine prochaine**	*lah suh-mehn proh-shehn*
a week from today	**d'aujourd'hui en huit**	*doh-zhoor-dwee ahn weet*
2 weeks from tomorrow	**de demain en quinze**	*duh duh-man ahn kanz*
during the week	**pendant la semaine**	*pahn-dahn lah suh-mehn*

MONTHS OF THE YEAR

January	**janvier**	*zhan-vee-yay*
February	**février**	*fay-vree-yay*
March	**mars**	*mahrss*
April	**avril**	*ah-vreel*
May	**mai**	*meh*
June	**juin**	*zhwan*
July	**juillet**	*zhwee-yeh*
August	**août**	*oo or oot*
September	**septembre**	*sehp-tahn-bruh*

October	**octobre**	*ohk-toh-bruh*
November	**novembre**	*noh-vahn-bruh*
December	**décembre**	*day-ssahn-bruh*
the month	**le mois**	*luh mwah*
2 months ago	**il y a deux mois**	*eel yah duh mwah*
last month	**le mois dernier**	*luh mwah dehr-nyay*
this month	**ce mois**	*suh mwah*
next month	**le mois prochain**	*luh mwah proh-shan*
during the month of	**pendant le mois de**	*pahn-dahn luh mwah duh*
since the month of	**depuis le mois de**	*duh-pwee luh mwah duh*
for the month of	**pour le mois de**	*poor luh mwah duh*
every month	**tous les mois**	*too lay mwah*
per month	**par mois**	*pahr mwah*
What is today's date?	**Quelle est la date d'aujourd'hui?** *kehl ay lah daht doh-zhoor-dwee?*	
Today is _____.	**C'est aujourd'hui _____.** *seht oh-zhoor-dwee*	
Monday, May 1	**lundi, le premier mai** *luhn-dee luh pruh-myay-meh*	
Tuesday, June 2	**mardi, le deux juin** *mahr-dee luh duh zhwan*	

NOTE: Use the ordinal number only for the first of the month.

the year	**l'an/l'année**	*lahn/lah-nay*
per year	**par an**	*pahr ahn*
all year	**toute l'année**	*toot lah-nay*

| every year | **chaque année** | *shahk ah-nay* |
| during the year | **pendant l'année** | *pahn-dahn lah-nay* |

THE FOUR SEASONS

spring	**le printemps**	*luh pran-tahn*
summer	**l'été**	*lay-tay*
autumn	**l'automne**	*loh-tohn*
winter	**l'hiver**	*lee-vehr*
in the spring	**au printemps**	*oh pran-tahn*
in the summer	**en été**	*ahn-nay-tay*
in the autumn	**en automne**	*ahn-noh-tohn*
in the winter	**en hiver**	*ahn nee-vehr*

WEATHER

What is the weather like?	**Quel temps fait-il?**	*kehl tahn feh-teel*
It is beautiful.	**Il fait beau.** *eel feh boh*
It is hot.	**Il fait chaud.** *eel feh shoh*
It is sunny.	**Il fait du soleil.** *eel feh dew soh-lehy*
It is bad.	**Il fait mauvais.** *eel feh moh-veh*
It is cold.	**Il fait froid.** *eel feh frwah*
It is cool.	**Il fait frais.** *eel feh freh*
It is windy.	**Il fait du vent.** *eel feh dew vahn*
It is foggy.	**Il fait du brouillard.** *eel feh dew broo-yahr*
It is snowing.	**Il neige.** *eel nehzh*
It is raining.	**Il pleut.** *eel pluh*

DIRECTIONS

the north	**le nord**	*luh nohr*
the south	**le sud**	*luh sewd*
the east	**l'est**	*lehsst*
the west	**l'ouest**	*lwehsst*

IMPORTANT SIGNS

À louer	*ah loo-ay*	For rent, hire
Ascenseur	*ah-sah<u>n</u>-ssuhr*	Elevator
Attention	*ah-tah<u>n</u>-ssyoh<u>n</u>*	Careful
À vendre	*ah vah<u>n</u>-druh*	For sale
Dames	*dahm*	Ladies
Danger	*dah<u>n</u>-zhay*	Danger
Danger de mort	*dah<u>n</u>-zhay duh mohr*	Danger of death
Défense de	*day-fah<u>n</u>ss duh*	Do not ___
Défense d'entrer	*day-fah<u>n</u>ss dah<u>n</u>-tray*	Do not enter
Défense de cracher	*day-fah<u>n</u>ss duh krah-shay*	No spitting
Défense de fumer	*day-fah<u>n</u>ss duh few-may*	No smoking
Défense de marcher sur l'herbe	*day-fah<u>n</u>ss duh mahr-shay sewr lehrb*	Keep off the grass
Eau non potable	*oh noh<u>n</u> poh-tah-bluh*	Don't drink the water
École	*ay-kohl*	School

Entrée	*ahn-tray*	Entrance
Entrée interdite	*ahn-tray an-tehr-deet*	No Entrance
Entrée libre	*ahn-tray lee-bruh*	Free Admission
Fermé	*fehr-may*	Closed
Fumeurs	*few-muhr*	Smokers
Hommes	*ohm*	Men
Hôpital	*oh-pee-tahl*	Hospital
Horaire	*oh-rehr*	Schedule
Toilettes	*twah-leht*	Washroom
Libre	*lee-bruh*	Free, Unoccupied
Messieurs	*meh-ssyuh*	Gentlemen
Ne pas toucher	*nuh pah too-shay*	Don't touch
Non fumeurs	*nohn few-muhr*	Non smokers
Occupé	*oh-kew-pay*	Occupied
Ouvert	*oo-vehr*	Open
Passage souterrain	*pah-ssahzh soo-teh-ran*	Underground passage
Poussez	*poo-ssay*	Push
Privé	*pree-vay*	Private
Quai/Voie	*kay/vwah*	Track, Platform
Renseignements	*rahn-sseh-nyuh-mahn*	Information
Réservé	*ray-zehr-vay*	Reserved
Salle d'attente	*sahl dah-tahnt*	Waiting room
Soldes	*sohld*	Sales
Sonnez	*soh-nay*	Ring
Sortie	*sohr-tee*	Exit

Sortie de secours	*sohr-tee duh suh-koor*	Emergency exit
Stationnement interdit	*stah-ssyohn-mahn an-tehr-dee*	No parking
Tirez	*tee-ray*	Pull
Toilettes	*twah-leht*	Toilets

COMMON ABBREVIATIONS

ACF	Automobile Club de France	Automobile Club of France
apr. J.-C.	après Jésus-Christ	A.D.
av. J.-C.	avant Jésus-Christ	B.C.
bd.	boulevard	boulevard
c.-à-d.	c'est-à-dire	that is to say, i.e.
CEE	Communauté économique européenne (Marché commun)	European Economic Community (Common Market)
CGT	Compagnie générale transatlantique	French Line
Cie.	compagnie	Company
EU	États-Unis	United States
h.	heure(s)	hour, o'clock
M.	Monsieur	Mr.
Mlle	Mademoiselle	Miss
MM	Messieurs	Gentlemen
Mme	Madame	Mrs.
ONU	Organisation des Nations Unies	United Nations
p.	page	page

p. ex.	**par exemple**	for example
P et T.	**Postes et Télécommunications**	Post Office and Telecommunications
RATP	**Régie Autonome des Transports Parisiens**	Paris Transport Authority
RD	**Route Départementale**	local road
RN	**Route Nationale**	national road
SA	**Société anonyme**	Ltd., Inc.
SI	**Syndicat d'initiative**	Tourist Information Office
SNCF	**Société Nationale des Chemins de Fer Français**	French National Railways
s.v.p.	**s'il vous plaît**	please

GERMAN

QUICK PRONUNCIATION GUIDE

VOWELS

Vowels may be long or short. A vowel is long when:

1. doubled (B<u>ee</u>thoven, B<u>oo</u>t, W<u>aa</u>ge)
2. followed by an h (Br<u>a</u>hms, <u>O</u>hm, F<u>e</u>hler)
3. followed by a single consonant (Sch<u>u</u>bert, M<u>o</u>zart, T<u>o</u>n)

When followed by two or more consonants, a vowel is usually short, as in B<u>a</u>ch.

VOWELS	SOUND IN ENGLISH	EXAMPLE
a	aa (**long**; <u>far</u>)	**haben** (*HAA-ben*)
	ah (**short**; h<u>o</u>t)	**hatte** (*HAH-teh*)
ä	ay (**long**; w<u>ay</u>)	**Bäder** (*BAY-duh*)
	eh (**short**; m<u>e</u>t)	**Gepäck** (*geh-PEHK*)
e	ay (**long**; h<u>ay</u>)	**leben** (*LAY-ben*)
	eh (**short**; <u>e</u>nd)	**helfen** (*HEHL-fen*)
	e (**unstressed syllables** ending in -<u>n</u>, -<u>l</u>, and -<u>t</u>, like -<u>en</u> in hidd<u>en</u>)	**lieben** (*LEE-ben*)
	uh (**unstressed syllables** ending in -<u>er</u>, moth<u>er</u>)	**Ritter** (*RIT-uh*)
i	ee (**long**; fl<u>ee</u>t)	**Ihnen** (*EE-nen*)
	i (**short**; w<u>i</u>t)	**wissen** (*VIss-en*)
ie	ee (always **long**; mart<u>i</u>ni)	**Liebe** (*LEE-beh*)
o	oh (**long**; r<u>o</u>se)	**Rose** (*ROH-zeh*)
	o (**short**; l<u>o</u>ve)	**komm** (*kom*)
ö	er (like h<u>er</u>, but sounded with the lips forward and rounded)	**hören** (*HER-en*)
u	oo (**long**; bl<u>oo</u>m)	**Schuh** (*shoo*)
	u (**short**; b<u>u</u>ll)	**Bulle** (*BUL-eh*)

VOWELS	SOUND IN ENGLISH	EXAMPLE
ü	ew (like dream, but with lips forward and rounded)	**Brüder** (*BREW-duh*)
y	ew (like the German ü)	**lyrisch** (*LEW-rish*)

DIPHTHONGS

LETTERS	SOUND IN ENGLISH	EXAMPLE
ai, ay ei, ey	eye (<u>eye</u>)	**schreiben** (*SHREYE-ben*)
au	ow (br<u>ow</u>n)	**braun** (*brown*)
äu, eu	oy (j<u>oy</u>)	**treu** (*troy*)

CONSONANTS

LETTER	SOUND IN ENGLISH	EXAMPLE
f, h, k, l, m, n, p, t, x	usually pronounced as in English	
b	p (between vowel and consonant or at end of word: map)	**Leib** (*leyep*)
	b (elsewhere as in English)	**bin** (*bin*)
c	ts (before e, i, ö, and ä: wits	**Cäsar** (*TSAY-zahr*)
ch	kh (strongly aspirated (breathy) sound; "Hawaiian hula-hula," or "Hugh")	**durch** (*doorkh*)
chs	k (kind)	**Lachs** (*lahks*)
d	t (between vowel and consonant and at end of word; cat)	**Hund** (*hunt*)
	d (otherwise: dollar)	**Dank** (*dank*)

VOWELS	SOUND IN ENGLISH	EXAMPLE
g	g (hard; gods)	**Geist** (geyest)
	k (at end of word; backpack)	**Tag** (taak)
	kh (words ending in ig; happy or whisky)	**windig** (VIN-dikh)
j	y (year)	**Jahr** (yaar)
qu	kv (k, followed by v as in veal)	**Quell** (kvehl)
r	r (preferably rolled in the throat, as in French, or trilled with the tip of the tongue, as in Spanish or Irish or Scottish brogues)	**Reise** (REYE-zeh)
s	z (preceding vowels or between them; zap)	**See** (zay)
	sh (at beginning of syllable, before p and t: shell)	**spielen** (SHPEE-len)
	s, ss (elsewhere: sing)	**Was ist das?** (vahs ist dahs)
ß, ss	s, ss (always: sell)	**weiß** (veyes)
		wissen (VI-ssen)
sch	sh (show)	**schlau** (shlow)
tsch	ch (cheer)	**Kitsch** (kich)
tz	ts (wits)	**Katze** (KAH-tseh)
v	f (father)	**Vater** (FAA-tuh)
	v (words of non-Germanic origin: violin)	**Violine** (vee-o-LEE-neh)
w	v (vest)	**Wasser** (VAH-suh)
z	ts (grits)	**Zeit** (tseyet)

THE BASICS FOR GETTING BY

MOST FREQUENTLY USED EXPRESSIONS

Yes.	**Ja.**	*yaa*
No.	**Nein.**	*neyen*
Maybe.	**Vielleicht**	*fee-LEYEKHT*
Never again!	**Nie wieder!**	*nee VEED-uh*
Please.	**Bitte.**	*BIT-eh*
Thank you.	**Danke.**	*DAHNK-eh*
Thank you very much.	**Vielen Dank.**	*FEEL-en dahnk*
You're (very) welcome.	**Bitte (sehr).**	*BIT-eh (zayr)*
Don't mention it.	**Gern geschehen.**	*gehrn ge-SHAY-en*
That'll be fine.	**Schon gut.**	*shon goot*
Excuse me.	**Verzeihung!**	*fehr-TSEYE-ung*
I'm sorry.	**Es tut mir leid.**	*ehs toot meer leyet*
Just a second.	**Augenblick mal!**	*OW-gen-blik maal*
That is (not) _____.	**Das ist (nicht) _____.**	*dahs ist (nikht)*
■ right	**richtig**	*RIKHT-ikh*
■ important	**wichtig**	*VIKHT-ikh*
■ good	**gut**	*goot*
■ true	**wahr**	*vaar*
■ beautiful	**schön** ·	*shern*
■ necessary	**nötig**	*NERT-ikh*

It doesn't matter.	**Das macht nichts.**	*dahs mahkht nikhts*
It's all the same to me.	**Das ist mir gleich.**	*dahs ist meer gleyekh*
(The) gentleman, Mr.	**(Der) Herr.**	*(dehr) hehrr*
(The) lady, Mrs.	**(Die) Frau.**	*(dee) frow*
(The) girl, Miss.	**(Das) Fräulein.**	*(dahs) FROY-leyen*
Good morning.	**Guten Morgen.**	*GOOT-en MORG-en*
Good afternoon.	**Guten Tag.**	*GOOT-en taak*
Good evening.	**Guten Abend.**	*GOOT-en AAB-ent*
Good night.	**Gute Nacht.**	*GOOT-eh nahkht*
Good-bye.	**Auf Wiedersehen!** *owf VEED-uh-zayen* **Auf Wiederschauen!** *owf VEED-uh-show-en* **Uf Wiederluege! (Swiss)** *uf VEED-uh-lueh-geh*	
See you soon.	**Bis bald.** *bis bahlt*	
See you later.	**Bis später.** *bis SHPAYT-uh*	
Till tomorrow.	**Bis morgen.** *bis MOR-gen*	
I speak little German.	**Ich spreche wenig Deutsch.** *ikh SHPREHKH-eh VAYN-ikh doytch*	
Do you speak English?	**Sprechen Sie Englisch?** *SHPREHKH-en zee EHNG-lish*	
You're speaking too fast.	**Sie sprechen zu schnell.** *zee SHPREHKH-en tsoo shnell*	
Please speak more slowly.	**Bitte sprechen Sie langsamer!** *BIT-eh SHPREKH-en zee LAHNG-zaam-uh*	
Please repeat.	**Wiederholen Sie bitte!** *VEED-uh-hoh-len zee BIT-eh*	
Do you understand?	**Verstehen Sie?** *fehr-SHTAY-en zee*	

I (don't) understand.	**Ich verstehe (nicht).** *ikh fehr-SHTAY-eh (nikht)*
What was that you said?	**Wie bitte?** *vee BIT-eh*
What does that mean?	**Was bedeutet das?** *vahss be-DOYT-et dahs*
How do you say that in German?	**Wie heißt das auf deutsch?** *Vee heyest dahs owf doytch*
Do you know . . . ?	**Wissen Sie . . . ?** *VISS-en zee*
I don't know.	**Ich weiß nicht.** *ikh veyess nikht*
What is that?	**Was ist das?** *vahs ist dahs*
Is that possible?	**Ist das möglich?** *ist dahs MERG-likh*
That is (im)possible.	**Das ist (un)möglich.** *Dahs ist (un)-MERG-likh*
I am an American. (-*in* for women)	**Ich bin Amerikaner (Amerikanerin).** *ikh bin aa-meh-ri-KAAN-uh (aa-meh-ri-KAAN-uh-rin)*
I am English.	**Ich bin Engländer. (Engländerin)** *ikh bin EHNG-lehnd-uh (EHNG-lehnd-uh-rin)*
I am Canadian.	**Ich bin Kanadier. (Kanadierin)** *ikh bin kah-NAA-diuh (kah-NAA-diuh-rin)*
I am Australian.	**Ich bin Australier. (Australierin)** *ikh bin ow-STRAA-liuh (ow-STRAA-liuh-rin)*
My name is . . .	**Ich heiße . . .** *ikh HEYESS-eh*
What's your name?	**Wie heißen Sie?** *vee HEYESS-en zee*
How are you? (How do you do?)	**Wie geht es Ihnen?** *vee gayt ehs EEn-en*
How are things?	**Wie geht's?** *vee gayts*
Fine, thank you. And you?	**Gut, danke.** **Und Ihnen?** *goot DAHNK-eh unt EEn-en*

How much does that cost?	**Wieviel kostet das?**	*VEE-feel KOST-et dahs*
I'm _____.	**Ich bin** _____	*ikh bin*
■ hungry	**hungrig**	*HUNG-rikh*
■ thirsty	**durstig**	*DOORST-ikh*
■ tired	**müde**	*MEWD-eh*
■ sick	**krank**	*krahnk*
Please bring me _____.	**Bitte bringen Sie mir** _____.	*BIT-eh BRING-en zee meer*

QUESTIONS

Why?	**Warum?**	*vah-RUM*
When?	**Wann?**	*vahn*
Where?	**Wo?**	*voh*
What?	**Was?**	*vahs*
How?	**Wie?**	*vee*
Who?	**Wer?**	*vayr*

PROBLEMS, PROBLEMS, PROBLEMS

I'm looking for _____.	**Ich suche** _____.	*ikh ZOOKH-eh*
■ my hotel	**mein Hotel**	*meyen ho-TEL*
■ my friends	**meine Freunde**	*MEYEN-eh FROYND-eh*
■ my suitcase	**meinen Koffer**	*MEYEN-en KOF-uh*
■ the railroad station	**den Bahnhof**	*dayn BAAN-hohf*
■ my husband	**meinen Mann**	*MEYEN-en mahn*
■ my wife	**meine Frau**	*MEYEN-eh frow*
■ my child	**mein Kind**	*meyen kint*
■ my bus	**meinen Bus**	*MEYEN-en bus*

I'm lost. (on foot)	**Ich habe mich verlaufen.** *ikh HAAB-eh mikh fehr- LOWF-en*
I'm lost. (driving)	**Ich habe mich verfahren.** *ikh HAAB-eh mikh fehr- FAAR-en*
Can you help me please?	**Können Sie mir bitte helfen?** *KERN-en zee meer BIT-eh HELF-en*
Does anyone here speak English?	**Spricht hier jemand Englisch?** *shprikht heer YAY-mahnt EHNG-lish*
Where is the American (British, Canadian, Australian) Consulate?	**Wo ist das amerikanische (britische, kanadische, australische) Konsulat?** *voh ist dahs a- meh-ri-KAAN-ish-eh (BRIT-ish-eh, kah- NAA-dish-eh, ow-STRAA-lish-eh) kon- zoo-LAAT*
Which way do I go?	**In welche Richtung soll ich gehen?** *in VELKH-eh RIKHT-ung zol ikh GAY-en*
■ to the left	**links** *links*
■ to the right	**rechts** *rehkhts*
■ straight ahead	**geradeaus** *ge-RAAD-eh-OWS*
_____ is stolen	**_____ ist gestohlen** *ist ge-SHTOHL- en*
■ my car	**mein Wagen** *meyen VAAG-en*
■ my briefcase	**meine Aktentasche** *MEYEN-eh AHKT-en-tahsh-eh*
■ my jewels	**mein Schmuck** *meyen shmuk*
■ my money	**mein Geld** *meyen gelt*
■ my suitcase	**mein Koffer** *meyen KOF-uh*
my ticket	**meine Fahrkarte** *MEYEN-eh FAAR-kahrt-eh*
■ my wallet	**meine Geldbörse** *MEYEN-eh GELT- berz-eh*
■ my watch	**meine Uhr** *MEYEN-eh oor*
Call the police!	**Rufen Sie die Polizei!** *ROOF-en zee dee pol-its-EYE*

NUMBERS

CARDINAL NUMBERS

0	**null**	*nul*
1	**eins**	*eyenss*
2	**zwei, zwo (over the telephone)**	*tsveye, tsvoh*
3	**drei**	*dreye*
4	**vier**	*feer*
5	**fünf**	*fewnf*
6	**sechs**	*zehks*
7	**sieben**	*ZEEB-en*
8	**acht**	*ahkht*
9	**neun**	*noyn*
10	**zehn**	*tsayn*
11	**elf**	*elf*
12	**zwölf**	*tsverlf*
13	**dreizehn**	*DREYE-tsayn*
14	**vierzehn**	*FEER-tsayn*
15	**fünfzehn**	*FEWNF-tsayn*
16	**sechzehn**	*ZEHKH-tsayn*
17	**siebzehn**	*ZEEP-tsayn*
18	**achtzehn**	*AHKHT-tsayn*
19	**neunzehn**	*NOYN-tsayn*
20	**zwanzig**	*TSVAHN-tsikh*
21	**einundzwanzig**	*EYEN-unt-tsvahn- tsikh*
22	**zweiundzwanzig**	*TSVEYE-unt- tsvahn-tsikh*

23	**dreiundzwanzig** *DREYE-unt-tsvahn-tsikh*
24	**vierundzwanzig** *FEER-unt-tsvahn- tsikh*
25	**fünfundzwanzig** *FEWNF-unt-tsvahn-tsikh*
26	**sechsundzwanzig** *ZEHKS-unt-tsvahn-tsikh*
27	**siebenundzwanzig** *ZEEB-en-unt-tsvahn-tsikh*
28	**achtundzwanzig** *AHKHT-unt-tsvahn-tsikh*
29	**neunundzwanzig** *NOYN-unt-tsvahn-tsikh*
30	**dreißig** *DREYESS-ikh*
31	**einundreißig** *EYEN-unt-dreyess-ikh*
40	**vierzig** *FEER-tsikh*
41	**einundvierzig** *EYEN-unt-feer-tsikh*
50	**fünfzig** *FEWNF-tsikh*
60	**sechzig** *ZEHKH-tsikh*
70	**siebzig** *ZEEP-tsikh*
80	**achtzig** *AHKH-tsikh*
90	**neunzig** *NOYN-tsikh*
100	**(ein)hundert** *(eyen)HUN-dehrt*
101	**hunderteins** *HUN-dehrt-eyenss*
102	**hundertzwei** *HUN-dehrt-tsveye*
200	**zweihundert** *TSVEYE-hun-dehrt*
300	**dreihundert** *DREYE-hun-dehrt*
400	**vierhundert** *FEER-hun-dehrt*
500	**fünfhundert** *FEWNF-hun-dehrt*

600	**sechshundert** *ZEHKS-hun-dert*
700	**siebenhundert** *ZEEB-en-hun-dehrt*
800	**achthundert** *AHKHT-hun-dehrt*
900	**neunhundert** *NOYN-hun-dehrt*
1000	**(ein)tausend** *(eyen)TOW-zehnt*
2000	**zweitausend** *TSVEYE-tow-zehnt*
1,000,000	**eine Million** *EYEN-eh mil-YOHN*
1,000,000,000	**eine Milliarde** *EYEN-eh mil-YAHRD-eh*

ORDINAL NUMBERS

first	**erst-**	*ayrst*
second	**zweit-**	*tsveyet*
third	**dritt-**	*drit*
fourth	**viert-**	*feert*
fifth	**fünft-**	*fewnft*
sixth	**sechst-**	*zehkst*
seventh	**siebt-**	*zeept*
eighth	**acht-**	*ahkht*
ninth	**neunt-**	*noynt*
tenth	**zehnt-**	*tsaynt*

WHEN YOU ARRIVE

PASSPORT, CUSTOMS

| Here is my passport. | **Hier ist mein Paß.** *heer ist meyen pahss* |
| Would you please stamp my passport? | **Würden Sie mir bitte meinen Paß stempeln?** *VEWRD-en zee meer BIT-eh MEYEN-ehn pahss SHTEMP-eln* |

I will not be working in Europe.	**In Europa werde ich nicht arbeiten.** *In OY-roh-paa VEHRD-eh ikh nikht AHR-beye-ten*
I'm traveling on vacation.	**Ich mache eine Ferienreise.** *ikh MAHKH-eh EYEN-eh FAIR-yen-reye-zeh*
I'm on a business trip.	**Ich bin auf Geschäfts reise hier.** *ikh bin owf geh-SHEHFTS-reye-zeh heer*
I'm visiting my relatives.	**Ich besuche meine Verwandten.** *ikh be-ZOOKH-eh MEYEN-eh fehr-VAHNT-en*
I'm just passing through.	**Ich bin nur auf der Durchreise.** *ikh bin noor owf dehr DOORKH-reye-zeh*
I'll be staying ___.	**Ich bleibe ___.** *ikh BLEYEB-eh*
■ a few days	**einige Tage** *EYEN-ig-eh TAAG-eh*
■ a few weeks	**einige Wochen** *EYEN-ig-eh VOKH-ehn*
■ a month	**einen Monat** *EYEN-en MOHN-aat*
I have nothing to declare.	**Ich habe nichts zu verzollen.** *ikh HAAB-eh nikhts tsoo fehr-TSOL-en*
Here is my luggage.	**Hier ist mein Gepäck.** *heer ist meyen geh-PEHK*
Do I have to pay duty on this?	**Ist dies zollpflichtig?** *ist dees TSOL-pflikh-tikh*
These are gifts.	**Das sind Geschenke.** *dahs zint ge-SHENK-eh*
This is for my personal use.	**Das ist für meinen persönlichen Gebrauch.** *dahs ist fewr MEYEN-en pehr-ZERN-likh-en ge-BROWKH*
May I close the bag now?	**Darf ich den Koffer (die Tasche) jetzt zumachen?** *dahrf ikh dayn KOF-uh (dee TASH-eh) yetst TSOO-mahkh-en*

BAGGAGE AND PORTERS

I'm looking for the luggage carts.	**Ich suche die Kofferkulis.** *ikh ZOOKH-eh dee KOF-uh-koo-lees*
I need a porter.	**Ich brauche einen Gepäckträger.** *ikh BROWKH-eh EYEN-en geh-PEHK-trayg-uh*
That's my (our) luggage.	**Das ist mein (unser) Gepäck.** *Dahs ist meyen (UNZ-uh) geh-PEHK*
Accompany us to the taxi, (the bus, the railroad entrance).	**Begleiten Sie uns zum Taxi, (Bus, Eisenbahneingang).** *beh-GLEYET-en zee uns tsoom TAHKS-ee (bus, EYEZ-en-baan-eyen-gahng)*
Be careful with that one!	**Vorsicht damit!** *FOR-zikht dah-MIT*
A suitcase is missing.	**Ein Koffer fehlt.** *eyen KOF-uh faylt*
Where is the lost and found?	**Wo ist das Fundbüro?** *voh ist dahs FUNT-bew-roh*
I'll carry this one myself.	**Diesen trag ich selber.** *DEEZ-en traag ikh ZELB-uh*
How much do I owe you?	**Wieviel macht das?** *VEE-feel mahkht dahs*

MONEY MATTERS

EXCHANGING MONEY

I want to change _____.	**Ich möchte _____ wechseln.** *ikh MERKH-teh VEHK-seln*
■ money	**Geld** *gehlt*

■dollars (pounds)	**Dollar (Pfund)** *DO-lahr (pfunt)*
■travelers' checks	**Reiseschecks** *REYEZ-eh-shehks*

What is the exchange rate for dollars (pounds)?

Wie ist der Wechselkurs für Dollar (Pfund)? *vee ist dehr VEHK-sel-koors fewr DO-lahr (pfunt)*

What commission do you charge?

Welche Gebühr erheben Sie? *VEHL-kheh geh-BEWR ehr-HAY-ben zee?*

Give me large (small) bills.

Geben Sie mir große (kleine) Scheine. *GAYB-en zee meer GROHSS-eh (KLEYEN-eh) SHEYEN-eh*

I also need some change.

Ich brauche auch etwas Kleingeld. *Ikh BROWKH-eh owkh ET-vahs KLEYEN-gelt*

I think you made a mistake.

Ich glaube, Sie haben sich verrechnet. *ikh GLOWB-eh zee HAAB-en zikh fehr-REKH-net*

I want to cash a personal check.

Ich möchte einen Barscheck einlösen. *ikh MERKHT-eh EYEN-eh BAAR-shehk EYEN-ler-zen*

AT THE HOTEL

RESERVATIONS–RECEPTION

I'd like a single (double) room for tonight.

Ich möchte ein Einzelzimmer (Doppelzimmer) für heute nacht. *ikh MERKHT-eh eyen EYEN-tsel-tsim-uh (DOP-el-tsim-uh) fewr HOYT-eh nahkht*

I want a room with (without) a private bath.

Ich möchte ein Zimmer mit (ohne) Privatbad. *Ikh MERKHT-eh eyen TSIM-uh mit (OHN-eh) pri-VAAT-baat*

I want a room with ____.

Ich möchte ein Zimmer mit ____. *ikh MERKHT-eh eyen TSIM-uh mit*

■ air conditioning	**Klimaanlage** *KLEEM-ah-ahn-laa-geh*
■ a balcony	**Balkon** *bahl-KOHN*
■ a bathtub	**einer Badewanne** *EYEN-uh BAAD-eh-vah-ne*
■ (color) television	**(Farb) Fernsehen** *faarp FEHRN-zayen*
■ a nice view	**schöner Aussicht** *SHERN-uh OWS-zikht*
■ private toilet	**eigenem WC** *EYEG-enem VAY-tsay*
■ radio	**Radio** *RAAD-ee-oh*
■ shower	**Dusche** *DOOSH-eh*
■ a shower on the floor	**Etagendusche** *ay-TAAZH-en-doosh-eh*
■ shower and toilet	**Dusche und WC** *DOOSH-eh unt VAY-tsay*
■ a telephone in the room	**Telephonanschluß** *TAYL-e-fohn-ahn-shluss*
■ twin beds	**zwei Betten** *tsveye BEHT-en*
■ a view of the sea	**Blick aufs Meer** *blik owfs mayr*
May I see the room?	**Darf ich mir das Zimmer ansehen?** *dahrf ikh meer dahs TSIM-uh AHN-zay-en*
I (don't) like it.	**Es gefällt mir (nicht).** *ehs ge-FEHLT meer (nikht).*
I'll take it (won't).	**Ich nehm's (nicht).** *ikh naymss (nikht)*
I (don't) have a reservation.	**Ich habe (nicht) reservieren lassen.** *ikh HAAB-eh (nikht) reh-zehr-VEER-en LASS-en*

May I leave this in your safe?	**Darf ich dies in Ihrem Tresor lassen?** *dahrf ikh dees in EE-rem treh-ZOHR LASS-en*
Would you have a room ____.	**Hätten Sie ein Zimmer ____.** *HEHT-en zee eyen TSIM-uh*
Would you have something ____.	**Hätten Sie etwas ____.** *HEHT-en zee ET-vahs*
■ in front	**vorne** *FORN-eh*
■ in back	**hinten** *HINT-en*
■ lower down	**weiter unten** *VEYET-uh UNT-en*
■ higher up	**weiter oben** *VEYET-uh OHB-en*
I want something ____.	**Ich will etwas ____.** *Ikh vill ET-vahs*
■ quieter	**Ruhigeres** *ROOH-i-geh-res*
■ bigger	**Größeres** *GRERSS-eh-res*
■ cheaper	**Billigeres** *BILL-i-geh-res*
■ better	**Besseres** *BESS-eh-res*
■ more elegant	**Eleganteres** *eh-lay-GAHNT-eh-res*
■ more modest	**Bescheideneres** *beh-SHEYED-e-neh-res*
If you have nothing more, could you call another hotel for me?	**Wenn Sie nichts mehr haben, könnten Sie ein anderes Hotel für mich anrufen?** *vehn zee nikhts mayr HAAB-en KERNT-en zee eyen AHND-eh-res ho-TEL fewr mikh AHN-roo-fen*
How much does it cost?	**Wieviel kostet es?** *VEE-feel KOST-et ehs*
Is breakfast (service, everything) included?	**Ist das Frühstück (Bedienung, alles) mit einbegriffen?** *ist dahs FREW-shtewk (beh-DEEN-ung, AH-les) mit EYEN-beh-gri-fen*

HOTEL SERVICES

I need _____.	**Ich brauche _____.** *ikh BROWKH-eh*
We need _____.	**Wir brauchen _____.** *veer BROWKH-en*
an ashtray	**einen Aschenbecher** *EYEN-en AHSH-ehn-bekhuh*
a blanket	**eine Decke** *EYEN-eh DEHK-eh*
matches	**Streichhölzer** *SHTREYEKH-herl-tsuh*
envelopes	**Briefumschläge** *BREEF-um-shlay-geh*
writing paper	**Schreibpapier** *SHREYEP-paa-peer*
postcards	**Postkarten** *POST-kaar-ten*
soap	**Seife** *ZEYEF-eh*
toilet paper	**Toilettenpapier** *toy-LET-en-paa-peer*
towels	**Tücher** *TEWKH-uh*
an extra bed	**ein zusätzliches Bett** *eyen TSOO-zehts-li-khes beht*
an extra pillow	**ein extra Kopfkissen** *eyen EHKS-traa KOPF-kiss-en*
a wastepaper basket	**einen Papierkorb** *EYEN-en paa-PEER-korp*
ice cubes	**Eiswürfel** *EYESS-vewr-fel*
more hangers	**mehr Kleiderbügel** *mayr KLEYED-uh-bew-gel*
What's the voltage here?	**Welche Stromspannung haben Sie hier?** *VEHLKH-eh SHTROHM-shpahn-ung HAAB-en zee heer*

May I leave this in your safe?	**Darf ich dies in Ihrem Tresor lassen?** *dahrf ikh dees in EE-rem treh-ZOHR LASS-en*
Where is ____?	**Wo ist ____?** *voh ist*
■ the elevator	**der Aufzug** *dehr OWF-tsook*
■ the bathroom	**das Bad** *dahs baat*
■ the shower	**die Dusche** *dee DOOSH-eh*
■ the breakfast room	**das Frühstückszimmer** *dahs FREW-shtewks-tsim-uh*
■ the dining room	**der Speisesaal** *dehr SHPEYEZ-eh-zaal*
■ the checkroom	**die Garderobe** *dee gahrd-eh-ROHB-eh*
■ the pool	**das Schwimmbad** *dahs SHVIM-baat*
■ the children's playroom	**der Aufenthaltsraum für Kinder** *dehr OWF-ent-hahlts-rowm fewr KIND-uh*
■ the telephone (book)	**das Telephon (buch)** *dahs TAY-leh-fohn (bookh)*
What's my room number?	**Welche Zimmernummer habe ich?** *VELKH-eh TSIM-uh-num-uh HAAB-eh ikh*
Shall I register now or later?	**Soll ich mich jetzt oder später eintragen?** *zol ikh mikh yehtst OHD-uh SHPAYT-uh EYEN-traa-gen*
I'll leave the key here.	**Ich lasse den Schlüssel hier.** *ikh LAHSS-eh dayn SHLEWSS-el heer*
Please wake me tomorrow at ____ o'clock.	**Bitte wecken sie mich morgen um ____ Uhr.** *BIT-eh VEHK-en zee mikh MORG-en um ____ oor*
Please don't forget.	**Bitte vergessen Sie es nicht.** *BIT-eh fehr-GESS-en zee ehs nikht*

I don't wish to be disturbed.	**Ich will nicht gestört werden.**	*Ikh vil nikht geh-SHTERT VAYRD-en*
Where is ____?	**Wo ist ____?**	*Voh ist*

■ the bellboy — **der Hotelpage** *dehr ho-TEL-paa-zheh*

■ the elevator operator — **der Liftjunge** *dehr LIFT-yun-geh*

■ the porter — **der Hausdiener** *dehr HOWS-dee-nuh*

■ the chambermaid — **das Zimmermädchen** *dahs TSIM-uh-mayd-khen*

■ the manager — **der Geschäftsführer** *dehr geh-SHEHFTS-few-ruh*

■ the switchboard operator — **die Telephonistin** *dee tay-leh-foh-NIST-in*

There is ____.	**Es gibt ____.**	*ehs gipt*

■ no hot water — **kein heißes Wasser** *keyen HEYESS-es VAHSS-uh*

■ no heat — **keine Heizung** *KEYEN-eh HEYETS-ung*

The room is dirty.	**Das Zimmer ist schmutzig.**	*dahs TSIM-uh ist SHMUTS-ikh*
The window (door, blind) is stuck.	**Das Fenster (die Tür, die Jalousie) klemmt.**	*dahs FENST-uh (dee tewr, dee zhah-loo-ZEE) klemt*
The ____ is defective.	**____ ist defekt.**	*ist deh-FEHKT*

■ air conditioning — **die Klimaanlage** *dee KLEE-mah-ahn-laa-geh*

■ fan — **der Ventilator** *dehr ven-tee-LAAT-or*

■ ventilator — **der Lüfter** *dehr LEWFT-uh*

▪the radio	**das Radio** *dahs RAAD-ee-oh*
▪television set	**der Fernseher** *dehr FEHRN-zay-uh*
▪the lamp	**die Lampe** *dee LAHMP-eh*
▪the plug	**die Steckdose** *dee SHTEK-doh-zeh*
▪the switch	**der Schalter** *dehr SHAHLT-uh*
▪the toilet	**die Toilette** *dee toy-LET-eh*

| The bathtub (the shower, the washbasin) is clogged. | **Die Badewanne (die Dusche, das Waschbecken) ist verstopft.** *dee BAAD-eh-vahn-eh (dee DOOSH-eh, dahs VAHSH-behk-en) ist fehr-SHTOPFT* |
| Do you have another room? | **Haben Sie ein anderes Zimmer?** *HAAB-en zee eyen AHND-eh-res TSIM-uh* |

BREAKFAST, ROOM SERVICE

Is breakfast included in the price of the room?	**Ist der Zimmerpreis mit Frühstück?** *ist dehr TSIM-uh-preyes mit FREW-shtewk*
Is an egg included?	**Ist ein Ei dabei?** *ist eyen eye dah-BEYE*
How much extra does the egg cost?	**Wieviel extra kostet das Ei?** *VEE-feel EKS-traa KOST-et dahs eye*
I want a soft-boiled egg.	**Ich möchte ein weichgekochtes Ei.** *ikh MERKHT-eh eyen VEYEKH-geh-kokh-tes eye*
▪a medium-boiled egg	**ein wachsweichgekochtes Ei** *eyen VAHKS-veyekh-geh-kokh-tes eye*
▪a hard-boiled egg	**ein hartgekochtes Ei** *eyen HAHRT-geh-kokh-tes eye*
I'd like ____.	**Ich möchte gerne ____.** *ikh MERKH-teh GEHRN-eh*

■ coffee	**Kaffee** *KAHF-fay*
■ tea	**Tee** *tay*
■ chocolate	**Schokolade** *shoko-LAAD-eh*
■ milk	**Milch** *milkh*
■ orange juice	**Apfelsinensaft** *AHP-fehl-zeen-en-zahft*
■ yoghurt	**Joghurt** *YOH-goort*
■ an omelette	**eine Omelette** *EYEN-eh omeh-LET-eh*
■ fried eggs	**Spiegeleier** *SHPEEG-ehl-eye-uh*
■ scrambled eggs	**Rühreier** *REWR-eye-uh*
■ bacon and eggs (ham)	**Eier mit Speck (Schinken)** *EYE-uh mit shpek (SHINK-en)*
I'd like more ____.	**Ich möchte mehr ____.** *ikh MERKHT-eh mayr*
■ butter	**Butter** *BUT-uh*
■ jam	**Marmelade** *mahr-meh-LAAD-eh*
■ sugar	**Zucker** *TSUK-uh*
■ cream	**Sahne** *ZAAN-eh*
■ bread	**Brot** *broht*
■ rolls	**Brötchen** *BRERT-khen*
■ honey	**Honig** *HOHN-ikh*
■ lemon	**Zitrone** *tsi-TROHN-eh*
Do you have room service?	**Gibt es Zimmerbedienung?** *gipt ehs TSIM-uh-be-dien-ung?*
How much does it cost with full room and board?	**Wieviel kostet es mit voller Verpflegung?** *VEE-feel KOST-et ehs mit FOL-uh fehr-PFLAYG-ung*
How much is half-board?	**Was ist der Preis für Halbpension?** *vahs ist dehr preyes fewr HAHLP-pehn-zee-ohn*

How long must I stay before I can get a reduction in price?	**Wie lange muß ich bleiben, bevor ich eine Preisermäßigung bekommen kann?** *vee LAHNG-eh muss ikh BLEYEB-en beh-FOR ikh EYEN-eh PREYESS-ehr-mayss-ig-ung beh-KOM-en kahn*
Come in.	**Herein!** *heh-REYEN*
Put it _____	**Stellen Sie es** *SHTEL-en zee ehs*
■ Over there.	**da drüben!** *daa DREWB-en*
■ On the table.	**Auf den Tisch.** *owf dayn tish*
■ Just a minute.	**Augenblick nur.** *OWG-en-blik noor*

OTHER ACCOMMODATIONS

Is there a youth hostel (a castle hotel, an inn) here?	**Gibt es eine Jugendherberge (ein Schloßhotel, ein Gasthaus) hier?** *gipt ehs EYEN-eh YOOG-ent-hehr-behr-geh (eyen SHLOSS-ho-tel, eyen GAHST-hows) heer*
I'm looking for a room in a boarding-house.	**Ich suche ein Zimmer in einer Pension.** *ikh ZOOKH-eh eyen TSIM-uh in EYEN-uh penz-YOHN*
Where is the local tourist office?	**Wo ist das Fremdenverkehrs-büro?** *voh ist dahs FREMD-en-fehr-kayrs-bew-roh*
I'd like to rent a house (a furnished apartment).	**Ich möchte ein Haus (eine Ferienwohnung) mieten.** *ikh MERKHT-eh eyen hows (EYEN-eh FEHR-yen-vohn-ung) MEET-en*
I need a living room, bedroom, and kitchen.	**Ich brauche ein Wohnzimmer, Schlafzimmer und Küche.** *ikh BROWKH-eh eyen VOHN-tsim-uh, SHLAAF-tsim-uh unt KEW-kheh*
How much is the rent?	**Was ist die Miete?** *vahs ist dee MEET-eh*

I'll be staying for ___.	**Ich bleibe ___.** *ikh BLEYEB-eh*
■ two weeks	**zwei Wochen** *tsveye VOKH-en*
■ one month	**einen Monat** *EYEN-en MOH-naat*
■ the whole season	**die ganze Saison** *dee GAHNTS-eh ZAY-zon*
I want something ___.	**Ich möchte etwas ___.** *ikh MERKHT-eh ET-vahs*
■ downtown	**im Zentrum** *im TSENT- room*
■ in the old part of town	**in der Altstadt** *in dehr AHLT-shtaht*
■ with modern conveniences	**mit modernem Komfort** *mit mod-EHRN-em kom-FOHR*

DEPARTURE

We're checking out tomorrow.	**Wir reisen morgen ab.** *veer REYEZ-en MORG-en ahp*
Are there any letters (messages) for me?	**Gibt es Briefe (Nachrichten) für mich?** *gipt ehs BREEF-eh (NAHKH-rikht-en) fewr mikh*
Please prepare my bill.	**Bitte bereiten Sie meine Rechnung vor.** *BIT-eh beh-REYET-en zee MEYEN-eh REKH-nung for*

TRAVELING AROUND TOWN

SUBWAYS, BUSES, AND STREETCARS

Where can I buy a ticket?	**Wo kann ich eine Fahrkarte kaufen?** *voh kahn ikh EYEN-eh FAAR-kahr-teh KOWF-en*

When does the next bus leave?	**Wann fährt der nächste Bus?** *vahn fayrt dehr NAYKST-eh bus*
Where is the bus stop?	**Wo ist die Bushaltestelle?** *voh ist dee BUS-hahl-teh-shteh-leh*
When does the last streetcar leave?	**Wann geht die letzte Straßen-bahn?** *vahn gayt dee LETST-eh SHTRAHSS-en-baan*
Where is the nearest subway station?	**Wo ist die nächste U-Bahn Station (Untergrundbahn)?** *voh ist dee NAYKH-steh oo-baan shtah-TSYOHN (UNT-uh-grunt-baan)*
How much is the fare?	**Wieviel kostet die Fahrt?** *VEE-feel KOST-et dee faart*
Which is the line that goes to _____?	**Welche Linie fährt nach _____?** *VEHLKH-eh LEEN-yeh fehrt nahkh*
Does this train go to _____?	**Fährt dieser Zug nach _____?** *fehrt DEEZ-uh tsook nahkh*
What's the next stop?	**Was ist die nächste Haltestelle?** *vahs ist dee NEHKHST-eh HAHLT-eh-shtel-eh*
Where should I get off?	**Wo muß ich aussteigen?** *voh muss ikh OWS-shteyeg-en*
Do I have to change trains?	**Muß ich umsteigen?** *muss ikh UM-shteyeg-en*
Please tell me when we get there.	**Bitte sagen Sie mir, wann wir dort ankommen.** *BIT-eh ZAAG-en zee meer vahn veer dort AHN-kom-en*

TAXIS

| Please call a taxi for me. | **Rufen Sie bitte eine Taxe für mich.** *ROOF-en zee BIT-eh EYEN-eh TAHKS-fewr mikh* |

How much is the ride to Wandsbek?	**Wieviel kostet die Fahrt nach Wandsbek?** *VEE-feel KOST-et dee faart nakh WAHNTS-behk?*
Drive me to the hotel (railroad station, airport).	**Fahren Sie mich zum Hotel (Bahnhof, Flughafen).** *FAAR-en zee mikh tsoom ho-TEL (BAAN-hohf, FLOOK-haa-fen)*
Please wait for me.	**Warten Sie auf mich bitte.** *VAART-en zee owf mikh BIT-eh*
I'm in a hurry.	**Ich hab's eilig.** *ikh hahps EYEL-ikh*
Is it still very far?	**Ist es noch sehr weit?** *ist ehs nokh zayr veyet*
Let me off at the next corner.	**Lassen Sie mich an der nächsten Ecke aussteigen!** *LASS-en zee mikh ahn dehr NAYKST-en EK-eh OWS-shteye-gen*

SIGHTSEEING

I'm looking for the Tourist Office.	**Ich suche das Fremden-verkehrsbüro.** *ikh ZOOKH-eh dahs FREHM-den-fehr-kayrs-bew-roh*
Is there a guided tour of the city? (bus tour)	**Gibt es eine Stadtrundfahrt?** *gipt ehs EYEN-eh SHTAHT-runt-faart*
Is there an English-speaking tour?	**Gibt es eine englischsprachige Führung?** *gipt ehs EYEN-eh ENG-lish-shpraa-khi-geh FEWR-ung*
I need a guidebook.	**Ich brauche einen Reiseführer.** *ikh BROWKH-eh EYEN-en REYEZ-eh-few-ruh*
What are the chief sights?	**Was sind die Haupt-sehenswürdigkeiten?** *vahs zint dee HOWPT-zay-ens-vewr-dikh-keye-ten*

Is (are) the _____ very far from here?	**Ist (sind) _____ sehr weit von hier?** *ist (zint) _____ zayr veyet fon heer*
■ abbey	**die Abtei** *dee ahp-TEYE*
■ amusement park	**der Vergnügungspark** *dehr fehr-GNEWG-ungks-paark*
■ artists' quarter	**das Künstlerviertel** *dahs KEWNST-lehr-feer-tel*
■ botanical garden	**der Botanische Garten** *dehr bo-TAAN-ish-eh GAART-en*
■ castle	**das Schloß/die Burg, Festung** *dahs shloss/dee boork, FEST-ung*
■ cathedral	**der Dom/die Kathedrale** *dehr dohm/dee kaa-tayd-RAAL-eh*
■ cemetery	**der Friedhof** *dehr FREET-hohf*
■ city center	**die Stadtmitte/das Zentrum** *dee SHTAHT-mit-eh/dahs TSENT-rum*
■ city hall	**das Rathaus** *dahs RAAT-hows*
■ church	**die Kirche** *dee KEERKH-eh*
■ commercial district	**das Geschäftsviertel** *dahs geh-SHEHFTS-feer-tel*
■ concert hall	**die Konzerthalle** *dee kon-TSAYRT-hah-leh*
■ docks	**die Hafenanlagen** *dee HAA-fen-ahn-laa-gen*
■ fountain	**der Springbrunnen** *dehr SHPR-ING-bru-nen*
■ gardens	**die Gärten/Grünanlagen** *dee GEHRT-en/GREWN-ahn-laa-gen*
■ library	**die Bibliothek** *dee bib-lee-oh-TAYK*
■ market	**der Markt** *dehr maarkt*

■ monastery	**das Kloster** *dahs KLOHST-uh*
■ monument	**das Denkmal** *dahs DEHNK-maal*
■ museum	**das Museum** *dahs moo-ZAY-um*
■ a nightclub	**ein Nachtlokal** *eyen NAHKHT-lo-kaal*
■ old part of town	**die Altstadt** *dee AHLT-shtaht*
■ open-air museum	**das Freilichtmuseum** *dahs FREYE-likht-moo-zay-um*
■ opera	**das Opernhaus** *dahs OHpehrn-howss*
■ palace	**das Schloß/Palais/der Palast** *dahs shloss/pah-LAY/dehr pah-LAHST*
■ ramparts	**die Stadtmauer** *dee STAHT-mow-uh*
■ river	**der Fluß** *dehr fluss*
■ ruins	**die Ruinen** *dee roo-EEN-en*
■ stadium	**das Stadion** *dahs SHTAAD-ee-ohn*
■ theater	**das Theater** *dahs tay-AAT-uh*
■ the tower	**der Turm** *dehr toorm*
■ the university	**die Universität** *dee u-nee-vayr-zi-TAYT*

Is it all right to go in now?	**Darf man jetzt 'rein?** *dahrf mahn yetst reyen*
What time does it open (close)?	**Um wieviel Uhr wird geöffnet (geschlossen)?** *um VEE-feel oor veert geh-ERF-net (geh-SHLOSS-en)*
Must children (students) pay full price?	**Müssen Kinder (Studenten) den vollen Preis bezahlen?** *MEWSS-en KIND-uh (shtu-DENT-en) dayn FOL-en preyess beh-TSAAL-en*

I want three tickets.	**Ich möchte drei Eintrittskarten.** *ikh MERKH-teh dreye EYEN-trits-kaar-ten*
Two adults and one child at half price.	**Zwei Erwachsene und ein Kind zum halben Preis.** *tsveye ehr-VAHKS-en-eh unt eyen kint tsoom HAHLB-en preyess*
Is taking photographs allowed?	**Darf man photographieren?** *dahr mahn foh-toh-grah-FEER-en*

PLANNING TRIPS

AT THE AIRPORT AND ON THE PLANE

Can I fly to Stuttgart directly from here?	**Kann ich von hier direkt nach Stuttgart fliegen?** *kahn ikh fon heer dee-REHKT naakh SHTUT-gahrt FLEEG-en*
Or do I have to change planes?	**Oder muß ich umsteigen?** *OHD-uh muss ikh UM-shteye-gen*
How much is a one-way trip (a round-trip)?	**Was kostet ein einfacher Flug (ein Rückflug)?** *vahs KOST-et eyen EYEN-fahkh-uh flook (eyen REWK-flook)*
When do I have to check in?	**Wann muß ich mich melden?** *vahn muss ikh mikh MEHLD-en*
At what time does it leave?	**Um wieviel Uhr ist der Abflug?** *um VEE-feel oor ist dehr AHP-flook*
I want a seat next to the window in the (non)smoking section.	**Ich möchte einen Fensterplatz (Nicht)Raucher haben.** *ikh MERKH-teh EYEN-en FEHNST-uh-plahts (nikht)ROWKH-uh HAAB-en*
When do we land?	**Wann landen wir?** *vahn LAHND-en veer*

Is there a meal served on flight number ____ ?	**Gibt es eine Mahlzeit auf Flug Nummer ____ ?** *gipt ehs EYEN-eh MAAL-tseyet owf flook NUM-uh*
I have only carry-on baggage.	**Ich habe nur Handgepäck.** *ikh HAAB-eh noor HAHNT-geh-pehk*
Please pass my film (camera) through by hand.	**Bitte reichen Sie mir meinen Film (meine Kamera).** *BIT-eh REYEKH-en zee meer MEYEN-en film (MEYEN-eh KAA-meh-raa)*

SHIPBOARD TRAVEL

Can I go by steamer from Düsseldorf to Cologne?	**Kann ich mit dem Rheindampfer von Düsseldorf nach Köln fahren?** *kahn ikh mit dem REYEN-dahmp-fuh fon DEWSS-el-dorf nahkh kerln FAAR-en*
When does the last ferry (the next boat) leave?	**Wann geht die letzte Fähre (das nächste Boot)?** *vahn gayt dee LEHTST-eh FAIR-eh (dahs NAYKST-eh boht)*
How long does the crossing to Helgoland take?	**Wie lange dauert die Überfahrt nach Helgoland?** *vee LAHNG-eh DOW-ehrt dee EWB-uh-faart nahkh HEHL-goh-lahnt*
I'd like a cabin ____ .	**Ich möchte eine Kabine ____ .** *ikh MERKHT-eh EYEN-eh kah-BEEN-eh*
■ in the luxury class	**in der Luxusklasse** *in dehr LUKS-us-klahss-eh*
■ in the first (second) class	**in der ersten (zweiten) Klasse** *in dehr EHRST-en (TSVEYET-en) KLAHSS-eh*
How long do we still have to stay on board?	**Wie lange müssen wir noch an Bord bleiben?** *vee LAHNG-eh MEWSS-en veer nokh ahn bort BLEYEB-en*

When do we have to board the ship again?	**Wann müssen wir wieder das Schiff besteigen?** *vahn MEWSS-en veer VEED-uh dahs shif be-STEYEG-en*
Do you have something for seasickness?	**Haben Sie etwas gegen Seekrankheit?** *HAAB-en zee ET-vahs GAYG-en ZAY-krahnk-heyet*

TRAINS

How do I get to the station from here?	**Wie komme ich zum Bahnhof von hier?** *vee KOM-eh ikh tsoom BAAN-hohf fon heer*
Is the station far from here? I'm on foot.	**Ist der Bahnhof weit von hier? Ich bin zu Fuß.** *ist dehr BAAN-hohf veyet fon heer? ikh bin tsoo fooss*
Where are the luggage lockers?	**Wo sind die Schließfächer?** *voh zint dee SHLEESS-fekh-uh*
Can you give me change for them?	**Können Sie mir dafür Kleingeld geben?** *KERN-en zee meer daa-FEWR KLEYEN-gelt GAYB-en*
Where is the ticket office?	**Wo ist der Fahrkartenschalter?** *voh ist dehr FAAR-kahr-ten-shahl-tuh*
A one way (a round trip) ticket to Heidelberg.	**Eine einfache Fahrkarte (eine Rückfahrkarte) nach Heidelberg.** *EYEN-eh EYEN-fahkh-eh FAAR-kahr-teh (EYEN-eh REWK-faar-kahr-teh) nahkh HEYED-el-behrk*
Can children travel at half price?	**Können Kinder zum halben Preis fahren?** *KERN-en KIND-uh tsoom HAHLB-en preyess FAAR-en*
What is the fare to Vienna?	**Was kostet die Fahrt nach Wien?** *vahs KOST-et dee faart nahkh veen*
Does the train stop in Linz?	**Hält der Zug in Linz?** *hehlt dehr tsook in lints*

On what platform does the train from Hamburg arrive?	**Auf welchem Bahnsteig kommt der Zug aus Hamburg an?** *owf WELKH-em BAAN-shteyek komt dehr tsook ows HAHM-boork ahn*
When does the next train for Zürich leave?	**Wann fährt der nächste Zug nach Zürich?** *vahn fehrt dehr NAYKST-eh tsook nahkh TSEW-rikh*
Is this car a smoker or nonsmoker?	**Ist dieser Wagen Raucher oder Nichtraucher?** *ist DEEZ-uh VAAG-en ROWKH-uh OHD-uh nikht ROWKH-uh*
Is this seat taken?	**Ist hier noch frei?** *ist heer nokh freye*
Do you have a time-table?	**Haben Sie einen Fahrplan?** *HAAB-en zee EYEN-en FAAR-plaan*
Is there a dining car?	**Gibt es einen Speisewagen?** *gipt ehs EIN-en SHPEYE-zeh-vaa-gen*
Is the train carrying a sleeping car?	**Führt der Zug einen Schlafwagen?** *fewrt dehr tsook EYEN-en SHLAAF-vaa-gen*
Or does it just have coaches?	**Oder hat er nur Liegewagen?** *OHD-uh haht ehr nur LEEG-eh-vaag-en*
All aboard!	**Einsteigen!** *EYEN-shteye-gen*
Where should I get off?	**Wo soll ich aussteigen?** *voh zol ikh OWS-shteye-gen*
Must I change trains?	**Muß ich umsteigen?** *muss ikh UM-steye-gen*
Can I take the express from Osna-brück to Bassum?	**Kann ich mit dem Fernschnellzug von Osnabrück nach Bassum fah-ren?** *kahn ikh mit daym FEHRN-shnel-tsook fon oss-nah-BREWK nakh BAHSS-um FAAR-en*
Or must I change to a local train?	**Oder muß ich in einen Personen-zug umsteigen?** *OHD-uh muss ikh in EYEN-en pehr-ZOHN-en-tsook UM-steye-gen*

ENTERTAINMENT AND DIVERSIONS

MOVIES, THEATERS, CONCERTS, OPERAS, OPERETTAS

I want to go to the movies tonight.	**Ich möchte heute abend ins Kino.** *ikh MERKHT-eh HOYT-eh AAB-ehnt ins KEEN-oh*
What sort of a movie is it?	**Was für ein Film ist es?** *vahs fewr eyen film ist ehs*
Is it a comedy (thriller, musical, Western)?	**Ist es eine Komödie (ein Krimi, Musical, Western)?** *ist ehs EYEN-eh ko-MERD-yeh (eyen KREEM-ee, "musical", VEHST-ehrn)*
I want to go to the theater (the concert).	**Ich möchte ins Theater (ins Konzert).** *ikh MERKHT-eh ins tay-AAT-uh (ins kon-TSEHRT)*
Do they speak English or German in the movie?	**Spricht man Englisch oder Deutsch im Film?** *sprikht mahn EHNG-lish OHD-uh doytsh im film*
What sort of a play is that?	**Was für ein Stück ist das?** *vahs fewr eyen shtewk ist dahs*
Is it a tragedy, comedy, or drama?	**Ist es ein Trauerspiel? Ein Lustspiel? Ein Schauspiel/Drama?** *ist ehs eyen TROW-ehr-shpeel eyen LUST-shpeel eyen SHOW-shpeel/DRAAM-ah*
Are the actors famous?	**Sind die Schauspieler berühmt?** *zint dee SHOW-shpeel-uh beh-REWMT*
Do you think I'll understand much of it?	**Glauben Sie, daß ich viel davon verstehen werde?** *GLOWB-en zee dahs ikh feel dah-FON fehr-SHTAY-en VEHRD-eh*
Is the theater far from here?	**Ist das Theater weit von hier?** *ist dahs tay-AAT-uh veyet von heer*

Is there a central box office for all the city's theaters?

Gibt es eine Zentralkasse für alle Theater der Stadt? *gipt ehs EYEN-eh tsen-TRAAL-kahss-eh fewr AHL-eh tay-AAT-uh dehr shtaht*

Can you get tickets for me?

Können Sie Karten für mich besorgen? *KERN-en zee KAART-en fewr mikh beh-ZORG-en*

When does the performance begin?

Wann beginnt die Vorstellung? *vahn beh-GINT dee FOR-shtel-ung*

I hope the performance isn't sold out.

Ich hoffe, die Vorstellung ist nicht ausverkauft. *ikh HOF-eh dee FOR-shtel-ung ist nikht OWSS-fehr-kowft*

Do you still have a good seat in the orchestra?

Haben Sie noch einen guten Platz im Parkett? *HAAB-en zee nokh EYEN-en GOOT-en plahts im pahr-KET*

■Down front

ganz vorne *gahnts FORN-eh*

■In the middle or in back

in der Mitte oder hinten *in dehr MIT-eh OHD-uh HINT-en*

I want three inexpensive but good seats in the second tier.

Ich möchte drei billige aber gute Plätze im zweiten Rang. *ikh MERKHT-eh drey BIL-ig-eh AAB-uh GOOT-eh PLEHTS-eh im TSVEYET-en rahng*

How expensive is it in the first row?

Wie teuer ist es in der ersten Reihe? *vee TOY-uh ist ehs in dehr EHRST-en REYE-eh*

Where is the cloakroom?

Wo ist die Garderobe? *voh ist dee gahr-deh-ROHB-eh*

How much does a program cost?

Was kostet ein Programm? *vahs KOST-et eyen proh-GRAHM*

Who's playing the lead?

Wer spielt die Hauptrolle? *vehr shpeelt dee HOWPT-rol-eh*

Who's singing (dancing, playing)?

Wer singt (tanzt, spielt)? *vehr zinkt (tahntst, shpeelt)*

Who's conducting?	**Wer dirigiert?** *vehr di-ree-GEERT*
I want to see a really sentimental operetta.	**Ich möchte eine wirklich schmalzige Operette sehen.** *ikh MERKHT-eh EYEN-eh VIRK-likh SHMAHLTS-ig-eh opeh-RET-eh ZAY-en*
Or maybe a ballet.	**Oder vielleicht ein Ballett.** *OHD-uh FEEL-eyekht eyen bah-LET*
Where and how can I get tickets for that?	**Wo und wie kann ich Karten dafür bekommen?** *Voh unt vee kahn ikh KAART-en dah-FEWR beh-KOM-en*

NIGHTCLUBS

I'd like to go to an interesting nightclub tonight.	**Ich möchte gerne in ein interessantes Nachtlokal heute abend gehen.** *ikh MERKHT-eh GEHRN-eh in eyen in-teh-ress-AHNT-es NAKHT-lo-kaal HOYT-eh AAB-ent GAY-en*
■ a beer or wine tavern with happy music	**Eine Bier- oder Weinstube mit fröhlicher Musik.** *EYEN-eh beer OHD-uh VEYEN-shtoob-eh mit FRER-likh-ehr moo-ZEEK*
■ a discotheque with young people	**Eine Diskothek mit jungen Leuten.** *EYEN-eh dis-koh-TAYK mit YUNG-en LOYT-en*
■ a lavish nightclub with a floor show	**ein Nachtlokal von Format mit Attraktionen.** *eyen NAHKHT-lo-kaal fon for-MAAT mit aht-rahk-tsee-OHN-en*
I want to shake my dancing legs.	**Ich will mein Tanzbein schwingen.** *ikh vil meyen TAHNTS-beyen SHVING-en*
Is a reservation necessary?	**Muß man reservieren lassen?** *muss mahn reh-zehr-VEER-en LASS-en*
Is evening dress required?	**Wird Abendgarderobe verlangt?** *veert AAB-ent-gaar-deh-roh-beh fehr-LAHNKT*

Where can I see folk dances?	**Wo kann ich Volkstänze sehen?** *voh kahn ikh FOLKS-tehn-tseh ZAY-en*
I'd like a good table.	**Ich möchte einen guten Tisch.** *ikh MERKHT-eh EYEN-en GOOT-en tish*
I want an adventure, but not an expensive evening.	**Ich will ein Abenteuer aber keinen teuren Abend.** *ikh vill eyen AAB-ehn-toy-uh AAB-uh KEYEN-en TOY-ren AAB-ent*
Is there a minimum?	**Gibt es eine Mindestgebühr?** *gipt ehs EYEN-eh MIND-ehst-geh-BEWR*

SPORTS

I'm looking for _____.	**Ich suche _____.** *ikh ZOOKH-eh*
■ a bowling alley	**eine Kegelbahn** *EYEN-eh KAYG-el-baan*
■ a tennis court	**einen Tennisplatz** *EYEN-en TEN-is-plahts*
■ a playing field	**einen Sportplatz** *EYEN-en SHPORT-plahts*
■ a golf course	**einen Golfplatz** *EYEN-en GOLF-plahts*
■ a gymnasium	**eine Turnhalle** *EYEN-eh TURN-hahl-eh*
■ a ju-jitsu school	**eine Jiu-Jitsu Schule** *EYEN-eh dshu-DSHIT-su SHUL-eh*
Are there rackets (clubs) for rent?	**Kann man Tennisschläger (Golfschläger) leihen?** *kahn mahn TEN-is-shlayg-uh (GOLF-shlayg-uh) LEYE-en*
How much does it cost per hour (round/day)?	**Wieviel kostet es pro Stunde (Runde/Tag)?** *vee-FEEL KOST-et ehs proh SHTUND-eh (RUND-eh/taak)*

SWIMMING

It's terribly hot today.	**Welche Hitze heute!** *VELKH-eh HITS-eh HOYT-eh*
Where can I find a swimming pool?	**Wo kann ich ein Schwimmbad finden?** *voh kahn ikh eyen SHVIM-baat FIND-en*
The hotel has an indoor swimming pool.	**Das Hotel hat ein Hallenbad.** *dahs ho-TEL haht eyen HAHL-en-baat*
I'm looking for an outdoor pool.	**Ich suche ein Freibad.** *ikh ZOOKH-eh eyen FREYE-baat*
Is there a thermal (mineral water) swimming pool in the area?	**Gibt es ein Thermalbad in der Gegend?** *gipt ehs eyen tayr-MAAL-baat in dehr GAYG-ent*
Is it heated?	**Ist es geheizt?** *ist ehs geh-HEYETST*
What's the water temperature?	**Welche Temperatur hat das Wasser?** *VELKH-eh tem-pay-raa-TOOR haht dahs VAHSS-uh*
How do I get there?	**Wie komme ich dort hin?** *vee KOM-eh ikh dort hin*
Is it warm?	**Ist es warm?** *ist ehs vahrm*
Cold?	**Kalt?** *kahlt*
When is low tide (high tide)?	**Wann ist Ebbe (Flut)?** *vahn ist EHB-eh (floot)*
Is there a lake in the area?	**Gibt es einen See in der Gegend?** *gipt ehs EYEN-en zay in dehr GAY-gent*
Is there a nudist beach in this area?	**Gibt es ein FKK Strandbad in dieser Gegend?** *gipt ehs eyen ef-kah-kah SHTRAHNT-baat in DEEZ-uh GAY-gent*
What's the admission charge?	**Was kostet der Eintritt?** *vahs KOST-et dehr EYEN-trit*

Do I have to join an organization?	**Muß ich einem Verein beitreten?** *muss ikh EYEN-em fehr-EYEN BEYE-trayt-en*
Is there a lifeguard?	**Gibt es einen Rettungsdienst?** *gipt ehs EYEN-en REHT-unks-deenst*
Is it safe to swim there?	**Kann man dort ohne Gefahr schwimmen?** *kahn mahn dort OHN-eh geh-FAAR SHVIM-en*
Can you swim in the river (pond)?	**Kann man im Fluß (Teich) schwimmen?** *kahn mahn im fluss (teyekh) SHVIM-en*
Is the water clean?	**Ist das Wasser rein?** *ist dahs VAHSS-uh reyen*
The pool is always too crowded.	**Das Schwimmbad ist immer zu voll.** *dahs SHVIM-baat ist IM-muh tsoo fol*
I want to enjoy nature's calm.	**Ich will die Ruhe der Natur genießen.** *ikh vil dee ROO-eh dehr naa-TOOR geh-NEESS-en*
Where can I get _____?	**Wo kann ich _____ bekommen?** *voh kahn ikh _____ beh-KOM-en*
■ an air mattress	**eine Luftmatratze** *EYEN-eh luft-maht-rahts-eh*
■ a chaise longue	**einen Liegestuhl** *EYEN-en LEEG-eh-shtool*
■ diving equipment	**eine Tauchausrüstung** *EYEN-eh TOWKH-owss-rewst-ung*
■ sunglasses	**eine Sonnenbrille** *EYEN-eh ZON-en-bril-eh*
■ suntan lotion	**Sonnencreme** *ZON-en-kraym*
■ a surfboard	**ein Surfbrett** *eyen "SURF"-breht*
■ waterskis	**Wasserschier** *VAHSS-uh-shee-uh*

Is there a sailing school here?	**Gibt es hier eine Segelschule?** *gipt ehs heer EYEN-eh ZAYG-ehl-shool-eh*

WINTER SPORTS

Are the very high passes still open to traffic?	**Sind die ganz hohen Pässe noch dem Verkehr offen?** *zint dee gahnts HOH-en PEHSS-eh nokh daym fehr-KAYR OFF-en*
Can you take the train there?	**Kann man mit dem Zug dort hinfahren?** *kahn mahn mit daym tsook dort HIN-faar-en*
Is there a cable car or cogwheel railway?	**Gibt es eine Seilschwebe- oder Bergbahn?** *gipt ehs EYEN-eh ZEYEL-shvayb-eh OHD-uh BAIRK-baan*
Are there ski lifts?	**Gibt es dort Schilifts?** *gipt ehs dort SHEE-lifts*
■chair lifts or T-bars	**Sessel-oder Schlepplifts** *ZEHSS-el OHD-uh SHLEP-lifts*
I need skiing lessons.	**Ich brauche Schiunterricht.** *ikh BROWKH-eh SHEE-un-tehr-rikht*
■skating lessons	**Unterricht im Schlittschuhlaufen** *UNT-ehr-rikht im SHLIT-shoo-lowf-en*
Is there a skating rink?	**Gibt es eine Eisbahn?** *gipt ehs EYEN-eh EYESS-baan*
■ an artificial skating rink?	**eine Kunsteisbahn?** *EYEN-eh KUNST-eyess-baan*
Is it possible to rent _____?	**Ist es möglich _____ zu mieten?** *ist ehs MERG-likh _____ tsoo MEET-en*
■ skiing equipment	**eine Schiausrüstung** *EYEN-eh SHEE-owss-rewst-ung*
■ a sled	**einen Schlitten** *EYEN-en SHLIT-en*

| poles | **Schistöcke** *SHEE-shterk-eh* |
| boots | **Stiefel** *SHTEEF-el* |

CAMPING

We're looking for a camping site around here.	**Wir suchen einen Campingplatz in der Nähe.** *veer ZUKH-en EYEN-en KEHMP-ing-plahts in dehr NAY-eh*
How far is it?	**Wie weit ist er?** *vee veyet ist ehr*
I hope it isn't too crowded.	**Hoffentlich ist er nicht zu voll.** *HOF-ent-likh ist ehr nikht tsoo fol*
Might it be possible to camp on your property?	**Dürften wir vielleicht auf Ihrem Grundstück zelten?** *DEWRFT-en veer feel-LEYEKHT owf EER-em GRUND-shtwek TSELT-en*
It's nice and quiet here (at your place).	**Bei Ihnen ist es schön ruhig.** *beye EEN-en ist ehs shern ROOH-ikh*
We're prepared to pay for peace and quiet.	**Wir sind bereit diese herrliche Ruhe zu bezahlen.** *veer zint beh-REYET DEEZ-eh HEHR-likh-eh ROO-eh tsoo beh-TSAAL-en*
Where can we spend the night?	**Wo können wir übernachten?** *voh KERN-en veer EWB-uh-nakht-en*
Where can we park our trailer?	**Wo können wir unseren Wohnwagen abstellen?** *voh KERN-en veer UN-zehr-en VOHN-vaag-en AHP-shtel-en*
How do we get to this camping place?	**Wie kommen wir zu diesem Campingplatz?** *vee KOM-en veer tsoo DEEZ-em KEHMP-ing-plahts*
Is there _____ there?	**Gibt es _____ dort?** *gipt ehs _____ dort*
drinking water	**Trinkwasser** *TRINK-vaass-uh*
running water	**fließendes Wasser** *FLEESS-end-es VAASS-uh*

■ a children's play-ground	**einen Spielplatz für Kinder** *EYEN-en SHPEEL-plahts fewr KIND-uh*
Are there _____?	**Gibt es _____?** *gipt es*
■ showers	**Duschen** *DOO-shen*
■ baths	**Bäder** *BAY-duh*
■ toilets	**Toiletten** *toy-LET-en*
■ tents	**Zelte** *TSELT-eh*
What does it cost per _____?	**Was kostet es pro _____?** *vahs KOST-et es proh*
■ person	**Person** *pehr-ZOHN*
■ car	**Wagen** *VAAG-en*
■ trailer	**Wohnwagen** *VOHN-vaag-en*
We'd like to stay _____ days (weeks).	**Wir möchten _____ Tage (Wochen) bleiben.** *veer MERKHT-en _____ TAAG-eh (VOKH-en) BLEYEB-en*
Can you recommend a region that's less overrun with tourists?	**Können Sie eine Gegend empfehlen, die weniger von Touristen überlaufen ist?** *KERN-en zee EYEN-eh GAYG-ent emp-FAYL-en dee VAYN-i-guh fon tu-RIST-en EWB-uh-lowf-en ist*

IN THE COUNTRYSIDE

Let's take a drive to no place special.	**Machen wir eine Fahrt ins Blaue.** *MAHKH-en veer EYEN-eh faart ins BLOW-eh*
Let's take a nice trip to the country.	**Machen wir einen schönen Ausflug aufs Land.** *MAHKH-en veer EYEN-en SHERN-en OWSS-flook owfs lahnt*
Let's look at forests and meadows.	**Sehen wir uns Wälder und Wiesen an.** *ZAY-en veer uns VEHLD-uh unt VEEZ-en ahn*

I want to see ruins and towers.	**Ich möchte Ruinen und Türme sehen.** *ikh MERKHT-eh roo-EEN-en unt TEWRM-eh ZAY-en*
I'd like to rent a car.	**Ich möchte einen Wagen mieten.** *ikh MERKHT-eh EYEN-en VAAG-en MEET-en*
How beautiful is (are) _____!	**Wie schön ist (sind) _____!** *vee shern ist (zint)*
■ the bridge	**die Brücke** *dee BREWK-eh*
■ the brook	**der Bach** *dehr bahkh*
■ the trees	**die Bäume** *dee BOYM-eh*
■ the village	**das Dorf** *dahs dorf*
■ the valley	**das Tal** *dahs taal*
I'm lost (driving).	**Ich habe mich verfahren.** *ikh HAAB-eh mikh fehr-FAAR-en*
I'm lost (walking).	**Ich habe mich verlaufen.** *ikh HAAB-eh mikh fehr-LOWF-en*
Can you show me the way to _____?	**Können Sie mir den Weg nach _____ zeigen?** *KERN-en zee meer dayn vayk nahkh _____ TSEYEG-en*
Where does _____ lead to?	**Wohin führt _____?** *VOH-hin fewrt*
■ this path	**dieser Weg** *DEEZ-uh vayk*
■ this road	**diese Straße** *DEEZ-eh SHTRAASS-eh*
■ this brook	**dieser Bach** *DEEZ-uh bahkh*
■ this stream	**dieser Strom** *DEEZ-uh shtrom*
Could you accompany me a bit if you're going that way?	**Könnten Sie mich ein Stück begleiten, wenn Sie denselben Weg haben?** *KERNT-en zee mikh eyen shtewk beh-GLEYET-en, ven zee dayn-ZELB-en vayk HAAB-en*

FOOD AND DRINK

DRINKING AND DINING

Is there a restaurant that serves local specialties?	**Gibt es ein Restaurant, das einheimische Spezialitäten serviert?** *gipt ehs eyen res-tow-RAHNG dahs EYEN-heye-mish-eh shpets-yah-li-TAYT-en zehr-VEERT*
Is there a good, not too expensive, German restaurant around here?	**Gibt es ein gutes, nicht zu teures deutsches Restaurant in der Nähe?** *gipt ehs eyen GOOT-es nikht tsoo TOYR-es DOY-ches res-tow-RAHNG in dehr NAY-eh*
Can you recommend an inexpensive restaurant _____?	**Können Sie mir ein preiswertes Restaurant empfehlen?** *KERN-en zee meer eyen PREYES-vehrt-es res-tow-RAHNG emp-FAYL-en*
with German specialties	**mit deutschen Spezialitäten** *mit DOY-chen shpets-yah-li-TAYT-en*
with local specialties	**mit hiesigen Spezialitäten** *mit HEEZ-ig-en shpehts-yah-li-TAYT-en*
I'm on a diet. The meat without sauce, please.	**Ich lebe Diät. Das Fleisch ohne Soße, bitte.** *ikh LAY-beh dee-AYT. dahs fleyesh OH-neh ZOHSS-eh BIT-eh*
Can they prepare a salt- and spice-free meal for me?	**Kann man mir ein Salz- und Gewürzfreies Essen vorbereiten?** *kahn mahn meer eyen zahlts unt ge-VEWRTS-freye-ehs EHSS-en for-be-REYET-en*
Do you have a table for me (us)?	**Haben Sie einen Tisch für mich (uns)?** *HAAB-en zee EYEN-en tish fewr mikh (uns)?*
Where are the toilets?	**Wo sind die Toiletten?** *voh zint dee toy-LET-en*

Where can I wash my hands?	**Wo kann ich mir die Hände waschen?** *voh kahn ikh meer dee HEHND-eh VAHSH-en*
Would we have to wait long?	**Müßten wir lange warten?** *MEWSST-en veer LAHNG-eh VAART-en*
I need (we need) another _____.	**Ich brauche (wir brauchen) noch _____.** *ikh BROWKH-eh (veer BROWKH-en) nokh _____.*

- spoon — **einen Löffel** *EYEN-en LERF-el*
- fork — **eine Gabel** *EYEN-eh GAAB-el*
- knife — **ein Messer** *eyen MESS-uh*
- glass — **ein Glas** *eyen glaas*
- plate — **einen Teller** *EYEN-en TEL-uh*
- chair — **einen Stuhl** *EYEN-en shtool*
- napkin — **eine Serviette** *EYEN-eh zehr-VYEHT-eh*

APPETIZERS

Aal in Gelee *aal in zheh-LAY*	eel in aspic (ballotine of eel)
Appetithäppchen *ah-peh-TEET-hehp-khyen*	canapés
Artischockenherzen in Öl *ahr-ti-SHOK-en-herts-en in erl*	hearts of artichokes in oil
Bismarckhering *BIS-mahrk-hayr-ing*	marinated herring with onions
Bückling *BEWK-ling*	kipper, bloater
Fleischpastete *FLEYESH-pahs-tayt-eh*	meat pie, meat loaf
Froschschenkel *FROSH-shehnk-el*	frogs' legs
Gänseleberpastete *GEHN-zeh-lay-buh-pahs-tayt-eh*	goose liver pâté

Gänseleber im eigenen Fett *GEHN-zeh-lay-buh im EYEG-en-en fet*	goose liver (cold) in its own fat
Geräucherte Gänsebrust *geh-ROYKH-ert-eh GEHN-zeh-brust*	smoked breast of goose
Gefüllte Champignons *geh-FEWLT-eh shahm-pin-YONGS*	stuffed mushrooms
Hoppel-Poppel *HOP-pel-POP-pel*	bacon or sausages in scrambled eggs
Hummer *HUM-uh*	lobster
Käsehäppchen *KAY-zeh-hehp-khyen*	bits of cheese
Katenschinken *KAAT-en-shink-en*	lightly smoked Westphalian ham
Kaviar mit Zwiebeln und Zitrone *KAA-viah mit TSVEEB-eln unt tsit-ROHN-eh*	caviar with onions and lemon
Königinpastete *KERN-eeg-in-pahs-tayt-eh*	mushrooms and bits of chicken and tongue in a puff-pastry shell
Krabben *KRAHB-en*	tiny shrimps
Krebs *krayps*	crawfish, crayfish, crab
Lachs *lahks*	salmon
Languste *lahn-GUS-teh*	spiny lobster
Makrele *mah-KRAY-leh*	mackerel
Matjeshering *MAH-tyehs-hayr-ing*	"maiden herring" (a young, white, salted herring usually served with new potatoes)
Russische Eier *RUSS-ish-eh EYE-uh*	Russian eggs (hard-boiled eggs with mayonnaise)

Rehpastete *RAY-pahs-tayt-eh*	venison pâté
Sardellen *zahr-DEL-en*	anchovies
Schinken *SHINK-en*	ham
Schnecken *SHNEHK-en*	snails
Soleier *ZOHL-eye-uh*	eggs boiled in brine
Spargelspitzen *SHPAHRG-el-shpits-en*	asparagus tips
Strammer Max *STRAHM-uh mahks*	well-seasoned diced pork served with eggs and onions
Verschiedene kleine Vorspeisen *fer-SHEED-en-eh KLEYE-neh for-SHPEYEZ-en*	various little appetizers (hors d'oeuvres)
Wurstsalat *VOORST-zah-laat*	cold cuts chopped and served with onions and oil

BEER

Beer may take a back seat to wine in the Rhineland and other wine-growing regions. Nevertheless, it is popular even there. Bavaria and Munich have long been associated with beer brewing, but Dortmund actually produces more beer than Munich. Local brews are found in all parts of German-speaking Europe. Some people affectionately refer to beer and other alcoholic beverages as **flüßiges Brot** (liquid bread).

Asking for a beer is simple:

Beer, please.	**Ein Bier, bitte.** *eyen beer BIT-eh*
You can have	
a bottle of beer	**eine Flasche Bier** *EYEN-eh FLAH-sheh beer*

a glass	**ein Glas**	*eyen glaas*
half a liter (about a pint)	**einen halben Liter**	*EYEN-en HAHLB-en LEET-uh*
a mug (quart)	**eine Maß**	*EYEN-eh maas*

You will also hear people ask for **ein Kleines** (a "short one") or **ein Seidel Bier,** which is usually about a pint, but can vary. In many places you will see beer steins. They are often colorfully decorated and sport sayings in praise of drink and love. Unless they are valuable antiques, you may be able to drink from one of them.

| May I please drink from the beautiful beer mug? | **Darf ich bitte aus dem schönen Steinkrug trinken?** *dahf ikh BIT-eh ows daym SHEWN-en SHTEYEN-krook TRINK-en* |

You may be familiar with some types of beer. Others may be new to you.

Altbier *AHLT-beer*	A bitter beer high in hops **(Hopfen),** said by some to be a tranquilizer
Alsterwasser *AHL-stuh-vahss-uh*	A light beer with a dash of lemonade ("lime lager" in England, *panaché* in France); in southern Germany it's known as **Radlermaß** *(RAA-dluh-maass),* but Hamburg's Alster river gives it its name in the north
Bockbier *BOK-beer* **Doppelbock** *DOPP-ehl-bok* **Märzenbier** *MEHRTS-en-beer*	Beers with a high alcohol and malt content

Malzbier *MAHLTS-beer*	A rather sweet, dark beer low in alcohol but not in calories
Pilsener *PILZ-en-uh*	A light beer originally brewed in Bohemia
Schlenkerle *SHLEHNK-ehr-leh*	A beer made of smoked hops, with a lightly smoked flavor, a specialty of Stuttgart
Weißbier *VEYESS-beer*	A pale ale brewed from wheat. **Berliner Weiße mit Schuß** (with a shot) is **Weißbier** with a dash of **Himbeersaft** (raspberry juice)

WINES

Do you have a wine list?	**Haben Sie eine Weinkarte?** *HAAB-en zee EYEN-eh VEYEN-kaart-eh*	
May I take a look at the wine list please.	**Darf ich mir bitte die Weinkarte ansehen?** *daarf ikh meer BIT-eh dee VEYEN-kaart-eh AHN-zay-en*	
What kinds of wine do you have?	**Was für Weine haben Sie?** *vahs fewr VEYEN-eh HAAB-en zee*	
a bottle of white wine (red) wine.	**eine Flasche Weißwein (Rotwein).** *EYEN-eh FLAHSH-eh VEYESS-veyen (ROHT-veyen)*	
another	**noch**	*nokh*
glass	**ein Glas**	*eyen glaas*
bottle	**eine Flasche**	*EYEN-eh FLAHSH-eh*
half-pint glass	**ein Viertel**	*eyen FEERT-el*
quarter-pint glass	**ein Achtel**	*eyen AHKHT-el*
liter	**einen Liter**	*EYEN-en LEET-uh*
carafe	**eine Karaffe**	*EYEN-eh kahr-AHF-eh*

AT THE RESTAURANT

COFFEE AND TEA

I would like _____.	**Ich möchte bitte _____.**	*ikh MERKHT-eh BIT-eh*
■ a cup of coffee	**eine Tasse Kaffee**	*EYEN-eh TAHSS-eh KAH-fay*
■ with cream	**mit Sahne**	*mit ZAAN-eh*
■ with milk	**einen Milchkaffee**	*EYEN-en MILKH-kah-fay*
■ black coffee	**einen Schwarzen**	*EYEN-en SHVAHRTS-en*
■ coffee with cream	**Braunen**	*BROWN-en*
■ espresso	**Espresso**	*es-PREHSS-oh*
■ iced coffee	**Eiskaffee**	*EYES-kah-fay*
A cup of tea _____	**Eine Tasse Tee**	*EYEN-eh TAHSS-eh tay*
■ with milk	**mit Milch**	*mit milkh*
■ with lemon	**mit Zitrone**	*mit tsi-TROHN-eh*

OTHER NONALCOHOLIC BEVERAGES

hot chocolate	**heiße Schoko-lade**	*HEYESS-eh SHO-ko-laad-eh*
(black, red) currant juice	**(schwarzer, rot-er) Johannis-beersaft**	*(SHVAHRTS-uh ROHT-uh) yo-HAHN-is-bayr-zahft*
mineral water	**Mineralwasser**	*min-eh-RAAL-vahs-uh*
orangeade	**Orangeade**	*or-ahn-ZHAAD-eh*
soda-water (artificially carbonated)	**Selterswasser**	*ZEHLT-uhs-vahs-uh*

soda water	**Sprudelwasser**	*SHPROOD-el-vahs-uh*
spring water	**Quellwasser**	*KVEL-vahs-uh*
apple juice	**Apfelsaft**	*AHPF-el-zahft*

SOUPS AND STEWS

| What is the soup of the day? | **Was ist die Tagessuppe?** *vahs ist dee TAA-gehs-zup-eh* |
| What soups do you have today? | **Was für Suppen gibt es heute?** *vas fewr ZUP-en geept ehs HOYT-eh?* |

Aalsuppe *AAL-zup-eh*	eel soup
Backerbsensuppe *BAHK-ehrps-en-zup-eh*	broth with croutons
Bauernsuppe *BOW-ern-zup-eh*	cabbage and sausage soup
Bohnensuppe *BOHN-en-zup-eh*	bean soup (usually with bacon)
Erbsensuppe *EHRP-sen-zup-eh*	pea soup
Fischsuppe *FISH-zup-eh*	fish soup
Fischbeuschelsuppe *FISH-boy-shel-zup-eh*	fish-roe soup with vegetables
Fridattensuppe *free-DAHT-en-zup-eh*	broth with pancake strips
Frühlingssuppe *FREW-lings-zup-eh*	spring vegetable soup
Grießnockerlsuppe *GREES-nok-ehrl-zup-eh*	semolina-dumpling soup
Gerstenbrühe *GEHRST-en-brew-eh*	barley broth
Gulaschsuppe *GOOL-ahsh-zup-eh*	stewed beef in a spicy soup
Hühnerreissuppe *HEWN-er-reyes-zup-eh*	chicken-rice soup
Hummersuppe *HUM-uh-zup-eh*	lobster soup

Kalte Obstsuppe, Kaltschale *KAHLT-eh OHPST-zup-eh, KAHLT-shahl-eh*	cold fruit soup, usually containing cream, beer, or wine
Kartoffelsuppe *kahr-TOF-el-zup-eh*	potato soup
Kartoffellauchsuppe *kahr-TOF-el-LOWKH-zup-eh*	potato-leek soup
Knödelsuppe *KNERD-el-zup-eh*	dumpling soup
Königinsuppe *KERN-ig-in-zup-eh*	contains beef, sour cream, and almonds
Kraftbrühe mit Ei *KRAFT-brew-eh mit eye*	beef consommé with raw egg
mit Topfteigerbsen *mit TOPF-teyek-ehrps-en*	with fried peas
mit Markknochen Einlage *mit MAHRK-knokh-en-EYEN-laag-eh*	with marrow-bone filling
Leberknödelsuppe *LAY-behr-knerd-el-zup-eh*	liver dumpling soup
Linsensuppe *LINZ-en-zup-eh*	lentil soup
Mehlsuppe Basler Art *MAYL-zup-eh BAAZL-uh aart*	cheese soup with flour, Basle style
Nudelsuppe *NOO-del-zup-eh*	noodle soup
Ochsenschwanzsuppe *OK-sen-shvahnts-zup-eh*	oxtail soup
Pichelsteiner Eintopf *PIKH-el-shteyen-uh EYEN-topf*	meat and vegetable stew
Schildkrötensuppe *SHILT-krert-en-zup-eh*	turtle soup
Schweinsragoutsuppe *SHVEYENS-rahgoo-zup-eh*	pork-ragout soup
Semmelsuppe *ZEH-mel-zup-eh*	dumpling soup
Serbische Bohnensuppe *ZERB-ish-eh BOHN-en-zup-eh*	spicy bean soup

Spargelsuppe	*SHPAHR-gel-zup-eh*	asparagus soup
Tomatensuppe	*toh-MAAT-en-zup-eh*	tomato soup
Zwiebelsuppe	*TSVEE-bel-zup-eh*	onion soup

MEATS

Bauernomelett	*BOW-ehrn-om-let*	bacon and onion omelet
Bauernschmaus	*BOW-ehrn-shmowss*	sauerkraut with smoked pork, sausages, dumplings, and potatoes
Bauernwurst	*BOW-ehrn-voorst*	pork sausage with mustard seeds and peppercorns
Berliner Buletten	*behr-LEEN-uh bul-EHT-en*	fried meat balls, Berlin style
Beuschel (Austria)	*BOY-shel*	veal lungs and heart (often finely chopped, then stewed)
Bratwurst	*BRAAT-voorst*	fried sausage
Bündnerfleisch (Swiss)	*BEWND-nehr-fleyesh*	thinly sliced, air-dried beef
deutsches Beefsteak	*DOY-ches BEEF-stayk*	Salisbury steak, hamburger
Eisbein	*EYES-beyen*	pig's knuckle
Faschiertes (Aust.)	*fah-SHEERT-es*	chopped meat
Fiakergulasch (Aust.)	*fee-AHK-uh-goo-lahsh*	goulash topped with a fried egg
Frikadellen	*fri-kah-DELL-en*	croquettes
gefülltes Kraut	*geh-FEWLT-es krowt*	cabbage leaves stuffed with chopped meat, rice, eggs, and bread crumbs

Gehacktes *ge-HAHKT-es*	chopped meat
Geschnetzeltes (Swiss) *ge-SHNEH-tsel-tes*	braised veal tips
Geselchtes *ge-ZEHLKHT-es*	salty smoked meat (pork)
Gulasch *GOO-lahsh*	beef stew with spicy paprika gravy
Hackbraten *HAHK-braat-en*	meatloaf
Hackfleisch *HAHK-fleyesh*	chopped meat
Hammelbraten *HAHM-el-braat-en*	roast mutton
Hammelkeule, Hammelschlegel *HAHM-el-koyl-eh, HAHM-el-shlay-gel*	leg of mutton
Hammelrippchen *HAHM-el-rip-khen*	mutton chops
Herz *hehrts*	heart
Holsteiner Schnitzel *HOL-shteyen-uh SHNITS-el*	breaded veal cutlet topped with a fried egg and often with bits of toast, anchovies, vegetables, etc.
Jungfernbraten *YUNG-fehrn-braat-en*	a crunchy roast suckling pig
Kalbsbraten *KAHLPS-braat-en*	roast veal
Kalbsbrust *KAHLPS-brust*	breast of veal
Kalbshachse *KAHLPS-hahks-eh*	veal shank
Kalbsmilch *KAHLPS-milkh*	sweetbreads
Karbonade *kahr-bo-NAAD-eh*	fried rib pork chops
Klöße *KLERSS-eh*	meatballs
Klößchen, Klößlein *KLERSS-khen/ KLERSS-leyen*	small meatballs
Kohl und Pinkel *kohl unt PINK-el*	smoked meat, cabbage, and potatoes

Kohlroulade *KOHL-roo-laad-eh*	stuffed cabbage
Königsberger Klops *KER-niks-behrg-uh Klops*	meatballs in caper sauce
Kutteln *KUT-ehln*	tripe
Lammkotelett *LAHM-kot-LET*	lamb chop
Leber *LAY-buh*	liver
Leberkäs *LAY-buh-kays*	meatloaf
Lendenbraten *LEHND-en-braat-en*	roast sirloin, tenderloin
Naturschnitzel *nah-TOOR-shni-tsel*	thick, unbreaded veal cutlet
Nieren *NEER-en*	kidneys
Pöckelfleisch *PER-kel-fleyesh*	pickled meat
Rinderbraten *RIND-uh-braat-en*	roast beef
Rindsstück *RINTS-shtewk*	steak, slice of beef
Rippensteak *RIP-ehn-shtayk*	rib steak
Rouladen *roo-LAAD-en*	vegetables rolled up in thick slices of beef or veal
Rumpfstück *RUMPF-shtewk*	rump steak
Sauerbraten *ZOW-ehr-braat-en*	marinated pot roast in a spicy brown gravy
Saure Nieren *ZOW-reh NEER-en*	kidneys in a sauce containing vinegar
Schlachtplatte *SHLAHKHT-plaht-eh*	mixed sausages and cold meats
Schmorfleisch *SHMOHR-fleyesh*	stewed meat
Schnitzel *SHNITS-el*	cutlet (usually veal)
Schweinskotelett *SHVEYENS-kot-let*	pork chop

Spanferkel *SHPAAN-fehr-kel*	suckling pig
Speck *shpehk*	bacon
(Steierische) Brettjause *SHTEYE-uh-rish-eh BREHT-yowz-eh*	(Styrian) cold cuts on a wooden platter
Sülze *ZEWLTS-eh*	headcheese ("brawn" in Britain)
Tafelspitz *TAAF-el-shpits*	Viennese boiled beef
Tartarensteak *tahr-TAAR-en-shtayk*	ground raw beef, seasoned variously
Wiener Schnitzel *VEEN-uh SHNITS-el*	breaded veal cutlet
Zigeuner Schnitzel *tsee-GOYN-uh SHNITS-el*	veal or pork cutlet in a sharp sauce
Zunge *TSUNG-eh*	tongue

POULTRY, GAME

Backhuhn *BAHK-hoon*	fried chicken
Brathuhn *BRAAT-hoon*	roast chicken
Entenbraten *EHNT-en-braat-en*	roast duck
Fasan *fah-ZAAN*	pheasant
Gänsebraten *GEHN-zeh-braat-en*	roast goose
Hähnchen *HAYN-khen*	small chicken
Hasenbraten *HAAZ-en-braat-en*	roast hare
Hasenpfeffer *HAAZ-en-pfeh-fuh*	spicy rabbit stew
Hirschbraten *HEERSH-braat-en*	venison
Hühnerbraten *HEWN-ehr-braat-en*	roast chicken
Hühnerkeule, Hühnerschlegel *HEWN-ehr-koyl-eh/SHLAY-gel*	drumstick, thigh
Kaninchen *kah-NEEN-khen*	rabbit

Rebhuhn *RAYP-hoon*	partridge
Rehrücken *RAY-rewk-en*	saddle of venison
Taube *TOW-beh*	pigeon, dove, squab
Truthahn *TROOT-haan*	turkey
Wachtel *VAHKHT-el*	quail
Wiener Backhendl *VEEN-uh BAHK-hen-del*	"southern fried chicken," Viennese style
Wildbraten *VILT-braat-en*	roast venison
Wildschweinrücken *VILT-shveyen-rewk-en*	saddle of wild boar

FISH, SEAFOOD

Aal *aal*	eel
Austern *OW-stern*	oysters
Barsch *bahrsh*	(lake) perch
Brachse/Brasse *BRAHKS-eh/BRAHSS-eh*	bream (similar to carp)
Brathering *BRAAT-hayr-ing*	fried sour herring
Dorsch *dorsh*	cod
Felchen *FEHL-khen*	whiting
Fischfrikadellen *FISH-fri-kah-dehl-en*	fish dumplings (croquettes)
Forelle *for-EHL-eh*	trout
Flunder *FLUND-uh*	flounder
Garnelen *gahr-NAYL-en*	shrimp, prawns
Haifischsteak *HEYE-fish-shtayk*	shark steak
Hecht *hekht*	pike
Heilbutt *HEYEL-but*	halibut
Hering *HAY-ring*	herring

Hummer *HUM-uh*		lobster
Jakobsmuscheln *YAA-kops-mush-eln*		scallops
Junger Hecht *YUNG-uh hekht*		pickerel
Kabeljau *KAA-bel-yow*		cod
Karpfen *KAHR-pfen*		carp
Kieler Sprotten *KEEL-uh SHPROT-en*		(Kiel) sprats
Krabben *KRAH-ben*		shrimp, prawn
Krebs *krayps*		crab
Lachs *lahks*		salmon
Languste *lahn-GOOST-eh*		lobster
Makrele *mah-KRAY-leh*		mackerel
Muscheln *MUSH-eln*		clams, cockles, mussels
Neunauge *NOYN-owg-eh*		lamprey eel
Rauch-, Räucher- *rowkh, ROY-khuh*		smoked
Rogen *ROH-gen*		roe
Rotbarsch *ROHT-bahrsh*		red sea bass
Schellfisch *SHEHL-fish*		haddock
Scholle *SHOL-eh*		flatfish, plaice
Schwertfisch *SHVAYRT-fish*		swordfish
Seebarsch *ZAY-bahrsh*		sea bass
Seezunge *ZAY-tsung-eh*		sole
Sojawalfischsteak *ZOH-yah-vaal-fish-stayk*		soya whale steak
Steinbutt *SHTEYEN-but*		turbot
Stint *shtint*		smelt
Stör *shterr*		sturgeon

VEGETABLES

I eat only vegetables.	**Ich esse nur Gemüse.** *ikh ESS-eh noor ge-MEWZ-eh*
I am a vegetarian.	**Ich bin Vegetarier.** *ikh bin veh-geh-TAAR-ee-uh*
What kind of vegetables are there?	**Was für Gemüse gibt es?** *vahs fewr ge-MEWZ-eh geept ehs*
What can you recommend?	**Was können Sie mir empfehlen?** *vahs KERN-en zee meer emp-FAYL-en*
There is:	**Es gibt:** *ehs geept*
We have:	**Wir haben:** *veer HAAB-en*

Auberginen *oh-behr-ZHEEN-en*	eggplant
Blumenkohl *BLOOM-en-kohl*	cauliflower
Bohnen *BOHN-en*	beans
Braunkohl *BROWN-kohl*	broccoli
Erbsen *EHRPS-en*	peas
Essiggurken *EHSS-ikh-goork-en*	sour pickles (gherkins)
Fisolen (Aust.) *fee-SOHL-en*	string beans, French beans
Gelbe Wurzeln *GEHLB-eh VOORTS-eln*	carrots
Gemischtes Gemüse *geh-MISHT-ehs ge-MEWZ-eh*	mixed vegetables
Grüne Bohnen *GREWN-eh BOHN-en*	green beans
Gurken *GOORK-en*	cucumbers
Häuptelsalat *HOYPT-el-zah-laat*	lettuce salad
Kabis, Kappes *KAHB-is, KAHP-es*	cabbage
Karfiol (Aust.) *kahr-fee-OHL*	cauliflower
Karotten *kahr-OT-en*	carrots

Knoblauch *KNOHP-lowkh*	garlic
Kohl *kohl*	cabbage
Kren (Aust.) *krayn*	horseradish
Kürbis *KEWR-biss*	pumpkin
Kukuruz (Aust.) *KOOK-oor-oots*	corn, maize
Lauch *lowkh*	leeks
Leipziger Allerlei *LEYEPTS-eeg-uh AHL-uh-leye*	carrots, peas, and asparagus
Mais *meyess*	corn, maize
Meerrettich *MAYR-reh-tikh*	horseradish
Mohrrüben *MOHR-rewb-en*	carrots
Paradeiser *pah-rah-DEYEZ-uh*	tomatoes
Pfifferlinge *PFIF-ehr-ling-eh*	chanterelle mushrooms
Pilze *PILTS-eh*	mushrooms
Radieschen *rah-DEES-khen*	radishes
Rosenkohl *ROHZ-en-kohl*	brussels sprouts
Rote Beten (Rüben) *ROHT-eh BAYT-en (REWB-en)*	beets
Rotkohl (Rotkraut) *ROHT-kohl (ROHT-krowt)*	red cabbage
Rübenkraut *REWB-en-krowt*	turnip tops
Schnittbohnen *SHNIT-bohn-en*	French beans
Schwarzwurzeln *SHVAHRTS-voorts-eln*	salsify
Spargelspitzen *SHPAARG-el-shpits-en*	asparagus tips
Spinat *shpeen-AAT*	spinach
Tomaten *to-MAAT-en*	tomatoes
Weiße Bohnen *VEYESS-eh BOHN-en*	white beans

Weiße Rüben	*VEYESS-eh REWB-en*	turnips
Weißkohl	*VEYESS-kohl*	cabbage
Zwiebeln	*TSVEEB-eln*	onions

NOTE: The many words in the list for cabbage (**Kohl** is the most important one) attest to its popularity and presence on German menus. Some of the terms are from regional dialects. In this and other lists, Austrian forms have sometimes been indicated. Often these forms will be found in neighboring Germany and Switzerland, too.

POTATOES, NOODLES

Bratkartoffeln	*BRAAT-kahr-tof-eln*	fried potatoes
Geröstel	*ge-RERST-el*	hashed-brown potatoes
Dampfnudeln	*DAHMPF-nood-eln*	steamed noodles,
Fadennudeln	*FAAD-en-nood-eln*	vermicelli
Kartoffel(n)	*kahr-TOF-el(n)*	potato(es)
■ **-bälle**	*-behl-eh*	balls
■ **-brei**	*-breye*	mashed
■ **-flocken**	*-flok-en*	flakes (potato crisps)
■ **-klöße**	*-klewss-eh*	dumplings
■ **-kroketten**	*-kroh-keht-en*	croquettes
■ **-mus**	*-moos*	mashed
■ **-puffer**	*-puf-uh*	fritters, potato pancakes
Krautkrapfen	*KROWT-krahp-fen*	cabbage fritters
Pellkartoffeln	*PEHL-kahr-tof-eln*	unpeeled boiled potatoes
Petersilienkartoffeln	*pay-tehr-ZEEL-yen-kahr-toff-eln*	parsleyed potatoes

Pommes frites *pom frit*	french fries
Röstkartoffeln *REWST-kahr-tof-eln*	fried potatoes
Rösti (Swiss) *REWST-ee*	hashed-brown potatoes
Salzkartoffeln *ZAHLTS-kahr-tof-eln*	boiled potatoes
Schlutzkrapfen (a South Tyrol specialty) *SHLUTS-krahpf-en*	ravioli filled with cottage cheese
Spätzle *SHPEHTS-leh*	thick noodles or Swabian dumplings
Teigwaren *TEYEKH-vaar-en*	pasta products, noodles

CHEESES

You may see a German cheese called **Frühstückskäse** (breakfast cheese) on your breakfast table along with several others, such as **Schmierkäse** (Smear Cheese) or **Streichkäse,** processed cheeses for spreading on your bread. One popular cheese you'll have no trouble identifying is called "Bavaria Blue." Bavaria is to German cheeses what Normandy and Wisconsin are to French and American cheeses. Yet cheese is made in most areas of Germany.

Cheeses are sometimes classified according to their fat content! **Doppelfett** (65%), **Überfett** (55%), **Vollfett** (45%), **Dreiviertelfett** (35%), **Halbfett** (25%), **Viertelfett** (15%), and **Mager** (less than 15%).

Connoisseurs distinguish between **Allgäuer Bergkäse, Emmenthaler,** and **Greyerzer** (Gruyères), but most of us would call them "Swiss cheese." Other well-known German, Austrian, and Swiss cheeses are **Alpenkäse, Bierkäse,** and **Stangenkäse. Edelpilzkäse,** a fine sharp cheese, and **Mondseerkäse** (similar to Limburger) are Austrian specialties. To appreciate the full range of German, Austrian, and Swiss cheeses, drop into a **Käsegeschäft** (a store that specializes in cheese). You may want to try a few in a restaurant.

We'll have the cheese platter, please.	**Wir nehmen den Käseteller, bitte.** *veer NAY-men dehn KAY-zeh-tell-uh, BIT-eh*

What kinds of cheeses are there on the cheese platter?	**Was für Käsesorten gibt es auf dem Käseteller?** *vahs fewr KAY-zeh-zort-en geept ehs owf dehm KAY-zeh-tell-uh*
Bring me a piece of cheese, please.	**Bringen Sie mir bitte ein Stück Käse!** *BRING-en zee meer BIT-eh eyen shtewk KAY-zeh*
Is the cheese soft or hard?	**Ist der Käse weich oder hart?** *ist dehr KAY-zeh veyekh OH-duh hahrt*
■ sharp or mild?	**scharf oder mild?** *shahrf OH-duh milt*

DESSERTS

Fürst Pückler is vanilla, chocolate, and strawberry ice cream together (Neapolitan). Besides **Erdbeereis** (strawberry ice cream), you will also find **Mokka-** (coffee), **Schokoladen-** (chocolate), **Vanille-** (vanilla), and **Zitroneneis** (lemon ice cream), and occasionally more exotic flavors. **Eis** *(eyess)* is used everywhere for "ice cream," although occasionally **Glace** *(GLAHS-eh)* is heard in Switzerland.

   Rote Grütze is a fresh berry pudding popular in the north. **Palatschinken** are particularly popular in the south. These crêpes can be filled with a variety of jams, cheeses, or even meats. **Apfelstrudel** is a popular delicate pastry filled with nuts, raisins, ham, and slices of apples. You may wish to try other varieties of strudel (poppy seed **[Mohn]**, cherry, etc.) In wine-growing regions, **Apfeltorte** (apple tart) can be a marvelously light combination of a thin whisper of crust, wine-soaked apples, sugar, and cinnamon, all topped by the omnipresent **Schlag** (whipped cream). **Kaiserschmarren** (literally, "imperial scraps") are shredded pancakes with raisins.

   Kuchen *(KOOKH-en)* means "cake," but you will see the word **Torte** (tart, *TOHR-teh*) more often. Many cakes have personalities and names of their own. For example:

Berliner *behr-LEEN-uh*	jam doughnut
Bienenstich *BEEN-en-shtikh*	honey-almond cake (literally "bee sting")

Gugelhupf *GOOG-el-hupf*	a round pound cake with a hole in the middle, often containing raisins and almonds (a Bavarian-Austrian specialty)
Hefekranz *HAY-feh-krahnts*	circular coffee cake
Mannheimer Dreck *MAHN-heyem-uh drehk*	chocolate-covered almond paste
(Weihnachts)stollen *(VEYE-nahkhts)shtol-en*	Christmas cake

FRUITS, NUTS

Ananas *AHN-ah-nahss*	pineapple
Apfel *AHPF-el*	apple
Apfelsine *ahpf-el-ZEEN-eh*	orange
Aprikosen *ahp-ree-KOHZ-en*	apricots
Banane *bah-NAAN-eh*	banana
Birne *BEERN-eh*	pear
Blaubeeren *BLOW-bayr-en*	blueberries (bilberries)
Brombeeren *BROM-bayr-en*	blackberries
Datteln *DAHT-ehln*	dates
Erdbeeren *AYRT-bayr-en*	strawberries
Feigen *FEYEG-en*	figs
Gemischte Nüsse *geh-MISHT-eh NEWSS-eh*	mixed nuts
Granatapfel *grah-NAAT-ahpf-el*	pomegranate
Haselnüsse *HAAZ-el-newss-eh*	hazelnuts
Heidelbeeren *HEYED-el-bayr-en*	blueberries (whortleberries)

Himbeeren *HIM-bayr-en*	raspberries
Holunderbeeren *hol-UND-uh-bayr-en*	elderberries
Johannisbeeren *yoh-HAHN-is-bayr-en*	currants
Kastanien *kahst-AAN-yen*	chestnuts
Kirschen *KEERSH-en*	cherries
Kokosnuß *KOHK-os-nuss*	coconut
Mandarine *mahn-dah-REEN-eh*	tangerine
Mandeln *MAHND-eln*	almonds
Marillen (Aust.) *mah-RIL-en*	apricots
Melone *meh-LOHN-eh*	cantaloupe
Nüsse *NEWSS-eh*	nuts
Pampelmuse *PAHMP-el-mooz-eh*	grapefruit
Pfirsich *PFEER-zikh*	peach
Pflaumen *PFLOW-men*	plums
Preiselbeeren *PREYE-zel-bayr-en*	cranberries
Quitte *KVIT-eh*	quince
Rauschbeeren *ROWSH-bayr-en*	cranberries, crawberries
Rhabarber *rah-BAHRB-uh*	rhubarb
Rosinen *roh-ZEEN-en*	raisins
Stachelbeeren *SHTAH-khel-bayr-en*	gooseberries
Studentenfutter *shtu-DENT-en-fut-uh*	"student fodder" (assorted nuts, raisins, seeds)
Südfrüchte *ZEWT-frewkht-eh*	tropical fruits
Trauben *TROWB-en*	grapes
Walnüsse *VAHL-newss-eh*	walnuts

Wassermelone *VAHSS-uh-meh-lohn-eh*	watermelon
Weichselkirschen *VEYEKS-el-keersh-en*	(sour) morello cherries
Weintrauben *VEYEN-trowb-en*	grapes
Zuckermelone *TSUK-uh-meh-lohn-eh*	honeydew melon
Zwetsch(g)en *TSVEHTSH-(g)en*	plums

EATING IN

I need ____.	**Ich brauche ____.** *ikh BROWKH-eh*
■ bread	**Brot** *broht*
■ butter	**Butter** *BUT-uh*
■ cheese	**Käse** *KAYZ-eh*
■ cold cuts	**Aufschnitt** *OWF-shnit*
■ cookies	**Kekse** *KAYKS-eh*
■ candy	**Konfekt** *kon-FEHKT*
■ a chocolate bar	**eine Tafel Schokolade** *EYEN-eh TAAF-el sho-ko-LAAD-eh*
■ a dozen eggs	**ein Dutzend Eier** *eyen DUTS-ent EYE-uh*
■ fruit	**Obst** *ohpst*
■ a bottle of milk	**eine Flasche Milch** *EYEN-eh FLAHSH-eh milkh*

If you ask for a **Pfund** or a **halbes Pfund** of something, you'll be getting more than a pound or half a pound, since the German **Pfund** is 500 grams (half a **Kilo**) and the American/English pound is 454 grams.

MEETING PEOPLE

GREETINGS AND INTRODUCTIONS

What's your name?	**Wie heißen Sie?**	*vee HEYESS-en zee*
My name is ___.	**Ich heiße ___.**	*ikh HEYESS-eh*
Pleased to meet you.	**Sehr erfreut.**	*zayr ehr-FROYT*
How do you do?	**Wie geht es Ihnen?**	*vee gayt es EEN-en*
How are things?	**Wie geht's?**	*vee gayts*
May I introduce ___?	**Darf ich ___ vorstellen?**	*dahrf ikh ___ FOHR-shtehl-en*
■ my husband	**meinen Mann**	*MEYEN-en mahn*
■ my wife	**meine Frau**	*MEYEN-eh frow*
■ my son	**meinen Sohn**	*MEYEN-en zohn*
■ my daughter	**meine Tochter**	*MEYEN-eh TOKHT-uh*
■ my friend	**meinen Freund**	*MEYEN-en froynd*
What's ___ name?	**Wie heißt ___?**	*vee heyesst ___*
■ your son's	**Ihr Sohn**	*eer zohn*
■ your daughter's	**Ihre Tochter**	*EER-eh TOKHT-uh*
■ your dog's	**Ihr Hund**	*eer hunt*

CONVERSATION

We have children the same age as yours.	**Wir haben Kinder im selben Alter.**	*veer HAAB-en KIND-uh im ZEHLB-en AHLT-uh*
Where are you from?	**Wo sind Sie her?**	*voh zint zee hayr*

I'm ____.	**Ich bin ____.** *ikh bin*
■ from America	**aus Amerika** *owss ah-MAY-ree-kah*
■ from the South	**aus den Südstaaten** *ows dayn ZEWT-shtaat-en*
■ from England	**aus England** *ows EHNG-lahnt*
■ from Canada	**aus Kanada** *ows KAH-nah-dah*
■ from Australia	**aus Australien** *ows ows-TRAAL-yen*

This is my first time in Germany.	**Dies ist das erste Mal, daβ ich in Deutschland bin.** *dees ist dahs EHRST-eh maal dahs ikh in DOYCH-lahnt bin*
I (don't) like everything.	**(Nicht) Alles gefällt mir.** *(nikht) AHL-es geh-FEHLT meer*
How long will you be staying?	**Wie lange bleiben Sie noch?** *vee LAHNG-eh BLEYEB-en zee nokh*
■ A few days.	**Einige Tage.** *EYEN-ig-eh TAAG-eh*
■ A week.	**Eine Woche.** *EYEN-eh VOKH-eh*
■ A month.	**Einen Monat.** *EYEN-en MOHN-aat*
Is your hotel far?	**Ist Ihr Hotel weit entfernt?** *ist eer ho-TEL veyet ehnt-FEHRNT*
Are you comfortable where you're staying?	**Sind Sie gut untergebracht?** *zint zee goot UNT-ehr-geh-brahkht?*
Would you like a picture?	**Möchten Sie ein Bild?** *MERKHT-en zee eyen bilt*
Stand here (there).	**Stellen sie sich dort hin.** *SHTEHL-en zee zikh dort hin*
Don't move.	**Keine Bewegung!** *KEYEN-eh beh-VAYG-ung*
Smile. That's it!	**Lächeln. Genau! (Richtig!)** *LEHKH-eln. geh-NOW (RIKHT-ikh)*

Would you take a picture of me (us)?	**Würden Sie mich (uns) photographieren?** *VEWRD-en zee mikh (uns) foh-toh-grah-FEER-en*
I'd like a picture of you, as a remembrance.	**Ich möchte ein Bild von Ihnen, als Andenken.** *ikh MERKHT-eh eyen bilt fon EEN-en, ahls AHN-denk-en*
I want a snapshot of you in front of the monument.	**Ich will Sie vor dem Denkmal knipsen.** *ikh vil zee for daym DEHNK-maal KNIPS-en*

DATING AND SOCIALIZING

Are you alone?	**Sind Sie allein?** *zint zee ah-LEYEN*
Or with your family?	**Oder mit der Familie?** *OHD-uh mit dehr fah-MEEL-yeh*
May I have this dance?	**Darf ich um diesen Tanz bitten?** *dahrf ikh um DEEZ-en tahnts BIT-en*
Would you like a drink (cigarette)?	**Möchten Sie ein Getränk (eine Zigarette)?** *MERKHT-en zee eyen geh-TREHNK (EYEN-eh tsi-gah-REHT-eh)*
Do you have a light?	**Haben Sie Feuer?** *HAAB-en zee FOY-uh*
Do you mind if I smoke?	**Macht es Ihnen etwas aus, wenn ich rauche?** *mahkht ehs EEN-en EHT-vahs ows vehn ikh ROWKH-eh*
Are you free this evening?	**Sind Sie heute abend frei?** *zint zee HOYT-eh AAB-ent freye*
Would you like to go for a walk with me?	**Möchten Sie einen Spaziergang mit mir machen?** *MERKHT-en zee EYEN-en shpah-TSEER-gahng mit meer MAHKH-en*
I'd like to show you the city.	**Ich möchte Ihnen gerne die Stadt zeigen.** *ikh MERKHT-eh EEN-en GEHRN-eh dee staht TSEYEG-en*
What's your telephone number?	**Wie ist Ihre Telephonnummer?** *vee ist EER-eh TAY-leh-fohn-num-uh*

May I invite you for _____?	**Darf ich Sie zu _____ einladen?** *dahrf ikh zee tsoo _____ EYEN-laad-en*
■ a glass of wine	**einem Glas Wein** *EYEN-em glaass veyen*
■ a cup of coffee	**einer Tasse Kaffee** *EYEN-uh TASS-eh KAH-fay*
What is your profession?	**Was sind Sie von Beruf?** *vahs zint zee fon beh-ROOF*
I'm a _____.	**Ich bin _____.** *ikh bin _____*
■ doctor	**Arzt (Ärztin)** *ahrtst (EHRTST-in)*
■ mechanic	**Mechaniker(in)** *meh-KHAA-ni-kehr(ein)*
■ teacher	**Lehrer(in)** *LAY-rehr(in)*
■ lawyer	**Rechtsanwalt(Rechtsanwältin)** *REHKHTS-ahn-vahlt(REHKHTS-ahn-vehlt-in)*
■ secretary	**Sekretär(in)** *zeh-kreh-TAYR(in)*
■ salesperson	**Verkäufer(in)** *fehr-KOY-fehr(in)*
■ businessperson	**Geschäftsmann(frau)** *geh-SHEHFTS-mahn(frow)*
■ student	**Student(in)** *shtoo-DEHNT(in)*
Do you love music (the theater, films)?	**Lieben Sie Musik (Theater, Filme)?** *LEEB-en zee moo-ZEEK (TAY-aat-uh, FILM-eh)*
I'll pick you up at your house (hotel).	**Ich hole Sie in Ihrem Haus (Hotel) ab.** *ikh HOHL-eh zee in EER-em hows (ho-TEL) ahp*
I'll wait for you in front of the theater (café).	**Ich warte auf Sie vor dem Theater (Cafe).** *ikh VAART-eh owf zee for daym TAY-aat-uh (kah-FAY)*
I thank you for your wonderful hospitality.	**Ich danke Ihnen für Ihre wunderbare Gastfreundlichkeit.** *ikh DAHNK-eh EEN-en fewr EER-eh VUND-uh-baar-eh GAHST-froynt-likh-keyet*

SHOPPING

GOING SHOPPING

I'm looking for ____.	**Ich suche ____.** *ikh ZOOKH-eh*
■ an antique shop	**ein Antiquitätengeschäft** *eyen ahn-ti-kvi-TAYT-en-geh-shehft*
■ an art dealer	**einen Kunsthändler** *EYEN-en KUNST-hehnt-luh*
■ a book store	**eine Buchhandlung** *EYEN-eh BOOKH-hahnt-lung*
■ a china shop	**einen Porzellanladen** *EYEN-en por-tseh-LAAN-laad-en*
■ a camera shop	**ein Photogeschäft** *eyen FOH-toh-geh-shehft*
■ a bakery	**eine Bäckerei** *EYEN-eh beh-keh-REYE*
■ a butcher shop	**einen Fleischerladen** *EYEN-en FLEYESH-ehr-laa-den*
■ a candy store	**einen Süßwarenladen** *EYEN-en SEWSS-vaa-ren-laa-den*
■ a clothing store	**ein Bekleidungsgeschäft** *eyen beh-KLEYED-ungs-geh-shehft*
for children	**Kinderbekleidungsgeschäft** *KIND-ehr-beh-kleyed-ungs-geh-shehft*
for women	**Damenbekleidungsgeschäft** *DAH-men-beh-kleyed-ungs-geh-shehft*
for men	**Herrenbekleidungsgeschäft** *HEHR-en-beh-kleyed-ungs-geh-shehft*

■ a delicatessen	**ein Delikatessengeschäft** *eyen deh-li-kah-TEHSS-en-geh-shehft*
■ a department store	**ein Warenhaus** *eyen VAAR-en-hows*
■ a drug store	**eine Drogerie/Apotheke** *EYEN-eh dro-geh-REE/ah-poh-TAYK-eh*
■ a dry cleaner's	**eine chemische Reinigung** *EYEN-eh KHAY-mi-sheh REYE-ni-gung*
■ a flower shop	**ein Blumengeschäft** *eyen BLOOM-en-geh-shehft*
■ a furrier	**einen Kürschner** *EYEN-en KEWRSH-nuh*
■ a gift (souvenir) shop	**einen Andenkenladen** *EYEN-en AHN-dehnk-en-laad-en*
■ a gourmet grocery store	**eine Feinkostwarenhandlung** *EYEN-eh FEYEN-kost-vaar-en-hahnt-lung*
■ a grocery store	**ein Lebensmittelgeschäft** *eyen LAYB-ens-mit-el-geh-shehft*
■ a hardware store	**eine Eisenwarenhandlung** *EYEN-eh EYEZ-en-vaar-en-hahnt-lung*
■ a health-food store	**ein Reformhaus** *eyen reh-FORM-hows*
■ a jewelry store	**einen Juwelier** *EYEN-en yu-veh-LEER*
■ a liquor store	**eine Spirituosenhandlung** *EYEN-eh shpee-ree-tu-OHZ-en-hahnt-lung*
■ a market	**einen Markt** *EYEN-en mahrkt*
■ a newsstand	**einen Zeitungsstand** *EYEN-en TSEYET-unks-shtahnt*
■ a pastry shop	**eine Konditorei** *EYEN-eyen-eh kon-dee-to-REYE*

■ a record store **ein Schallplattengeschäft** *eyen SHAHL-plaht-en-geh-shehft*

■ a shoe store **ein Schuhgeschäft** *eyen SHOO-geh-shehft*

■ a shopping center **ein Einkaufszentrum** *EYEN-kowfs-tsent-rum*

■ a supermarket **einen Supermarkt** *EYEN-en ZOOP-uh-mahrkt*

■ a tobacco shop **einen Tabakladen** *EYEN-en TAA-bahk-laad-en*

■ a toy shop **ein Spielwarengeschäft** *eyen SHPEEL-vaar-en-geh-shehft*

■ a wine merchant **eine Weinhandlung** *EYEN-eh VEYEN-hahnt-lung*

BOOKS

Where is the largest bookstore here?
Wo ist hier die größte Buchhandlung? *voh ist heer dee GRERST-eh BOOKH-hahnt-lung*

I'm looking for a copy of ____.
Ich suche ein Exemplar von ____. *ikh ZOOKH-eh eyen eks-ehm-PLAAR fon*

Do you have books (novels) in English?
Haben Sie Bücher (Romane) in Englisch? *HAAB-en zee BEWKH-uh (roh-MAAN-eh) in EHNG-lish*

I'd like an English and German edition of *Grimm's Fairy Tales.*
Ich möchte eine englische und eine deutsche Ausgabe von *Grimms Märchen.* *ikh MERKHT-eh EYEN-eh EHNG-lish-eh unt EYEN-eh DOYCH-eh OWSS-gaab-eh fon grimms MAYRKH-en*

I need a guidebook.
Ich brauche einen Reiseführer. *ikh BROWKH-eh EYEN-en REYEZ-eh-fewr-uh*

Can you recommend a good grammar to me?	**Können Sie mir eine gute Grammatik empfehlen?** *KERN-en zee meer EYEN-eh GOOT-eh grah-MAH-tik ehmp-FAYL-en*
I'm looking for ____.	**Ich suche ____.** *ikh ZOOKH-eh* ____.
■ a pocket dictionary	**ein Taschenwörterbuch** *eyen TAHSH-en-vert-ehr-bookh*
■ a German-English dictionary	**ein deutsch-englisches Wörterbuch** *eyen doytsh-EHNG-lishes vert-ehr-bookh*
■ a map of the city	**einen Stadtplan** *EYEN-en SHTAHT-plaan*

CLOTHING

Please show me ____.	**Zeigen Sie mir bitte ____.** *TSEYEG-en zee meer BIT-eh* ____
■ a belt	**einen Gürtel** *EYEN-en GEWRT-el*
■ a blouse	**eine Bluse** *EYEN-eh BLOOZ-eh*
■ a cap	**eine Mütze** *EYEN-eh MEWTS-eh*
■ a brassiere	**einen Büstenhalter** *EYEN-en BEWST-en-hahlt-uh*
■ a coat	**einen Mantel** *EYEN-en MAHNT-el*
■ dancing shoes	**Tanzschuhe** *TAHNTS-shoo-eh*
■ a dress	**ein Kleid** *eyen kleyet*
■ furs	**Pelze** *PELTS-eh*
■ an evening gown	**ein Abendkleid** *eyen AAB-ent-kleyet*
■ gloves	**Handschuhe** *HAHNT-shoo-eh*
■ a hat	**einen Hut** *EYEN-en hoot*

■ a jacket	**eine Jacke** *EYEN-eh YAHK-eh*
■ knitwear	**Stricksachen** *SHTRIK-zahkh-en*
■ lingerie	**Damenunterwäsche** *DAAM-en-un-tehr-vehsh-eh*
■ pants	**eine Hose** *EYEN-eh HOHZ-eh*
■ a mink coat	**einen Nerzmantel** *EYEN-en NEHRTS-mahn-tel*
■ panties	**einen Schlüpfer** *EYEN-en SHLEWPF-uh*
■ panty hose	**eine Strumpfhose** *EYEN-eh SHTRUMPF-hohz-eh*
■ a raincoat	**einen Regenmantel** *EYEN-en RAYG-en-mahn-tel*
■ a scarf	**ein Halstuch** *eyen HAHLS-tookh*
■ a shirt	**ein Hemd** *eyen hemt*
■ a pair of shoes	**ein Paar Schuhe** *eyen paar SHOO-eh*
■ shorts	**kurze Unterhosen** *KURTS-eh UN-tehr-hohz-en*
■ a skirt	**einen Rock** *EYEN-en rok*
■ a slip	**einen Unterrock** *EYEN-en UN-tehr-rok*
■ slippers	**Hausschuhe** *HOWS-shoo-eh*
■ socks	**Socken** *ZOK-en*
■ stockings	**Strümpfe** *SHTREWMPF-eh*
■ a man's suit	**einen Anzug** *EYEN-en AHN-tsook*
■ a woman's suit	**ein Kostüm** *eyen kos-TEWM*
■ a sweater	**einen Pullover** *EYEN-en pul-OHV-uh*
■ a tie	**eine Krawatte** *EYEN-eh krah-VAHT-eh*

■ an undershirt	**ein Unterhemd** *eyen UN-tehr-hehmt*
■ underwear	**Unterwäsche** *UN-tehr-vehsh-eh*
Is there a sale to-day?	**Gibt's heute einen Verkauf?** *gipts HOYT-eh EYEN-en fehr-KOWF*
Is this really a close-out sale?	**Ist das wirklich ein Schluβver-kauf?** *ist dahs VIRK-likh eyen SHLUSS-fehr-kowf*
Are there any special sale items?	**Was für Angebote gibt's?** *vahs fewr AHN-geh-boht-eh gipts*
Do you know of a store that might have a large stock of ____?	**Kennen Sie ein Geschäft, das ein reichhaltiges Lager an ____ hätte?** *KEN-en zee eyen geh-SHEHFT dahs eyen REYEKH-hahl-ti-ges LAAG-uh ahn ____ HEHT-eh*
Do you have the same thing with short (long) sleeves?	**Haben Sie dasselbe mit kurzen (langen) Ärmeln?** *HAAB-en zee dahs-ZELB-eh mit KOORTS-en (LAHNG-en) EHRM-ehln*
I'd like something ____.	**Ich möchte etwas ____.** *ikh MERKHT-eh EHT-vahs*
■ less expensive	**Billigeres** *BIL-ig-ehr-es*
■ more elegant	**Eleganteres** *eh-lay-GAHNT-ehr-es*
■ of better quality	**von besserer Qualität** *fon BEHSS-ehr-uh kvah-li-TAYT*
■ more cheerful	**Heitereres** *HEYET-ehr-ehr-es*
■ more youthful	**Jugendlicheres** *YOOG-ent-li-kher-es*
■ else	**anderes** *AHND-ehr-es*
■ bigger	**Größeres** *GRERSS-ehr-es*
■ smaller	**Kleineres** *KLEYEN-ehr-es*
I (don't) like it.	**Es gefällt mir (nicht).** *ehs geh-FEHLT meer (nikht).*

This is too _____.	**Dies ist zu _____.** *deess ist tsoo _____.*
■ thick	**dick** *dik*
■ thin	**dünn** *dewn*
■ expensive	**teuer** *TOY-uh*
■ dark	**dunkel** *DUNK-el*
■ light	**hell** *hel*

It's very elegant, but I don't want to spend a fortune on it.

Es ist sehr elegant, aber ich will kein Vermögen dafür ausgeben. *ehs ist zayr eh-lay-GAHNT AAB-uh ikh vil keyen fehr-MERG-en dah-FEWR OWS-gay-ben*

COLORS

I like the material, but I don't like the color.

Der Stoff gefällt mir, aber nicht die Farbe. *dehr shtof geh-FEHLT meer, AAB-uh nikht die FAARB-eh*

Would you have it in _____?	**Hätten Sie es vielleicht in _____?** *HEHT-en zee ehs fee-LEYEKHT in*
■ black	**schwarz** *shvaarts*
■ blue	**blau** *blow*
■ brown	**braun** *brown*
■ gray	**grau** *grow*
■ green	**grün** *grewn*
■ pink	**rosa** *ROH-zaa*
■ red	**rot** *roht*
■ white	**weiß** *veyess*
■ yellow	**gelb** *gehlp*

■ A lighter (darker) blue (brown, green).	**Ein helleres (dunkleres) Blau (Braun, Grün).** *eyen HEL-ehr-es (DUNK-lehr-es) blow (brown, grewn)*

FIT, ALTERATIONS

Please take my measurements (for a dress).	**Bitte nehmen Sie mir Maß (zu einem Kleid).** *BIT-eh NAYM-en zee meer maass (tsoo EYEN-em kleyet)*
I think my size is 40.	**Ich glaube, ich habe Grösse vierzig.** *ikh GLOWB-eh ikh HAAB-eh GRERSS-eh FEER-tsikh*
I'd like to try it on.	**Ich möchte es anprobieren.** *ikh MERKHT-eh ehs AHN-proh-beer-en*
It fits badly in the shoulders.	**Es sitzt schlecht in den Schultern.** *ehs zitst shlehkht in dayn SHUL-tehrn*
The sleeves are too narrow (wide).	**Die Ärmel sind zu eng (weit).** *dee EHRM-el zint tsoo ehng (veyet)*
It needs alterations.	**Es braucht Änderungen.** *ehs browkht EHND-eh-rung-en*
Can you alter it?	**Können Sie es ändern?** *KERN-en zee ehs EHND-ehrn*
Can I return this?	**Kann ich dies zurückgeben?** *kahn ikh dees tsoo-REWK-gayb-en*
It fits very well.	**Es paßt sehr gut.** *ehs pahsst zayr goot*
It doesn't fit.	**Es paßt nicht.** *ehs pahsst nikht*
I'll take it.	**Ich nehm's.** *ikh naymss*
Please wrap it well.	**Bitte packen Sie es gut ein.** *BIT-eh PAHK-en zee ehs goot eyen*
Please giftwrap it.	**Bitte packen Sie es als Geschenk ein.** *BIT-eh PAHK-en zee ehs ahls geh-SHEHNK eyen*
Please give me some shoelaces too.	**Geben Sie mir bitte auch Schnürsenkel.** *GAYB-en zee meer BIT-eh owkh SHNEWR-zenk-el*

| That's all I need to-day. | **Heute brauche ich sonst nichts mehr.** *HOYT-eh browkh ikh zonst nikhts mayr* |

REGIONAL CLOTHES

Trachten (local peasant costumes) are still seen in various parts of German-speaking Europe. Best known are the **Lederhosen** and **Dirndlkleider** of Alpine areas, standard apparel for performers and vocalists in Bavarian bands in nightspots all over the world. Adaptations of **Dirndl** dresses often appear in the collections of prominent designers.

Where can I buy regional costumes?	**Wo kann ich hier Trachten kaufen?** *voh kahn ikh heer TRAHKHT-en KOWF-en*
I'm looking for ____.	**Ich suche ____.** *ikh ZOOKH-eh*
■ a dirndl dress	**ein Dirndlkleid** *eyen DEERNDL-kleyet*
■ leather short pants	**Lederhosen** *LAYD-uh-hohz-en*
■ a loden cloak (flowing, and usually hunter's green)	**einen Lodenmantel** *EYEN-en LOHD-en-mahnt-el*
■ a Tyrolean hat	**einen Tirolerhut** *EYEN-en tee-ROHL-uh-hoot*
■ a waterproof woolen overcoat	**einen Wetterfleck** *EYEN-en VEHT-uh-flehk*
■ embroidered articles	**Stickereien** *SHTIK-eh-reye-en*
■ linen goods	**Leinenzeug** *LEYEN-en-tsoyk*

You may want a **Tiroler Pfeife** (pipe) to accompany your Tyrolean hat, and perhaps a **Gamsbart** (chamois brush) to pin on the hat. They are widely sold in souvenir shops.

JEWELRY

What sort of jewelry do you have?	**Was für Schmucksachen haben Sie?** *vahs fewr SHMUK-zahkh-en HAAB-en zee*
Please show me _____.	**Zeigen Sie mir bitte _____.** *TSEYEG-en zee meer BIT-eh _____*
■ a bracelet	**ein Armband** *eyen AHRM-bahnt*
■ a brooch	**eine Brosche** *EYEN-eh BROSH-eh*
■ a chain	**ein Kettchen** *eyen KET-khen*
■ cufflinks	**Manschettenknöpfe** *mahn-SHEHT-en-knerpf-eh*
■ a goblet	**einen Becher** *EYEN-en BEHKH-uh*
■ earrings	**Ohrringe** *OHR-ring-eh*
■ a necklace	**eine Halskette** *EYEN-eh HAHLS-ket-eh*
■ a pin	**eine Anstecknadel** *EYEN-eh AHN-shtehk-naad-el*
■ a ring	**einen Ring** *EYEN-en ring*
■ an engagement ring	**einen Verlobungsring** *EYEN-en fehr-LOHB-unks-ring*
■ a wedding ring	**einen Ehering** *EYEN-en AY-eh-ring*
■ a tie pin	**eine Krawattennadel** *EYEN-eh krah-VAHT-en-naad-el*
■ a tiara	**eine Tiara** *EYEN-eh tee-AAR-ah*
■ a wristwatch	**eine Armbanduhr** *EYEN-eh AHRM-bahnt-oor*
Is this _____?	**Ist dies in _____?** *ist dees in _____*
■ gold	**Gold** *golt*

■ platinum	**Platin** *plah-TEEN*
■ silver	**Silber** *ZILB-uh*
■ stainless steel	**rostfreiem Stahl** *ROST-freye-em shtahl*

Is it in gold or just gold plate?	**Ist es in Gold oder nur vergoldet?** *ist ehs in golt OHD-uh noor fehr-GOLD-et*
silver plate	**versilbert** *fehr-ZILB-ehrt*
■ How many carats is it?	**Wieviel Karat hat es?** *VEE-feel kah-RAAT haht ehs*
■ I collect precious stones.	**Ich sammle Edelsteine.** *ikh ZAHM-leh AY-del-shteyen-eh*
■ Semiprecious stones, too.	**Halbedelsteine auch.** *HAHLP-ay-del-shteyen-eh owkh*
I'm looking for ____.	**Ich suche ____.** *ikh ZOOKH-eh ____*
■ amber jewelry	**Bernsteinschmuck** *BEHRN-shteyen-shmuk*
■ an amethyst	**einen Amethyst** *EYEN-en ah-meh-THEWST*
■ diamonds	**Diamanten** *dee-ah-MAHNT-en*
■ emeralds	**Smaragde** *smah-RAHKT-eh*
■ hematite	**Blutstein** *BLOOT-shteyen*
■ ivory	**Elfenbein** *EHLF-en-beyen*
■ jade	**Jade** *YAAD-eh*
■ onyx	**Onyx** *OH-niks*
■ pearls	**Perlen** *PEHRL-en*
■ rubies	**Rubine** *ru-BEEN-eh*
■ sapphires	**Saphire** *zah-FEER-eh*
■ topazes	**Topase** *toh-PAAZ-eh*

RECORDS AND TAPES

Is there a record shop in the neighborhood?	**Gibt's ein Schallplattengeschäft in der Nähe?** *gipts eyen SHAHL-plaht-en-geh-shehft in dehr NAY-eh*
Do you have albums of opera highlights?	**Haben Sie Opernquerschnitte?** *HAAB-en zee OHP-ehrn-kvehr-shnit-eh*
I'm interested in _____.	**Ich interessiere mich für _____.** *ikh in-teh-reh-SEER-eh mikh fewr _____*
▪ brass-band music	**Blasmusik** *BLAAS-moo-zeek*
▪ chamber music	**Kammermusik** *KAHM-uh-moo-zeek*
▪ classical music	**klassische Musik** *KLAHS-ish-eh moo-ZEEK*
▪ folk music	**Volksmusik** *FOLKS-moo-zeek*
▪ folksongs (dances)	**Volkslieder (tänze)** *FOLKS-leed-uh (TEHNTS-eh)*
▪ the latest hits	**die allerneusten Schlager** *die AHL-ehr-noyst-en SHLAAG-uh*
▪ golden oldies	**"Evergreens"** *Evergreens*
▪ easy listening	**Unterhaltungsmusik** *UNT-ehr-hahlt-unks-moo-zeek*
▪ pop music	**Pop-Musik** *POP-moo-zeek*
Do you have historic recordings of DGG and Telefunken?	**Haben Sie historische Aufnahmen von DGG und Telefunken?** *HAAB-en zee his-TOHR-ish-eh OWF-naam-en fon DAY-gay-gay unt TAY-leh-funk-en*

NEWSPAPERS AND MAGAZINES

Do you have stamps?	**Haben Sie auch Briefmarken?** *HAAB-en zee owkh BREEF-maark-en*

Do you sell booklets of tickets for the streetcars?	**Verkaufen Sie Fahrscheinhefte für die Straßenbahnen?** *fehr-KOW-fen zee FAAR-sheyen-heft-eh fewr dee SHTRAASS-en-baan-en*
Do you have newspapers (magazines, periodicals) in English?	**Haben Sie Zeitungen (Illustrierten, Zeitschriften) in Englisch?** *HAAB-en zee TSEYET-ung-en (il-us-TREERT-en, TSEYET-shrift-en) in EHNG-lish*
Do you have other postcards besides these?	**Haben Sie noch andere Postkarten als diese?** *HAAB-en zee nokh AHND-eh-reh POST-kaart-en ahls DEEZ-eh*
How much is that?	**Was macht das?** *vahs mahkht dahs*

PHOTOGRAPHIC SUPPLIES

Where can I find a camera shop?	**Wo finde ich ein Photogeschäft?** *voh FIND-eh ikh eyen FOH-toh-geh-shehft*
How quickly can you develop these films?	**Wie schnell können Sie diese Filme entwickeln?** *vee shnel KERN-en zee DEEZ-eh FILM-eh ehnt-VIK-ehln*
Here are a black-and-white and two color films.	**Hier haben Sie einen schwarz-weißen und zwei Farbfilme.** *heer HAAB-en zee EYEN-en SHVAHRTS-veyess-en unt tsveye FAHRP-filmeh*
I want a print of each negative.	**Ich möchte einen Abzug von jedem Negativ.** *ikh MERKHT-eh EYEN-en AHP-tsook fon YAYD-em NEH-gah-teef*
I want this picture enlarged.	**Ich möchte dieses Bild vergrößern lassen.** *ikh MERKHT-eh DEEZ-es bilt fehr-GRERSS-ehrn LASS-en*
■ with a glossy finish	**Hochglanz** *HOHKH-glahnts*
■ with a matte finish	**matt** *maht*

Is there an extra charge for developing?

Kostet das Entwickeln extra?
KOST-et dahs ehnt-VIK-eln EKS-traa

I want prints only of the exposures that turned out well.

Ich möchte nur von den gut gelungenen Aufnahmen Abzüge haben.
ikh MERKHT-eh noor fon dayn goot geh-LUNG-en-en OWF-naam-en AHP-tsewg-eh HAAB-en

I need a roll of color film for slides.

Ich brauche einen Farbfilm für Farbdias. *ikh BROWKH-eh EYEN-en FAHRP-film fewr FAHRP-dee-ahs*

What inexpensive (expensive) cameras do you sell?

Was für billige (teure) Kameras verkaufen Sie? *vahs fewr BIL-ig-eh (TOY-reh) KAHM-eh-raas fehr-KOWF-en zee*

HANDICRAFTS, TOYS, SOUVENIRS

I'd like to buy a gift (souvenir).

Ich möchte gerne ein Geschenk (Andenken) kaufen. *ikh MERKHT-eh GEHRN-eh eyen geh-SHENK (AHN-dehnk-en) KOWF-en*

I don't want to spend more than ____ on it.

Ich will nicht mehr als ____ dafür ausgeben. *ikh vil nikht mayr ahls ____ dah-FEWR OWS-gayb-en*

What do you have in ____?

Was haben Sie an ____? *vahs HAAB-en zee ahn ____*

■ leather goods

Lederwaren *LAYD-uh-vaar-en*

■ glassware

Glaswaren *GLAAS-vaar-en*

Are these little spoons genuine silver?

Sind diese Löffelchen echt Silber? *zint DEEZ-eh LERF-el-khen ehkht ZILB-uh*

How old is this beer stein?

Wie alt ist dieser Bierkrug? *vee ahlt ist DEEZ-uh BEER-krook*

Is this ____?	**Ist dies ____?** *ist dees ____*
■handcarved	**handgeschnitzt** *HAHNT-geh-shnitst*
■handpainted	**handgemalt** *HAHNT-geh-maalt*
Is this made of wood (paper, metal, copper, pewter)?	**Ist dies aus Holz (Papier, Metall, Kupfer, Zinn)?** *ist dees ows holts (pah-PEER, meh-TAHL, KUP-fuh, tsin)*
What kinds of toys do you have?	**Was für Spielzeuge haben Sie?** *vahs fewr SHPEEL-tsoyg-eh HAAB-en zee*
Please receipt this bill.	**Bitte, quittieren Sie diese Rechnung.** *BIT-eh kvi-TEER-en zee DEEZ-eh REHKH-nung*
I don't want any trouble at customs.	**Ich will keine Schwierigkeiten beim Zoll haben.** *ikh vil KEYEN-eh SHVEE-rikh-keyet-en beyem tsol HAAB-en*

STATIONERY ITEMS

I'm looking for ____.	**Ich suche ____.** *ikh ZOOKH-eh ____*
■ ball-point pens	**Kugelschreiber** *KOOG-el-shreyeb-uh*
■ a deck of playing cards	**Spielkarten** *SHPEEL-kaart-en*
■ envelopes	**Umschläge** *UM-shlayg-eh*
■ an eraser	**einen Radiergummi** *EYEN-en rah-DEER-gu-mee*
■ glue	**Leim** *leyem*
■ notebooks	**Notizhefte** *noh-TEETS-hehft-eh*
■ pencils	**Bleistifte** *BLEYE-shtift-eh*

■ a ruler	**ein Lineal** *eyen lee-nay-AAL*
■ tape	**Klebestreifen** *KLAYB-eh-shtreyef-en*
■ some string	**Schnur** *schnoor*
■ thumbtacks	**Reißzwecken** *REYESS-tsvehk-en*
■ typing paper	**Schreibmaschinenpapier** *SHREYEP-mah-sheen-en-pah-peer*
■ a writing pad	**einen Schreibblock** *EYEN-en SHREYEP-blok*
■ airmail writing paper	**Luftpost Briefpapier** *LUFT-post BREEF-pah-peer*
■ Scotch tape	**Tesafilm** *TAY-zaa-film*

TOBACCO

I'd like a pack (carton) of cigarettes.	**Ich möchte eine Schachtel (Stange) Zigaretten.** *ikh MERKHT-eh EYEN-eh SHAHKHT-el (SHTAHNG-eh) tsee-gah-REHT-en*
■ filtered	**mit Filter** *mit FILT-uh*
■ unfiltered	**ohne Filter** *OHN-eh FILT-uh*
■ menthol	**Mentholzigaretten** *mehn-TOHL-tsee-gah-REHT-en*
■ king-size	**extra lang** *EKS-traa lahng*
■ reduced nicotine	**nikotinarm** *ni-koh-TEEN-ahrm*
What kind of mild (strong) cigarettes do you have here?	**Was für milde (starke) Zigaretten gibt es hier?** *vahs fewr MILD-eh (SHTAHRK-eh) tsee-gah-REHT-en gipt ehs heer*
I'd like to try a few brands.	**Ich möchte einige Marken versuchen.** *ikh MERKHT-eh EYEN-ig-eh MAHRK-en fehr-ZOOKH-en*

What American cigarettes do you have?	**Was für amerikanische Zigaretten haben Sie?** *vahs fewr ah-meh-ree-KAAN-ish-eh tsee-gah-REHT-en HAAB-en zee*
What sort of pipe tobacco do you have?	**Was für Pfeifentabak haben Sie?** *vahs fewr PFEYEF-en-tah-bahk HAAB-en zee*
I need _____.	**ich brauche _____.** *ikh BROWKH-eh*
■ chewing tobacco	**Kautabak** *KOW-tah-bahk*
■ cigars	**Zigarren** *tsee-GAHR-en*
■ snuff	**Schnupftabak** *SHNUPF-tah-bahk*
■ a cigarette holder	**eine Zigarettenspitze** *EYEN-eh tsee-gah-REHT-en-shpits-eh*
■ flints	**Feuersteine** *FOY-uh-shteyen-eh*
■ a cigarette lighter	**ein Feuerzeug** *eyen FOY-uh-tsoyk*
■ pipe cleaners	**Pfeifenreiniger** *PFEYEF-en-reye-nig-uh*
■ matches	**Streichhölzer** *SHTREYEKH-herlts-uh*
At home I smoke only low-nicotine cigarettes.	**Zu Hause rauche ich nur nikotinarme Zigaretten.** *tsoo HOW-zeh ROWKH-eh ikh noor ni-ko-TEEN-ahrm-eh tsee-gah-REHT-en*

FOOD AND HOUSEHOLD ITEMS

I'd like _____.	**Ich möchte _____.** *ikh MERKHT-eh*
■ a bar of soap	**ein Stück Seife** *eyen shtewk ZEYEF-eh*
■ a bottle of juice	**eine Flasche Saft** *EYEN-eh FLAHSH-eh zahft*

■ a box of cereal | **ein Karton Müsli** *eyen kahr-TONG MEWS-lee*

■ a can (tin) of tomato sauce | **eine Dose Tomatensoße** *EYEN-eh DOHZ-eh toh-MAAT-en-zohss-eh*

■ a dozen eggs | **ein Dutzend Eier** *eyen DUTS-ehnt EYE-uh*

■ a jar of coffee | **ein Glas Kaffee** *eyen glahs KAH-fay*

■ a kilo of potatoes (just over 2 pounds) | **ein Kilo Kartoffeln** *eyen KEE-loh kahr-TOF-eln*

■ a half-kilo of cherries (just over 1 pound) | **ein halbes Kilo Kirschen** *eyen HAHLB-es KEE-loh KEERSH-en*

■ a liter of milk (about 1 quart) | **ein Liter Milch** *eyen LEET-uh milkh*

■ a package of candies | **ein Paket Bonbons** *eyen pah-KAYT bong-BOHNGS*

■ a hundred grams of cheese (about $\frac{1}{4}$ pound) | **hundert Gramm Käse** *HUN-dehrt grahm KAYZ-eh*

■ a roll of toilet paper | **eine Rolle Toilettenpapier** *EYEN-eh ROL-eh toy-LEHT-en-pah-peer*

■ a kilo of butter | **ein Kilo Butter** *eyen KEE-loh BUT-uh*

■ two hundred grams (about $\frac{1}{2}$ pound) of cookies | **zweihundert Gramm Kekse** *TSVEYE-hun-dehrt grahm KAYKS-eh*

■ a hundred grams of bologna | **hundert Gramm Fleischwurst** *HUN-dehrt grahm FLEYESH-voorst*

NOTE: Common measurements for purchasing foods are a kilo or fractions thereof, and 100 (**einhundert**), 200 (**zweihundert**), and 500 (**fünfhundert**) grams.

TOILETRIES

I'm looking for ____.	**Ich suche** ____. *ikh ZOOKH-eh*
■ a brush	**eine Bürste** *EYEN-eh BEWRST-eh*
■ cleansing cream	**Reinigungscreme** *REYEN-ig-ungs-kraym*
■ cologne	**Kölnisch Wasser** *KERLN-ish VAHS-uh*
■ a comb	**einen Kamm** *EYEN-en kahm*
■ a deodorant	**ein Desodorans** *eyen dehz-oh-doh-RAHNTS*
■ (disposable) diapers	**(wegwerfbare) Windeln** *(VEHK-vehrf-baar-eh) VIND-eln*
■ a file	**eine Feile** *EYEN-eh FEYEL-eh*
■ eye liner	**einen Lidstift** *EYEN-en LEED-shtift*
■ eye shadow	**einen Lidschatten** *EYEN-en LEED-shaht-en*
■ eyebrow pencil	**einen Augenbrauenstift** *EYEN-en OWG-en-brow-en-shtift*
■ foot powder	**Fußpuder** *FOOSS-pood-uh*
■ hair pins	**Haarklemmen** *HAAR-klem-en*
■ hair spray	**Haarspray** *HAAR-shpray*
■ lipstick	**einen Lippenstift** *EYEN-en LIP-en-shtift*
■ mascara	**Wimperntusche** *VIMP-ehrn-tush-eh*
■ a mirror	**einen Spiegel** *EYEN-en SHPEEG-el*
■ mouthwash	**Mundwasser** *MUNT-vahs-uh*

▪nail clippers	**eine Nagelzange** *EYEN-eh NAAG-el-tsahng-eh*
▪nail polish	**Nagellack** *NAAG-el-lahk*
▪nail polish remover	**Nagellackentferner** *NAAG-el-lahk-ehnt-fehrn-uh*
▪nail scissors	**eine Nagelschere** *EYEN-eh NAAG-el-shayr-eh*
▪a razor	**einen Rasierapparat** *EYEN-en rah-ZEER-ah-pah-raat*
▪razor blades	**Rasierklingen** *rah-ZEER-kling-en*
▪rouge	**Schminke/Rouge** *SHMINK-eh/roozh*
▪sanitary napkins	**Damenbinden** *DAAM-en-bind-en*
▪shampoo	**ein Haarwaschmittel** *eyen HAAR-vahsh-mit-el*
▪shaving lotion	**Rasierwasser** *rah-ZEER-vahs-uh*
▪shaving cream	**Rasiercreme** *rah-ZEER-kraym*
▪soap	**Seife** *ZEYEF-eh*
▪a sponge	**einen Schwamm** *EYEN-en shvahm*
▪tissues	**Papiertücher** *pah-PEER-tewkh-uh*
▪toilet paper	**Toilettenpapier** *toy-LEHT-en-pah-peer*
▪a toothbrush	**eine Zahnbürste** *EYEN-eh TSAAN-bewrst-eh*
▪toothpaste	**Zahnpasta** *TSAAN-pahs-tah*
▪tweezers	**eine Pinzette** *EYEN-eh pin-TSEHT-eh*

PERSONAL CARE AND SERVICES

BARBER SHOP

I must go to the barber.	**Ich muß zum Friseur.** *ikh muss tsoom free-ZEHR*
Is there one in the hotel?	**Gibt's einen im Hotel?** *gipts EYEN-en im ho-TEL*
I don't want to wait long.	**Ich will nicht lange warten.** *ikh vil nikht LAHNG-eh VAART-en*
Give me a shave, please.	**Rasieren, bitte.** *rah-ZEER-en BIT-eh*
I want a haircut, please.	**Haare schneiden, bitte.** *HAAR-eh SHNEYED-en BIT-eh*
(Not too) short in back, long in front.	**(Nicht zu) kurz hinten, lang vorne.** *(nikht tsoo) koorts HINT-en, lahng FORN-eh*
Take a little more off on top.	**Nehmen Sie oben ein bißchen mehr weg.** *NAYM-en zee OHB-en eyen BISS-khen mayr vehk*
Nothing more on the sides.	**Nichts mehr an den Seiten.** *nikhts mayr ahn dayn ZEYET-en*
That's enough.	**Das genügt.** *dahs ge-NEWKT*
Just use the scissors, please.	**Nur mit der Schere, bitte.** *noor mit dehr SHAYR-eh BIT-eh*
Don't use the machine.	**Keine Maschine, bitte.** *KEYEN-eh mah-SHEEN-eh BIT-eh*
Please, just a light trim.	**Bitte nur ausputzen.** *BIT-eh noor OWS-puts-en*

Especially the neck.	**Besonders im Nacken.** *beh-ZOND-ehrs im NAHK-en*
Please trim my _____.	**Bitte stutzen Sie mir _____.** *BIT-eh SHTUTS-en zee meer*
■ beard	**den Bart** *dayn baart*
■ moustache	**den Schnurrbart** *dayn SCHNOOR-baart*
■ sideburns	**die Koteletten** *dee kot-eh-LEHT-en*
Please bring me a hand mirror.	**Bringen Sie mir bitte einen Handspiegel.** *BRING-en zee meer BIT-eh EYEN-en HAHNT-shpeeg-el*
How much do I owe you?	**Was schulde ich Ihnen?** *vahs SHULD-eh ikh EEN-en*
Is the service included?	**Ist die Bedienung inbegriffen?** *ist dee beh-DEEN-ung IN-beh-grif-en*

AT THE BEAUTY PARLOR

Is there a beauty parlor around here?	**Gibt es einen Damensalon hier in der Nähe?** *gipt ehs EYEN-en DAAM-en-zaa-long heer in dehr NAY-eh*
I'd like to make an appointment for today (tomorrow).	**Ich möchte mich für heute (morgen) anmelden.** *ikh MERKHT-eh mikh fewr HOYT-eh (MORG-en) AHN- meld-en*
I'd like _____.	**Ich möchte _____.** *ikh MERKHT-eh _____*
Can you give me _____?	**Können Sie mir _____ geben?** *KERN-en zee meer _____ GAYB-en*
■ a color rinse	**eine Farbspülung** *EYEN-eh FAHRP-shpewl-ung*
■ a face pack	**eine Gesichtsmaske** *EYEN-eh geh-ZIKHTS-mahsk-eh*

■ a manicure (pedicure)   **eine Maniküre (Pediküre)** *EYEN-eh MAHN-i-kewr-eh (PAYD-i-kewr-eh)*

■ a mudbath   **ein Schlammbad** *eyen SHLAHM-baat*

■ a facial massage   **eine Gesichtsmassage** *EYEN-eh geh-ZIKHTS-mah-sazh-eh*

■ a permanent   **eine Dauerwelle** *EYEN-eh DOW-uh-vehl-eh*

■ a touch up   **eine Auffrischung** *EYEN-eh OWF-frish-ung*

Just a shampoo and set, please.   **Nur Waschen und Legen, bitte.** *noor VAHSH-en unt LAYG-en BIT-eh*

No, don't cut it.   **Nein, nicht schneiden.** *neyen, nikht SHNEYED-en*

I don't like the color any more.   **Die Farbe gefällt mir nicht mehr.** *dee FAARB-eh geh-FEHLT meer nikht mayr*

This time I'm going to try _____.   **Diesmal versuche ich _____.** *DEES-maal fehr-ZOOKH-eh ikh*

■ auburn   **kastanienbraun** *kahs-TAAN-yen-brown*

■ light blond   **hellblond** *hel blont*

■ dark blond   **dunkelblond** *DUNK-el blont*

■ brunette   **braun** *brown*

■ a darker color   **eine dunklere Farbe** *EYEN-eh DUNK-lehr-eh FAARB-eh*

■ a lighter color   **eine hellere Farbe** *EYEN-eh HEL-ehr-eh FAARB-eh*

■ the same color   **dieselbe Farbe** *DEE-zehlb-eh FAARB-eh*

■ something exotic   **etwas Exotisches** *EHT-vahs eks-OHT-ish-es*

I'd like to look at the color chart again.	**Ich möchte mir nochmal die Farbtabelle ansehen.** *ikh MERKHT-eh meer NOKH-maal dee FAARP-tah-bel-eh AHN-zay-en*
Not too much hairspray.	**Nicht zu viel Haarspray.** *nikht tsoo feel HAAR-shpray*
No hairspray please.	**Kein Haarspray, bitte.** *keyen HAAR-shpray BIT-eh*
More hairspray.	**Mehr Haarspray.** *mayr HAAR-shpray*
Do you carry wigs?	**Führen Sie Perücken?** *FEWR-en zee peh-REWK-en*
I want a new hairdo.	**Ich will eine neue Frisur.** *ikh vil EYEN-eh NOY-eh free-ZOOR*
Something striking.	**Etwas Auffallendes.** *EHT-vahs OWF-fahl-ehnd-es*
Something wild.	**Etwas ganz Tolles.** *EHT-vahs gahnts TOL-es*
With curls.	**Mit Löckchen.** *mit LERK-khen*
With waves.	**Mit Wellen.** *mit VEL-en*
In a bun on top or behind.	**In einem Knoten oben oder hinten.** *in EYEN-em KNOHT-en OHB-en OHD-uh HINT-en*

SHOE REPAIRS

Can you fix these shoes (boots) right now?	**Können Sie gleich jetzt diese Schuhe (Stiefel) reparieren?** *KERN-en zee gleyekh yetst DEEZ-eh SHOO-eh (SHTEEF-el) reh-pah-REER-en*

They need new (half)soles and heels.	**Sie brauchen neue (Halb)sohlen und Absätze.** *zee BROWKH-en NOY-eh (hahlp)ZOHL-en unt AHP-zehts-eh*
I can come back in an hour.	**Ich kann in einer Stunde zurückkommen.** *ikh kahn in EYEN-uh SHTUND-eh tsoo-REWK-kom-en*
Please shine them also.	**Bitte putzen Sie sie auch.** *BIT-eh PUTS-en zee zee owkh*
Will they be ready by Friday?	**Sind sie bis Freitag fertig?** *zint zee bis FREYE-taak FEHRT-ikh*

LAUNDRY AND DRY CLEANING

Hotel signs in several languages will often inform you that it's strictly **verboten** to use electric heaters, wash clothes, etc. Yet, many people do wash out small items. Some hotels have laundry and dry-cleaning services, sometimes with multi-lingual lists. If not, ask:

Is there a laundry (dry cleaner's) near-by?	**Gibt es eine Wäscherei (chemi-sche Reinigung) in der Nähe?** *gipt ehs EYEN-eh vehsh-eh-REYE (KHAY-mi-sheh REYE-ni-gung) in dehr NAY-eh?*
Can these clothes be washed (ironed, cleaned) for me?	**Kann man mir diese Kleider waschen (bügeln, reinigen)?** *kahn mahn meer DEEZ-eh KLEYED-uh VAHSH-en (BEWG-eln, REYE-nig-en)*
Could I have it today (tomorrow, the day after tomorrow)?	**Könnte ich's schon heute (morgen, übermorgen) haben?** *KERNT-eh ikhs shon HOYT-eh (MORG-en, EWB-uh-morg-en) HAAB-en*
I absolutely must have it ____.	**Ich muß es unbedingt ____ haben.** *ikh muss ehs UN-beh-dingt ____ HAAB-en*

■ as soon as possible   **so bald wie möglich** *zoh bahlt vee MERG-likh*

■ tonight   **vor heute abend** *for HOYT-eh AAB-ehnt*

■ tomorrow   **vor morgen** *for MORG-en*

■ next week   **vor nächste Woche** *for NAYKHST-eh VOKH-eh*

■ the day after tomorrow   **vor übermorgen** *for EWB-uh-morg-en*

When will you bring it (them) back?   **Wann werden Sie es (sie) zurückbringen?** *vahn VEHRD-en zee ehs (zee) tsoo-REWK-bring-en*

When will it be ready?   **Wann wird es fertig sein?** *vahn virt ehs FEHR-tikh zeyen*

Here's a nasty spot too.   **Hier ist auch ein verflixter Fleck.** *heer ist owkh eyen fehr-FLIKST-uh flek*

Can you remove it?   **Können Sie ihn entfernen?** *KERN-en zee een ehnt-FAYR-nen*

When will you bring it back?   **Wann können Sie es zurückbringen?** *vahn KERN-en zee ehs tsoo-REWK-bring-en*

When will it be ready?   **Wann wird es fertig sein?** *vahn virt ehs FEHR-tikh zeyen*

This isn't my laundry.   **Dies ist nicht meine Wäsche.** *dees ist nikht MEYEN-eh VEHSH-eh*

WATCH REPAIRS

Is it worth getting this watch fixed?   **Lohnt es sich diese Uhr reparieren zu lassen?** *lohnt ehs zikh DEEZ-eh oor reh-pah-REER-en tsoo LASS-en*

I dropped it.   **Ich habe sie fallen lassen.** *ikh HAAB-eh zee FAHL-en LAS⟨*

Then repair and clean the watch (clock).	**dann reparieren und reinigen Sie die Uhr.** *dahn reh-pah-REER-en unt REYEN-ig-en zee dee oor*
How long do you need for that?	**Wie lange brauchen Sie dafür?** *vee LAHNG-eh BROWKH-en zee dah-FEWR*

CAMERA REPAIRS

Can you fix this (movie) camera?	**Können Sie diese (Film) Kamera reparieren?** *KERN-en zee DEEZ-eh (film) KAH-meh-raa reh-pah-REER-en*
How much would it cost to have this camera repaired?	**Wieviel würde es kosten, diese Kamera reparieren zu lassen?** *VEE-feel VEWRD-eh ehs KOST-en DEEZ-eh KAH-meh-raa reh-pah-REER-en tsoo LASS-en*
Would it take long?	**Würde es lange dauern?** *VEWRD-eh ehs LAHNG-eh DOW-ehrn*
The film doesn't advance	**Der Film dreht sich nicht weiter.** *dayr film drayt zikh nikht VEYET-uh*
May I have an estimate?	**Können Sie mir einen Kostenanschlag geben?** *KERN-en zee meer EYEN-en KOST-en-ahn-shlaak GAYB-en*
May I have a receipt?	**Darf ich eine Quittung haben?** *dahrf ikh EYEN-eh KVIT-ung HAAB-en*
When can I come and get it?	**Wann kann ich sie wieder abholen?** *vahn kahn ikh zee VEED-uh AHP-hohl-en*
I need it as soon as possible.	**Ich brauche sie sobald wie möglich.** *ikh BROWKH-eh zee zoh-BAHLT vee MERG-likh*

MEDICAL CARE

PHARMACY

Where can I find the nearest (all-night) pharmacy?	**Wo finde ich die nächste Apotheke (mit Nachtdienst)?** *voh FIND-eh ikh dee NAYKST-eh ah-poh-TAYK-eh (mit NAHKHT-deenst)*
At what time does it open (close)?	**Um wieviel Uhr wird geöffnet (geschlossen)?** *um VEE-feel oor veert geh-ERF-net (geh-SHLOSS-en)*
I'm looking for something for ____.	**Ich suche etwas gegen ____.** *ikh ZOOKH-eh EHT-vahs GAYG-en*
▪ a cold	**eine Erkältung** *EYEN-eh ehr-KEHLT-ung*
▪ lack of appetite	**Appetitslosigkeit** *ah-peh-TEETS-loh-zikh-keyet*
▪ constipation	**Verstopfung** *fehr-SHTOPF-ung*
▪ a cough	**Husten** *HOOST-en*
▪ a fever	**Fieber** *FEEB-uh*
▪ diarrhea	**Durchfall** *DOORKH-fahl*
▪ a hangover	**Kater** *KAAT-uh*
▪ indigestion	**Magenverstimmung** *MAAG-en-fehr-shtim-ung*
▪ hay fever	**Heuschnupfen** *HOY-shnupf-en*
▪ headache	**Kopfschmerzen** *KOPF-shmehrts-en*
▪ insomnia	**Schlaflosigkeit** *SHLAAF-loh-zikh-keyet*
▪ motion sickness	**Reisekrankheit** *REYEZ-eh-krahnk-heyet*
▪ insect bites	**Insektenstiche** *in-ZEHKT-en-shtikh-eh*

■ prickly heat	**Hitzblattern** *HITS-blaht-ehrn*
■ a blister	**eine Blase** *EYEN-eh BLAAZ-eh*
■ a burn	**eine Brandwunde** *EYEN-eh BRAHNT-vund-eh*
■ sunburn	**Sonnenbrand** *ZON-en-brahnt*
■ a toothache	**Zahnschmerzen** *TSAAN-shmehrts-en*
Can you fill this prescription for me now?	**Können Sie mir dieses Rezept jetzt machen?** *KERN-en zee meer DEEZ-es reh-TSEPT yetst MAAKH-en*
It's urgent.	**Es ist dringend.** *ehs ist DRING-ent*
How long will it take?	**Wie lange wird's dauern?** *vee LAHNG-eh veerts DOW-ehrn*
I'll wait.	**Ich warte darauf.** *ikh VAART-eh dah-ROWF*
When can I pick it up?	**Wann kann ich's abholen?** *vahn kahn ikhs AHP-hohl-en*
I need _____.	**Ich brauche _____.** *ikh BROWKH-eh*
■ an antacid	**Magentabletten** *MAAG-en-tahb-leht-en*
■ an antiseptic	**ein Antiseptikum** *eyen ahn-tee-ZEP-ti-kum*
■ aspirin	**Aspirin** *ah-spee-REEN*
■ bandages	**Verbandzeug** *fehr-BAHNT-tsoyk*
■ Band Aids	**Heftpflaster** *HEHFT-pflahst-uh*
■ a contraceptive	**ein Verhütungsmittel** *eyen fehr-HEWT-ungs-mit-el*
■ corn plasters	**Hühneraugenpflaster** *HEWN-ehr-owg-en-pflahst-uh*
■ cotton balls	**Wattebäusche** *VAHT-eh-boysh-eh*
■ cough drops	**Hustenbonbons** *HOOST-en-bon-bongs*

■ ear drops	**Ohrentropfen**	*OHR-en-tropf-en*
■ eye drops	**Augentropfen**	*OWG-en-tropf-en*
■ herbal teas	**Kräutertees**	*KROY-tehr-tayss*
■ first-aid kit	**einen Verbandkasten**	*EYEN-en fehr-BAHNT-kahst-en*
■ iodine	**Jod**	*yoht*
■ an (herbal) laxative	**ein (Kräuter) Abführmittel**	*eyen (KROYT-ehr) AHP-fewr-mit-el*
■ talcum powder	**Talkumpuder**	*TAHLK-um-pood-uh*
■ a thermometer	**ein Thermometer**	*eyen ther-mo-MAYT-uh*
■ throat lozenges	**Halspastillen**	*HAHLS-pahs-til-en*
■ tranquilizers	**ein Beruhigungsmittel**	*eyen beh-ROO-i-gungs-mit-el*
■ vitamins	**Vitamine**	*vee-taa-MEEN-eh*

WITH THE DOCTOR

I think I'm sick.	**Ich glaube, ich bin krank.** *ikh GLOWB-eh ikh bin krahnk*
I need a doctor.	**Ich brauche einen Arzt.** *ikh BROWKH-eh EYEN-en ahrtst*
Is there a doctor here who speaks English?	**Gibt's hier einen Arzt, der Englisch spricht?** *gipts heer EYEN-en ahrtst dehr EHNG-lish shprikht*
Where is his office?	**Wo ist seine Praxis?** *voh ist SEYEN-eh PRAHK-siss*
What are his office hours?	**Was sind seine Sprechstunden?** *vahs zint ZEYEN-eh SHPREKH-shtund-en*
Could the doctor come to me in my hotel?	**Könnte der Arzt zu mir ins Hotel kommen?** *KERNT-eh dehr ahrtst tsoo meer ins ho-TEL KOM-en*

I have _____.	**Ich habe** _____. *ikh HAAB-eh*
■ an abscess	**einen Abszeß** *EYEN-en ahps-TSESS*
■ a broken leg	**einen Beinbruch** *EYEN-en BEYEN-brukh*
■ a bruise	**eine Quetschung** *EYEN-eh KVETSH-ung*
■ a burn	**eine Brandwunde** *EYEN-eh BRAHNT-vund-eh*
■ a cold	**eine Erkältung** *EYEN-eh ehr-KEHLT-ung*
■ constipation	**Verstopfung** *fehr-SHTOPF-ung*
■ cramps	**Krämpfe** *KREHMPF-eh*
■ a cut	**eine Schnittwunde** *EYEN-eh SHNIT-vund-eh*
■ diarrhea	**Durchfall** *DOORKH-fahl*
■ dysentery	**Ruhr** *roor*
■ fever	**Fieber** *FEEB-uh*
■ a fracture	**einen Bruch** *EYEN-en brookh*
■ an eye inflammation	**eine Augenentzündung** *EYEN-eh OWG-en-ehnt-tsewnd-ung*
■ a lump	**eine Beule** *EYEN-eh BOYL-eh*
■ a sore throat	**Halsschmerzen** *HAHLS-shmehrts-en*
■ a skin disease	**eine Hautkrankheit** *EYEN-eh HOWT-krahnk-heyet*
■ a stomach ulcer	**ein Magengeschwür** *eyen MAAG-en-geh-shvewr*
■ a sty	**einen Augenliderbrand** *EYEN-en OWG-en-leed-ehr-brahnt*

◼ a swelling	**eine Schwellung** *EYEN-eh SHVEL-ung*
◼ a wound	**eine Wunde** *EYEN-eh VUND-eh*
◼ a veneral disease	**eine Geschlechtskrankheit** *EYEN-eh geh-SHLEKHTS-krahnk-heyet*
◼ a head (back) ache	**Kopf (Rücken) schmerzen** *kopf (REWK-en) SHMERTS-en*
I have chills.	**Mich fröstelt.** *mikh FRERST-elt*
It hurts me here.	**Hier tut es weh.** *heer toot ehs vay*
I hurt all over.	**Es tut mir überall weh.** *ehs toot meer EWB-ehr-ahl vay*
My _____ hurts (hurt).	**Mein(e) _____ tut (tun) mir weh.** *meyen(eh) _____ toot (toon) meer vay*
◼ my ankle	**mein Knöchel** *meyen KNERKH-el*
◼ my arm	**mein Arm** *meyen ahrm*
◼ my ear	**mein Ohr** *meyen ohr*
◼ my eye	**mein Auge** *meyen OWG-eh*
◼ my face	**mein Gesicht** *meyen geh-ZIKHT*
◼ my finger	**mein Finger** *meyen FING-uh*
◼ my foot	**mein Fuß** *meyen fooss*
◼ my glands	**meine Drüsen** *MEYEN-eh DREWZ-en*
◼ my hand	**meine Hand** *MEYEN-eh hahnt*
◼ my hip joint	**mein Hüftgelenk** *meyen HEWFT-geh-lehnk*
◼ my heel	**meine Ferse** *MEYEN-eh FEHRZ-eh*
◼ my leg	**mein Bein** *meyen beyen*

■ my nose   **meine Nase** *MEYEN-eh NAAZ-eh*

■ my ribs   **meine Rippen** *MEYEN-eh RIP-en*

■ my shoulder   **meine Schulter** *MEYEN-eh SHULT-uh*

■ my stomach   **mein Magen** *meyen MAAG-en*

■ my toe   **meine Zehe** *MEYEN-eh TSAY-eh*

■ my wrist   **mein Handgelenk** *meyen HAHNT-geh-lenk*

I've had this pain since yesterday.   **Seit gestern habe ich diese Schmerzen.** *zeyet GEHST-ehrn HAAB-eh ikh DEEZ-eh SHMEHRTS-en*

I've been suffering from this disease for some time.   **Seit einiger Zeit leide ich an dieser Krankheit.** *zeyet EYE-ni-guh tseyet LEYED-eh ikh ahn DEEZ-uh KRAHNK-heyet*

Can you prescribe sleeping pills for me?   **Können Sie mir Schlaftabletten verschreiben?** *KERN-en zee meer SHLAAF-tah-blet-en fehr-SHREYEB-en*

I have heart trouble.   **Ich bin herzkrank.** *ikh bin HEHRTS-krahnk*

Do I have to go to the hospital?   **Muß ich ins Krankenhaus?** *muss ikh ins KRAHNK-en-howss*

When can I continue my trip?   **Wann kann ich meine Reise fortsetzen?** *vahn kahn ikh MEYEN-eh REYEZ-eh FORT-zets-en*

DOCTOR'S INSTRUCTIONS

Please open your mouth.   **Öffnen Sie bitte den Mund.** *ERFN-en zee BIT-eh dayn munt*

Breathe deeply and cough please.   **Tief atmen und husten, bitte.** *teef AHT-men unt HOOST-en, BIT-eh*

Get (un)dressed.	**Ziehen Sie sich an (aus).** *TSEE-en zee zikh ahn (owss)*
Lie down a moment please.	**Legen Sie sich bitte einen Augenblick hin.** *LAYG-en zee zikh BIT-eh EYEN-en OWG-en-blik hin*
Get up.	**Stehen Sie auf.** *SHTAY-en zee owf*

PATIENT

Are you going to give me a prescription for it?	**Verschreiben Sie mir etwas dafür?** *fehr-SHREYEB-en zee meer EHT-vahs dah-FEWR*
How often must I take this medicine (these pills)?	**Wie oft muß ich dieses Medikament (diese Pillen) nehmen?** *vee oft muss ikh DEEZ-es may-di-kah-MENT (DEEZ-eh PIL-en) NAYM-en*
Must I stay in bed? How long?	**Muß ich im Bett bleiben? Wie lange?** *muss ikh im bet BLEYEB-en? vee LAHNG-eh*
Thank you for everything, doctor.	**Ich danke Ihnen vielmals, Herr (Frau) Doktor.** *ikh DAHNK-eh EEN-en FEEL-maals hehr (frow) DOK-tor*
How much do I owe you for your services?	**Wieviel bin ich Ihnen schuldig?** *vee-FEEL bin ikh EEN-en SHULD-ikh*

NOTE: Often both a Germanic and a Latin or Greek derivative exist for the same thing. Pneumonia, for example, is both **Lungenentzündung** and **Pneumonie.** Use the medical term you know, and chances are the doctor will recognize it.

IN THE HOSPITAL (ACCIDENTS)

Help me, quick!	**Helfen Sie mir, schnell!** *HELF-en zee meer, shnel*
It's urgent.	**Es ist dringend.** *ehs ist DRING-ehnt*
Call a doctor immediately.	**Rufen Sie sofort einen Arzt.** *ROOF-en zee zoh-FORT EYEN-en ahrtst*

Get an ambulance.	**Holen Sie einen Krankenwagen.** *HOHL-en zee EYEN-en KRAHNK-en-vaag-en*
Take me (him) to the hospital.	**Bringen Sie mich (ihn) ins Krankenhaus.** *BRING-en zee mikh (een) ins KRAHNK-en-howss*
I need first aid.	**Ich brauche erste Hilfe.** *ikh BROWKH-eh EHRST-eh HILF-eh*
I'm bleeding.	**Ich blute.** *ikh BLOOT-eh*
I've (he's) lost a lot of blood.	**Ich habe (er hat) viel Blut verloren.** *ikh HAAB-eh (ehr haht) feel bloot fehr-LOHR-en*
I think something is broken (dislocated).	**Ich glaube, es ist etwas gebrochen (verrenkt).** *ikh GLOWB-eh ehs ist EHT-vahs geh-BROKH-en (fehr-REHNKT)*

AT THE DENTIST

Unfortunately I must go to the dentist.	**Leider muß ich zum Zahnarzt.** *LEYED-uh muss ikh tsoom TSAAN-ahrtst*
Do you know a good one?	**Kennen Sie einen guten?** *KEN-en zee EYEN-en GOOT-en*
I have a toothache that's driving me crazy.	**Ich habe wahnsinnige Zahnschmerzen.** *ikh hahp VAAN-zi-nig-eh TSAAN-shmehrts-en*
I've lost a filling (crown).	**Ich habe eine Plombe (Krone) verloren.** *ikh hahp EYEN-eh PLOMB-eh (KROHN-eh) fehr-LOHR-en*
I broke a tooth on hard nuts.	**Ich habe mir an harten Nüßen einen Zahn ausgebissen.** *ikh hahp meer ahn HAHRT-en NEWSS-en EYEN-en tsaan OWSS-geh-biss-en*
I can't chew.	**Ich kann nicht kauen.** *ikh kahn nikht KOW-en*

My gums are bleeding.	**Das Zahnfleisch blutet.** *dahs TSAAN-fleyesh BLOOT-et*	
Do I have an abscess?	**Habe ich einen Abszeß?** *hahb ikh EYEN-en ahps-TSESS*	
Can the tooth be saved?	**Ist der Zahn noch zu retten?** *ist dehr tsaan nokh tsoo RET-en*	
I just want a temporary filling (treatment).	**Ich möchte nur eine provisorische Füllung (Behandlung).** *ikh MERKHT-eh noor EYEN-eh pro-vee-ZOR-ish-eh FEWL-ung (beh-HANT-lung)*	
Can you fix ___ ?	**Können Sie ___ reparieren?** *KERN-en zee ___ reh-pah-REER-en*	
■ this denture	**dieses Gebiß** *DEEZ-es geh-BISS*	
■ these false teeth	**diesen Zahnersatz** *DEEZ-en TSAAN-ehr-zahts*	
How much do I owe you for your services?	**Wieviel bin ich Ihnen schuldig?** *VEE-feel bin ikh EEN-en SHULD-ikh*	

WITH THE OPTICIAN

I'd like to get these glasses repaired.	**Diese Brille möchte ich reparieren lassen.** *DEEZ-eh BRIL-eh MERKHT-eh ikh reh-pah-REER-en LAHSS-en*
Can you put in a new lens for the broken one?	**Können Sie das gebrochene Glas auswechseln?** *KERN-en zee dahs geh-BROKH-en-eh glaas OWSS-vehks-eln*
The screw must be replaced.	**Die Schraube muß ersetzt werden.** *dee SHROWB-eh muss ehr-ZETST VAYRD-en*
It fell out.	**Sie ist herausgefallen.** *zee ist hehr-OWSS-geh-fahl-en*
Could you repair them right away?	**Können Sie sie gleich jetzt reparieren?** *KERN-en zee zee gleyekh yetst reh-pah-REER-en*

I can wait.	**Ich kann warten.** *ikh kahn VAART-en*
I need them.	**Ich brauche sie.** *ikh BROWKH-eh zee*
I have no others.	**Ich habe keine andere.** *ikh hahp KEYEN-eh AHN-deh-reh*

COMMUNICATIONS

POST OFFICE

I must mail some letters.	**Ich muß einige Briefe auf die Post tragen.** *ikh muss EYE-ni-geh BREEF-eh owf dee post TRAAG-en*
I want to send (mail) these postcards home.	**Ich will diese Postkarten mit der Post nach Hause schicken.** *ikh vil DEEZ-eh POST-kart-en mit dehr post nahkh HOWZ-eh SHIK-en*
I want to mail these packages home.	**Ich möchte diese Pakete mit der Post nach Hause schicken.** *ikh MERKHT-eh DEEZ-eh pah-KAYT-eh mit dehr post nahkh HOWZ-eh SHIK-en*
Where is the post office?	**Wo ist das Postamt?** *voh ist dahs POST-ahmt*
Where can I find a mailbox?	**Wo finde ich einen Briefkasten?** *voh FIND-eh ikh EYEN-en BREEF-kahst-en*
What is the postage on ___ to the U.S. (England, Canada, Australia)?	**Was kostet ___ nach USA (England, Kanada, Australien)?** *vahs KOST-et ___ nahkh oo-ess-aa (EHNG-lahnt, KAA-naa-dah, owss-TRAAL-yen)*
■ a letter	**ein Brief** *eyen breef*
■ an airmail letter	**ein Luftpostbrief** *eyen LUFT-post-breef*

■ a registered letter	**ein Einschreibebrief** *eyen EYEN-shreyeb-eh-breef*
■ a special delivery letter	**ein Eilbrief** *eyen EYEL-breef*
■ a postcard	**eine Postkarte** *EYEN-eh POST-kaart-eh*
■ this package	**dieses Paket** *DEEZ-es pah-KAYT*
Can I have this letter (this package) insured?	**Kann ich diesen Brief (dieses Paket) versichern lassen?** *kahn ikh DEEZ-en breef (DEEZ-es pah-KAYT) fehr-ZIKH-ehrn LAHSS-en*
When will it arrive?	**Wann wird's ankommen?** *vahn veerts AHN-kom-en*
Where is the _____ window?	**Wo ist der Schalter für _____?** *voh ist dehr SHAHLT-uh fewr*
■ general delivery	**postlagernde Sendungen** *POST-laa-gehrnd-eh ZEHND-ung-en*
■ money orders	**Postanweisungen** *POST-ahn-veyez-ung-en*
■ stamps	**Briefmarken** *BREEF-mahrk-en*
Are there any stamp dealers in this town?	**Gibt es Briefmarkenhändler in dieser Stadt?** *gipt ehs BREEF-mahrk-en-hehnt-luh in DEEZ-uh shtaht*
Please let me have _____.	**Geben Sie mir bitte _____.** *GAYB-en zee meer BIT-eh*
■ eight envelopes	**acht Umschläge** *ahkht UM-shlayg-eh*
■ twenty (air mail) stamps	**zwanzig (Luftpost) Briefmarken** *TSVAHN-tsikh (LUFT-post) BREEF-mahrk-en*
Are there any letters for me?	**Ist Post für mich da?** *ist post fewr mikh daa*
My name is _____.	**Ich heiße _____.** *ikh HEYESS-eh*

TELEGRAMS

Where can I send a telegram?	**Wo kann ich ein Telegramm aufgeben?** *vo kahn ikh eyen tay-leh-GRAHM OWF-gayb-en*
I'd like to send a telegram (night letter) to ____.	**Ich möchte ein Telegramm (Brieftelegramm) nach ____ aufgeben.** *ikh MERKHT-eh eyen tay-leh-GRAHM (BREEF-tay-leh-grahm) nakh ____ OWF-gayb-en*
How much is it per word?	**Was kostet es pro Wort?** *vahs KOST-et ehs proh vort*
Please let me have a form.	**Geben Sie mir bitte ein Formular.** *GAYB-en zee meer BIT-eh eyen for-mu-LAAR*
I want to send it collect.	**Ich möchte, daß der Empfänger es bezahlt.** *ikh MERKHT-eh dahs dehr ehmp-FEHNG-uh ehs beh-TSAALT*

TELEPHONE

I'm looking for ____.	**Ich suche ____.** *ikh ZOOKH-eh*
■ a telephone booth	**eine Telefonzelle** *EYEN-eh tay-leh-FOHN-tsel-eh*
■ a telephone directory	**ein Telefonbuch** *eyen tay-leh-FOHN-bookh*
May I use your phone?	**Darf ich Ihr Telefon benutzen?** *dahrf ikh eer tay-leh-FOHN beh-NUTS-en*
Here is the number.	**Hier ist die Nummer.** *heer ist dee NUM-uh*
Can you help me?	**Können Sie mir helfen?** *KERN-en zee meer HELF-en*

It's a local call.	**Es ist ein Ortsgespräch.** *ehs ist eyen ORTS-geh-shpraykh*
◾ a long-distance call	**ein Ferngespräch** *eyen FEHRN-geh-shpraykh*
◾ a person-to-person call	**ein Gespräch mit Voranmeldung** *eyen geh-SHPRAYKH mit FOHR-ahn-mehld-ung*
◾ a collect call	**ein R-Gespräch** *eyen ehr-geh-SHPRAYKH*
Can you dial direct?	**Kann man durchwählen?** *kahn mahn DOORKH-vayl-en*
Operator, please get me number _____.	**Fräulein, verbinden Sie mich bitte mit der Nummer ____.** *FROY-leyen, fehr-BIND-en zee mikh BIT-eh mit dehr NUM-uh*
May I speak to Mr. (Mrs., Miss) ____?	**Darf ich bitte Herrn (Frau, Fräulein) ____ sprechen?** *dahrf ikh BIT-eh hehrn (frow, FROY-leyen) ____ SHPREHKH-en*
Speak louder (more slowly).	**Sprechen Sie lauter (langsamer).** *SHPREHKH-en zee LOWT-uh (LAHNG-zaam-uh)*
Don't hang up.	**Bleiben Sie am Apparat.** *BLEYEB-en zee ahm ah-pah-RAAT*
The line is busy.	**Die Leitung ist besetzt.** *dee LEYET-ung ist beh-ZEHTST*
You gave me the wrong number.	**Sie haben mich falsch verbunden.** *zee HAAB-en mikh fahlsh fehr-BUND-en*
I'll call again later.	**Später rufe ich noch einmal an.** *SHPAYT-uh roof ikh nokh EYEN-maal ahn*
I'd like to leave a message.	**Ich möchte etwas ausrichten lassen.** *ikh merkht EHT-vahs OWSS-rikht-en LAHSS-en*

DRIVING A CAR

ROAD SIGNS

AUF 8 KM	For 8 Kilometers
AUSFAHRT FREI HALTEN	Keep Driveway Clear
BLAUE ZONE	Blue Parking Zone (requires special parking disk)
DURCHGANGS-VERKEHR	Through Traffic
EINBAHN-STRASSE	One-way Street
EINFAHRT FREI HALTEN	Do Not Block Entrance
EINORDNEN	Get in Lane
ENDE DES PARK-VERBOTS	End of No Parking Zone
_____ (NICHT) ER-LAUBT	_____ (not) Allowed
FROSTSCHÄDEN	Frost Damage
FUSSGÄNGER-ZONE	Pedestrian Zone
GEFÄHRLICHES GEFÄLLE	Dangerous Descent
GEFÄHRLICHE STEIGUNG	Dangerous (steep) Hill
HALT, POLIZEI	Stop, Police
HUPEN VERBO-TEN	No Honking
KEIN DURCH-GANG FÜR FUSS-GÄNGER	Closed to Pedestrians

KURZPARKZONE	Limited Parking Zone
LANGSAM FAH-REN	Drive Slowly
LAWINENGE-FAHR	Danger of Avalanche
LINKS FAHREN	Keep Left
LKW	Alternate Truck Route
NUR FÜR AN-LIEGER	Residents Only
PARKEN VERBO-TEN	No Parking
RECHTS FAHREN	Keep Right
SCHLECHTE FAHRBAHN	Bad Road Surface
SCHULE	School
SPURRILLEN	Grooves in Road
STEINSCHLAG	Falling Rocks
STRASSENAR-BEITEN AUF 5 KILOMETER	Road Work for 5 Kilometers
UMLEITUNG	Detour
VERKEHRSSTAU AUF 15 KILOME-TER	Traffic Backups (jams) for the Next 15 Kilometers
_____ VERBOTEN	_____ Not Allowed
VORSICHT	Caution

CAR RENTALS

I need _____.	**Ich brauche**	*ikh BROWKH-eh*
▪ a car	**einen Wagen**	*EYEN-en VAAG-en*

No U-turn

No passing

Border crossing

Traffic signal ahead

Speed limit

Traffic circle (roundabout)
ahead

Minimum speed limit

All traffic turns left

End of no passing zone

One-way street

Detour

Danger ahead

Entrance to expressway

Expressway ends

Guarded railroad crossing

Yield

Stop

Right of way

Dangerous intersection ahead

Gasoline (petrol) ahead

Parking

No vehicles allowed

Dangerous curve

Pedestrian crossing

Oncoming traffic has right of way

No bicycles allowed

No parking allowed

No entry

No left turn

■ a motorcycle	**ein Motorrad** *eyen moh-TOHR-raat*
■ a bicycle	**ein Fahrrad** *eyen FAAR-raat*
Is there a car rental office nearby?	**Gibt es eine Autovermietung in der Nähe?** *gipt ehs EYEN-eh OW-toh-fehr-meet-ung in dehr NAY-eh*
I need a big (small) car.	**Ich brauche einen großen (klein-en) Wagen.** *ikh BROWKH-eh EYEN-en GROHSS-en (KLEYEN-en) VAAG-en*
How much does it cost per ____?	**Wieviel kostet es pro ____?** *VEE-feel KOST-et ehs proh*
■ day	**Tag** *taak*
■ week	**Woche** *VOKH-eh*
■ month	**Monat** *MOH-naat*
■ kilometer	**Kilometer** *kee-loh-MAYT-uh*
How much is the insurance?	**Was kostet die Versicherung?** *vahs KOST-et dee fehr-ZIKH-ehr-ung*
Do I have to pay for gas?	**Muß ich das Benzin bezahlen?** *muss ikh dahs behn-TSEEN beh-TSAAL-en*
Do I have to leave a deposit?	**Muß ich etwas hinterlegen?** *muss ikh EHT-vahs hin-tehr-LAYG-en*
Even with this credit card?	**Selbst mit dieser Kreditkarte?** *zehlpst mit DEEZ-uh kray-DIT-kaart-eh*
I want to rent the car here and leave it in Munich.	**Ich will das Auto hier mieten und es in München wieder abgeben.** *ikh vil dahs OW-toh heer MEET-en unt ehs in MEWN-khen VEED-uh AHP-gayb-en*
Is there an additional charge for that?	**Entstehen mir dadurch zusätzliche Kosten?** *ehnt-SHTAY-en meer daa-DURKH TSOO-zehts-likh-eh KOST-en*
What kind of gasoline does it use?	**Mit welchem Benzin fährt der Wagen?** *mit VEHLKH-em behn-TSEEN fayrt dehr VAAG-en*

Here is my driver's license.	**Hier haben Sie meinen Führerschein.** *heer HAAB-en zee MEYEN-en FEWR-ehr-sheyen*

ON THE ROAD

Pardon me.	**Entschuldigen Sie, bitte.** *ehnt-SHULD-ig-en zee BIT-eh*
Is this the road to _____?	**Ist dies die Straße nach _____?** *ist dees dee SHTRAASS-eh nahkh*
Where does this road lead?	**Wohin führt diese Strasse?** *VOH-hin fewrt DEEZ-eh SHTRAASS-eh*
How do we get to _____?	**Wie kommen wir nach _____?** *Vee KOM-en veer nahkk*
Is this road shorter (longer)?	**Ist diese Straße kürzer (länger)?** *ist DEEZ-eh SHTRAASS-eh KEWRTS-ehr (LEHNG-ehr)*
Is it still very far to _____?	**Ist es noch sehr weit nach _____?** *ist ehs nokh zayr veyet nahkh*
What's the next town called?	**Wie heißt der nächste Ort?** *vee heyesst dehr NAYKST-eh ort*
Do you have a road map?	**Haben Sie eine Autokarte?** *HAAB-en zee EYEN-eh OW-toh-kaart-eh*
Can you show it to me on the map?	**Können Sie ihn mir auf der Karte zeigen?** *KERN-en zee een meer owf dehr KAART-eh TSEYEG-en*
Shall I drive straight ahead?	**Soll ich geradeaus fahren?** *zol ikh geh-RAAD-eh-owss FAAR-en*
Where must I turn?	**Wo muß ich abbiegen?** *voh muss ikh AHP-beeg-en*
Left?	**Links?** *links*
Right?	**Rechts?** *rehkhts*

AT THE SERVICE STATION

I'm looking for a gas station.	**Ich suche eine Tankstelle.** *ikh ZOOKH-eh EYEN-eh TAHNK-shtehl-eh*
Where is the nearest gas station (with service)?	**Wo ist die nächste Tankstelle (mit Bedienung)?** *voh ist dee NAYKST-eh TAHNK-shtehl-eh (mit beh-DEEN-ung)*
Fill it up, please.	**Voll, bitte.** *fol, BIT-eh*
Give me twenty-five liters.	**Geben Sie mir fünfundzwanzig Liter.** *GAYB-en zee meer FEWNF-unt-tsvahn-tsikh LEET-uh*
▮ regular	**Normal** *nor-MAAL*
▮ super	**Super** *ZOOP-uh*
Please check the oil and water.	**Bitte kontrollieren Sie Ölstand und Wasser.** *BIT-eh kon-tro-LEER-en zee ERL-shtahnt unt VAHSS-uh*
Please check ____.	**Prüfen Sie bitte ____.** *PREWF-en zee BIT-eh*
▮ the battery	**die Batterie** *dee bah-teh-REE*
▮ the brakes	**die Bremsen** *dee BREHM-zen*
▮ the carburetor	**den Vergaser** *dayn fehr-GAAZ-uh*
▮ the spark plugs	**die Zündkerzen** *dee TSEWNT-kehrts-en*
▮ the ignition system	**die Zündung** *dee TSEWND-ung*
▮ the lights	**die Beleuchtung** *dee beh-LOYKHT-ung*
▮ the tires	**die Reifen** *dee REYEF-en*
▮ the spare tire	**den Ersatzreifen** *dayn ehr-ZATS-reyef-en*
▮ the tire pressure	**den Reifendruck** *dayn REYEF-en-druk*

ACCIDENTS, REPAIRS

My car has broken down.	**Mein Wagen hat eine Panne.** *meyen VAAG-en haht EYEN-eh PAHN-eh*
It overheats.	**Er ist überhitzt.** *ehr ist EWB-uh-hitst*
I have a flat tire.	**Der Reifen ist kaputt.** *dehr REYEF-en ist kah-PUT*
The car is stuck.	**Der Wagen ist verklemmt.** *dehr VAAG-en ist fehr-KLEHMT*
Is there a garage (for repairs) near here?	**Gibt es eine Reparaturwerkstatt in der Nähe?** *gipt ehs EYEN-eh reh-paa-rah-TOOR-vehrk-shtaht in dehr NAY-eh*
Can you help me?	**Können Sie mir helfen?** *KERN-en zee meer HELF-en*
I have no tools.	**Ich habe keine Werkzeuge.** *ikh HAAB-eh KEYEN-eh VEHRK-tsoyg-eh*
I can't change the tire.	**Ich kann den Reifen nicht wechseln.** *ikh kahn dayn REYEF-en nikht VEHKS-eln*
I need a mechanic (a tow truck).	**Ich brauche einen Mechaniker (Abschleppwagen).** *ikh BROWKH-eh EYEN-en meh-KHAA-nik-uh (AHP-shlehp-vaag-en)*
Can you lend me ____?	**Können Sie mir ____ leihen?** *KERN-en zee meer ____ LEYE-en*
■ a flashlight	**eine Taschenlampe** *EYEN-eh TAHSH-en-lahmp-eh*
■ a hammer	**einen Hammer** *EYEN-en HAHM-uh*
■ a jack	**einen Wagenheber** *EYEN-en VAAG-en-hayb-uh*

■ a monkey wrench	**einen Schraubenschlüssel** *EYEN-en SHROWB-en-shlewssel*
■ pliers	**eine Zange** *EYEN-eh TSAHNG-eh*
■ a screwdriver	**einen Schraubenzieher** *EYEN-en SHROWB-en-tsee-uh*
Can you fix the car?	**Können Sie den Wagen reparieren?** *KERN-en zee dayn VAAG-en ray-paa-REER-en*
Do you have the part?	**Haben Sie das Ersatzteil?** *HAAB-en zee dahs ehr-ZAHTS-teyel*
I need _____.	**Ich brauche _____.** *ikh BROWKH-eh*
■ a bulb	**eine Birne** *EYEN-eh BIRN-eh*
■ a filter	**einen Filter** *EYEN-en FILT-uh*
■ a fuse	**eine Sicherung** *EYEN-eh ZIKH-ehr-ung*
I think there's something wrong with _____.	**Ich glaube, es ist irgend etwas mit _____ verkehrt.** *ikh GLOWB-eh, ehs ist EER-gehnt EHT-vahs mit _____ fehr-KAYRT*
■ the directional signals	**den Blinklichtern** *dayn BLINK-likht-ehrn*
■ the electrical system	**der elektrischen Anlage** *dehr eh-LEHK-trish-en AHN-lahg-eh*
■ the fan	**dem Ventilator** *daym ven-ti-LAAT-ohr*
■ the fan belt	**dem Keilriemen** *daym KEYEL-reem-en*
■ the fuel pump	**der Benzinpumpe** *dehr behn-TSEEN-pump-eh*
■ the gear shift	**der Gangschaltung** *dehr GAHNG-shahlt-ung*

■ the headlights	**den Scheinwerfern** *dayn SHEY-EN-vehr-fehrn*
■ the horn	**der Hupe** *der HOOP-eh*
■ the ignition	**der Zündung** *dehr TSEWND-ung*
■ the radio	**dem Radio** *daym RAA-dee-oh*
■ the starter	**dem Anlasser** *daym AHN-lahss-uh*
■ the steering wheel	**dem Steuerrad** *daym SHTOY-uh-raat*
■ the tail light	**dem Schlußlicht** *daym SHLUSS-likht*
■ the transmission	**dem Getriebe** *daym geh-TREEB-eh*
■ the water pump	**der Wasserpumpe** *dehr VAHSS-uh-pump-eh*
■ the windshield (windscreen) wiper	**dem Scheibenwischer** *daym SHEYEB-en-vish-uh*
Can you look at ____?	**Können Sie sich ____ ansehen?** *KERN-en zee zikh ____ AHN-zay-en*
■ the brakes	**die Bremsen** *dee BREHM-zen*
■ the bumper	**die Stoßstange** *dee SHTOHSS-shtahng-eh*
■ the exhaust	**den Auspuff** *daym OWS-puf*
■ the fender	**den Kotflügel** *dayn KOT-flewg-el*
■ the gas tank	**den Benzintank** *dayn behn-TSEEN-tahnk*
■ the hood	**die Kühlerhaube** *dee KEWL-ehr-howb-eh*
■ the trunk	**den Kofferraum** *dayn KOHF-uh-rowm*
Can you repair it temporarily?	**Können Sie es provisorisch reparieren?** *KERN-en zee ehs pro-vi-ZOHR-ish ray-paa-REER-en*

How long will it take?	**Wie lange dauert's?** *vee LAHNG-eh DOW-ehrts*
Couldn't it possibly be done today?	**Geht's vielleicht doch heute noch?** *gayts fee-LEYEKHT dokh HOYT-eh nokh*
Is everything OK now?	**Ist jetzt alles in Ordnung?** *ist yetst in AH-lehs ORT-nung*
How much do I owe you?	**Was schulde ich Ihnen?** *vahs SHULD-eh ikh EEN-en*

GENERAL INFORMATION

TELLING TIME

What time is it?	**Wieviel Uhr ist es?** *VEE-feel oor ist ehs*
■ hour	**Stunde** *SHTUND-eh*
■ minute	**Minute** *mi-NOOT-eh*
■ second	**Sekunde** *zeh-KUN-deh*
■ half an hour	**eine halbe Stunde** *EYEN-eh HAHLB-eh SHTUND-eh*
■ an hour and a half	**anderthalb Stunden** *AHN-dehrt-haalp SHTUND-en*
At what time shall we meet?	**Um wieviel Uhr treffen wir uns?** *um VEE-feel oor TREHF-en veer uns*

Telling time in conversation is done as in English.

| We'll eat at eight (o'clock). | **Wir essen um acht (Uhr).** *veer ESS-en um ahkht (oor)* |

12:20 can be expressed as

twenty after twelve	**zwanzig nach zwölf**	*TSVAHNTS-ikh nahkh tsverlf*
or		
twelve twenty	**zwölf Uhr zwanzig**	*tsverlf oor TSVAHNTS-ikh*

1:30 is either

one-thirty	**ein Uhr dreißig**	*eyen oor DREYSS-ikh*
or		
half an hour (30 minutes) to two	**halb zwei**	*hahlp tsveye*

German usually focuses not on the hour completed but on the hour coming up.

4:30 (half an hour to five)	**halb fünf**	*hahlp fewnf*
7:30 (half an hour to eight)	**halb acht**	*hahlp ahkht*

The easiest way for you to tell the time in German is to state the hour (**ein Uhr, zwei Uhr, drei Uhr,** etc.) and then the minutes (from 1 to 60).

9:37	**neun Uhr siebenunddreißig**	*noyn oor ZEEB-en-unt-dreyess-ikh*

Nach (after) and **vor** (to, before) are not difficult either.

eight to three (2:52)	**acht vor drei**	*ahkht for drey*
five to seven (6:55)	**fünf vor sieben**	*fewnf for ZEEB-en*
nine after four (4:09)	**neun nach vier**	*noyn nahkh feer*
a quarter after three (3:15)	**viertel nach drei**	*FEERT-el nahkh dreye*

Timetables use the 24 hour clock, so that the next hour after 12 noon is 13 (1:00 p.m.). Thus 2:00 p.m. is **vierzehn Uhr**, and so on.

My train leaves at 8:20 p.m.	**Mein Zug fährt um zwanzig Uhr zwanzig.** *meyen tsook fayrt um TSVAHN-tsikh oor TSVAHN-tsikh*

DAYS OF THE WEEK

Today is _____.	**Heute ist _____.**	*HOYT-eh ist*
■ Monday	**Montag**	*MOHN-taak*
■ Tuesday	**Dienstag**	*DEENS-taak*
■ Wednesday	**Mittwoch**	*MIT-vokh*
■ Thursday	**Donnerstag**	*DON-ehrs-taak*
■ Friday	**Freitag**	*FREYE-taak*
■ Saturday	**Samstag/Sonnabend**	*ZAHMS-taak/ ZON-aab-ent*
■ Sunday	**Sonntag**	*ZON-taak*
yesterday	**gestern**	*GEST-ehrn*
the day before yesterday	**vorgestern**	*FOHR-gest-ehrn*
tomorrow	**morgen**	*MORG-en*
the day after tomorrow	**übermorgen**	*EWB-ehr-morg-en*
in the morning (afternoon, evening)	**am Morgen (Nachmittag, Abend)**	*ahm MORG-en (NAHKH-mit-taak, AAB-ent)*
mornings	**morgens**	*MORG-ens*
evenings	**abends**	*AAB-ents*
all day	**den ganzen Tag**	*dayn GAHNTS-en taak*
tonight	**heute abend**	*HOYT-eh AAB-ent*

| this afternoon | **heute nachmit-tag** | *HOYT-eh NAHKH-mit-taak* |
| every day | **jeden Tag** | *YAYD-en taak* |

MONTHS OF THE YEAR

January	**Januar/Jänner** (Austria)	*YAA-noo-aar/YEH-nehr*
February	**Februar**	*FAY-broo-aar*
March	**März**	*mehrts*
April	**April**	*ah-PRIL*
May	**Mai**	*meye*
June	**Juni**	*YOON-ee*
July	**Juli**	*YOOL-ee*
August	**August**	*ow-GUST*
September	**September**	*zep-TEHM-buh*
October	**Oktober**	*ok-TOH-buh*
November	**November**	*no-VEHM-buh*
December	**Dezember**	*deh-TSEHM-buh*
What is today's date?	**Der wievielte ist heute?**	*dehr VEE-feelt-eh ist HOYT-eh*
Today is May 3.	**Heute ist der 3. Mai.**	*HOYT-eh ist dehr DRIT-eh meye*
March 8	**der 8. März**	*dehr AHKHT-eh mehrts*
monthly	**monatlich**	*MOHN-aat-likh*
this month	**in diesem Monat**	*in DEEZ-em MOHN-aat*
next month	**im nächsten Monat**	*im NAYKHST-en MOHN-aat*

last month	**im letzten Monat**	*im LETST-en MOHN-aat*
two months ago	**vor zwei Monaten**	*for tsveye MOHN-aaten*

THE FOUR SEASONS

spring	**der Frühling**	*dehr FREW-ling*
summer	**der Sommer**	*dehr ZOM-uh*
autumn	**der Herbst**	*dehr hehrpst*
winter	**der Winter**	*dehr VINT-uh*
during the spring	**während des Frühlings**	*VEHR-ent dehs FREW-lings*
every summer	**jeden Sommer**	*YAYD-en ZOM-uh*
in the winter	**im Winter**	*im VINT-uh*

THE WEATHER

How is the weather today?	**Wie ist das Wetter heute?** *vee ist dahs VEHT-uh HOYT-eh*
The weather is good (bad).	**Es ist gutes (schlechtes) Wetter.** *ehs ist GOOT-es (SHLEHKHT-es) VEHT-uh*
What splendid (horrible) weather!	**Was für ein herrliches (scheußliches) Wetter!** *vahs fewr eyen HEHR-likh-es (SHOYSS-likh-es) VEHT-uh*
It is _____.	**Es ist _____.** *ehs ist*
■ hot	**heiß** *heyess*

■ warm	**warm** *vaarm*
■ cold	**kalt** *kahlt*
■ cool	**kühl** *kewl*
■ sunny	**sonnig** *ZON-ikh*
■ windy	**windig** *VIND-ikh*
It's raining (snowing).	**Es regnet (schneit).** *ehs RAYG-net (shneyet)*

IMPORTANT SIGNS

Abfahrten	Departures
Achtung	Attention
Angebot	Featured item (in a sale)
Aufzug	Elevator
Ausfahrt	Highway Exit
Ausgang	Exit
Auskunft	Information
Ausverkauf	Clearance sale
Ausverkauft	Sold out
Baden verboten	No swimming
Belegt	Filled Up
Besetzt	Occupied
Betreten des Rasens verboten	Keep off the grass
Damentoilette	Ladies' room
Drücken	Push
Einfahrt	Highway Entrance
Eingang	Entrance
Eintritt frei	No Admission Charge

Frei	Vacant
Für Unbefugte verboten	No Trespassing
Gefahr	Danger
Geöffnet von ___ bis ___	Open from ___ to ___
Geschlossen	Closed
Geschlossene Gesellschaft	Private party
Heiß	Hot
Kalt	Cold
Herrentoilette	Men's room
Kasse	Cashier
Kein Zutritt	No entry
Lebensgefahr	Mortal danger
Lift	Elevator
Nicht berühren	Do not touch
Nichtraucher	Nonsmoking compartment (section)
Notausgang	Emergency exit
Privatstrand	Private beach
Privatweg	Private road
Rauchen verboten	No smoking
Raucher	Smoking compartment
Reserviert	Reserved
Schlußverkauf	Final sale
Unbefugtes Betreten verboten	No trespassing
___ verboten	___ prohibited
Vorsicht	Caution
Vorsicht, Bissiger Hund	Beware of the dog
Ziehen	Pull
Zimmer frei	Room(s) to let
Zu den Bahnsteigen	To the railroad platforms

EMERGENCY TELEPHONE NUMBERS

Police	110 (Germany)
	133 (Austria)
	117 (Switzerland)
Fire	112 (Germany)
	122 (Austria)
	118 (Switzerland)

SOME COMMON ABBREVIATIONS

Abt.	Abteilung	compartment
ACS	Automobil-Club der Schweiz	Automobile Association of Switzerland
ADAC	Allgemeiner Deutscher Automobil Club	General Automobile Association of Germany
Bhf	Bahnhof	railway station
BRD	Bundesrepublik Deutschland	Federal Republic of Germany (West Germany)
BMW	Bayerische Motorenwerke	Bavarian Motor Works
CDU	Christlich-Demokratische Union	Christian Democratic Union
DB	Deutsche Bundesbahn	West German Railways
DBP	Deutsche Bundespost	West German Postal Service
DDR	Deutsche Demokratische Republik	German Democratic Republic (East Germany)
DZT	Deutsche Zentrale für Tourismus	German National Tourist Board
d.h.	das heißt	that is (i.e.)
e.V.	eingetragener Verein	registered association (corporation)

FKK	Freikörperkultur	Free Physical Culture (nudism)
Frl.	Fräulein	Miss
GmbH	Gesellschaft mit beschränkter Haftung	limited-liability corporation
Hr.	Herr	Mr.
JH	Jugendherberge	youth hostel
km	Kilometer	kilometer
KG	Kommanditgesellschaft	limited partnership
LKW	Lastkraftwagen	truck
Mill.	Million	million
ÖAMTC	Österreichischer Automobil- Motorrad- und Touring- Club	Austrian Automobile, Motorcycle, and Touring Association
ÖBB	Österreichische Bundesbahnen	Austrian Federal Railroad
PKW	Personenkraftwagen	passenger car
PTT	Post, Telefon, Telegraph	Postal, Telephone, and Telegraph Office
SBB	Schweizerische Bundesbahnen	Swiss Federal Railways
SPD	Sozialdemokratische Partei Deutschlands	Social Democratic Party of Germany
Str.	Straße	street
TCS	Touring-Club der Schweiz	Swiss Touring Association
usf./usw.	und so fort/und so weiter	et cetera (etc.)
Ztg.	Zeitung	newspaper
z.Z.	zur Zeit	at the present time

ITALIAN

QUICK PRONUNCIATION GUIDE

ITALIAN LETTER(S)	SOUND IN ENGLISH	EXAMPLE
VOWELS		
a	ah (y<u>a</u>cht)	**casa** *(kAH-sah)*, house
è	eh (n<u>e</u>t)	**lèggere** *(lEH-jeh-reh)*, to read
e	ay (h<u>ay</u>)	**mela** *(mAY-lah)*, apple
i	ee (f<u>ee</u>t)	**libri** *(lEE-bree)*, books
o	oh (r<u>o</u>pe)	**boccone** *(boh-kOH-neh)*, mouthful
u	oo (c<u>oo</u>l)	**tutto** *(tOOt-toh)*, everything
CONSONANT SOUNDS		
ci	chee (<u>chee</u>se)	**cinema** *(chEE-nay-mah)*, movies
ce	chay (<u>ch</u>air)	**piacere** *(pee-ah-chAY-reh)*, pleasure
ca	kah (<u>c</u>ot)	**casa** *(kAH-sah)*, house
co	koh (<u>c</u>old)	**cotto** *(kOHt-toh)*, cooked
che	kay (<u>k</u>ent)	**perché** *(pehr-kAY)*, because
chi	key (<u>k</u>ey)	**pochi** *(pOH-key)*, few
gi	jee (<u>j</u>eep)	**giro** *(jEE-roh)*, turn
ge	jay (<u>g</u>eneral)	**generale** *(jay-nay-rAH-leh)*, general
gh	gh (spa<u>gh</u>etti)	**spaghetti** *(spah-ghAYt-tee)*
gli	ll (mi<u>lli</u>on)	**egli** *(AY-ly-ee)*, he **bottiglia** *(boht-tEE-ly-ee-ah)*, bottle
gn	ny (ca<u>ny</u>on)	**magnifico** *(mah-ny-EE-fee-koh)*, magnificent
qu	koo (<u>qu</u>iet)	**àquila** *(AH-koo-ee-lah)*, eagle
sce	sh (fi<u>sh</u>)	**pesce** *(pAY-sheh)*, fish
sci		**sciòpero** *(shee-OH-peh-roh)*, strike
z or zz	ts (ea<u>ts</u>)	**pizza** *(pEE-tsah)*, pizza **zero** *(tsEH-roh)*, zero

THE BASICS FOR GETTING BY

MOST FREQUENTLY USED EXPRESSIONS

The following are expressions you'll use over and over—the fundamentals of polite conversation, the way to express what you want or need, and some simple question tags that you can use to construct all sorts of questions. We suggest you become very familiar with these phrases.

Yes	**Sì**	*see*
No	**No**	*noh*
Maybe	**Forse**	*fOHr-seh*
Please	**Per piacere**	*pEHr pee-ah-chAY-reh*
Thank-you (very much)	**(Mille) grazie**	*(mEEl-leh) grAH-tsee-eh*
You're welcome	**Prego**	*prEh-goh*
Excuse me	**Mi scusi**	*mee skOO-see*
I'm sorry	**Mi dispiace**	*mee dee-spee-AH-cheh*
Just a second	**Un momento**	*OOn-moh-mEHn-toh*
That's all right, okay	**Va bene**	*vah bEH-neh*
It doesn't matter	**Non importa**	*nohn eem-pOHr-tah*
Good morning (afternoon)	**Buon giorno**	*boo-OHn jee-OHr-noh*
Good evening (night)	**Buona sera (notte)**	*boo-Oh-nah sAY-rah (nOHt-teh)*
Sir	**Signore**	*see-ny-OH-reh*
Madame	**Signora**	*see-ny-OH-rah*
Miss	**Signorina**	*see-ny-oh-rEE-nah*
Good-bye	**Arrivederci**	*ahr-ree-veh-dAYr-chee*

254 • THE BASICS FOR GETTING BY

See you later (so long)	**A più tardi (ciao)**	*ah pee-OO tAHr-dee (chee-AH-oh)*
See you tomorrow	**A domani**	*ah doh-mAH-nee*
Do you speak English?	**Parla inglese?**	*pAHr-lah een-glAY-seh*
I don't speak Italian.	**Io non parlo italiano.**	*EE-oh nohn pAHr-loh ee-tah-lee-AH-noh*
I speak a little Italian.	**Parlo poco l'italiano.**	*pAHr-loh pOH-koh lee-tah-lee-AH-noh*
Is there anyone here who speaks English?	**C'è qualcuno qui che parla inglese?**	*chEH koo-ahl-kOO-noh koo-EE kay pAHr-lah een-glAY-seh*
Do you understand?	**Capisce? (ha capito)?**	*kah-pEE-sheh (ah kah-pEE-toh)*
I understand.	**Capisco (ho capito).**	*kah-pEE-skoh (oh kah-pEE-toh*
I don't understand.	**Non capisco (non ho capito).**	*nohn kah-pEE-skoh (nohn oh kah-pEE-toh)*
What does that mean?	**Che cosa significa (quello)?**	*kay kOH-sah see-ny-EE-fee-kah (koo-AYl-loh)*
What? What did you say?	**Che? Che cosa ha detto?**	*kAY kay KOH-sah ah dAYt-toh*
What do you call this (that) in Italian?	**Come si chiama questo (quello) in italiano?**	*kOH-meh see key-AH-mah koo-AYs-toh (koo-AYl-loh) een ee-tah-lee-AH-noh*
Please speak slowly.	**Per piacere parli lentamente.**	*pehr pee-ah-chAY-reh pAHr-lee lehn-tah-mEHn-teh*
Please repeat that.	**Lo ripeta per favore.**	*loh ree-pEH-tah pehr fah-vOH-reh*
I'm American (English) (Australian) (Canadian).	**Sono americano(a) (inglese) (australiano) (canadese).**	*sOH-noh ah-meh-ree-kAH-noh (nah) (een-glAY-seh) (ah-oos-trah-lee-AH-noh) (kah-nah-dAY-seh)*

My name is ____.	**Mi chiamo ____.** *mee kee-AH-moh*
What's your name?	**Lei, scusi, come si chiama?** *lEH-ee, skOO-see, kOH-meh see key-AH-mah*
How are you?	**Come sta?** *kOH-meh stAH*
How's everything?	**Come va?** *kOH-meh vAH*
Very well, thanks. And you?	**Molto bene, grazie. E lei?** *mOHl-toh bEH-neh, grAH-tsee-eh. Ay lEH-ee*
Where is ____?	**Dove si trova ____?** *dOH-veh see trOH-vah*
▪ the bathroom	**un gabinetto (una toilette)** *oon gah-bee-nAYt-toh (oo-nah too-ah-lEHt)*
▪ the dining room (restaurant)	**un ristorante** *oon rees-toh-rAHn-teh*
▪ the entrance	**l'ingresso** *leen-grEHs-soh*
▪ the exit	**l'uscita** *loo-shEE-tah*
▪ the telephone	**un telefono** *oon teh-lEH-phoh-noh*
I'm lost.	**Non so dove mi trovo.** *nohn sOH dOH-veh mee trOH-voh*
We are lost.	**Non sappiamo dove ci troviamo.** *nohn sahp-pee-AH-moh dOH-veh chee troh-vee-AH-moh*
Where are ____?	**Dove sono ____?** *dOH-veh sOH-noh*
I am looking for ____.	**Sto cercando ____.** *stOH chehr-kAHn-doh*
Which way do I go?	**In che direzione devo andare?** *een-kAY dee-reh-tsee-OH-neh dAY-voh ahn-dAH-reh*
▪ to the left	**a sinistra** *ah see-nEE-strah*
▪ to the right	**a destra** *ah dEH-strah*
▪ straight ahead	**sempre diritto** *sehm-preh dee-rEEt-toh*
▪ around the corner	**all'angolo (della via)** *ahl-lAHn-goh-loh (dAYl-lah vEE-ah)*

the first street on the right	**la prima strada a destra** *lah prEE-mah strAH-dah ah dEH-strah*
How much is it?	**Quanto costa?** *koo-AHn-toh kOH-stah*
I'd like ____.	**Vorrei ____.** *vohr-rEH-ee*
Please bring me ____.	**Per piacere mi porti ____.** *pehr pee-ah-chAY-reh mee pOHr-tee*
Please show me (please let me see) ____.	**Per piacere mi mostri (per piacere mi fa vedere) ____.** *pehr pee-ah-chAY-reh mee mOH-stree (mee fah veh-dEH-reh)*
Here it is.	**Eccolo(a).** *EH-koh-loh(ah)*
I'm hungry.	**Ho fame.** *oh fAH-meh*
I'm thirsty.	**Vorrei bere (ho sete).** *vohr-rEH-ee bAY-reh (oh sAY-teh)*
I'm tired.	**Mi sento stanco(a).** *mee sEHn-toh stAHn-koh(ah)*
What's that?	**Che cos'è quello(a)?** *kay ko-sEH koo-AYl-loh (lah)*
What's up?	**(Che) cosa succede?** *(kay) kOH-sah soo-chEH-deh*
I (don't) know.	**(Non) lo so.** *(nohn) loh sOH*

QUESTIONS

Where is ____?	**Dov'è ____?**	*doh-vEH*
When?	**Quando?**	*koo AHn-doh*
How?	**Come?**	*kOH-meh*
How much?	**Quanto?**	*koo-AHn-toh*
Who?	**Chi?**	*key*
Why?	**Perchè?**	*pehr-kAY*
Which?	**Quale?**	*koo-AH-leh*

PROBLEMS, PROBLEMS, PROBLEMS

Watch out! Be careful!	**Attenzione! Stia attento(a)!** *ah-tehn-tsee-OH-neh stEE-ah aht-tEHn-toh(ah)*
Hurry up!	**Si sbrighi!** *see sbrEE-ghee*
Look!	**Guardi!** *goo-AHr-dee*
Wait!	**Aspetti un momento!** *ah-spEHt-tee oon moh-mEHn-toh*
Fire!	**Al fuoco!** *AHl foo-OH-koh*
Leave me alone!	**Mi lasci in pace!** *mee lAH-shee een pAH-cheh*
Help, police!	**Aiuto, polizia!** *ah-ee-OO-toh poh-lee-tsEE-ah*
I'm going to call a cop!	**Adesso chiamo un poliziotto!** *ah-dEHs-soh key-AH-moh oon poh-lee-tsee-OHt-toh*
He has stolen _____.	**Mi ha rubato _____.** *mee ah roo-bAH-toh*
I have lost _____.	**Ho perduto _____.** *OH pehr-dOO-toh*
▪ my car	**la (mia) auto** *lah (mEE-ah) AH-oo-toh*
▪ my passport	**il (mio) passaporto** *eel (mEE-oh) pahs-sah-pOHr-toh*
▪ my purse	**la (mia) borsa** *lah (mEE-ah) bOHr-sah*
▪ my suitcase	**la (mia) valigia** *lah (mEE-ah) vah-lEE-jee-ah*
▪ my wallet	**il (mio) portafoglio** *eel (mEE-oh) pohr-tah-fOH-ly-ee-oh*
▪ my watch	**l'orologio (il mio orologio)** *loh-roh-lOH-jee-oh (eel mEE-oh oh-roh-lOH-jee-oh)*

I want to go ____.	**Voglio andare ____.** *vOH-ly-ee-oh ahn-dAH-reh*
■ to the American (British) (Australian) (Canadian) Consulate.	**al Consolato Americano (Inglese) (Australiano) (Canadese).** *ahl kohn-soh-lAH-toh ah-meh-ree-kAH-noh (een-glAY-seh) (ah-oo-strah-lee-ah-noh) (kah-nah-dAY-seh)*
■ *to the police station	**all'ufficio di polizia (al Commissariato)** *ahl-loof-fEE-chee-oh dee poh-lee-tsEE-ah (ahl kohm-mees-sah-ree-AH-toh)*
I need help, quick!	**Ho bisogno d'aiuto, subito!** *oh bee-sOH-ny-oh dah-ee-OO-toh, sOO-bee-toh*
Can you help me, please?	**Può aiutarmi, per favore?** *poo-OH ah-ee-oo-tAHr-mee pehr fah-vOH-reh*
Does anyone here speak English?	**Qui c'è qualcuno che parla inglese?** *Koo-EE chEH koo-ahl-kOO-noh kay pAHr-lah een-glAY-seh*
I need an interpreter.	**Ho bisogno di un interprete.** *oh bee-sOH-ny-oh dee oon een-TEHR-preh-teh*

*NOTE: In small towns and villages without a local police force, ask to go to **la caserma dei carabinieri**.

NUMBERS

CARDINAL NUMBERS

0	**zero** *tsEH-roh*
1	**uno** *OO-noh*
2	**due** *dOO-eh*
3	**tre** *trEH*
4	**quattro** *koo-AHt-troh*
5	**cinque** *chEEn-koo-eh*
6	**sei** *sEH-ee*

7	**sette** *sEHt-teh*
8	**otto** *OHt-toh*
9	**nove** *nOH-veh*
10	**dieci** *dee-EH-chee*
11	**undici** *OOn-dee-chee*
12	**dodici** *dOH-dee-chee*
13	**tredici** *trEH-dee-chee*
14	**quattordici** *koo-aht-tOHr-dee-chee*
15	**quindici** *koo-EEn-dee-chee*
16	**sedici** *sAY-dee-chee*
17	**diciassette** *dee-chee-ahs-sEHt-teh*
18	**diciotto** *dee-chee-OHt-toh*
19	**diciannove** *dee-chee-ahn-nOH-veh*
20	**venti** *vAYn-tee*
21	**ventuno** *vayn-tOO-noh*
22	**ventidue** *vayn-tee-dOO-eh*
23	**ventitrè** *vayn-tee-trEH*
24	**ventiquattro** *vayn-tee-koo-AHt-troh*
25	**venticinque** *vayn-tee-chEEn-koo-eh*
26	**ventisei** *vayn-tee-sEH-ee*
27	**ventisette** *vayn-tee-sEHt-teh*
28	**ventotto** *vayn-tOHt-toh*
29	**ventinove** *vayn-tee-nOH-veh*
30	**trenta** *trEHn-tah*
40	**quaranta** *koo-ah-rAHn-tah*
50	**cinquanta** *cheen-koo-AHn-tah*
60	**sessanta** *sehs-sAHn-tah*

70	**settanta**	*seht-tAHn-tah*
80	**ottanta**	*oht-tAHn-tah*
90	**novanta**	*noh-vAHn-tah*
100	**cento**	*chEHn-toh*
101	**centouno**	*chEHn-toh OO-noh*
102	**centodue**	*chEHn-toh dOO-eh*
200	**duecento**	*doo-eh-chEHn-toh*
300	**trecento**	*treh-chEHn-toh*
400	**quattrocento**	*koo-aht-troh-chEHn-toh*
500	**cinquecento**	*cheen-koo-eh-chEHn-toh*
600	**seicento**	*seh-ee-chEHn-toh*
700	**settecento**	*seht-teh-chEHn-toh*
800	**ottocento**	*oht-toh-chEHn-toh*
900	**novecento**	*noh-veh-chEHn-toh*
1.000	**mille**	*mEEl-leh*
2.000	**duemila**	*dOO-eh mEE-lah*
1.000.000	**un milione**	*OOn mee-lee-OH-neh*
2.000.000	**due milioni**	*dOO-eh mee-lee-OH-nee*

ORDINAL NUMBERS

first	**primo**	*prEE-moh*
second	**secondo**	*seh-kOHn-doh*
third	**terzo**	*tEHr-tsoh*
fourth	**quarto**	*koo-AHr-toh*
fifth	**quinto**	*koo-EEn-toh*
sixth	**sesto**	*sEHs-toh*
seventh	**settimo**	*sEHt-tee-moh*

eighth	**ottavo**	*oht-tAH-voh*
ninth	**nono**	*nOH-noh*
tenth	**decimo**	*dEH-chee-moh*
the last one	**l'ultimo**	*lOOl-tee-moh*
once	**una volta**	*oo-nah vOHl-tah*
twice	**due volte**	*dOO-eh vOHl-teh*
three times	**tre volte**	*trEH vOHl-teh*

FRACTIONS

half of _____.	**la metà di _____.**	*lah meh-tAH dee*
▪ half of the money	**la metà dei soldi**	*lah meh-tAH day-ee sOHl-dee*
half a _____.	**mezzo**	*mEH-tsoh*
▪ half a kilo	**mezzo chilo**	*mEH-tsoh kEE-loh*
a fourth (quarter)	**un quarto**	*oon koo-AHr-toh*
a dozen	**una dozzina**	*oo-nah doh-tsEE-nah*
▪ a dozen oranges	**una dozzina d'arance**	*oo-nah doh-tsEE-nah dah-rAHn-cheh*
100 grams	**un etto**	*oon EHt-toh*
200 grams	**due etti**	*dOO-eh EHt-tee*
350 grams	**tre etti e mezzo**	*treh EHt-tee ay mEH-tsoh*
a pair (of)	**un paio (di)**	*oon pAH-ee-oh (dee)*
▪ a pair of shoes	**un paio di scarpe**	*oon pAH-ee-oh dee skAHr-peh*

WHEN YOU ARRIVE

PASSPORT AND CUSTOMS

My name is _____.	**Mi chiamo _____.** *mee key-AH-moh*
I'm American (British) (Australian) (Canadian).	**Sono americano(a) (inglese) (australiano-a) (canadese).** *sOH-noh ah-meh-ree-kAH-noh(ah) (een-glAY-seh) (ah-oo-strah-lee-AH-noh-ah) (kah-nah-dAY-seh)*
My address is _____.	**Il mio indirizzo è _____.** *eel mEE-oh een-dee-rEE-tsoh EH*
I'm staying at _____.	**Starò a _____.** *stah-rOH ah*
Here is (are) _____.	**Ecco _____.** *EHk-oh*
my documents	**i (miei) documenti)** *ee (mee-EH-ee) doh-koo-mEHn-tee*
my passport	**il (mio) passaporto** *eel (mEE-oh) pahs-sah-pOHr-toh*
my I.D. card	**la (mia) carta d'identità** *lah (mEE-ah) kAHr-tah dee-dehn-tee-tAH*
I'm _____.	**Sono _____.** *sOH-noh*
on a business trip	**in viaggio d'affari** *een vee-AH-jee-oh dahf-fAH-ree*
on vacation	**in vacanza** *een vah-kAHn-tsah*
visiting relatives (friends)	**venuto(a) a trovare i parenti (gli amici)** *sOH-noh vay-nOO-toh(ah) ah troh-vAH-reh ee pah-rEHn-tee (ly-ee ah-mEE-chee)*
just passing through	**solo di passaggio** *sOH-loh dee pahs-sAH-jee-oh*
I'll be staying here for _____.	**Resterò qui _____.** *ray-steh-rOH koo-EE pehr*

▪ a few days	**alcuni giorni** *ahl-kOO-nee jee-OHr-nee*
▪ a few weeks	**alcune settimane** *ahl-kOO-neh seht-tee-mAH-neh*
▪ a week	**una settimana** *oo-nah seht-tee-mAH-nah*
▪ a month	**un mese** *oon mAY-seh*
I'm traveling ____.	**Sto viaggiando.** *stOH vee-ah-jee-AHn-doh*
▪ alone	**da solo(a)** *dah sOH-loh(ah)*
▪ with my husband	**con mio marito** *kOHn mEE-oh mah-rEE-toh*
▪ with my wife	**con mia moglie** *kOHn mEE-ah mOH-ly-ee-eh*
▪ with my family	**con la mia famiglia** *kOHn lah mEE-ah fah-mEE-ly-ee-ah*
▪ with my friend	**con il mio amico (la mia amica)** *kOHn eel mEE-oh ah-mEE-koh (lah mEE-ah ah-mEE-kah)*
These are my bags.	**Queste sono le mie valigie.** *koo-AYs-teh sOH-noh leh mEE-eh vah-lEE-jee-eh*
I have nothing to declare.	**Non ho nulla da dichiarare.** *nohn oh nOOl-lah dah dee-key-ah-rAH-reh*
I only have ____.	**Ho solo ____.** *oh sOH-loh*
▪ a carton of cigarettes	**una stecca di sigarette** *oo-nah stAYk-kah dee see-gah-rAYt-teh*
▪ a bottle of whisky	**una bottiglia di whisky** *oo-nah boht-tEE-ly-ee-ah dee oo-EE-skey*
They're gifts.	**Sono regali.** *sOH-noh reh-gAH-lee*

They're for my personal use.	**Sono cose di uso personale.** *sOH-noh kOH-seh dee OO-soh pehr-soh-nAH-leh*
Do I have to pay duty?	**Devo pagare dogana?** *dAY-voh pah-gAH-reh doh-gAH-nah*
May I close the bag now?	**Posso chiudere la valigia adesso?** *pOHs-soh key-OO-deh-reh lah vah-lEE-jee-ah ah-dEHs-soh*

BAGGAGE AND PORTERS

Where can I find a baggage cart?	**Dove posso trovare un carrello portabagagli?** *dOH-veh pOHs-soh troh-vAH-reh oon kahr-rEHl-loh (pohr-tah-bah-gAH-ly-ee)*
I need a porter.	**Ho bisogno di un portabagagli.** *oh bee-sOH-ny-oh dee oon pohr-tah-bah-gAH-ly-ee*
Porter!	**Portabagagli!** *pohr-tah-bah-gAH-ly-ee*
These are our (my) bags.	**Queste sono le nostre (mie) valigie.** *koo-AYs-teh sOH-noh leh nOH-streh (mEE-eh) vah-lEE-jee-eh*
That big (little) one.	**Quella grande (piccola).** *koo-AYl-lah grAHn-deh (pEEk-koh-lah)*
These two black (green) ones.	**Queste due nere (verdi).** *koo-AYs-teh dOO-eh nAY-reh (vAYr-dee)*
Put them here (there).	**Le metta qui (lì).** *leh mAYt-tah koo-EE (lEE)*
Be careful with that one!	**Stia attento a quella lì!** *stEE-ah aht-tEHn-toh ah koo-AYl-lah lEE*
I'll carry this one myself.	**Questa la porto io.** *koo-AYs-tah lah pOHr-toh ee-oh*
I'm missing a suitcase.	**Mi manca una valigia.** *mee mAHn-cah oo-nah vah-lEE-jee-ah*

How much do I owe you?	**Quanto le devo?** *koo-AHn-toh leh dAY-voh*
Thank-you (very much). This is for you.	**(Molte) grazie. Questo è per Lei.** *(mOHl-teh) grAH-tsee-eh Koo-AYs-toh EH pehr lEH-ee*
Where can I get a bus (taxi) to the city?	**Dove posso prendere l'autobus (il tassì) per andare in città?** *dOH-veh pOHs-soh prAYn-deh-reh lAH-oo-toh-boos (eel tahs-sEE) pehr ahn-dAH-reh een cheet-tAH*

MONEY MATTERS

EXCHANGING MONEY

Where is the currency exchange (bank)?	**Dov'è l'ufficio di cambio (la banca)?** *doh-vEH loof-fEE-chee-oh dee kAHm-bee-oh (lah bAHn-kah)*
I wish to change ____.	**Desidero cambiare ____.** *day-sEE-deh-roh kahm-bee-AH-reh*
▪ money	**il denaro** *eel deh-nAH-roh*
▪ dollars (pounds)	**i dollari (le sterline)** *ee-dOHl-lah-ree (le stehr-lEE-neh)*
▪ traveler's checks	**traveler's checks (assegni da viaggiatori)** *(ahs-sEH-ny dah vee-ah jee-ah tOH-ree)*
May I cash a personal check?	**Posso cambiare un assegno personale?** *pOHs-soh kahm-bee-AH-reh oon ahs-sEH-ny-ee-oh pehr-soh-nAH-leh*
What time do they open (close)?	**A che ora aprono (chiudono)?** *ah kay OH-rah AH-proh-noh (key-OO-doh-noh)*
Where is the cashier's window?	**Dov'è lo sportello del cassiere?** *doh-vEH loh spohr-tEHl-loh dayl kahs-see-AY-reh*

What's the current exchange rate for dollars (pounds)?	**Qual è il cambio corrente del dollaro (della sterlina)?** *koo-ahl-EH eel kAHm-bee-oh kohr-rEHn-teh dayl dOHl-lah-roh (dAYl-lah stehr-lEE-nah)*
What commission do you charge?	**Quale percentuale vi fate pagare?** *koo-AH-leh pehr-chehn-too-AH-leh vee fAH-teh pah-gAH-reh*
Where do I sign?	**Dove debbo firmare?** *dOH-veh dAYb-boh feer-mAH-reh*
I'd like the money _____.	**Vorrei i soldi _____.** *vohr-rEH-ee ee sOHl-dee*
▪ in large (small) bills	**in grosse (piccole) banconote** *een grOHs-seh (pEEk-oh-leh) bahn-koh-nOH-teh*
▪ in small change	**in spiccioli** *een spee-chee-oh-lee*
Give me two twenty (thousand)-lire bills.	**Mi dia due biglietti da ventimila lire.** *mee dEE-ah dOO-eh bee-ly-ee-AYt-tee dah vayn-tee mEE-lah lEE-reh*
▪ fifty thousand lire	**cinquanta mila lire** *cheen-koo-AHn-tah mEE-lah lEE-reh*
▪ one hundred thousand lire	**centomila lire** *chehn-toh-mEE-lah lEE-reh*
Do you accept credit cards?	**Si accettano carte di credito?** *see ah-chEHt-tah-noh kAHr-teh dee-krEH-dee-toh*

AT THE HOTEL

I'd like a single (double) room for tonight.	**Vorrei una camera singola (doppia) per stanotte.** *vohr-rEH-ee oo-nah kAH-meh-rah sEEn-goh-lah (dOHp-pee-ah) pehr stah-nOHt-teh*
How much is the room _____?	**Quant'è la camera _____?** *koo-ahn-tEH lah kAH-meh-rah*

with a shower	**con doccia** *kohn dOH-chee-ah*
with a private bath	**con bagno proprio (privato)** *kohn bAH-ny-oh prOH-pree-oh (pree-vAH-toh)*
with a balcony	**con terrazzino** *kohn tehr-rah-tsEE-noh*
facing the sea	**che dia sul mare** *kay dEE-ah sool mAH-reh*
facing (away from) the street	**che (non) dia sulla strada** *kay (nohn) dEE-ah sOOl-lah strAH-dah*
facing the court-yard	**che dia sul cortile** *kay dEE-ah sOOl kohr-tEE-leh*
Does it have ____?	**Ha ____?** *AH*
air-conditioning	**l'aria condizionata** *lAH-ree-ah kohn-dee-tsee-oh-nAH-tah*
hot water	**l'acqua calda** *lAH-koo-ah kAHl-dah*
television	**la televisione** *lah teh-leh-vee-see-OH-neh*
I (don't) have a reservation.	**(Non) ho prenotazione.** *(nohn) OH preh-noh-tah-tsee-OH-neh*
Could you call another hotel to see if they have something?	**Potrebbe telefonare a un altro hotel per vedere se hanno qualcosa?** *poh-trAYb-beh teh-leh-foh-nAH-reh ah oon AHl-troh oh-tEHl pehr vay-dAY-reh say AHn-noh koo-ahl-kOH-sah*
May I see the room?	**Potrei vedere la camera?** *poh-trEH-ee veh-dAY-reh lah kAH-meh-rah*
I (don't) like it.	**(Non) mi piace.** *(nohn) mee pee-AH-cheh*
Do you have something ____?	**Ha qualche cosa ____?** *ah koo-AHl-keh kOH-sah*
better	**di meglio** *dee mEH-ly-ee-oh*

■ larger	**più grande**	*pee-OO grAHn-deh*
■ smaller	**più piccolo**	*pee-OO pEEk-koh-loh*
■ cheaper	**meno costoso**	*mAY-noh koh-stOH-soh*
■ quieter	**più quieto (tranquillo)**	*pee-OO quee-EH-toh (trahn-hoo-EEl-loh)*

What floor is it on? **A che piano è?** *ah kay pee-AH-noh EH*

Is there an elevator (lift)? **C'è l'ascensore?** *chEH lah-shehn-sOH-reh*

How much is the room _____? **Quanto si paga per una camera _____?** *koo-AHn-toh see pAH-gah pehr OO-nah kAH-meh-rah*

■ with the American plan (three meals a day) **con pensione completa** *kohn pehn-see-OH-neh kohm-plEH-tah*

■ with breakfast **con colazione** *kohn koh-lah-tsee-OH-neh*

■ with no meals **senza i pasti** *sEHn-tsah ee pAH-stee*

Is everything included? **È tutto compreso?** *EH tOOt-toh kohm-prAY-soh*

The room is very nice. I'll take it. **La camera è molto bella. La prendo.** *lah kAH-meh-rah EH mOHl-toh bEHl-lah lah prAYn-doh*

We'll be staying _____. **Resteremo _____.** *rehs-teh-rAY-moh*

■ one night **una notte** *OO-nah nOHt-teh*

■ a few nights **alcune notti** *ahl-kOO-neh nOHt-tee*

■ one week **una settimana** *OO-nah sayt-tee-mAH-nah*

How much do you charge for children? **Quanto fanno pagare per i bambini?** *koo-AHn-toh fAHn-noh pah-gAH-reh pehr ee bahm-bEE-nee*

Could you put another bed in the room?	**Si potrebbe avere un altro letto nella camera?** *see poh-trAYb-beh ah-vAY-reh oon-AHl-troh lEHt-toh nAYl-lah kAH-meh-rah*
Is there a charge? How much?	**C'è da pagare? Quanto?** *chEH dah pah-gAH-reh koo-AHn-toh*

OTHER ACCOMMODATIONS

I'm looking for ____.	**Sto cercando ____.** *stOH chehr-kAHn-doh*
■ a boardinghouse	**una pensione** *oo-nah pehn-see-OH-neh*
■ a private house	**una casa privata (un villino)** *oo-nah kAH-sah pree-vAH-tah (oon veel-lEE-noh)*
I want to rent an apartment.	**Voglio affittare un appartamento.** *vOH-ly-ee-oh ahf-feet-tAH-reh oon ahp-pahr-tah-mEHn-toh*
I need a living room, bedroom, and kitchen.	**Ho bisogno di salotto, camera da letto, e cucina.** *oh bee-sOH-ny-oh dee sah-lOHt-toh, kAH-meh-rah dah lEHt-toh, ay koo-chEE-nah*
Do you have a furnished room?	**Ha una camera ammobiliata?** *AH oo-nah kAH-meh-rah ahm-moh-bee-lee-AH-tah*
How much is the rent?	**Quant'è d'affitto?** *koo-ahn-tEH dahf-fEEt-toh*
I'll be staying here for ____.	**Resterò qui ____.** *rehs-teh-rOH koo-EE*
■ two weeks	**due settimane** *dOO-eh seht-tee-mAH-neh*
■ one month	**un mese** *oon mAY-seh*
■ the whole summer	**tutta l'estate** *tOOt-tah leh-stAH-teh*
I want a place ____.	**Voglio abitare ____.** *vOH-ly-ee-oh ah-bee-tAH-reh*

■ that's centrally located	**al centro** *ahl chAYn-troh*
■ near public transportation	**vicino ai servizi di trasporti pubblici** *vee-chEE-noh AH-ee sayr-vEE-tsee dee trah-spOHr-tee pOOb-blee-chee*
Is there a youth hostel around here?	**C'è un ostello per la gioventù qui vicino?** *chEH oon oh-stAYl-loh pehr lah jee-oh-vehn-tOO koo-EE vee-chEE-noh*

ORDERING BREAKFAST

We'll have breakfast in the room.	**Faremo colazione in camera.** *fah-rAY-moh koh-lah-tsee-OH-neh een kAH-meh-rah*
Please send up _____.	**Per favore mandino _____.** *pehr fah-vOH-reh mAHn-dee-noh*
■ one (two) coffee(s)	**un (due) caffè** *oon (dOO-ee) kahf-fEH*
■ tea	**un tè** *oon tEH*
■ hot chocolate	**una cioccolata calda** *OO-nah chee-oh-koh-lAH-tah kAHl-dah*
■ a sweet roll (brioche)	**un berlingozzo (brioche)** *oon behr-leen-gOH-tsoh (brEE-osh)*
■ fruit (juice)	**un (succo di) frutta** *oon (sOO-koh-dee) frOOt-tah*
I'll eat breakfast downstairs.	**Mangerò la colazione giù.** *mahn-jeh-rOH lah koh-lah-tsee-OH-neh jee-OO*
We'd both like _____.	**Noi due desideriamo _____.** *nOH-ee dOO-eh deh-see-deh-ree-AH-moh*
■ bacon and eggs	**uova al tegamino con pancetta** *oo-OH-vah ahl teh-gah-mEE-noh kohn pahn-chAYt-tah*

■ scrambled (fried, boiled) eggs **uova al tegamino strapazzate (fritte, alla coque)** *oo-OH-vah ahl teh-gah-mEE-noh strah-pah-tsAH-teh (frEEt-teh) (ahl-lah kOHk)*

■ toast **pan tostato** *pAHn toh-stAH-toh*

■ jam (marmalade) **marmellata** *mahr-mehl-lAH-tah*

HOTEL SERVICES

Where is ____? **Dov'è ____?** *doh-vEH*

■ the dining room **la sala da pranzo** *lah sAH-lah dah prAHn-tsoh*

■ the bathroom **il bagno? (la toilette)** *eel bAH-ny-oh (lah too-ah-lEHt)*

■ the elevator (lift) **l'ascensore** *lah-shehn-sOH-reh*

■ the phone **il telefono** *eel teh-lEH-foh-noh*

What is my room number? **Qual è il numero della mia camera?** *koo-ah-lEH eel nOO-meh-roh dAYl-lah mEE-ah kAH-meh-rah*

May I please have my key? **Può darmi la chiave, per favore?** *poo-OH dAHr-mee lah key-AH-veh pehr fah-vOH-reh*

I've lost my key. **Ho perduto la chiave.** *oh pehr-dOO-toh lah key-AH-veh*

I need ____. **Ho bisogno di ____.** *oh bee-sOH-ny-oh dee*

■ a bellhop **un fattorino** *oon faht-toh-rEE-noh*

■ a chambermaid **una cameriera** *oo-nah kah-meh-ree-EH-rah*

Please send ____ to my room. **Per piacere mi mandi ____ in camera.** *pehr pee-ah-chAY-reh mee mAHn-dee ____ een kAH-meh-rah*

a towel	**un asciugamano** *oon ah-shoo-gah-mAH-noh*
a bar of soap	**una saponetta** *oo-nah sah-poh-nAYt-tah*
some hangers	**delle grucce (degli attaccapanni)** *dAYl-lay grOO-cheh (dAY-ly-ee aht-AHk-kah-pAHn-nee)*
a pillow	**un cuscino** *oon koo-shEE-noh*
a blanket	**una coperta** *oo-nah koh-pEHr-tah*
some ice cubes	**dei cubetti di ghiaccio** *day-ee koo-bAYt-tee dee ghee-AH-chee-oh*
some ice water	**dell'acqua ghiacciata** *dayl-lAH-koo-ah ghee-ah-chee-AH-tah*
a bottle of mineral water	**una bottiglia d'acqua minerale** *OO-nah boht-tEE-ly-ee-ah dAH-koo-ah mee-neh-rAH-leh*
an ashtray	**un portacenere** *oon pohr-tah-chAY-nay-reh*
toilet paper	**della carta igienica** *dayl-lah kAHr-tah ee-jee-EH-nee-kah*
a reading lamp	**una lampada per la lettura** *OO-nah lAHm-pah-dah pehr lah leht-tOO-rah*
an electric adaptor	**un trasformatore elettrico** *oon trahs-fohr-mah-tOH-reh ay-lEHt-tree-koh*
Who is (was) it?	**Chi è (era)?** *key-EH (EH-rah)*
Just a minute.	**Un momento.** *oon moh-mEHn-toh*
Come in.	**Entri (venga).** *AYn-tree (vEHn-gah)*
Put it on the table.	**Lo metta sul tavolo.** *loh mAYt-tah sool tAH-voh-loh*
Please wake me tomorrow at ____.	**Per favore mi svegli domani alle ____.** *pehr fah-vOH-reh mee svAY-ly-ee doh-mAH-nee AHl-leh*

COMPLAINTS

There is no ___.	**Manca ___.** *mAHn-kah*
▪ running water	**l'acqua corrente** *lAH-koo-ah kohr-rEHn-teh*
▪ hot water	**l'acqua calda** *lAH-koo-ah kAHl-dah*
▪ electricity	**la luce elettrica** *lah lOO-cheh eh-lEHt-tree-kah*
The ___ doesn't work.	**___ non funziona.** *nohn foon-tsee-OH-nah*
▪ air-conditioning	**l'aria condizionata** *lAH-ree-ah kohn-dee-tsee-oh-nAH-tah*
▪ fan	**il ventilatore** *eel vehn-tee-lah-tOH-reh*
▪ faucet	**il rubinetto** *eel roo-bee-nAYt-toh*
▪ light	**la luce** *lah lOO-cheh*
▪ radio	**la radio** *lah rAH-dee-oh*
▪ electric socket	**la presa della corrente** *lah prAY-sa dehl-lah kohr-rEHn-teh*
▪ light switch	**l'interruttore** *leen-tehr-root-tOH-reh*
▪ television	**la televisione** *lah teh-leh-vee-see-OH-neh*
Can you fix it?	**Può farlo(la) riparare?** *poo-OH fAHr-loh(ah) ree-pah-rAH-reh*
The room is dirty.	**La camera è sporca.** *lah kAH-meh-rah EH spOHr-kah*
Can you clean it ___?	**Può farla pulire ___?** *poo-OH fAHr-lah poo-lEE-reh*
▪ now	**subito** *sOO-bee-toh*
▪ as soon as possible	**il più presto possibile** *eel pee-OO prEH-stoh pohs-sEE-bee-leh*

AT THE DESK

Are there (any) ____ for me?	**Ci sono ____ per me?** *chee sOH-noh ____ payr mAY*
■ letters	**(delle) lettere** *(dAYl-leh) lAYt-teh-reh*
■ messages	**(dei) messaggi** *(day-ee) mehs-sAH-jee*
■ packages	**(dei) pacchi** *(day-ee) pAH-key*
■ postcards	**(delle) cartoline postali** *(dAYl-leh) kahr-toh-lEE-neh poh-stAH-lee*
Did anyone call for me?	**Mi ha cercato qualcuno?** *mee-AH chehr-kAH-toh koo-ahl-kOO-noh*
I'd like to leave this in your safe.	**Vorrei lasciare questo nella sua cassaforte.** *vohr-rEH-ee lah-shee-AH-reh koo-AYs-toh nAYl-lah sOO-ah kahs-sah-fOHr-teh*
Will you make this call for me?	**Può farmi questa telefonata?** *poo-OH fAHr-mee koo-AYs-tah teh-leh-foh-nAH-tah*

CHECKING OUT

I'd like the bill, please.	**Vorrei il conto per favore.** *vohr-rEH-ee eel kOHn-toh pehr fah-vOH-reh*
I'll be checking out today (tomorrow).	**Pagherò e partirò oggi (domani).** *pah-gheh-rOH ay pahr-tee-rOH OH-jee (doh-mAH-nee)*
Please send someone up for our baggage.	**Per favore mandi qualcuno a prendere le valigie.** *pehr fah-vOH-reh mAHn-dee koo-ahl-kOO-noh ah prAYn-deh-reh leh vah-lEE-jee-eh*

GETTING AROUND TOWN

THE SUBWAY (UNDERGROUND)

Is there a subway (underground) in this city?	**C'è una metropolitana in questa città?** *chEH oo-na meh-troh-poh-lee-tAH-nah een koo-AYs-tah cheet-tAH*
Do you have a map showing the stops?	**Ha una cartina che indica le fermate della metropolitana?** *ah oo-nah kahr-tEE-nah kay EEn-dee-kah lay fayr-mAH-teh dAYl-lah meh-troh-poh-lee-tAH-nah*
Where is the closest subway (underground) station?	**Dov'è la stazione più vicina della metropolitana?** *doh-vEH lah stah-tsee-OH-neh pee-OO vee-chEE-nah dAYl-lah meh-troh-poh-lee-tAH-nah*
How much is the fare?	**Quanto costa il biglietto?** *koo-AHn-toh kOHs-tah eel bee-ly-ee-AYt-toh*
Where can I buy a token (a ticket)?	**Dove posso comprare un gettone (un biglietto)?** *dOH-veh pOHs-soh kohm-prAH-reh oon jee-eht-tOH-neh (oon bee-ly-ee-AYt-toh)*
Which is the train that goes to _____?	**Qual è il treno che va a _____?** *koo-ah-lEH eel trEH-noh keh vah ah*
Does this train go to _____?	**Questo treno va a _____?** *koo-AYs-toh trEH-noh vAH ah*
How many more stops?	**Quante fermate ancora?** *koo-AHn-teh fehr-mAH-teh ahn-kOH-rah*
What's the next station?	**Qual è la prossima stazione?** *koo-ah-lEH lah prOHs-see-mah stah-tsee-OH-neh*
Where should I get off?	**Dove dovrei scendere?** *dOH-vay doh-vrEH-ee shAYn-deh-reh*

Do I have to change trains?	**Devo cambiare treno?** *dAY-voh kahm-bee-AH-reh trEH-noh*
Please tell me when we get there.	**Può farmi sapere quando siamo arrivati(e).** *poo-OH fAHr-mee sah-pAY-reh koo-AHn-doh see-AH-moh ahr-rEE-vah-tee(eh)*

THE BUS (STREETCAR, TRAM)

Where is the bus stop (bus terminal)?	**Dov'è la fermata dell'autobus (il capolinea)?** *doh-vEH lah fehr-mAH-tah dayl-lAH-oo-toh-boos (eel kah-poh-lEE-neh-ah)*
Which bus (trolley) do I take to get to _____?	**Quale autobus (tram) devo prendere per andare a _____?** *koo-AH-leh AH-oo-toh-boos (trAH-m) dAY-voh prAYn-deh-reh pehr ahn-dAH-reh ah*
In which direction do I have to go?	**In quale direzione devo andare?** *een koo-AH-leh dee-reh-tsee-OH-neh dAY-voh ahn-dAH-reh*
How often do the buses run?	**Ogni quanto tempo passano gli autobus?** *OH-ny-ee koo-AHn-toh tEHm-poh pAHs-sah-noh ly-ee AH-oo-toh-boos*
Do you go to _____?	**Va a _____?** *vAH ah*
I want to go to _____.	**Voglio andare a _____.** *vOH-ly-ee-oh ahn-dAH-reh ah*
Is it far from here?	**È lontano da qui?** *EH lohn-tAH-noh dah koo-EE*
How many stops are there?	**Quante fermate ci sono?** *koo-AHn-teh fehr-mAH-teh chee sOH-noh*
Do I have to change buses?	**Devo cambiare autobus?** *dAY-voh kahm-bee-AH-reh AH-oo-toh-boos*
How much is the fare?	**Quanto costa il biglietto?** *koo-AHn-toh kOH-stah eel bee-ly-ee-AYt-toh*

Where do I get off?	**Dove devo scendere?** *dOH-vay dAY-voh shAYn-deh-reh*
Please tell me where to get off.	**Può dirmi dove devo scendere?** *poo-OH dEEr-mee dOH-veh dAY-voh shAYn-deh-reh*

TAXIS

Is there a taxi stand near here?	**C'è un posteggio dei taxi qui vicino?** *chEH oon poh-stAY-jee-oh dAY-ee tahs-sEE koo-EE vee-chEE-noh*
Please get me a taxi.	**Per favore mi chiami un taxi.** *pehr fah-vOH-reh mee key-AH-mee oon tahs-sEE*
Taxi! Are you free?	**Taxi! È libero?** *tahs-sEE EH lEE-beh-roh*
Take me (I want to go) _____.	**Mi porti (voglio andare) _____.** *mee pOHr-tee (vOH-ly-ee-oh ahn-dAH-reh)*
▪ to the airport	**all'aeroporto** *ahl-lah-eh-roh-pOHr-toh*
▪ to this address	**a questo indirizzo** *ah koo-AYs-toh een-dee-rEE-tsoh*
▪ to the station	**alla stazione** *AHl-lah stah-tsee-OH-neh*
▪ to _____ Street	**in via _____** *een vEE-ah*
Do you know where it is?	**Sa dove si trova?** *sah dOH-veh see trOH-vah*
How much is it to _____?	**Qual è la tariffa per _____?** *koo-ah-lEH lah tah-rEEf-fah pehr*
Faster! I'm in a hurry.	**Più presto (veloce)! Ho fretta.** *pee-OO prEH-stoh (veh-lOH-cheh) oh frAYt-tah*
Please drive slower.	**Per cortesia guidi più piano.** *pehr kohr-tay-sEE-ah goo-EE-dee pee-OO pee-AH-noh*

Stop here at the corner.	**Si fermi qui all'angolo.** *see fAYr-mee koo-EE ahl-lAHn-goh-loh*
Stop at the next block.	**Si fermi alla prossima via.** *see fAYr-mee AHl-lah prOHs-see-mah vEE-ah*
Wait for me. I'll be right back.	**Mi aspetti. Torno subito.** *mee ah-spEHt-tee tOHr-noh sOO-bee-toh*
I think you are going the wrong way.	**Penso che lei stia andando nella direzione sbagliata.** *pEHn-soh kay lEH-ee stEE-ah ahn-dAHn-doh nAYl-lah dee-reh-tsee-OH-neh sbah-ly-ee-AH-tah*
How much do I owe you?	**Quanto le devo?** *koo-AHn-toh leh dAY-voh*
This is for you.	**Questo è per lei.** *koo-AYs-toh EH pehr lEH-ee*

SIGHTSEEING AND TOURS

Where is the Tourist Information Office?	**Dov'è l'Ente Locale (Nazionale) per il Turismo?** *doh-vEH lEHn-teh loh-kAH-leh (nah-tsee-oh-nAH-leh) pehr eel too-rEEs-moh*
Where can I buy an English guidebook?	**Dove posso comprare una guida turistica in inglese?** *dOH-veh pOHs-soh kohm-prAH-reh OO-nah goo-EE-dah too-rEEs-tee-kah een een-glAY-seh*
I need an English-speaking guide.	**Ho bisogno di una guida che parli inglese.** *oh bee-sOH-ny-oh dee oo-nah goo-EE-dah kay pAHr-lee een-glAY-seh*
How much does he charge ____?	**Quanto si fa pagare ____?** *koo-AHn-toh see fah pah-gAH-reh*
▪ per hour	**all'ora** *ahl-lOH-rah*

■ per day	**al giorno** *ahl jee-OHr-noh*
When does the tour begin?	**Quando inizia il tour (la gita)?** *koo-AHn-doh ee-nEE-tsee-ah eel tOOr (lah jEE-tah)*
How long is the tour?	**Quanto dura il tour (la gita)?** *koo-AHn-toh dOO-rah eel tOOr (lah jEE-tah)*
There are two (four, six) of us.	**Siamo in due (quattro, sei).** *see-AH-moh een-dOO-eh (koo-AHt-troh, sEH-ee)*
What are the main attractions?	**Quali sono le principali attrazioni?** *koo-AH-lee sOH-noh leh preen-cee-pAH-lee aht-trah-tsee-OH-nee*
We are here for one (two) day(s) only.	**Saremo qui un giorno (due giorni) soltanto.** *sah-rAY-moh koo-EE oon gee-OHr-noh (dOO-eh jee-OHr-nee) sohl-tAHn-toh*
Are there trips through the city?	**Si fanno (dei tour) delle gite turistiche della città?** *see fAHn-noh (day tOOr) dAYl-leh jEE-teh too-rEE-stee-keh dAYl-lah cheet-tAH*
Where do they leave from?	**Da dove iniziano i tour (le gite)?** *dah dOH-veh ee-nEE-tsee-ah-noh ee tOOr (leh jEE-teh)*
We want to see _____.	**Vogliamo vedere _____.** *voh-ly-ee-AH-moh vay-dAY-reh*
■ the botanical garden	**il giardino botanico** *eel jee-ahr-dEE-noh boh-tAH-nee-koh*
■ the business center	**il centro commerciale** *eel chAYn-troh kohm-mehr-chee-AH-leh*
■ the castle	**il castello** *eel kahs-tEHl-loh*
■ the cathedral	**la cattedrale** *lah kaht-teh-drAH-leh*
■ the church	**la chiesa** *lah key-EH-sah*
■ the concert hall	**la sala dei concerti** *lah sAH-lah dAY-ee kohn-chEHr-tee*

■ the downtown area	**la zona del centro**	*lah tsOH-nah dayl chAYn-troh*
■ the fountains	**le fontane**	*leh fohn-tAH-neh*
■ the library	**la biblioteca**	*lah bee-blee-oh-tEH-kah*
■ the main park	**il parco principale**	*eel pAHr-koh preen-chee-pAH-leh*
■ the main square	**la piazza principale**	*lah pee-AH-tsah preen-chee-pAH-leh*
■ the market	**il mercato**	*eel mehr-kAH-toh*
■ the mosque	**la moschea**	*lah moh-skEH-ah*
■ the museum (of fine arts)	**il museo (delle belle arti)**	*eel moo-sEH-oh (dAYl-leh bEHl-leh AHr-tee)*
■ a nightclub	**un night (locale notturno)**	*oon nAH-eet (loh-kAH-leh noht-tOOr-noh)*
■ the old part of town	**la parte vecchia della città**	*lah pAHr-teh vEHk-key-ah dAYl-la cheet-tAH*
■ the opera	**il teatro dell'opera**	*eel teh-AH-troh dayl-lOH-peh-rah*
■ the palace	**il palazzo**	*eel pah-lAH-tsoh*
■ the stadium	**lo stadio**	*loh stAH-dee-oh*
■ the synagogue	**la sinagoga**	*lah see-nah-gOH-gah*
■ the university	**l'università**	*loo-nee-vehr-see-tAH*
■ the zoo	**il giardino zoologico (lo zoo)**	*eel jee-ahr-dEE-no tsoh-oh-lOH-jee-koh (loh tsOH-oh)*
Is it all right to go in now?	**Si può entrare adesso?**	*see poo-OH ehn-trAH-reh ah-dEHs-soh*
Is it open (closed)?	**È aperto (chiuso)?**	*EH ah-pEHr-toh (key-OO-soh)*

At what time does it open (close)?	**A che ora aprono (chiudono)?** *ah kay OH-rah AH-proh-noh (key-OO-doh-noh)*
What's the admission price?	**Quant'è l'entrata?** *koo-ahn-tEH lehn-trAH-tah*
How much do children pay?	**Quanto pagano i bambini?** *koo-AHn-toh pAH-gah-noh ee bahm-bEE-nee*
Can they go in free? Until what age?	**Possono entrare gratis? Fino a quale età?** *pOHs-soh-noh ehn-trAH-reh grAH-tees fEE-noh ah koo-AH-leh eh-tAH*
Is it all right to take pictures?	**Si possono fare fotografie?** *see pOHs-soh-noh fAH-reh foh-toh-grah-fEE-eh*
How much extra does it cost to take pictures?	**Quanto costa in più per fare delle fotografie?** *koo-AHn-toh kOHs-tah een pee-OO pehr fAH-reh dAYl-leh foh-toh-grah-fEE-eh*
I do (not) use a flash attachment.	**Io (non) uso il flash.** *EE-oh (nohn) OO-soh eel flEH-sh*

PLANNING A TRIP

AIR SERVICES

When is there a flight to _____?	**Quando c'è un volo per _____?** *koo-AHn-doh chEH oon vOH-loh pehr*
I would like _____.	**Vorrei _____.** *vohr-rEH-ee*
▪ a round-trip (one-way) ticket_____.	**un biglietto di andata e ritorno (di andata)** *oon bee-ly-ee-AYt-toh dee ahn-dAH-tah ay ree-tOHr-noh (dee ahn-dAH-tah)*
▪ in tourist class	**in classe turistica** *een klAHs-seh too-rEE-stee-kah*

■ in first class	**in prima classe** _een prEE-mah klAHs-seh_
I would like a seat _____.	**Vorrei un posto_____.** _vohr-rEH-ee OOn pOH-stoh_
■ in the (non)smoking section	**tra i (non)fumatori** _trAH ee (nohn)foo-mah-tOH-ree_
■ next to the window	**accanto al finestrino** _ah-kAHn-toh ahl fee-neh-strEE-noh_
■ on the aisle	**vicino al corridoio** _vee-chEE-noh ahl kohr-ree-dOH-ee-oh_
What is the fare?	**Qual è il prezzo del biglietto?** _koo-ah-lEH eel prEH-tsoh dAYl bee-ly-ee-EHt-toh_
Are meals served?	**Sono inclusi i pasti?** _sOH-noh een-klOO-see ee pAH-stee_
When does the plane leave (arrive)?	**A che ora parte (arriva) l'aereo?** _ah kay OH-rah pAHr-teh (ahr-ree-vAH) lah-EH-reh-oh_
When must I be at the airport?	**Quando dovrò trovarmi all'aeroporto?** _koo-AHn-doh doh-vrOH troh-vAHr-mee ahl-lah-eh-roh-pOHr-toh_
What is my flight number?	**Qual è il (mio) numero di volo?** _koo-AH-lEH eel (mEE-oh) nOO-meh-roh dee vOH-loh_
What gate do we leave from?	**Qual è la nostra porta d'uscita?** _koo-ah-lEH lah nOH-strah pOHr-tah doo-shEE-tah_
I want to confirm (cancel) my reservation for flight _____.	**Desidero confermare (cancellare) la mia prenotazione per il volo _____.** _day-sEE-deh-roh kohn-fayr-mAH-reh (kahn-chehl-lAH-reh) lah mEE-ah preh-noh-tah-tsee-OH-neh pehr eel vOH-loh_
I'd like to check my bags.	**Vorrei consegnare le valigie.** _vohr-rEH-ee kohn-say-ny-AH-reh leh vah-lEE-jee-eh_

I have only carry-on baggage.	**Ho soltano bagagli a mano.** *oh sohl-tAHn-toh bah-gAH-ly-ee ah MAH-noh*
Please pass my film (camera) through by hand.	**Per piacere mi passi il rollino.(la macchina fotografica) a mano** *pehr pee-ah-chAY-reh, mee pAHs-see eel rohl-lEE-noh (lah mAH-kee-nah foh-toh-grAH-fee-koh) ah MAH-noh*

TRAIN SERVICE

Where is the train station?	**Dov'è la stazione ferroviaria?** *doh-vEH lah stah-tsee-OH-neh fehr-roh-vee-AH-ree-ah*
When does the train for (from) ____ leave (arrive)? •	**Quando parte (arriva) il treno per (da) ____.** *koo-AHn-doh pAHr-teh (ahr-rEE-vah) eel trEH-noh pehr (dah)*
Does this train stop at ____?	**Questo treno si ferma a ____?** *koo-AYs-toh trEH-noh see fAYr-mah ah*
I would like ____.	**Vorrei ____.** *vohr-rEH-ee*
▪ a first (second)-class ticket for ____.	**un biglietto di prima (seconda) classe per ____.** *oon bee-ly-ee-AYt-toh dee prEE-mah (say-kOHn-dah) klAHs-seh pehr*
▪ a half-price ticket	**un biglietto a tariffa ridotta** *oon bee-ly-ee-AYt-toh ah tah-rEEf-fah ree-dOHt-tah*
▪ a one-way (round-trip) ticket	**un biglietto di andata (andata e ritorno)** *oon bee-ly-ee-AYt-toh dee ahn-dAH-tah (ahn-dAH-tah ay ree-tOHr-noh)*
▪ with supplement (for the rapid train)	**con supplemento rapido** *kohn soop-pleh-MEN-toh rAH-pee-doh*
▪ with reserved seat	**con prenotazione** *kohn prey-noh-tAH-tzee-oh-neh*
Is the train late?	**Il treno è in ritardo?** *eel trEH-noh EH een ree-tAHr-doh*

How long does it stop?	**Quanto tempo si ferma?** *koo-AHn-toh tEHm-poh see fAYr-mah*
Is there time to get a bite?	**C'è tempo per comprare un boccone?** *chEH tEHm-poh pehr kohm-prAH-reh oon boh-kOH-neh*
Is there a dining car (a sleeping car)?	**C'è un vagone ristorante (un vagone letto)?** *chEH oon vah-gOH-neh ree-stoh-rAHn-teh (oon vah-gOH-neh lEHt-toh)*
Is this an express (local) train?	**È questo un (treno) rapido (locale)?** *EH koo-AYs-toh oon (trEH-noh) rAH-pee-doh (loh-kAH-leh)*
Do I have to change trains?	**Debbo cambiar treno?** *dAYb-boh kahm-bee-AHr trEH-noh*
Is this seat taken?	**È occupato questo posto?** *EH oh-koo-pAH-toh koo-AYs-toh pOH-stoh*
Excuse me, but you are in my seat.	**Mi scusi ma lei ha occupato il mio posto.** *mee skOO-see mah lEH-ee ah oh-koo-pAH-toh eel mEE-oh pOHs-toh*
Where is the train station?	**Dov'è la stazione ferroviaria?** *doh-vEH lah stah-tsee-OH-neh fehr-roh-vee-AH-ree-ah*
When does the train for (from) _____ leave (arrive)?	**Quando parte (arriva) il treno per (da) _____.** *koo-AHn-doh pAHr-teh (ahr-rEE-vah) eel trEH-noh pehr (dah)*
Does this train stop at _____?	**Questo treno si ferma a _____?** *koo-AYs-toh trEH-noh see fAYr-mah ah*

SHIPBOARD TRAVEL

| Where is the port (dock)? | **Dov'è il porto (molo)?** *doh-vEH eel pOHr-toh (mOH-loh)* |
| When does the next boat leave for _____? | **Quando parte il prossimo battello per _____?** *koo-AHn-doh pAHr-teh eel prOHs-see-moh baht-tEHl-loh* |

How long does the crossing take?	**Quanto dura la traversata?** *koo-AHn-toh dOO-rah lah trah-vehr-sAH-tah*
Do we stop at any other ports?	**Ci fermiamo in qualche altro porto?** *chee fayr-mee-AH-moh een koo-AHl-keh AHl-troh pOHr-toh*
How long will we remain in the port?	**Quanto tempo resteremo in porto?** *koo-AHn-toh tEHm-poh reh-stay-rEH-moh een pOHr-toh*
When do we land?	**Quando sbarcheremo?** *koo-AHn-do sbahr-keh-rAY-moh*
At what time do we have to go back on board?	**A che ora ritorniamo a bordo?** *ah kay OH-rah ree-tohr-nee-AH-moh ah bOHr-doh*

ENTERTAINMENT AND DIVERSIONS

MOVIES, THEATER, CONCERTS, OPERA, BALLET

Let's go to the ____.	**Andiamo al ____.** *ahn-dee-AH-moh ahl*
■ movies (cinema)	**cinema** *chEE-neh-mah*
■ theater	**teatro** *teh-AH-troh*
What are they showing today?	**Che spettacoli ci sono oggi?** *kay speht-tAH-koh-lee chee sOH-noh OH-jee*
Is it a ____?	**È ____?** *EH*
■ mystery	**un giallo** *oon jee-AHl-loh*
■ comedy	**una commedia** *OO-na kohm-mEH-dee-ah*
■ drama	**un dramma** *oon drAHm-mah*

■ romance	**un romanzo** *oon roh-mAHn-tsoh·*
■ Western	**un western** *oon oo-EH-stehrn*
■ war film	**un film di guerra** *oon fEElm dee goo-EHr-ra*
■ science fiction film	**un film di fantascienza** *oon fEElm dee fahn-tah-shee-EHn-tsah*
Is it in English?	**È parlato in inglese?** *EH pahr-lAH-toh een een-glAY-seh*
Has it been dubbed?	**È stato doppiato?** *EH stAH-toh dohp-pee-AH-toh*
Where is the box office?	**Dov'è il botteghino?** *doh-vEH eel boht-tay-ghEE-noh*
What time does the (first) show begin?	**A che ora comincia lo (il primo) spettacolo?** *ah kay OH-rah koh-mEEn-chee-ah loh (eel prEE-moh) speht-tAH-koh-loh*
What time does the (last) show end?	**A che ora finisce lo (l'ultimo) spettacolo?** *ah kay OH-rah fee-nEE-sheh loh (lOOl-tee-moh) speht-tAH-koh-loh*
I want a seat near the middle (front, rear).	**Desidero un posto al centro (davanti, dietro).** *day-sEE-deh-roh oon-pOHs-toh ahl chAYn-troh (dah-vAHn-tee, dee-EH-troh)*
Can I check my coat?	**Posso consegnare (lasciare) il mio cappotto?** *pOHs-soh kohn-seh-ny-ee-AH-reh (lah-shee-AH-reh) eel mEE-oh kahp-pOHt-toh*
I need ___ tickets for tonight (tomorrow night).	**Mi occorrono ___ biglietti per stasera (domani sera).** *mee oh-kOHr-roh-noh dOO-eh bee-ly-ee-AYt-tee pehr stah-sAY-rah (doh-mAH-nee sAY-rah)*
■ two orchestra seats	**due poltrone d'orchestra** *doo-eh pohl-trOH-neh dohr-kEHs-trah*

▇ two box seats	**due poltrone nei palchi** *doo-eh pohl-trOH-neh nAY-ee pAHl-kee*
▇ two mezzanine seats	**due poltrone** *doo-eh pohl-trOH-neh*
▇ two gallery seats	**due posti in galleria** *doo-eh pOHs-tee een gahl-leh-rEE-ah*
How much are the front-row seats?	**Qual è il prezzo dei posti di prima fila?** *koo-ah-lEH eel prEH-tsoh dAY-ee pOH-stee dee prEE-mah fEE-lah*
What are the least expensive seats?	**Quali sono i posti meno costosi?** *koo-AH-lee sOH-noh ee pOH-stee mAY-noh koh-stOH-see*
Are there any seats for tonight's performance?	**Ci sono posti per lo spettacolo di stasera?** *chee sOH-noh pOH-stee pehr loh speht-tAH-koh-loh dee stah-sEH-rah*
We would like to attend ____.	**Vorremmo assistere ad ____.** *vohr-rEHm-moh ahs-sEE-steh-reh ahd*
▇ a ballet	**un balletto** *oon bahl-lAYt-toh*
▇ a concert	**un concerto** *oon kohn-chEHr-toh*
▇ an opera	**un'opera** *oo-nOH-peh-rah*
What are they playing (singing)?	**Che cosa recitano (cantano)?** *kay kOH-sah rEH-chee-tah-noh (kAHn-tah-noh)*
Who is the conductor?	**Chi è il direttore d'orchestra?** *key-EH eel dee-reht-tOH-reh dohr-kEH-strah*
I prefer ____.	**Preferisco ____.** *preh-feh-rEE-skoh*
▇ classical music	**la musica classica** *lah mOO-see-kah clAHs-see-kah*
▇ popular music	**la musica popolare** *lah mOO-see-kah poh-poh-lAH-reh*
▇ folk dance	**la danza folcloristica** *lah dAHn-tsah fohl-kloh-rEE-stee-kah*
▇ ballet	**il balletto** *eel bahl-lAYt-toh*

When does the season begin (end)?	**Quando cominicia (finisce) la stagione (lirica)?** *koo-AHn-doh koh-mEEn-chee-ah (fee-nEE-sheh) lah stah-jee-OH-neh (lEE-ree-kah)*
Should I get the tickets in advance?	**Debbo comprare i biglietti in anticipo?** *dAYb-boh kohm-prAH-reh ee bee-ly-ee-AYt-tee een ahn-tEE-chee-poh*
Do I have to dress formally?	**È prescritto l'abito da sera?** *EH preh-skrEEt-toh lAH-bee-toh dah sAY-rah*
May I buy a program?	**Posso comprare il programma di sala?** *pOHs-soh kohm-prAH-reh eel proh-grAHm-mah dee sAH-lah*
What opera (ballet) are they performing?	**Quale opera (balletto) danno?** *koo-AH-leh OH-peh-rah (bahl-lAYt-toh) dAHn-noh*
Who's singing (tenor, soprano, baritone, contralto)?	**Chi sta cantando (il tenore, il soprano, il baritono, il contralto)?** *key stah kahn-tAHn-doh (eel teh-nOH-reh, eel soh-prAH-noh eel bah-rEE-toh-noh, eel kohn-trAHl-toh)*

NIGHTCLUBS, DANCING

Let's go to a nightclub.	**Andiamo al night.** *ahn-dee-AH-moh ahl nAH-eet*
Is a reservation necessary?	**È necessaria la prenotazione?** *EH neh-chehs-sAH-ree-ah lah preh-noh-tah-tsee-OH-neh*
We haven't gotten a reservation.	**Non abbiamo la prenotazione.** *nohn ahb-bee-AH-moh lah preh-noh-tah-tsee-OH-neh*
Is there a good discotheque here?	**C'è una buona discoteca qui?** *chEH OO-nah boo-OH-nah dee-skoh-tEH-kah koo-EE*

Is there dancing at the hotel?	**Si balla in albergo (all'hotel)?** *see bAHl-lah een ahl-bEHr-goh (ahl-loh-tEHl)*
We'd like a table near the dance floor.	**Vorremmo un tavolo vicino alla pista (di ballo).** *vohr-rEHm-moh oon tAH-voh-loh vee-chEE-noh AHl-lah pEE-stah (dee bAHl-loh)*
Is there a minimum (cover charge)?	**C'è un prezzo minimo (per il tavolo)?** *chEH oon prEH-tsoh mEE-nee-moh (pehr eel tAH-voh-loh)*
Where is the checkroom?	**Dov'è il guardaroba?** *doh-vEH eel goo-ahr-dah-rOH-bah*
At what time does the floor show go on?	**A che ora comincia lo spettacolo (di varietà)?** *ah kay OH-rah koh-mEEn-chee-ah loh speht-tAH-koh-loh dee vah-ree-eh-tAH*

SPECTATOR SPORTS

I'd like to watch a soccer game.	**Vorrei vedere una partita di calcio.** *vohr-rEH-ee veh-dAY-reh OO-nah pahr-tEE-tah dee kAHl-chee-oh*
Where's the stadium?	**Dov'è lo stadio?** *doh-vEH loh stAH-dee-oh*
When does the first half begin?	**Quando inizia il primo tempo?** *koo-AHn-doh ee-nEE-tsee-ah eel prEE-moh tEHm-poh*
What teams are going to play?	**Quali squadre giocheranno?** *koo-AH-lee skoo-AH-dreh jee-oh-keh-rAHn-noh*
Who is playing ____?	**Chi è ____?** *key EH*
center	**il centroavanti** *eel chehn-troh-ah-vAHn-tee*

| ■ fullback | **il terzino** *eel tehr-tsEE-noh* |
| ■ halfback | **il libero** *eel lEE-beh-roh* |

Who is playing wing? **Chi sta all'ala?** *key stAH ahl-lAH-lah*

Go! **Forza!** *fOHr-tsah*

What was the score? **Qual è stato il punteggio?** *koo-ah-lEH stAH-toh eel poon-tAY-jee-oh*

Is there a racetrack here? **C'è un ippodromo qui?** *chEH oon eep-pOH-droh-moh koo-EE*

ACTIVE SPORTS

Do you play tennis? **Gioca a tennis?** *jee-OH-kah ah tEHn-nees*

I (don't) play very well. **(Non) gioco molto bene.** *(nohn) jee-OH-koh mOHl-toh bEH-neh*

Do you play singles (doubles)? **Gioca il singolo (in doppio)?** *jee-OH-kah eel sEEn-goh-loh (een dOHp-pee-oh)*

Do you know where there is a court? **Sa dove c'è un campo da tennis?** *sAH doh-veh-chEH oon kAHm-poh dah tEHn-nees*

Is it a private club? I'm not a member. **È un club privato? Io non sono socio.** *EH oon clEHb pree-vAH-toh? EE-oh nohn sOH-noh sOH-chee-oh*

How much do they charge per hour? **Quanto si paga all'ora?** *koo-AHn-toh see pAH-gah ahl-lOH-rah*

Can I rent a racquet? **Posso affittare una racchetta?** *pOHs-soh ahf-feet-tAH-reh OO-nah rahk-kAYt-tah*

Do you sell balls for a hard (soft) surface? **Vendono palle per fondo duro (morbido)?** *vAYn-doh-noh pAHl-leh pehr fOHn-doh dOO-roh (mOHr-bee-doh)*

Let's rally first to warm up.	**Prima scambiamo qualche battuta per riscaldarci.** *prEE-mah skahm-bee-AH-moh koo-AHl-keh baht-tOO-tah pehr rees-kahl-dAHr-chee*
I serve (you serve) first.	**Io servo (lei serve) per primo.** *EE-oh sEHr-voh (lEH-ee sEHr-veh) pehr prEE-moh*
You play very well.	**Lei gioca molto bene.** *lEH-ee jee-OH-kah mOHl-toh bEH-neh*
You've won. Let's play another set.	**Lei ha vinto. Giochiamo un altro set.** *lEH-ee ah vEEn-toh jee-oh-key-AH-moh oon-AHl-troh seht*
Let's play another set.	**Giochiamo un altro set.** *jee-oh-key-AH-moh oon-AHl-troh seht*
Do you know where there is a handball (squash) court?	**Sa dov'è un campo cintato per giocare a palla a muro (squash)?** *sah doh-vEH oon kAHm-poh cheen-tAH-toh pehr jee-oh-kAH-reh ah pAHl-lah ah mOO-roh (squash)*
Are there racquetball courts?	**Ci sono campi per giocare a palla a muro con la racchetta?** *chee sOH-noh kAHm-pee pehr jee-oh-kAH-reh ah pAHl-lah ah mOO-roh kohn lah rah-kAYt-tah*
Where is a safe place to run (to jog)?	**Dov'è un posto buono dove si può correre (fare del footing)?** *doh-vEH oon pOHs-toh boo-OH-noh dOH-veh see poo-OH kOHr-reh-reh (fAH-reh dayl fOO-teeng)*
Where is there a health club?	**Dove si può trovare un centro fitness?** *doh-veh see poo-OH troh-vAH-reh oon chAYn-tro feet-nEHs*
Where can I play bocci?	**Dove posso giocare alle bocce?** *dOH-veh pOHs-soh jee-oh-kAH-reh AHl-leh bOH-cheh*

AT THE BEACH/POOL

Let's go to the beach (to the pool).	**Andiamo alla spiaggia (in piscina).** *ahn-dee-AH-moh AHl-lah spee-AH-jee-ah (een pee-shEE-nah)*
Which bus will take us to the beach?	**Quale autobus ci porterà alla spiaggia?** *koo-AH-leh AH-oo-toh-boos chee pohr-teh-rAH AHl-lah spee-AH-jee-ah*
Is there an indoor (outdoor) pool in the hotel?	**C'è una piscina coperta (scoperta) nell'hotel?** *chEH OO-nah pee-shEE-nah koh-pEHr-tah (skoh-pEHr-tah) nayl-loh-tEHl*
I (don't) know how to swim well.	**(Non) so nuotare bene.** *(nohn) soh noo-oh-tAH-reh bEH-neh*
I just want to stretch out in the sand.	**Voglio solo stendermi sulla sabbia.** *vOH-ly-ee-oh sOH-loh stEHn-dehr-mee sOOl-lah sAHb-bee-ah*
Is it safe to swim here?	**Si può nuotare qui senza pericolo?** *see poo-OH noo-oh-tAH-reh koo-EE sEHn-tsah peh-rEE-koh-loh*
Is it dangerous for children?	**È pericoloso per i bambini?** *EH peh-ree-koh-lOH-soh pehr ee bahm-bEE-nee*
Is there a lifeguard?	**C'è un bagnino?** *chEH oon bah-ny-EE-noh*
Where can I get ____?	**Dove posso trovare ____?** *dOH-vey pOHs-soh troh-vAH-reh*
an air mattress	**un materassino pneumatico** *oon mah-teh-rahs-sEE-noh p-neh-oo-mAH-tee-koh*
a bathing suit	**un costume da bagno** *oon koh-stOO-meh dah bAH-ny-oh*

a beach ball	**un pallone per la spiaggia** *oon pahl-lOH-neh pehr lah spee-AH-jee-ah*
a beach chair	**una sedia per la spiaggia** *OO-nah sEH-dee-ah pehr lah spee-AH-jee-ah*
a beach towel	**una tovaglia da spiaggia** *OO-nah toh-vAH- ly-ee-ah dah spee-AH- jee-ah*
diving equipment	**un equipaggiamento subacqueo** *oon ay-koo-ee-pah-jee-ah-mEHn-toh soob-AH-koo-eh-oh*
sunglasses	**degli occhiali da sole** *dAY-ly-ee oh-key-AH-lee dah sOH-leh*
suntan lotion	**una lozione per l'abbronzatura** *OO-nah loh-tsee-OH-neh pehr lahb-brohn-tsah-tOO-rah*
water skis	**degli sci acquatici?** *dAY-ly-ee shEE ah- koo-AH-tee-chee*

ON THE SLOPES

Which ski area do you recommend?	**Quali campi di sci consiglia?** *koo-AH-lee kAHm-pee dee shee kohn-sEE-ly-ee-ah*
I am a novice (intermediate, expert) skier.	**Sono uno sciatore (una sciatrice) principiante, dilettante, esperto(a).** *sOH-noh oo-noh shee-ah-tOH-reh (oo-nah shee-ah-trEE-ceh) preen-chee-pee-AHn-teh, dee-leht-tAHn-teh, ehs-pEHr-toh(ah)*
What kind of lifts are there?	**Come sono le sciovie?** *kOH-meh sOH-noh leh shee-oh-vEE-eh*
How much does the lift cost?	**Quant'è il biglietto per la sciovia?** *koo-ahn-tEH eel bee-ly-ee-AYt-toh pehr lah shee-oh-vEE-ah*
Do they give lessons?	**Danno lezioni?** *dAHn-noh leh-tsee-OH-nee*

Is there enough snow this time of the year?	**C'è abbastanza neve in questo periodo dell'anno?** *chEH ahb-bah-stAHn-tsah nAY-veh een koo-AY-stoh peh-rEE-oh-doh dayl-lAHn-noh*
Is there any cross-country skiing?	**C'è anche lo sci di fondo?** *chEH AHn-keh loh shee dee fOHn-doh*
Where can I stay at the summit?	**Sulla cima dove posso trovare alloggio?** *sool-lah chEE-mah dOH-veh pOHs-soh troh-vAH-reh ahl-lOH-jee-oh*
Can I rent ____ there?	**Posso affittare ____ sul posto?** *pOHs-soh ahf-feet-tAH-reh sOOl pOH-stoh*
◾ equipment	**l'attrezzatura** *laht-treh-tsah-tOO-rah*
◾ poles	**le racchette da sci** *leh rah-kAYt-teh dah shEE*
◾ skis	**gli sci** *ly-ee shEE*
◾ ski boots	**gli scarponi da sci** *ly-ee skahr-pOH-nee dah shEE*

ON THE LINKS

Is there a golf course here?	**C'è un campo di golf (qui)?** *chEH oon kAHm-poh dee gOHlf (koo-EE)*
Can one rent clubs?	**Si possono affittare le mazze?** *see pOHs-soh-noh ahf-feet-tAH-reh leh mAH-tseh*

CAMPING

Is there a camping area near here?	**C'è un campeggio qui vicino?** *chEH oon kahm-pAY-jee-oh koo-EE vee-chEE-noh*
Do we pick our own site?	**Possiamo scegliere il posto che ci piace?** *pohs-see-AH-moh shay-ly-ee-EH-reh eel pOHs-toh kay chee pee-AH-cheh*

We only have a tent.	**Noi abbiamo solo una tenta.** *nOH-ee ahb-bee-AH-moh sOH-loh OO-nah tEHn-tah*
Where is it on this map?	**Dov'è su questa cartina?** *doh-vEH soo koo-AY-stah kahr-tEE-nah*
Can we park our trailer (caravan)?	**Possiamo posteggiare la nostra roulotte?** *pohs-see-AH-moh poh-steh-jee-AH-reh lah nOH-strah roo-lOH-te*
Can we camp for one night only?	**Possiamo accamparci per una notte solamente?** *pohs-see-AH-moh ahk-kahm-pAHr-chee pehr OO-nah nOHt-teh soh-lah-mEHn-teh*
Is (are) there _____?	**C'è (ci sono) _____?** *cheh (chee sOH-noh)*
▪ drinking water	**acqua potabile** *AH-koo-ah poh-tAH-bee-leh*
▪ showers	**docce?** *dOH-cheh*
▪ fireplaces	**caminetti** *kah-mee-nAYt-tee*
▪ picnic tables	**tavoli per il pic-nic** *tAH-voh-lee pehr eel peek-nEEk*
▪ electricity	**l'elettricità** *leh-leh-tree-chee-tAH*
▪ a grocery store	**un negozio di generi alimentari** *oon nay-gOH-tsee-oh dee jEH-neh-ree ah-lee-mehn-tAH-ree*
▪ a children's play-ground	**un posto dove far giocare i bambini** *oon pOH-stoh dOH-veh fahr jee-oh-kAH-reh ee bahm-bEE-nee*
▪ flush toilets	**gabinetti** *gah-bee-nAYt-tee*
How much do they charge per person? (per car)?	**Quanto si paga a persona? (per macchina)?** *koo-AHn-toh see pAH-gah ah pehr-sOH-nah (pehr mAHk-key-nah)*
We intend to stay _____ days (weeks).	**Pensiamo di stare _____ giorni (settimane).** *pehn-see-AH-moh dee stAH-reh jee-OHr-nee (seyt-tee-mAH-neh)*

IN THE COUNTRYSIDE

Are there tours to the countryside?	**Si organizzano gite in campagna?** *see ohr-gah-nEE-tsah-noh jEE-teh een kahm-pAH-ny-ah*
What a beautiful landscape!	**Che bel panorama!** *kay bEHl pah-noh-rAH-mah*
Where does this path lead to?	**Dove porta questo sentiero?** *dOH-veh pOHr-tah koo-AY-stoh sehn-tee-EH-roh*
What kind of a tree is this?	**Che pianta è questa?** *kay pee-AHn-tah EH koo-AYs-tah*
These gardens are beautiful.	**Questi giardini sono belli.** *koo-AYs-tee jee-ahr-dEE-nee sOH-noh bEHl-lee*

FOOD AND DRINK

Bar or Snack Bar	Ice cream, coffee, pastries, and drinks are served. This is also a favorite place for a quick breakfast consisting of a hot, foamy **cappuccino** and a **mottino,** or a **maritozzo,** a **cornetto,** a **tramezzino,** or other pastry.
Trattoria or Osteria	Small, family-operated inn serving simple but delicious local dishes prepared while you wait.
Tavola Calda	Small, self-service cafeteria with simple, hot dishes that you choose from a hot table. In some places local specialties and dishes from other countries are prepared.
Rosticceria	Generally a take-out place for grilled meats.

Pizzeria	Small, family-operated pizza parlor. Local pizza specialties and other simple dishes are served. In some places they are called **pizzeria-rosticceria**, where you can sit and enjoy a nice meal.
Autogrill	A self-service cafeteria or snack area on the **autostrade** (motorway, turnpike) with bar, restaurant, tourist market, souvenirs, telephones, and bedrooms.
Ristorante	Elegant place classified by stars (some restaurants are rated according to their decor, others by the quality of their cuisine). *Often closed on Mondays.*

THE MENU

Many restaurants offer a special plate of the day (**il piatto del giorno**) or have a tourist menu at a set price (**il menù turistico a prezzo fisso**). These are usually very good values. You should also watch for the specialty of the chef or of the restaurant (**la specialità del cuoco o del ristorante**). Often the local wine is included in the price of a meal (**vino incluso**).

The bill may or may not include a service charge (**servizio**), which is usually 12 to 15 percent of the bill. Other items that may appear on the bill are the tip (**mancia**), bread and cover charge (**pane e coperto**), and a surcharge (**supplemento**). Even if the service and tip are included, you should leave some remaining change; it is a token of your appreciation for good service and excellent food.

EATING OUT

Do you know a good restaurant?	**Scusi, conosce un buon ristorante?** *skOO-see koh-nOH-sheh oon boo-OHn ree-stoh-rAHn-teh*
Is it very expensive (dressy)?	**È molto costoso (elegante)?** *eh mohl-toh koh-stOH-soh (eh-leh-gAHn-teh)*

Do you know a restaurant that serves typical dishes?	**Conosce un ristorante tipico (del luogo)?** *koh-nOH-sheh oon res-toh-rAHn-teh tEE-pee-koh (dAYl loo-OH-goh)*
Waiter!	**Cameriere!** *kah-meh-ree-EH-reh*
A table for two please.	**Un tavolo per due, per favore.** *oon tAH-voh-loh pehr dOO-eh peh fah-vOH-reh*
▪ in the corner	**all'angolo** *ahl-lAHn-goh-loh*
▪ near the window	**vicino alla finestra** *vee-chee-noh AHl-lah fee-nEHs-trah*
▪ on the terrace	**sul terrazzo** *sOOl tehr-rAH-tsoh*
I'd like to make a reservation ____.	**Vorrei fare una prenotazione ____.** *vohr-rEH-ee fAH-reh oon-ah preh-noh-tah-tsee-OH-neh*
▪ for tonight	**per stasera** *pehr stah-sAY-rah*
▪ for tomorrow evening	**per domani sera** *pehr doh-mAH-nee sAY-rah*
▪ for two (four) persons	**per due (quattro) persone** *pehr dOO-eh (koo-AHt-troh) pehr-SOH-neh*
▪ at 8 p.m.	**per le venti** *pehr leh vAYn-tee*
▪ at 8:30 p.m.	**per le venti e trenta** *pehr leh vAYn-tee ay trEHn-tah*
We'd like to have lunch (dinner) now.	**Vorremmo pranzare adesso.** *vohr-rAYm-moh prahn-tsAH-reh ah-dEHs-soh*
The menu, please.	**Il menù, per piacere.** *eel may-noo pehr pee-ah-chAY-reh*
I'd like the set menu.	**Vorrei il menù turistico. (Il menù a prezzo fisso.)** *vohr-rEH-ee eel meh-nOO too-rEEs-tee-koh (eel meh-nOO ah prEH-tsoh fEEs-soh)*
What's today's special?	**Qual è il piatto del giorno?** *koo-ah-lEH eel pee-AHt-toh dayl jee-OHr-noh*

What do you recommend?	**Che cosa mi consiglia lei?** *kay kOH-sah mee kohn-sEE-ly-ee-ah lEH-ee*
What's the house specialty?	**Qual è la specialità della casa?** *koo-ah-lEH lah speh-chee-ah-lee-tAH dayl-lah kAH-sah*
Do you serve children's portions?	**Si servono porzioni per bambini?** *see sEHr-voh-noh pohr-tsee-OH-nee pehr bahm-bEE-nee*
I'm (not) very hungry.	**(Non) ho molta fame.** *(nohn) oh mOHl-tah fAH-meh*
Are the portions small (large)?	**Le porzioni sono piccole (grandi)?** *leh pohr-tsee-OH-nee sOH-noh pEE-koh-leh (grAHn-dee)*
To begin with, please bring us ____.	**Per cominciare, ci porti ____.** *pehr koh-meen-chee-AH-reh chee pOHr-tee*
▪ an aperitif	**un aperitivo** *oon ah-peh-ree-tEE-voh*
▪ a cocktail	**un cocktail** *oon kOHk-tayl*
▪ some white (red) wine	**del vino bianco (rosso)** *dayl vEE-noh bee-AHn-koh (rOHs-soh)*
▪ some water	**dell'acqua** *dayl-LAH-koo-ah*
▪ a bottle of mineral water, with (without) gas	**una bottiglia d'acqua minerale gassata (naturale)** *oo-nah boht-tEE-ly-ee-ah dAH-koo-ah mee-neh-rAH-leh gahs-sAH-tah (nah-too-rAH-leh)*
▪ a beer	**una birra** *OO-nah bEEr-rah*
I'd like to order now.	**Vorrei ordinare adesso** *vohr-rEH-ee ohr-dee-nAH-reh ah-dEHs-soh*
I'd like ____.	**Vorrei ____.** *vohr-rEH-ee*
Do you have a house wine?	**Hanno il vino della casa?** *AHn-noh eel VEE-noh dAYl-lah kAH-sah*

Is it dry (mellow, sweet)?	**È vino secco (amabile, dolce)?** *EH vEE-noh sAY-koh (ah-mAH-bee-leh, dOHl-cheh)*
Please also bring us _____.	**Per piacere ci porti anche _____.** *pehr pee-ah-chAY-reh chee pOHr-tee AHn-keh*
▪a roll	**un panino** *oon pah-nEE-noh*
▪bread	**il pane** *eel pAH-neh*
▪bread and butter	**pane e burro** *pAH-neh ay bOOr-roh*
Waiter, we need _____.	**Cameriere(a), abbiamo bisogno di _____.** *kah-meh-ree-EH-reh(a) ahb-bee-AH-moh bee-sOH-ny-oh dee*
▪a knife	**un coltello** *oon kohl-tEHl-loh*
▪a fork	**una forchetta** *oo-nah fohr-kAYt-tah*
▪a spoon	**un cucchiaio** *oon koo-key-AH-ee-oh*
▪a teaspoon	**un cucchiaino** *oon koo-key-ah-EE-noh*
▪a soup spoon	**un cucchiaio per la minestra (il brodo)** *oon koo-key-AH-ee-oh pehr lah mee-nEHs-trah (eel brOH-doh)*
▪a glass	**un bicchiere** *oon bee-key-EH-reh*
▪a cup	**una tazza** *oo-nah tAH-tsah*
▪a saucer	**un piattino** *oon pee-aht-tEE-noh*
▪a plate	**un piatto** *oon pee-AHt-toh*
▪a napkin	**un tovagliolo** *oon toh-vah-ly-ee-OH-loh*
▪toothpicks	**gli stuzzicadenti** *ly-ee stOO-tsee-kah-dEHn-tee*

APPETIZERS (STARTERS)

acciughe	*ah-chee-OH-gheh*	anchovies

antipasto misto	*ahn-tee-pAHs-toh mEEs-toh*	assorted appetizers
carciofi	*kahr-chee-OH-fee*	artichoke
mortadella	*mohr-tah-dEHl-lah*	cold sausage, similar to bologna
prosciutto crudo	*proh-shee-OOt-toh krOO-doh*	raw cured ham
tartufi	*tahr-tOO-fee*	truffles (white)

SOUPS

brodo di manzo	*brOH-doh dee mAHn-tsoh*	broth, generally meat-based
brodo di pollo	*brOH-hod dee pOHl-loh*	chicken broth
brodo magro di vegetali	*brOH-doh mAH-groh dee veh-jeh-tAH-lee*	vegetable broth
crema di ____	*krEH-mah dee*	creamed ____ soup
buridda	*boo-rEEd-dah*	fish stew
cacciucco	*kah-chee-OO-koh*	seafood chowder
minestra in brodo	*mee-nEHs-trah een brOH-doh*	pasta in broth
minestrone	*mee-nehs-trOH-neh*	thick vegetable soup
zuppa di ____	*tsOOp-pah dee*	thick soup

PASTA OR RICE COURSE

A pasta course usually precedes your entree, so it is usually a small serving offered as in special presentation. Since the varieties of pasta are almost endless, you'll find them offered on menus as **agnellotti, cappelletti, fettuccine, lasagne, tagliatelle, tortellini,** and many more. It will be sauced, perhaps with a cream and cheese mixture or served with tomato sauce. It may also be stuffed or baked, or served in a soup.

In parts of northern Italy, rice is often substituted for pasta. These dishes are generally less well known, but are no less tasty. Generally you'll find on a menu as a plain rice dish **(riso)** or as a **risotto,** a creamy rice mixture often combined with cheese, fruit, vegetables, or meat.

A few other "pasta" dishes you will find on some menus are **polenta** *(poh-lEHn-tah)*—a cornmeal mush often sliced and served with sausages or chicken—and **gnocchi** *(ny-OH-key)*—dumplings made from potatoes and often mixed with spinach, cheese, or cornmeal. Egg dishes are also often offered for this course. A **frittata** *(free-tAH-tah)* is an omelet, often filled with vegetables.

ENTREES (MEAT AND FISH DISHES)

acciughe	*ah-chee-OO-gheh*	anchovies
anguille	*ahn-goo-EEl-leh*	eel
aragosta	*ah-rah-gOHs-tah*	lobster (spiny)
aringa	*ah-rEEn-gah*	herring
affumicata	*ahf-foo-mee-kAH-tah*	smoked
baccalà	*bah-kah-lAH*	dried salt cod
branzino (nasello)	*brahn-tsEE-noh (nah-sEHl-loh)*	bass (hake)
calamari (seppie)	*kah-lah-mAH-ree (sAYp-pee-eh)*	squid
cozze	*kOH-tseh*	mussels
gamberetti	*gAHm-beh-rAY-tee*	prawns
granchi	*grAHn-key*	crabs

lumache	*loo-mAH-keh*	snails
merluzzo	*mayr-lOOt-tsoh*	cod
ostriche	*OHs-tree-keh*	oysters
polipo	*pOH-lee-poh*	octopus
salmone	*sahl-mOH-neh*	salmon
sardine	*sahr-dEE-neh*	sardines
scampi	*skAHm-pee*	shrimps
sogliola	*sOH-ly-ee-oh-lah*	flounder (sole)
trota	*trOH-tah*	trout
tonno	*tOHn-noh*	tuna
vongole	*vOHn-goh-leh*	clams
trance di pesce alla griglia	*trAHn-cheh dee pAY-sheh AHl-lah grEE-ly-ee-ah*	grilled fish steaks
fritto misto di pesce	*frEEt-toh mEEs-toh dee pAY-sheh*	mised fried fish
agnello (abbacchio)	*ah-ny-EHl-loh (ahb-bAH-key-oh)*	lamb
capretto	*kah-prAHy-toh)*	goat
maiale	*mah-ee-AH-leh*	pork
manzo	*mAHn-tsoh*	beef
montone	*mohn-tOH-neh*	mutton
vitello	*vee-tEHl-loh*	veal
affettati	*ahf-fayt-tAH-tee*	cold cuts
costate	*kohs-tAH-teh*	chops
animelle	*ah-nee-mEHl-leh*	sweetbreads
cervello	*chehr-vEHl-loh*	brains
fegato	*fAY-gah-toh*	liver

bistecca	*bees-tAY-kah*	steak
lingua	*lEEn-goo-ah*	tongue
pancetta	*pahn-chAYt-tah*	bacon
polpette	*pohl-pAYt-teh*	meatballs
prosciutto cotto	*proh-shee-OOt-toh kOHt-toh*	ham (cooked)
rognoni	*roh-ny-OH-nee*	kidneys
anitra	*AH-nee-trah*	duck
beccaccia	*bay-kAH-chee-ah*	woodcock
cappone	*kahp-pOH-neh*	capon
carne di cervo	*kAHr-neh dee chEHr-voh*	venison
coniglio	*koh-nEE-ly-ee-oh*	rabbit
fagiano	*fah-jee-AH-noh*	pheasant
faraona	*fah-rah-OH-nah*	guinea fowl
lepre	*lEH-preh*	hare
oca	*OH-kah*	goose
pernice	*pehr-nEE-cheh*	partridge
piccioncino	*pEE-chee-ohn-chEE-noh*	squab (pigeon)
pollo	*pOHl-loh*	chicken
porcellino di latte	*pohr-chehl-lEE-noh dee lAHz-teh*	suckling pig
quaglia	*koo-AH-ly-ee-ah*	quail
tacchino	*tah-kEY-noh*	turkey
Is it _____?	**È_____?** *eh*	
baked	**cotta al forno** *kOHt-tah ahl fOHr-noh*	
boiled	**lessa** *lAYs-sah*	

■ braised (stewed)	**brasata** *brah-sAH-tah*
■ broiled (grilled)	**ai ferri** *AH-ee fEHr-ree*
■ roasted	**arrosto** *ahr-rOH-stoh*
grilled	**alla griglia** *AHl-lah grEE-ly-ee-ah*
poached	**bollita** *bohl-lEE-tah*
I like the meat ____.	**La carne mi piace ____.** *lah kAHr-neh mee pee-AH-cheh*
■ well done	**ben cotta** *bEHn kOHt-tah*
■ medium	**cotta a puntino** *kOHt-tah ah poon-tEE-noh*
■ rare	**al sangue** *ahl sAHn-goo-eh*
■ tender	**tenera** *tEH-neh-rah*

VEGETABLES

asparagi	*ahs-pAH-rah-jee*	asparagus
carciofi	*kahr-chee-OH-fee*	artichoke
carote	*kah-rOH-teh*	carrots
cavoli	*kAH-voh-lee*	cabbage
cavolfiori	*kah-vohl-fee-OH-ree*	cauliflower
cetriolo	*cheh-tree-OO-loh*	cucumber
ceci	*chay-chee*	chick-peas
fagioli	*fah-jce-oh-lEE*	beans (dried)
fagiolini	*fah-jee-oh-lEE-nee*	green beans
fave	*fAH-veh*	broad beans
finocchi	*fee-nOH-key*	fennel
funghi	*fOOn-ghee*	mushrooms
lattuga	*laht-tOO-gah*	lettuce

lenticchie	*len-tEE-key-eh*	lentils
granturco	*grahn-tOO-rkoh*	corn (maize)
melanzana	*meh-lAHn-tsah-nah*	eggplant (aubergine)
peperoni	*peh-peh-rOH-nee*	pepper
patate	*pah-tAH-teh*	potatoes
patatine fritte	*pah-tah-tEE-neh frEEt-teh*	French fries (chips)
piselli	*pee-sEHl-lee*	peas
pomodoro	*poh-moh-dOH-roh*	tomato
porcini	*pohr-chee-nee*	wild mushroom, similar to cepes
sedano	*sAY-dah-noh*	celery
spinaci	*spee-nAH-chee*	spinach
zucchini	*tsoo-key-nee*	green squash (courgettes)

SEASONINGS

I'd like ____.	**Vorrei ____.**	*vohr-rEH-ee*
butter	**burro**	*bOOr-roh*
horseradish	**rafano**	*rAH-fah-noh*
ketchup	**ketchup**	*keh-chOHp*
margarine	**margarina**	*mahr-gah-rEE-nah*
mayonnaise	**maionese**	*mah-ee-oh-nAY-seh*
mustard	**senape, mostarda**	*sEH-nah-peh, moh-stAHr-dah*
olive oil	**olio d'oliva**	*OH-lee-oh doh-lEE-vah*
pepper (black)	**pepe (nero)**	*pAY-peh (nAY-roh)*
pepper (red)	**pepe (rosso)**	*pAY-peh (rOHs-soh)*

■ salt	**sale**	*sAH-leh*
■ sugar	**zucchero**	*tsOO-keh-roh*
■ saccharin	**saccarina, dolci-ficante (Sweet and Low)**	*sah-kah-rEE-nah, dohl-chee-fee-kAHn-teh*
■ vinegar	**aceto**	*ah-chAY-toh*

CHEESE COURSE

Is the cheese ____?	**È il formaggio ____?**	*eh eel fohr-mAH-jee-oh*
■ mild	**dolce**	*dOHl-cheh*
■ sharp	**piccante**	*pee-kAHn-teh*
■ hard	**duro**	*dOO-roh*
■ soft	**molle**	*mOHl-leh*

FRUITS AND NUTS

What kind of fruit do you have?	**Che frutta c'è?**	*kay frOOt-tah chEH*
albicocca	*ahl-bee-kOH-kah*	apricot
ananasso	*ah-nah-nAHs-soh*	pineapple
anguria	*ahn-gOO-ree-ah*	watermelon
arancia	*ah-rAHn-chee-ah*	orange
castagne	*kahs-tAH-ny-eh*	chestnuts
cedro	*chAY-droh*	lime
ciliege	*chee-lee-EH-jee-eh*	cherries
datteri	*dAHt-teh-ree*	dates
fichi	*fEE-key*	figs
fragole	*frAH-goh-leh*	strawberries
lampone	*lahm-pOH-neh*	raspberry

limone	*lee-mOH-neh*	lemon
mandarini	*mahn-dah-rEE-nee*	tangerines
mandorle	*mAHn-dohr-leh*	almonds
mela	*mAY-lah*	apple
more	*mOH-reh*	mulberries
noci	*nOH-chee*	nuts
nocciole	*noh-chee-OH-leh*	hazelnuts (filberts)
melone	*meh-lOH-neh*	melon
pera	*pAY-rah*	pear
pesca	*pAYs-kah*	peach
pompelmo	*pohm-pEHl-moh*	grapefruit
prugne	*prOO-ny-eh*	plum
uva	*OO-vah*	grape

DESSERT—SWEETS

torta	*tOHr-tah*	cake
dolci	*dOHl-chee*	sweets
macedonia di frutta	*mah-cheh-dOH-nee-ah dee frOOt-tah*	fresh fruit salad
mousse al cioc-colato	*mOOs ahl chee-oh-koh lAH-toh*	chocolate mousse
crema inglese	*krEH-mah een-glAY-seh*	custard
crostata	*kroh-stAH-tah*	pie
budino	*boo-dEE-noh*	pudding
▪ **di pane**	*dee pAH-neh*	bread
▪ **di crema**	*dee krEH-mah*	cream

■ **di riso**	*dee rEE-soh*	rice
crema di cara-mello	*crEH-mah dee kah-rah-mEHl-loh*	caramel custard
gelato	*jeh-lAH-toh*	ice cream
■ **al cioccolato**	*ahl chee-oh-koh-lAH-toh*	chocolate
■ **alla vaniglia**	*AHl-lah vah-nEE-ly-ee-ah*	vanilla
■ **alla fragola**	*AHl-lah frAH-goh-lah*	strawberry
■ **di caffè (con panna)**	*dee kahf-fEH (kOHn pAHn-nah)*	coffee (with whipped cream)

SPECIAL CIRCUMSTANCES

I don't want anything fried (salted).	**Non posso mangiare cose fritte (salate).** *nohn pOHs-soh mahn-jee-AH-reh kOH-seh frEEt-teh (sah-lAH-teh)*
I cannot eat anything made with ____.	**Non posso mangiare niente fatto con ____.** *nohn pOHs-soh mahn-jee-AH-reh nee-EHn-teh fAHt-toh kohn*
Is this very spicy?	**Questo è molto piccante?** *koo-AY-stoh eh mohl-toh pee-kAHn-teh*
Do you have any dishes without meat?	**Hanna piatti (cibi) senza carne?** *AHn-noh pee-AHt-tee (chEE-bee) sEHn-tsah kAHr-neh*

BEVERAGES

Waiter, please bring me ____.	**Cameriere(a), per piacere mi porti ____.** *kah-meh-ree-EH-reh(ah), pehr pee-ah-chAY-reh mee pOHr-tee*

coffee (regular or American)	**caffè**	*kahf-fEH*
▦ with milk	**caffelatte**	*kahf-fEH-lAHt-teh*
▦ with sugar	**con zucchero**	*kOHn tsOO-keh-roh*
▦ without sugar	**senza zucchero**	*sEHn-tsah tsOO-keh-roh*
▦ with saccharin	**con saccarina**	*kohn sah-kah-rEE-nah*
▦ with cream	**con panna**	*kOHn pAHn-nah*
Italian coffee	**espresso**	*ehs-prEHs-soh*
▦ with anisette	**corretto all'anisetta**	*kohr-rEHt-toh ahl-lah-nee-sAYt-tah*
iced (coffee)	**freddo**	*frAYd-doh*
tea	**tè**	*tEH*
▦ with milk	**con latte**	*kOHn lAHt-teh*
▦ with lemon	**con limone**	*kOHn lee-mOH-neh*
▦ with sugar	**con zucchero**	*kOHn tsOO-keh-roh*
▦ iced	**con ghiaccio**	*kOHn ghee-AH-chee-oh*
water	**acqua**	*AH-koo-ah*
▦ cold	**fredda**	*frAYd-dah*
▦ iced	**con ghiaccio**	*kOHn ghee-AH-chee-oh*
▦ mineral	**minerale**	*mee-neh-rAH-leh*
(with gas)	**gassata**	*gahs-sAH-tah*
(without gas)	**naturale**	*nah-too-rAH-leh*

a glass of ____.	un bicchiere di ____.	oon bee-key-EH-reh dee
milk (cold)	latte (fresco)	lAHt-teh (frAY-skoh)
malted milk	latte con malto	lAHt-teh kOHn mAHl-toh
milk shake	frullato di latte	frool-lAH-toh dee lAHt-teh
orangeade	aranciata	ah-rahn-chee-AH-tah
punch	punch	pOHn-ch
soda	bibita anal-colica (soda)	bEE-bee-tah ah-nahl-kOH-lee-kah
(fruit) juice	succo di (frutta)	sOO-koh dee (frOOt-tah)
lemonade	limonata	lee-moh-nAH-tah

SETTLING UP

The check, please.	Il conto, per favore.	eel kOHn-toh, pehr fah-vOH-reh
Separate checks.	Conti separati.	kOHn-tee seh-pah-rAH-tee
Is the service included?	È incluso il servizio?	EH een-klOO-soh eel sehr-vEE-tsee-oh
I haven't ordered this.	Non ho ordinato questo.	nohn oh ohr-dee-nAH-toh koo-AY-stoh
I don't think the bill is right.	Non penso che il conto sia corretto.	nohn pEHn-soh kay eel kOHn-toh sEE-ah kor-rEHt-toh
We're in a hurry.	Abbiamo fretta.	ahb-bee-AH-moh frAYt-tah
This is for you.	Questo è per lei.	koo-AY-stoh EH pehr lEH-ee

MEETING PEOPLE

SMALL TALK

My name is ____.	**Il mio nome è ____.** *eel mEE-oh nOH-meh EH*
Do you live here?	**Lei abita qui?** *lEH-ee AH-bee-tah koo-EE*
Where are you from?	**Lei di dov'è?** *lEH-ee dee doh-vEH*
I am ____.	**Vengo ____.** *vEHn-goh*
▪ from the United States	**dagli Stati Uniti** *dAH-ly-ee stAH-tee oo-nEE-tee*
▪ from Canada	**dal Canadà** *dAHl kah-nah-dAH*
▪ from England	**dall'Inghilterra** *dahl-lEEn-gheel-tEHr-rah*
▪ from Australia	**dall'Australia** *dahl-lah-oos-trAH-lee-ah*
I like Italy (Rome) very much.	**L'Italia (Roma) mi piace moltissimo.** *lee-tAH-lee-ah (rOH-mah) mee pee-AH-cheh mohl-tEEs-see-moh*
I would like to go there.	**Mi piacerebbe andarci.** *mee pee-ah-cheh-rAYb-beh ahn-dAHr-chee*
How long will you be staying?	**Quanto tempo resterà qui?** *koo-AHn-toh tEHm-poh reh-steh-rAH koo-EE*
I'll stay for a few days (a week).	**Resterò alcuni giorni (una settimana).** *reh-steh-rOH ahl-kOO-nee jee-OHr-nee (OO-na seht-tee-mAH-nah)*
What hotel are you staying at?	**In quale hotel (albergo) sta?** *een koo-AH-leh oh-tEHl (ahl-bEHr-goh) stAH*
What do you think of it?	**Che ne pensa?** *kay nay pEHn-sah*

I (don't) like it very much.	**(Non) mi piace tanto.** *(nohn) mee pee-AH-cheh tAHn-toh*
I think it's ____.	**Penso che sia ____.** *pEHn-soh kay sEE-ah*
■ beautiful	**bello** *bEHl-loh*
■ interesting	**interessante** *een-teh-rehs-sAHn-teh*
■ magnificent	**splendido (magnifico)** *splEHn-dee-doh (mah-ny-EE-fee-koh)*
■ wonderful	**stupendo** *stoo-pEHn-doh*
May I introduce ____?	**Posso presentarle ____?** *pOHs-soh preh-sehn-tAHr-leh*
■ my brother (sister)	**mio fratello (mia sorella)** *mEE-oh frah-tEHl-loh (mEE-ah soh-rEHl-lah)*
■ my father (mother)	**mio padre (mia madre)** *mEE-oh pAH-dreh (mEE-ah mAH-dreh)*
■ my friend	**il mio amico** *eel mEE-oh ah-mEE-koh*
■ my husband (wife)	**mio marito (mia moglie)** *mEE-oh mah-rEE-toh (mEE-ah mOH-ly-ee-eh)*
■ my sweetheart	**il mio ragazzo (la mia ragazza)** *eel mEE-oh rah-gAH-tsoh (lah mEE-ah rah-gAH-tsah)*
■ my son (daughter)	**mio figlio (mia figlia)** *mEE-oh fEE-ly-ee-oh (mEE-ah fEE-ly-ee-ah)*
Glad to meet you.	**Piacere. Lieto(a) di conoscerla.** *pee-ah-chAY-reh.lee-EH-toh(ah) dee koh-nOH-shehr-lah*
How do you do?	**Come sta?** *kOH-meh stah*
I am a ____.	**Sono ____.** *sOH-noh*
teacher	**maestro(a)** *mah-AYs-troh(ah)*
doctor	**dottore (dottoressa)** *doht-tOH-reh (doht-toh-rAYs-sah)*

lawyer	**avvocato (avvocatessa)** *ahv-voh-kAH-toh (ahv-voh-kah-tAYs-sah)*
businessperson	**una persona d'affari** *oo-nah pehr-sOH-nah dahf-fAH-ree*
student	**studente (studentessa)** *stoo-dEHn-teh (stoo-dehn-tAYs-sah)*
Would you like a picture (snapshot)?	**Vuole che le scatti una foto (un'instantanea)?** *voo-OH-leh kay leh skAHt-tee OO-nah fOH-toh (oon-een-stahn-tAH-neh-ah)*
Stand here (there).	**Si metta qui (lì).** *see mAYt-tah koo-EE (lEE)*
Don't move.	**Non si muova.** *nohn see moo-OH-vah*
Smile. That's it.	**Sorrida. Ecco fatto.** *sohr-rEE-dah. EH-koh fAHt-toh*
Will you take a picture of me (us)?	**Può farmi (farci) una foto?** *poo-OH fAHr-mee (fAHr-chee) OO-nah fOH-toh*

DATING AND SOCIALIZING

May I have this dance?	**Le piacerebbe ballare con me?** *leh pee-ah-cheh-rAYb-beh bahl-lAH-reh kohn mAY*
With pleasure.	**Con piacere.** *kohn pee-ah-chAY-reh*
Would you like a drink (a cigarette)?	**Potrei offrirle da bere (una sigaretta)?** *poh-trEH-ee ohf-frEEr-leh dah bAY-reh (OO-na see-gah-rAYt-tah)*
Do you have a light (matches)?	**Ha un accendino (un fiammifero)?** *ah oon ah-chayn-dEE-noh (oon fee-ahm-mEE-feh-roh)*
Do you mind if I smoke?	**Le dispiace se fumo?** *leh dee-spee-AH-cheh say fOO-moh*

May I call you?	**Posso telefonarle?** *pOHs-soh teh-leh-foh-nAHr-leh*
May I take you home?	**L'accompagno a casa?** *lahk-kohm-pAH-ny-oh ah kAH-sah*
Are you doing anything tomorrow?	**Che fa domani?** *kay fAH doh-mAH-nee*
Are you free this evening?	**È libero(a) stasera?** *EH lEE-beh-roh(ah) stah-sAY-rah*
Would you like to go to ____ together?	**Le piacerebbe andare insieme a ____?** *leh pee-ah-cheh-rEHb-beh ahn-dAH-reh een-see-EH-meh ah*
I'll wait for you in front of the hotel.	**L'aspetterò davanti all'hotel (all'albergo).** *lah-speht-teh-rOH dah-vAHn-tee ahl-loh-tEHl (ahl-lahl-bEHr-goh)*
I'll pick you up at your house (hotel).	**La verrò a prendere a casa sua (all'hotel).** *lah vehr-rOH ah prAYn-day-reh ah kAH-sah sOO-ah (ahl-loh-tEHl)*
What is your telephone number?	**Qual è il suo numero di telefono?** *koo-ahl-EH eel sOO-oh nOO-meh-roh dee teh-lEH-foh-noh*
Here's my telephone number (address).	**Ecco il mio numero di telefono (indirizzo).** *EHk-koh eel mEE-oh nOO-meh-roh dee teh-lEH-foh-noh (een-dee-rEE-tsoh)*
Will you write to me?	**Mi scriverà?** *mee skree-veh-rAH*
I'm single (married).	**Sono scapolo (nubile) (sposato[a]).** *sOH-noh scAH-poh-loh nOO-bih-leh (spoh-sAH-toh[ah])*
Is your husband (wife) here?	**Sta qui suo marito (la signora)?** *stAH koo-EE sOO-oh mah-rEE-toh (lah see-ny-OH-rah)*

I'm here with my family.	**Sono qui con la mia famiglia.** *sOH-noh koo-EE kohn lah mEE-ah fah-mEE-ly-ee-ah*
Do you have any children?	**Ha bambini?** *AH bahm-bEE-nee*
How many?	**Quanti?** *koo-AHn-tee*
How old are they?	**Quanti anni hanno?** *koo-AHn-tee AHn-nee AHn-noh*

SAYING GOOD-BYE

Nice to have met you.	**È stato un piacere conoscerla.** *EH stAH-toh oon pee-ah-chAY-reh koh-nOH-shehr-lah*
The pleasure was mine.	**Il piacere è stato mio.** *eel pee-ah-chAY-reh EH stAH-toh mEE-oh*
Regards to ____.	**Saluti a ____.** *sah-lOO-tee ah*
Thanks for the evening.	**Grazie della serata.** *grAH-tsee-eh dAYl-lah say-rAH-tah*
I must go home now.	**Adesso devo andarmene a casa.** *ah-dEHs-soh dAY-voh ahn-dAHr-meh-neh ah kAH-sah*
You must come to visit us.	**Deve venire a farci visita.** *dAY-veh veh-nEE-reh ah fAHr-chee vEE-see-tah*

SHOPPING

GOING SHOPPING

Where can I find ____?	**Dove posso trovare ____?** *dOH-veh pOHs-soh troh-vAH-reh*
■ a bakery	**un fornaio** *oon fohr-nAH-ee-oh*
■ a bookstore	**una libreria** *OO-nah lee-bray-rEE-ah*

■ a butcher	**una macelleria** *OO-nah mah-chehl-leh-rEE-ah*
■ a camera shop	**un negozio di fotocine** *oon neh-gOH-tsee-oh dee foh-toh-chEE-neh*
■ a candy store	**un sale e tabacchi** *oon sAH-leh ay tah-bAH-key*
■ a clothing store	**un negozio di abbigliamento** *oon neh-gOH-tsee-oh dee ahb-bee-ly-ee-ah-mEHn-toh*
■ for children's clothes	**per bambini** *pehr bahm-bEE-nee*
■ men's store	**per uomini** *pehr oo-OH-mee-nee*
■ women's boutique	**per signore** *pehr see-ny-OH-reh*
■ a delicatessen	**una salumeria** *OO-nah sah-loo-meh-rEE-ah*
■ a department store	**i grandi magazzini** *ee grAHn-dee mah-gah-tsEE-nee*
■ a pharmacy (chemist)	**una farmacia** *OO-nah fahr-mah-chEE-ah*
■ a florist	**un fioraio** *oon fee-oh-rAH-ee-oh*
■ a gift (souvenir) shop	**un negozio di regali (souvenir)** *oon neh-gOH-tsee-oh dee reh-gAH-lee (soo-vay-nEEr)*
■ a grocery store	**un negozio di alimentari** *oon neh-gOH-tsee-oh dee ah-lee-mehn-tAH-ree*
■ a hardware store (ironmonger)	**un negozio di ferramenta** *oon neh-gOH-tsee-oh dee fehr-rah-mEHn-tah*
■ a jewelry store	**una gioielleria** *OO-nah jee-oh-ee-ehl-leh-rEE-ah*
■ a liquor store	**una enoteca** *OO-nah eh-noh-tEH-kah*

▪ a newsstand	**un'edicola (il giornalaio)** *oo-neh-dEE-koh-lah (eel jee-ohr-nah-lAH-ee-oh)*
▪ a record store	**un negozio di dischi** *oon nay-gOH-tsee-oh dee dEE-skey*
▪ a supermarket	**un supermercato** *oon soo-pehr-mehr-kAH-toh*
▪ a tobacco shop	**una tabaccheria** *OO-nah tah-bahk-keh-rEE-ah*
▪ a toy store	**un negozio di giocattoli** *oon neh-gOH-tsee-oh dee jee-oh-kAHt-toh-lee*
▪ a wine merchant	**una mescita, una cantina, una enoteca** *OO-nah mAY-shee-tah OO-nah kahn-tEE-nah OO-nah eh-noh-tEH-kah*
Young man, can you wait on me?	**Giovanotto, può occuparsi di me?** *jee-oh-vah-nOHt-toh poo-OH ohk-koo-pAHr-see dee meh*
Miss, can you help me?	**Signorina, può aiutarmi?** *see-ny-oh-rEE-nah poo-OH ah-ee-oo-tAHr-mee*
Do you take credit cards?	**Accettano carte di credito?** *ah-chEHt-tah-noh kAHr-teh dee crEH-dee-toh*
Can I pay with a traveler's check?	**Posso pagare con un traveler's check?** *pOHs-soh pah-gAH-reh kohn oon trAH-veh-lehs chEH-keh*

BOOKS

Is there a store that carries English-language books?	**C'è un negozio dove si vendono libri in lingua inglese?** *chEH oon neh-gOH-tsee-oh dOH-veh see vAYn-doh-noh lEE-bree een lEEn-goo-ah een-glAY-seh*

What is the best (biggest) bookstore here?	**Dov'è la migliore (la più grande) libreria qui?** *doh-vEH lah mee-ly-ee-OH-reh (lah pee-OO grAHn-deh) lee-breh-rEE-ah koo-EE*
I'm looking for a copy of ____.	**M'interessa una copia di ____.** *meen-teh-rEHs-sah OO-nah kOH-pee-ah dee*
The author of the book is ____.	**L'autore del libro è ____.** *lah-oo-tOH-reh dayl lEE-broh EH*
I don't know the title (author).	**Non conosco il titolo (l'autore).** *nohn koh-nOH-skoh eel tEE-toh-loh (lah-oo-tOH-reh)*
I'm just looking.	**Sto solo guardando.** *stoh sOH-loh goo-ahr-dAHn-doh*
Do you have books (novels) in English?	**Ha libri (romanzi) in inglese?** *ah lEE-bree (roh-mAHn-tsee) een een-glAY-seh*
I want ____.	**Desidero ____.** *deh-sEE-deh-roh*
▪ a guide book	**una guida** *OO-nah goo-EE-dah*
▪ a map of this city	**una pianta di questa città** *OO-nah pee-AHn-tah dee koo-AYs-tah cheet-tAH*
▪ a pocket dictionary	**un dizionario tascabile** *oon dee-tsee-oh-nAH-ree-oh tah-skAH-bee-leh*
▪ an Italian-English dictionary	**un dizionario Italiano-Inglese** *oon dee-tsee-oh-nAH-ree-oh ee-tah-lee-AH-noh een-glAY-seh*
Where can I find ____?	**Dove posso trovare ____?** *dOH-veh pOHs-soh troh-vAH-reh*
▪ detective stories	**romanzi gialli** *roh-mAHn-tsee jee-AHl-lee*
▪ comics	**fumetti** *foo-mAYt-tee*
▪ history books	**libri di storia** *lEE-bree dee stOH-ree-ah*

■ short stories	**una raccolta di novelle** *OO-nah rahk-kOHl-tah dee noh-vEHl-leh*
■ cookbooks	**libri di cucina** *lEE-bree dee koo-chEE-nah*
I'll take these books.	**Prendo questi libri.** *prAYn-doh koo-AYs-tee lEE-bree*
Will you wrap them, please?	**Me l'incarta, per favore?** *meh leen-kAHr-tah pehr fah-vOH-reh*

CLOTHING

Would you please show me _____?	**Per favore, può mostrarmi _____?** *pehr fah-vOH-reh poo-OH moh-strAHr-mee*
■ a belt for man (lady)	**una cintura per uomo (per signora)** *OO-nah cheen-tOO-rah pehr oo-OH-moh (pehr see-ny-OH-rah)*
■ a blouse	**una blusa (camicetta)** *OO-nah blOO-sah (kah-mee-chAYt-tah)*
■ a bra	**un reggiseno** *oon reh-jee-sAY-noh*
■ a dress	**una veste** *OO-nah vEH-steh*
■ an evening gown	**un abito da sera** *oon AH-bee-toh dah sAY-rah*
■ leather (suede) gloves	**dei guanti di pelle (scamosciata)** *dAY-ee goo-AHn-tee dee pEHl-leh (skah-moh-shee-AH-tah)*
■ handkerchiefs	**dei fazzoletti** *dAY-ee fah-tsoh-lAYt-tee*
■ a hat	**un cappello** *oon kahp-pEHl-loh*
■ a jacket	**una giacca** *OO-nah jee-AHk-kah*
■ an overcoat	**un soprabito** *oon soh-prAH-bee-toh*

pants	**dei pantaloni**	*dAY-ee pahn-tah-lOH-nee*
panty hose	**un collant**	*oon koh-lAHn*
a raincoat	**un impermeabile**	*oon eem-pehr-meh-AH-bee-leh*
a robe (for lady)	**una vestaglia**	*OO-nah veh-stAH-ly-ee-ah*
a robe (for man)	**una veste da camera**	*OO-nah vEH-steh dah kAH-meh-rah*
a shirt	**una camicia**	*OO-nah kah-mEE-chee-ah*
(a pair of) shoes	**un paio di scarpe**	*oon pAH-ee-oh dee skAHr-peh*
shorts (briefs)	**dei pantaloncini (delle mutande)**	*dAY-ee pahn-tah-lohn-chEE-nee (dAYl-leh moo-tAHn-deh)*
a skirt	**una gonna**	*OO-nah gOHn-nah*
a slip	**una sottoveste**	*oo-nah soht-toh-vEH-steh*
slippers	**delle pantofole**	*dAYl-leh pahn-tOH-foh-leh*
socks	**dei calzini**	*dAY-ee kahl-tsEE-nee*
(nylon) stockings	**delle calze (di nylon)**	*dAYl-leh kAHl-tseh (dee nAH-ee-lohn)*
a suit	**un vestito**	*oon veh-stEE-toh*
a sweater	**una maglia**	*OO-nah mAH-ly-ee-ah*
a tie	**una cravatta**	*OO-nah krah-vAHt-tah*
an undershirt	**una canottiera**	*OO-nah kah-noht-tee-EH-rah*
a tee-shirt	**una maglietta**	*OO-nah mah-ly-ee-AYt-tah*

underwear	**della biancheria intima** *dAYl-lah bee-ahn-keh-rEE-ah EEn-tee-mah*
a wallet	**un portafoglio** *oon pohr-tah-fOH-ly-ee-oh*
Is there a special sale today?	**Oggi c'è una vendita d'occasione?** *OH-jee chEH OO-nah vAYn-dee-tah dohk-kah-see-OH-neh*
I'd like a shirt with short (long) sleeves.	**Vorrei una camicia con le maniche corte (lunghe).** *vohr-rEH-ee OO-nah kah-mEE-chee-ah kOHn leh mAH-nee-keh kOHr-teh (lOOn-gheh)*
Do you have anything _____?	**Ha qualche cosa _____?** *AH koo-AHl-keh kOH-sah*
cheaper	**più a buon mercato** *pee-OO ah boo-OHn mehr-kAH-toh*
else	**d'altro** *dAHl-troh*
larger	**più grande** *pee-OO grAHn-deh*
less expensive	**meno costoso** *mAY-noh koh-stOH-soh*
longer	**più lungo** *pee-OO lOOn-goh*
of better quality	**di migliore qualità** *dee mee-ly-ee-OH-reh koo-ah-lee-tAH*
shorter	**più corto** *pee-OO kOHr-toh*
smaller	**più piccolo** *pee-OO pEE-koh-loh*
I don't like the color.	**Non mi piace il colore.** *nohn mee pee-AH-cheh eel koh-lOH-reh*
Do you have it in _____?	**Lo ha in _____?** *loh AH een*
black	**nero** *nAY-roh*
blue	**blu** *blOO*
brown	**marrone** *mahr-rOH-neh*

gray	**grigio** *grEE-jee-oh*
green	**verde** *vAYr-deh*
pink	**rosa** *rOH-sah*
red	**rosso** *rOHs-soh*
white	**bianco** *bee-AHn-koh*
yellow	**giallo** *jee-AHl-loh*

SALE SIGNS

SVENDITA	(sale)
SALDI DI FINE STAGIONE	(end of season sale)
LIQUIDAZIONE	(everything must go)
VENDITA TOTALE	
PREZZI FISSI	(fixed prices)

I want something in _____.	**Voglio qualche cosa** _____. *vOH-ly-ee-oh koo-AHl-keh kOH-sah*
chiffon	**di chiffon** *dee sheef-fOHn*
corduroy	**di velluto a coste** *dee vehl-lOO-toh ah kOH-steh*
cotton	**di cotone** *dee koh-tOH-neh*
denim	**di denim** *dee dEH-nim*
felt	**di feltro** *dee fAYl-troh*
flannel	**di flanella** *dee flah-nEHl-lah*
gabardine	**di gabardine** *dee gah-bahr-dEE-neh*
lace	**in pizzo** *een pEE-tsoh*
leather	**in pelle** *een pEHl-leh*

■ linen	**di lino** *dee lEE-noh*
■ nylon	**di nylon** *dee nAH-ee-lohn*
■ permanent press	**con piega permanente** *kOHn pee-EH-gah pehr-mah-nEHn-teh*
■ satin	**di raso** *dee rAH-soh*
■ silk	**di seta** *dee sAY-tah*
■ suede	**di renna** *dee rAYn-nah*
■ terrycloth	**in tessuto spugnoso** *een tehs-sOO-toh spoo-ny-OH-soh*
■ velvet	**di velluto** *dee vehl-lOO-toh*
■ wool	**di lana** *dee lAH-nah*
■ synthetic (polyester)	**in poliestere** *een poh-lee-EH-steh-reh*
■ wash-and-wear	**che non si stira** *kay nohn see stEE-rah*
Show me something _____.	**Mi faccia vedere qualche cosa** _____. *mee fAH-chee-ah veh-dAY-reh koo-AHl-kay kOH-sah*
■ in solid color	**a tinta unita** *ah tEEn-tah oo-nEE-tah*
■ with stripes	**a righe** *ah rEE-gheh*
■ with polkadots	**a pallini** *ah pahl-lEE-nee*
■ in plaid	**a quadri** *ah koo-AH-dree*
Please take my measurements.	**Può prendermi le misure?** *poo-OH prEHn-dayr-mee leh mee-sOO-reh*
I take size (my size is) _____.	**La mia taglia è** _____. *lah mEE-ah tAH-ly-ee-ah EH*
■ small	**piccola** *pEEk-koh-lah*
■ medium	**media** *mEH-dee-ah*
■ large	**grande** *grAHn-deh*
Can I try it on?	**Posso provarmelo(la)?** *pOHs-soh proh-vAHr-meh-loh(lah)*

Can you alter it?	**Può aggiustarmelo(la)?** *poo-OH ah-jee-oo-stAHr-meh-loh(lah)*
Can I return the article (if I change my mind)?	**(Se non mi va), posso portarlo indietro?** *(say nOHn mee vAH) pOHs-soh pohr-tAHr-loh een-dee-EH-troh*
Do you have something hand made?	**Non c'è nulla che sia fatto a mano?** *nOHn chEH nOOl-lah kay sEE-ah fAHt-toh ah mAH-noh*
The zipper doesn't work.	**La cerniera non funziona.** *lah chehr-nee-EH-rah nohn fOOn-tsee-OH-nah*
It doesn't fit me.	**Non mi sta bene.** *nohn mee stAH bEH-neh*
It fits very well.	**Mi sta molto bene.** *mee stAH mOHl-toh bEH-neh*
I'll take it.	**Lo(la) prendo.** *loh(lah) prAYn-doh*
Will you wrap it?	**Me lo(la) impacchetta?** *meh loh(lah) eem-pahk-kEHt-tah*
I'd like to see the pair of shoes (boots) in the window.	**Vorrei vedere il paio di scarpe (stivali) in vetrina.** *vohr-rEH-ee veh-dAY-reh eel pAH-ee-oh dee skAHr-peh (stee-vAH-lee) een vay-trEE-nah*
They're too narrow (wide).	**Sono troppo strette (larghe).** *sOH-noh trOHp-poh strAYt-teh (lAHr-gheh)*
They pinch me.	**Mi stanno strette.** *mee stAHn-noh strAYt-teh*
They fit me.	**Mi stanno bene.** *mee stAHn-noh bEH-neh*
I'll take them.	**Le compro.** *leh kOHm-proh*
I also need shoelaces.	**Ho bisogno anche dei lacci.** *oh bee-sOH-ny-oh AHn-keh dAY-ee lAH-chee*
That's all I want for now.	**Questo è tutto quello che voglio per ora.** *koo-AYs-toh EH tOOt-toh koo-AYl-loh kay vOH-ly-ee-oh pehr OH-rah*

ELECTRICAL APPLIANCES

I want to buy ____.	**Vorrei comprare** ____. *vohr-rEH-ee kohm-prAH-reh*
▨ a battery	**una pila** *OO-nah pEE-lah*
▨ an electric shaver	**un rasoio elettrico** *oon rah-sOH-ee-oh eh-lEHt-tree-koh*
▨ a hair dryer	**un asciugacapelli** *oon ah-shee-oo-gah-kah-pAYl-lee*
▨ a (portable) radio	**una radio (portatile)** *OO-nah rAH-dee-oh (pohr-tAH-tee-leh)*
▨ a tape recorder	**un registratore** *oon reh-jee-strah-tOH-reh*

FOODS AND HOUSEHOLD ITEMS

I'd like ____.	**Vorrei** ____. *vohr-rEH-ee*
▨ a bar of soap	**una saponetta** *oo-nah sah-poh-nEHt-tah*
▨ a bottle of juice	**un succo di frutta** *oon sOO-koh dee frOOt-tah*
▨ a box of cereal	**una scatola di cereali** *oo-nah skAH-toh-lah dee cheh-reh-AH-lee*
▨ a can (tin) of to-mato sauce	**una scatola di conserva di pomo-doro** *oo-nah skAH-toh-lah dee kohn-sEHr-vah dee poh-moh-dOH-roh*
▨ a dozen eggs	**una dozzina d'uova** *oo-nah doh-tsEE-nah doo-OH-vah*
▨ a jar of coffee	**un vasetto di caffè** *oon vah-sAYt-toh dee kahf-fEH*
▨ a kilo of potatoes (just over 2 pounds)	**un chilo di patate** *oon kEE-loh dee pah-tAH-teh*

▨ a half kilo of cherries (just over one pound)

mezzo chilo di ciliege *mEH-tsoh kEE-loh dee chee-lee-EH-jeh*

▨ a liter of milk (about 1 quart)

un litro di latte *oon LEE-troh dee lAHt-teh*

▨ a package of candies

un pacchetto di caramelle *oon pah-kAYt-toh dee kah-rah-mEHl-leh*

▨ 100 grams of cheese (about ¼ pound)

cento grammi di formaggio (un etto) *chEHn-toh grAHm-mee dee fohr-mAH-jee-oh (oon EHt-toh)*

▨ a roll of toilet paper

un rotolo di carta igienica *oon rOH-toh-loh dee kAHr-tah ee-jee-EH-nee-kah*

I'd like a kilo (about 2 pounds) of oranges.

Vorrei un chilo di arance. *vohr-rEY-ee oon kEY-loh dee ah-rAHn-chay*

▨ a half kilo of butter

mezzo chilo di burro. *mAY-tsoh kEY-loh dee bOOr-roh*

▨ 200 grams (about ½ pound) of cookies

due etti di biscotti *dOO-eh EHt-tee dee bees-kOHt-tee*

▨ 100 grams (about ¼ pound) of bologna

un etto di mortadella *oon EHt-toh dee mohr-tah-dAYl-lah*

What is this (that)?

Che cosa è questo (quello)? *kay kOH-sah EH koo-AY-stoh (koo-AYl-loh)*

Is it fresh?

È fresco? *EH frAY-skoh*

JEWELRY

I'd like to see ____.

Vorrei vedere ____. *vohr-rEH-ee veh-dAY-reh*

▨ a bracelet

un braccialetto *oon brah-chee-ah-lAYt-toh*

■ a brooch	**un fermaglio (una spilla)** *oon fehr-mAH-ly-ee-oh (OO-nah spEE-lah)*
■ a chain	**una catenina** *OO-nah kah-teh-nEE-nah*
■ a charm	**un ciondolo** *oon chee-OHn-doh-loh*
some earrings	**degli orecchini** *dAY-ly-ee oh-rehk-kEE-nee*
■ a necklace	**un monile** *oon moh-nEE-leh*
■ a pin	**una spilla** *OO-nah spEEl-lah*
■ a ring	**un anello** *oon ah-nEHl-loh*
■ a rosary	**una corona del rosario** *OO-nah koh-rOH-nah dayl roh-sAH-ree-oh*
■ a (wrist) watch	**un orologio da polso** *oon oh-roh-lOH-jee-oh dah pOHl-soh*
Is this _____?	**Questo è _____?** *koo-AY-stoh EH*
■ gold	**d'oro** *dOH-roh*
■ platinum	**di platino** *dee plAH-tee-noh*
■ silver	**d'argento** *dahr-jEHn-toh*
■ stainless steel	**d'acciaio inossidabile** *dah-chee-AH-ee-oh ee-nohs-see-dAH-bee-leh*
Is it solid or gold plated?	**È oro massiccio oppure oro placcato?** *EH OH-roh mahs-sEE-chee-oh ohp-pOO-reh OH-roh plahk-kAH-toh*
How many carats is it?	**Di quanti carati è?** *dee koo-AHn-tee kah-rAH-tee EH*
What is that (precious) stone?	**Che pietra (preziosa) è?** *kay pee-Eh-trah (preh-tsee-OH-sah) EH*
I want _____.	**Vorrei (voglio) _____.** *vohr-rEH-ee (vOH-ly-ee-oh)*
■ a coral	**un corallo** *oon koh-rAHl-loh*
■ an amethyst	**un'ametista** *oo-nah-meh-tEE-stah*

▪ an aquamarine	**un'acquamarina** *oo-nah-koo-ah-mah-rEE-nah*
▪ a diamond	**un diamante** *oon dee-ah-mAHn-teh*
▪ an emerald	**uno smeraldo** *OO-noh smeh-rAHl-doh*
▪ an enamel	**uno smalto** *OO-noh smAHl-toh*
▪ ivory	**una cosa d'avorio** *OO-nah kOH-sah dah-vOH-ree-oh*
▪ jade	**una giada** *OO-nah jee-AH-dah*
▪ onyx	**un 'onice** *oon-OH-nee-cheh*
▪ pearls	**delle perle** *dAYl-leh pEHr-leh*
▪ a ruby	**un rubino** *oon roo-bEE-noh*
▪ a sapphire	**uno zaffiro** *OO-noh tsahf-fEE-roh*
▪ a topaz	**un topazio** *oon toh-pAH-tsee-oh*
▪ turquoise	**un turchese** *oon toor-kAY-seh*
How much is it?	**Quanto costa?** *koo-AHn-toh kOH-stah*

RECORDS AND TAPES

Is there a record shop around here?	**C'è un negozio di dischi qui vicino?** *chEH oon neh-GOH-tsee-oh dee dEE-skee koo-EE vee-chEE- noh*
Do you have an L.P. (45 r.p.m.) of ____?	**Ha un microsolco (a quarantacinque giri) di ____?** *Ah oon mee-kroh-sOHl-koh (ah koo-ah-rAHn-tah-chEEn-koo-eh jEE-ree) dee*
I'd like to buy ____.	**Vorrei comprare ____.** *vohr-rEH-ee kohm-prAH-reh*
▪ cassettes	**delle cassette** *dAYl-leh kahs-sAYt-teh*
▪ records	**dei dischi** *dAY-ee dEE-skee*

◼ tapes	**dei nastri** *dAY-ee nAH-stree*
Where is the ____ section?	**Dov'è la sezione ____?** *doh-vEH lah seh-tsee-OH-neh*
◼ classical music	**di musica classica** *dee mOO-see-kah clAHs-see-kah*
◼ popular music	**di musica popolare** *dee mOO-see-kah poh-poh-lAH-reh*
◼ latest hits	**degli ultimi successi** *dAY-ly-ee OOl-tee-mee soo-chEHs-see*
◼ Italian music	**della musica italiana** *dAYl-lah mOO-see-kah ee-tah-lee-AH-nah*
◼ opera	**di musica d'opera** *dee mOO-see-kah dOH-peh-rah*

NEWSPAPERS AND MAGAZINES

Do you carry English newspapers (magazines)?	**Ha giornali (riviste) in inglese?** *a jee-ohr-nAH-lee (ree-vEE-steh) een een-glAY-seh*
I'd like to buy some (picture) postcards.	**Vorrei comprare delle cartoline (illustrate).** *vohr-rEH-ee kohm-prAH-reh dAYl-leh kahr-toh-lEE-neh (eel-loo-strAH-teh)*
Do you have stamps?	**Ha francobolli?** *AH frahn-koh-bOHl-lee*
How much is it?	**Quant'è?** *koo-ahn-tEH*

PHOTOGRAPHIC SUPPLIES

| Where is there a camera shop? | **Dov'è un negozio di fotocine (macchine fotografiche)?** *doh-vEH oon nay-GOH-tsee-oh dee foh-toh-chEE-neh (mAHk-kee-neh foh-toh-grAH-fee-keh)* |

Do they develop films?	**Sviluppano i rullini?** *svee-lOOp-pah-noh ee rool-lEE-nee*
How much does it cost to develop a roll?	**Quanto costa far sviluppare un rullino?** *koo-AHn-toh kOH-stah fahr svee-loop-pAH-reh oon rool-lEE-noh*
I want one print of each.	**Voglio una copia per ogni fotografia.** *vOH-ly-ee-oh OO-nah kOH-pee-ah pehr OH-ny-ee foh-toh-grah-fEE-ah*
I want ____.	**Vorrei (voglio) ____.** *vohr-rEH-ee (vOH-ly-ee-oh)*
an enlargement	**un ingrandimento** *oon een-grahn-dee-mEHn-toh*
with a glossy (matte) finish	**su carta lucida (opaca, matta)** *soo kAHr-tah lOO-chee-dah (oh-pAH-kah, mAHt-tah)*
I want a roll of color (black and white) film.	**Voglio un rullino a colori (in bianco e nero).** *vOH-ly-ee-oh oon rool-lEE-noh ah koh-lOH-ree (een bee-AHn-koh ay nAY-roh)*
I want a roll of 20 (36) exposures (for slides).	**Vorrei un rullino (per diapositive) di venti, trentasei pose.** *vohr-rEH-ee oon rool-lEE-noh (pehr dee-ah-poh-see-tEE-veh) dee vAYn-tee, trehn-tah-sEH-ee pOH-seh*
I want a filmpack ____.	**Vorrei (voglio) un rullino per istantanee (poloroid).** *vohr-rEH-ee (vOH-ly-ee-oh) oon rool-lEE-noh pehr ee-stahn-tAH-neh-eh (poloroid)*
When can I pick up the pictures?	**Quando vengo a ritirarle?** *koo-AHn-doh vEHn-goh ah ree-tee-rAHr-leh*
I want an expensive (inexpensive) camera.	**Voglio una buona macchina fotografica (a buon mercato).** *vOH-ly-ee-oh OO-nah boo-OH-nah mAHk-kee-nah foh-toh-grAH-fee-kah (ah boo-OHn mayr-kAH-toh)*

SOUVENIRS, HANDICRAFTS

I'd like ____.	**Vorrei ____.** *vohr-rEH-ee*
a pretty gift	**un bel regalo** *oon bEHl reh-gAH-loh*
a small gift	**un regalino** *oon reh-gah-lEE-noh*
a souvenir	**un souvenir** *oon soo-veh-nEEr*

It's for ____.   **È per ____.** *EH pehr*

I don't want to spend more than 20 (30) dollars.   **Non voglio spendere più di venti (trenta) dollari.** *nohn vOH-ly-ee-oh spEHn-deh-reh pee-OO dee vAYn-tee (trEHn-tah) dOHl-lah-ree*

Could you suggest something?   **Potrebbe suggerirmi qualche cosa?** *poh-trAYb-beh soo-jeh-rEEr-mee koo-AHl-keh kOH-sah*

Would you show me your selection of ____?   **Che cosa potrebbe mostrarmi di ____?** *kay kOH-sah poh-trAYb-beh moh-strAHr-mee dee*

blown glass	**vetro soffiato** *vAY-troh sohf-fee-AH-toh*
carved object	**legno intagliato** *lAY-ny-oh een-tah-ly-ee-AH-toh*
crystal	**cristallo** *kree-stAHl-loh*
earthenware (pottery)	**ceramiche** *cheh-rAH-mee-keh*
fans	**ventagli** *vehn-tAH-ly-ee*
jewelry	**oggetti preziosi** *oh-jEHt-tee preh-tsee-OH-see*
lace	**pizzi** *pEE-tsee*
leathergoods	**articoli in pelle** *ahr-tEE-koh-lee een pEHl-leh*
liqueurs	**liquori** *lee-koo-OH-ree*

◼ musical instruments	**strumenti musicali**	*stroo-mEHn-tee moo-see-kAH-lee*
◼ perfumes	**profumi**	*proh-fOO-mee*
◼ (miniature) pictures	**quadretti (in miniatura)**	*koo-ah-drAYt-tee (een mee-nee-ah-tOO-rah)*
◼ posters	**affissi, manifesti, poster**	*ahf-fEEs-see, mah-nee-fEH-stee, pOH-stehr*
◼ religious articles	**articoli religiosi**	*ahr-tEE-koh-lee reh-lee-jee-OH-see*
◼ local handicrafts	**prodotti dell'artigianato locale?**	*proh-dOHt-tee dayl-lahr-tee-jee-ah-nAH-toh loh-kAH-leh*

STATIONERY ITEMS

I want to buy ____.	**Voglio comprare ____.**	*vOH-ly-ee-oh kohm-prAH-reh*
◼ a ball-point pen	**una penna a sfera**	*OO-nah pAYn-nah ah sfEH-rah*
◼ a deck of cards	**un mazzo di carte**	*oon mAH-tsoh dee kAHr-teh*
◼ envelopes	**delle buste**	*dAYl-leh bOO-steh*
◼ an eraser	**una gomma per cancellare**	*OO-nah gOHm-mah pehr kahn-chehl-lAH-reh*
◼ glue	**della colla**	*dAYl-lah kOHl-lah*
◼ a notebook	**un taccuino**	*oon tahk-koo-EE-noh*
◼ pencils	**delle matite**	*dAYl-leh mah-tEE-teh*
◼ a pencil sharpener	**un temperamatite**	*oon tehm-peh-rah-mah-tEE-teh*
◼ a ruler	**una riga**	*OO-nah rEE-gah*
◼ Scotch tape	**un nastro adesivo (uno scotch)**	*oon nAH-stroh ah-deh-sEE-voh (OO-noh skO-ch)*

▪ some string	**del filo** *dayl fEE-loh*
▪ typing paper	**della carta per battere a macchina** *dAYl-lah kAHr-tah pehr bAHt-teh-reh ah mAH-kee-nah*
▪ wrapping paper	**della carta da imballaggio** *dAYl-lah kAHr-tah dah eem-bahl-lAH-jee-oh*
▪ a writing pad	**un blocchetto di carta** *oon blohk-kAYt-toh dee kAHr-tah*
▪ writing paper	**della carta da scrivere** *dAYl-lah kAHr-tah dah scrEE-veh-reh*

TOBACCO

A pack (carton) of cigarettes, please.	**Un pacchetto (una stecca) di sigarette, per piacere.** *oon pah-kAYt-toh (OO-nah stAYk-kah) dee see-gah-rAYt-teh, pehr pee-ah-chAY-reh*
▪ filtered	**con filtro** *kOHn fEEl-troh*
▪ unfiltered	**senza filtro** *sEHn-tsah fEEl-troh*
▪ menthol	**alla menta** *ahl-lah mEHn-tah*
▪ king-size	**lunghe** *lOOn-gheh*
Are these cigarettes (very) strong (mild)?	**Sono (molto) forti (leggere) queste sigarette?** *sOH-noh (mOHl-toh) fOHr-tee (leh-jEH-reh) koo-AY-steh see-gah-rAYt-teh*
Do you have American cigarettes?	**Ha sigarette americane?** *AH see-gah-rAYt-teh ah-meh-ree-kAH-neh?*
What brand?	**Di che marca?** *dee kay mAHr-kah*
Please give me a pack of matches also.	**Mi dia anche una scatola di fiammiferi, per piacere.** *mee dEE-ah AHn-kay OO-nah skAH-toh-lah dee fee-ahm-mEE-fay-ree pehr pee-ah-chAY-reh*

Do you sell ___?	**Vendono ___?** *vAYn-doh-noh*
chewing tobacco	**tabacco da masticare** *tah-bAHk-koh dah mah-stee-kAH-reh*
cigarette holders	**portasigarette** *pohr-tah-see-gah-rAYt-teh*
cigars	**sigari** *sEE-gah-ree*
flints	**pietrine** *pee-eh-trEE-neh*
lighter fluid	**benzina per accendini?** *behn-tsEE-nah pehr ah-chen-dEE-nee*
pipes	**pipe** *pEE-peh*
pipe tobacco	**tabacco da pipa** *tah-bAHk-koh dah pEE-pah*
snuff	**tabacco da fiuto** *tah-bAHk-koh dah fee-OO-toh*

TOILETRIES

Do you have ___?	**Ha ___?** *ah*
bobby pins	**delle forcine** *dAYl-leh fohr-chEE-neh*
a brush	**una spazzola** *OO-nah spAH-tsoh-lah*
cleansing cream	**della crema detergente** *dAYl-lah crEH-mah day-tehr-jEHn-teh*
a comb	**un pettine** *oon pEHt-tee-neh*
a deodorant	**un deodorante** *oon deh-oh-doh-rAHn-teh*
(disposable) diapers	**dei pannolini usa e getta** *dAY-ee pahn-noh-lEE-nee OO-sah ay jEHt-tah*
emery boards	**delle limette per le unghie** *dAYl-leh lee-mEHt-teh pehr leh OOn-ghee-eh*

▩ eye liner	**un eye liner** *oon "eye liner"*
▩ eye shadow	**l'ombretto** *lohm-brAYt-toh*
▩ eyebrow pencil	**una matita per le sopracciglia** *OO-nah mah-tEE-tah pehr leh soh-prah-chEE-ly-ee-ah*
▩ hair spray	**della lacca per capelli** *dAYl-la lAHk-kah pehr kah-pAYl-lee*
▩ lipstick	**il lipstick (rossetto per le labbra)** *eel "lipstick" (rohs-sEHt-toh pehr leh lAHb-brah)*
▩ make-up	**il make-up (trucco)** *eel "make up" (trOOk-koh)*
▩ mascara	**del mascara** *dAYl mah-skAH-rah*
▩ a mirror	**uno specchio** *OO-noh spEHk-key-oh*
▩ mouthwash	**del disinfettante per la bocca** *dayl dee-seen-feht-tAHn-teh pehr lah bOHk-kah*
▩ nail clippers	**dei tagliaunghie** *dAY-ee tah-ly-ee-ah-OOn-ghee-eh*
▩ a nail file	**una limetta per le unghie** *OO-nah lee-mAYt-tah pehr leh OOn-ghee-eh*
▩ nail polish	**dello smalto per le unghie** *dAYl-loh smAHl-toh pehr leh OOn-ghee-eh*
▩ nail polish remover	**dell'acetone** *dayl-lah-cheh-tOH-neh*
▩ a razor	**un rasoio di sicurezza** *oon rah-sOH-ee-oh dee see-koo-rAY-tsah*
▩ razor blades	**delle lamette** *dAYl-leh lah-mAYt-teh*
▩ rouge	**il rossetto (belletto)** *eel rohs-sEHt-toh (behl-lEHt-toh)*
▩ sanitary napkins	**degli assorbenti (igienici)** *dAY-ly-ee ahs-sohr-bEHn-tee (ee-jee-EH-nee-chee)*

(cuticle) scissors	**delle forbicine**	*dAYl-leh fohr-bee-chEE-neh*
shampoo	**dello shampoo**	*dAYl-loh shee-AHm-poh*
shaving lotion	**un dopobarba**	*oon doh-poh-bAHr-bah*
soap	**del sapone**	*dayl sah-pOH-neh*
a sponge	**una spungna**	*OO-nah spOO-ny-ah*
tampons	**dei tamponi**	*dAY-ee tahm-pOH-nee*
tissues	**dei fazzolettini di carta**	*dAY-ee fah-tsoh-leht-tEE-nee dee kAHr-tah*
toilet paper	**della carta igienica**	*dAYl-lah kAHr-tah ee-jee-EH-nee-kah*
a toothbrush	**uno spazzolino per i denti**	*OO-noh spah-tsoh-lEE-noh pehr ee dEHn-tee*
toothpaste	**un dentifricio**	*oon dEHn-tee-frEE-chee-oh*
tweezers	**delle pinzette**	*dAYl-leh peen-tsEHt-teh*

PERSONAL CARE AND SERVICES

AT THE BARBER

Where is there a good barbershop?	**Dove potrei trovare (una buona barberia) un buon parrucchiere?** *dOH-veh poh-trEH-ee troh-vAH-reh (OO-nah boo-OH-nah bahr-beh-rEE-ah) oon boo-OHn pahr-rook-key-EH-reh*
Do I have to wait long?	**C'è da aspettare molto?** *chEH dah-speht-tAH-reh mOHl-toh*
Am I next?	**È arrivato il mio turno?** *EH ahr-ree-vAH-toh eel mEE-oh tOOr-noh*

I want a shave.	**Voglio farmi la barba.** *vOH-ly-ee-oh fAHr-mee lah bAHr-bah*
I want a haircut.	**Voglio un taglio di capelli.** *vOH-ly-ee-oh oon tAH-ly-ee-oh dee kah-pAYl-lee*
Short in back, long in front.	**Corti dietro, lunghi davanti.** *kOHr-tee dee-EH-troh, lOOn-ghee dah-vAHn-tee*
Leave it long.	**Me li lasci lunghi.** *meh-lee lAH-shee lOOn-ghee*
I want it (very) short.	**Li voglio (molto) corti.** *lee vOH-ly-ee-oh (mOHl-toh) kOHr-tee*
You can cut a little _____.	**Me li può tagliare un po' _____.** *meh lee poo-OH tah-ly-ee-AH-reh oon pOH*
▧ in back	**di dietro** *dee dee-EH-troh*
▧ in front	**sul davanti** *sool dah-vAHn-tee*
▧ off the top	**sopra** *sOH-prah*
Cut a little bit more here.	**Tagli un po' di più qui (per favore).** *tAH-ly-ee oon pOH dee pee-OO koo-EE (pehr fah-vOH-reh)*
That's enough.	**Basta così.** *bAH-stah koh-sEE*
Use the scissors only.	**Usi solamente le forbici.** *OO-see soh-lah-mEHn-teh leh fOHr-bee-chee*
I'd like a razor cut.	**Vorrei un taglio al rasoio.** *vohr-rEH-ee oon tAH-ly-ee-oh ahl rah-sOH-ee-oh*
Please trim _____.	**Può spuntarmi _____.** *poo-OH spoon-tAHr-mee*
▧ my beard	**il pizzo (la barba)** *eel pEE-tsoh (lah bAHr-bah)*
▧ my moustache	**i baffi** *ee bAHf-fee*
▧ my sideburns	**le basette** *leh bah-sAYt-teh*

Where's the mirror?	**Dov'è lo specchio?** *doh-vEH loh spEHK-key-oh*
How much do I owe you?	**Quanto le devo?** *koo-AHn-toh leh dAY-voh*
Is service included?	**È incluso il servizio?** *EH een-klOO-soh eel sehr-vEE-tzee-oh*

AT THE BEAUTY PARLOR

Is there a beauty parlor (hairdresser) near the hotel?	**C'è una parrucchiera vicino all'albergo?** *chEH OO-nah pahr-rook-key-EH-rah vee-chEE-noh ahl-lahl-bEHr-goh*
I'd like an appointment for this afternoon (tomorrow).	**Vorrei un appuntamento per questo pomeriggio (per domani).** *vohr-rEH-ee oon ahp-poon-tah-mEHn-toh pehr koo-AYs-toh poh-meh-rEE-jee-oh (pehr doh-mAH-nee)*
Can you give me ____?	**Può farmi ____?** *poo-OH fAHr-mee*

▦ a color rinse	**un cachet** *oon kah-shEH*
▦ a facial massage	**un massaggio facciale** *oon mahs-sAH-jee-oh fah-chee-AH-leh*
▦ a haircut	**un taglio di capelli** *oon tAH-ly-ee-oh dee kah-pAYl-lee*
▦ a manicure	**la manicure** *lah mah-nee-kOO-reh*
▦ a permanent	**una permanente** *OO-nah pehr-mah-nAYn-teh*
▦ a shampoo	**lo shampoo** *loh shee-AH-mpoh*
▦ a wash and set	**shampoo e messa in piega** *shee-AH-mpoh ay mAYs-sah een pee-AY-gah*

I'd like to see a color chart.	**Vorrei vedere il cartellino dei colori.** *vohr-rEH-ee veh-dAY-reh eel kahr-tehl-lEE-noh dAY-ee koh-lOH-ree*
I want _____.	**Voglio _____.** *vOH-ly-ee-oh*
auburn	**un color rame** *oon koh-lOHr rAH-meh*
(light) blond	**un biondo (chiaro)** *oon bee-OHn-doh (key-AH-roh)*
brunette	**un bruno** *oon brOO-noh*
a darker color	**un colore più scuro** *oon koh-lOH-reh pee-OO skOO-roh*
a lighter color	**un colore più chiaro** *oon koh-lOH-reh pee-OO key-AH-roh*
the same color	**lo stesso colore** *loh stAYs-soh koh-lOH-reh*
Don't apply any hair-spray.	**Non mi metta nessuna lacca.** *nohn mee mEHt-tah nays-sOO-nah lAHk-kah*
Not too much hair-spray.	**Non troppa lacca.** *nohn trOHp-pah lAHk-kah*
I want my hair _____.	**Vorrei (voglio) i capelli _____.** *vohr-rEH-ee (vOH-ly-ee-oh) ee kah-pEHl-lee*
with bangs	**con la frangia** *kohn lah frAHn-jee-ah*
in a bun	**a nodo (a crocchia)** *ah nOH-doh (ah krOHk-key-ah)*
in curls	**a boccoli** *ah bOHk-koh-lee*
with waves	**ondulati** *ohn-doo-lAH-tee*
Where's the mirror?	**Dov'è lo specchio?** *doh-vEH loh spEHk-key-oh*

How much do I owe you?	**Quanto le devo?** *koo-AHn-toh leh dAY-voh*
Is service included?	**È incluso il servizio?** *EH een-klOO-soh eel sehr-vEE-tzee-oh*

LAUNDRY AND DRY CLEANING

Where is the nearest laundry (dry cleaner's)?	**Dov'è la lavanderia (la tintoria) più vicina?** *Doh-vEH lah lah-vahn-deh-rEE-ah (lah teen-toh-rEE-ah) pee-OO vee-chEE-nah*
I have a lot of (dirty) clothes to be ____.	**Ho molta biancheria (sporca) da ____.** *oh mOHl-tah bee-ahn-keh-rEE-ah (spOHr-kah) dah*
dry cleaned	**lavare a secco** *lah-vAH-reh ah sAYk-koh*
washed	**lavare** *lah-vAH-reh*
mended	**rammendare** *rahm-mehn-dAH-reh*
ironed	**stirare** *stee-rAH-reh*
Here's the list:	**Ecco l'elenco:** *EHk-koh leh-lEHn-koh*
3 shirts (men's)	**tre camicie (da uomo)** *tray kah-mee-cheh (dah oo-OH-moh)*
12 handkerchiefs	**dodici fazzoletti** *dOH-dee-chee fah-tsoh-lAYt-tee*
6 pairs of socks	**sei paia di calzini** *sAY-ee pAH-ee-ah dee kahl-tsEE-nee*
1 blouse (nylon)	**una blusa (di nylon)** *oo-nah blOO-sah (dee nAH-ee-lohn)*
4 shorts	**quattro mutande** *koo-AHt-tro moo-tAHn-deh*

■ 1 pyjamas	**due pigiama** *dOO-eh pee-jee-AH-mah*
■ 2 suits	**due vestiti** *dOO-eh veh-stEE-tee*
■ 3 ties	**tre cravatte** *tray krah-vAHt-teh*
■ 2 dresses (cotton)	**due vesti (di cotone)** *dOO-eh veh-stee (dee koh-tOH-neh)*
■ 2 skirts	**due gonne** *dOO-eh gOHn-neh*
■ 1 sweater (wool)	**una maglia (di lana)** *oo-na mAH-ly-ah (dee lAH-nah)*
■ 1 pair of gloves	**un paio di guanti** *oon pAH-ee-oh dee goo-AHn-tee*

I need them for ____.	**Mi occorrono per ____.** *mee ohk-kOHr-roh-noh pehr*
■ as soon as possible	**al più presto possibile** *ahl pee-OO preh-stoh pohs-see-bee-leh*
■ tonight	**stasera** *stah-sAY-ra*
■ tomorrow	**domani** *doh-mAH-nee*
■ next week	**la settimana prossima** *lah seht-tee-mAH-nah prOHs-see-mah*
■ the day after tomorrow	**dopodomani** *doh-poh doh-mAH-nee*

When will you bring it (them) back?	**Quando lo (li) riporterà?** *koo-AHn-doh loh (lee) ree-pohr-teh-rAH*
When will it be ready?	**Quando sarà pronto?** *koo-AHn-doh sah-rAH prOHn-toh*
There's a button missing.	**Manca un bottone.** *mAHn-kah oon boht-tOH-neh*
Can you sew it on?	**Può riattaccarlo?** *poo-OH ree-aht-tahk-kAHr-loh*
This isn't my laundry.	**Questa non è la mia biancheria.** *koo-AYs-tah nohn EH lah mEE-ah bee-ahn-keh-rEE-ah*

SHOE REPAIRS

Can you fix these shoes (boots)?

Può ripararmi queste scarpe (questi stivali)? *poo-OH ree-pah-rAHr-mee koo-AYs-teh skAHr-peh (koo-AY-stee-vAH-lee)*

Put on (half) soles and rubber heels.

Ci metta le (mezze) suole e i tacchi di gomma. *chee mEHt-tah leh (mEH-tseh) soo-OH-leh ay ee tAH-key dee gOHm-mah*

I'd like to have my shoes shined too.

Vorrei anche che mi lucidasse le scarpe. *vohr-rEH-ee AHn-keh kay mee loo-chee-dAHs-seh leh skAHr-peh*

When will they be ready?

Quando saranno pronte? *koo-AHn-doh sah-rAHn-noh prOHn-teh*

I need them by Saturday (without fail).

Mi occorrono per sabato (assolutamente). *mee ohk-kOHr-roh-noh pehr sAH-bah-toh (ahs-soh-loo-tah-mEHn-teh)*

WATCH REPAIRS

Can you fix this watch (alarm clock) (for me)?

(Mi) può aggiustare quest'orologio (questa sveglia)? *(mee) poo-OH ah-jee-oo-stAH-reh koo-ay-stoh-roh-lOH-jee-oh (koo-AY-stah svAY-ly-ee-ah)*

Can you clean it?

Può pulirlo(la)? *poo-OH poo-lEEr-loh(lah)*

I dropped it.

L'ho lasciato(a) cadere. *lOH lah-shee-AH-toh(tah) kah-dAY-reh*

It's running slow (fast).

Va piano (in anticipo). *vAH pee-AH-noh (een ahn-tEE-chee-poh)*

It's stopped.

S'è fermato(a). *sEH fehr-mAH-toh(tah)*

I wind it everyday.	**Lo (la) carico ogni giorno.** *loh (lah) kAH-ree-koh OH-ny-ee jee-OHr-noh*
I need ____.	**Ho bisogno di ____.** *oh bee-sOH-ny-oh dee*
▩ a crystal, glass	**un vetro** *oon vAY-troh*
▩ an hour hand	**una lancetta delle ore** *OO-nah lahn-chAYt-tah dAYl-leh OH-reh*
▩ a minute hand	**una lancetta dei minuti** *OO-nah lahn-chAYt-tah dAY-ee mee-nOO-tee*
▩ a second hand	**una lancetta dei secondi** *OO-nah lahn-chAYt-tah dAY-ee seh-kOHn-dee*
▩ a stem	**una vite** *oo-nah vEE-teh*
▩ a spring	**una molla** *OO-nah mOHl-lah*
▩ a battery	**una pila** *oo-nah pEE-lah*
When will it be ready?	**Quando sarà pronto?** *koo-AHn-doh sah-rAH prOHn-toh*
May I have a receipt?	**Posso avere la ricevuta?** *pOHs-soh ah-vAY-reh lah ree-cheh-vOO-tah*

CAMERA REPAIRS

Can you fix this camera (movie camera)?	**Può aggiustare questa macchina fotografica (questa cinepresa)?** *poo-OH ah-jee-oo-stAH-reh koo-AY-stah mAH-kee-nah foh-toh-grAH-fee-kah (koo-AY-stah chee-neh-prAY-sah)*
The film doesn't advance.	**Si è bloccato il rullino.** *see EH bloh-kAH-toh eel rool-lEE-noh*
I think I need new batteries.	**Penso di aver bisogno delle pile nuove.** *pEHn-soh dee ah-vAYr bee-sOH-ny-ee-oh dAYl-leh pEE-leh noo-OH-veh*

How much will the repair cost?	**Quanto mi costerà farla aggiustare?** *koo-AHn-toh mee-koh-steh-rAH fAHr-lah ah-jee-oo-stAH-reh*
When can I come and get it?	**Quando posso venire a ritirarla?** *koo-AHn-doh pOHs-soh veh-nEE-reh ah ree-tee-rAHr-lah*
I need it as soon as possible.	**Ne ho bisogno al più presto possibile.** *nay oh bee-sOH-ny-ee-oh ahl pee-OO prEH-stoh pohs-sEE-bee-leh*

MEDICAL CARE

THE PHARMACY

Where is the nearest (all night) pharmacy (chemist)?	**Dov'è la farmacia (notturna) più vicina?** *doh-vEH lah fahr-mah-chEE-ah (noht-tOOr-nah) pee-OO vee-chEE-nah*
At what time does the pharmacy open (close?)	**A che ora apre (chiude) la farmacia?** *ah kay OH-rah AH-preh (key-OO-deh) lah fahr-mah-chEE-ah*
I need something for _____.	**Ho bisogno di qualche cosa per _____.** *oh bee-sOH-ny-ee-oh dee koo-AHl-keh kOH-sah pehr*
■ a cold	**il raffreddore** *eel rahf-frehd-dOH-reh*
■ constipation	**la stitichezza** *lah stee-tee-kAY-tsah*
■ a cough	**la tosse** *lah tOHs-seh*
■ diarrhea	**la diarrea** *lah dee-ahr-rEH-ah*
■ a fever	**la febbre** *lah fEHb-breh*
■ hay fever	**una rinite da fieno** *OO-nah ree-nEE-teh dah fee-EH-noh*
■ a headache	**il mal di testa** *eel mAHl dee tEH-stah*
■ insomnia	**l'insonnia** *leen-sOHn-nee-ah*

◼ sunburn	**la scottatura solare** *lah skoht-tah-tOO-rah soh-lAH-reh*
◼ motion sickness	**il mal d'auto (di mare)** *eel mAHl dAH-oo-toh (dee mAH-reh)*
◼ a toothache	**il mal di denti** *eel mAHl dee dEHn-tee*
◼ an upset stomach	**il mal di stomaco** *eel mAHl dee stOH-mah-koh*
I do not have a prescription.	**Non ho la ricetta medica.** *nohn OH lah ree-chEHt-tah mEH-dee-kah*
May I have it right away?	**Posso averla subito?** *pOHs-soh ah-vAYr-lah sOO-bee-toh*
It's an emergency.	**È un'emergenza.** *eH oo-neh-mehr-jEHn-tsah*
How long will it take?	**Quanto tempo ci vorrà** *koo-AHn-toh tEHm-poh chee vohr-rAH*
When can I come for it?	**Quando potrò venire a prenderla?** *koo-AHn-doh poh-trOH veh-nEE-reh ah prAYn-dehr-lah*
I would like _____.	**Vorrei _____.** *vohr-rEH-ee*
◼ adhesive tape	**un nastro adesivo** *oon nAH-stroh ah-deh-sEE-voh*
◼ alcohol	**dell'alcool** *dayl-lAHl-koh-ohl*
◼ an antacid	**un antiacido** *oon ahn-tee-AH-chee-doh*
◼ an antiseptic	**un antisettico** *oon ahn-tee-sEHt-tee-koh*
◼ aspirins	**delle aspirine** *dAYl-leh ah-spee-rEE-neh*
◼ Band-Aids	**dei cerotti** *dAY-ee cheh-rOHt-tee*
◼ contraceptives	**dei contraccettivi** *dAY-ee kohn-trah-chEHt-tee-vee*

corn plasters	**dei callifughi** *dAY-ee kahl-lEE-foo-ghee*
cotton balls	**del cotone idrofilo** *dayl koh-tOH-neh ee-drOH-fee-loh*
cough drops/syrup	**delle pasticche (dello sciroppo) per la tosse** *dAYl-leh pah-stEEk-keh (dAHl-loh shee-rOHp-poh) pehr lah tOHs-seh*
ear drops	**delle gocce per gli orecchi** *dAYl-leh gOH-cheh pehr ly-ee oh-rAYk-key*
eye drops	**del collirio** *dayl kohl-lEE-ree-oh*
iodine	**della tintura di iodio** *dAYl-lah teen-tOO-rah dee ee-OH-dee-oh*
a (mild) laxative	**un lassativo (leggero)** *oon lahs-sah-tEE-voh (lay-jEH-roh)*
milk of magnesia	**della magnesia** *dAYl-lah mah-ny-ee-EH-see-ah*
prophylactics	**dei profilattici** *dAY-ee proh-fee-lAHt-tee-chee*
sanitary napkins	**degli assorbenti (igienici)** *dAY-ly-ee ahs-sohr-bEHn-tee (ee-jee-EH-nee-chee)*
suppositories	**delle supposte** *dAYl-leh soop-pOH-steh*
talcum powder	**del borotalco** *dayl boh-roh-tAHl-koh*
tampons	**dei tamponi** *dAY-ee tahm-pOH-nee*
a thermometer	**un termometro** *oon tehr-mOH-meh-troh*
vitamins	**delle vitamine** *dAYl-leh vee-tah-mEE-neh*

WITH THE DOCTOR

I don't feel well.	**Non mi sento bene.** *nohn mee sEHn-toh bEH-neh*
I need a doctor right away.	**Ho bisogno urgente del medico.** *oh bee-sOH-ny-ee-oh oor-jEHn-teh dayl mEH-dee-koh*
Do you know a doctor who speaks English?	**Conosce un dottore che parla inglese?** *koh-nOH-sheh oon doht-tOH-reh kay pAHr-lah een-glAY-seh*
Where is his office (surgery)?	**Dov'è il suo ambulatorio?** *doh-vEH eel sOO-oh ahm-boo-lah-tOH-ree-oh*
Will the doctor come to the hotel?	**Il dottore potrà venire all'hotel?** *eel doht-tOH-reh poh-trAH veh-NEE-reh ahl-loh-tEHl*
I feel dizzy.	**Mi gira la testa (ho le vertigini).** *mee jEE-rah lah tEH-stah (oh leh vehr-tEE-jee-nee)*
I feel weak.	**Mi sento debole.** *mee sEHn-toh dAY-boh-leh*

PARTS OF THE BODY

head	**la testa**	*lah tEH-stah*
face	**il viso**	*eel vEE-soh*
ear	**l'orecchio**	*loh-rAY-key-oh*
eye	**l'occhio**	*lOH-key-oh*
nose	**il naso**	*eel nAH-soh*
mouth	**la bocca**	*lah bOH-kah*
tooth	**il dente**	*eel dEHn-teh*
throat	**la gola**	*lah gOH-lah*
neck	**il collo**	*eel kOHl-loh*

shoulder	**la spalla**	*lah spAHl-lah*
breast	**il petto**	*eel pEHt-toh*
heart	**il cuore**	*eel koo-OH-reh*
arm	**il braccio**	*eel brAH-chee-oh*
elbow	**il gomito**	*eel gOH-mee-toh*
wrist	**il polso**	*eel pOHl-soh*
hand	**la mano**	*lah mAH-noh*
appendix	**l'appendicite**	*lahp-pehn-dee-chEE-teh*
liver	**il fegato**	*ell fEH-gah-toh*
hip	**l'anca**	*l'AHn-kah*
leg	**la gamba**	*lah gAHm-bah*
knee	**il ginocchio**	*eel jee-nOH-key-oh*
ankle	**la caviglia**	*lah kah-vEE-ly-ah*
foot	**il piede**	*eel pee-EH-deh*
skin	**la pelle**	*lah pEHl-leh*

I (think) have ____.	**(Credo che) ho ____.**	*(kreh-doh kay) oh*
■ an abscess	**un ascesso**	*oon ah-shEHs-soh*
■ a broken bone	**una frattura**	*OO-nah frat-tOO-rah*
■ a bruise	**una contusione**	*OO-nah kohn-too-see-OH-neh*
■ a burn	**un'ustione**	*oo-noo-stee-oH-neh*
■ something in my eye	**qualche cosa nell'occhio**	*koo-AHl-keh kOH-sah nayl-lOHk-key-oh*
■ the chills	**i brividi**	*ee brEE-vee-dee*
■ a cold	**un raffreddore**	*oon rahf-frehd-dOH-reh*

constipation	**stitichezza** *stee-tee-kAY-tsah*
stomach cramps	**crampi allo stomaco** *krAHm-pee AHl-loh stOH-mah-koh*
a cut	**una ferita (un taglio)** *OO-nah feh-rEE-tah (oon tAH-ly-ee-oh)*
diarrhea	**la diarrea** *lah dee-ahr-rEH-ah*
a fever	**la febbre** *la fEHb-breh*
a headache	**un mal di testa** *oon mAHl dee tEH-stah*
an infection	**un'infezione** *oo-neen-feh-tsee-OH-neh*
a lump	**un gonfiore** *oon gohn-fee-OH-reh*
a sore throat	**un mal di gola** *oon mAHl dee gOH-lah*
a stomachache	**un mal di stomaco** *oon mAHl dee stOH-mah-koh*
rheumatism	**i reumatismi** *ee reh-oo-mah-tEE-smee*

TELLING THE DOCTOR

It hurts me here.	**Mi fa male qui.** *mee fah mAH-leh koo-EE*
I've had this pain since yesterday.	**Ho questo dolore da ieri.** *oh koo-AY-stoh doh-lOH-reh dah ee-EH-ree*
There's a (no) history of asthma (diabetes) in my family.	**(Non) c'è anamnesi di asma (diabete) nella mia famiglia.** *(nohn) chEH ah-nahm-nEH-see dee AH-smah (dee-ah-bEH-teh) nAYl-lah mEE-ah fah-mEE-ly-ee-ah*
I'm (not) allergic to antibiotics (penicillin).	**(Non) sono allergico agli antibiotici (alla penicillina).** *(nohn) sOH-noh ahl-lEHr-jee-koh AH-ly-ee ahn-tee-bee-OH-tee-chee (AHl-lah peh-nee-cheel-lEE-nah)*

I have a pain in my chest.	**Ho un dolore al petto.** *oh oon doh-lOH-reh ahl pEHt-toh*
I had a heart attack _____.	**Ho avuto un attacco cardiaco _____.** *oh ah-vOO-toh oon aht-tAHk-koh kahr-dEE-ah-koh*
last year	**l'anno scorso** *lAHn-noh skOHr-soh*
(three) years ago	**(tre) anni fa** *trEH AHn-nee fah*
I'm taking this medicine (insulin).	**Sto prendendo questa medicina (insulina).** *stOH prehn-dEHn-doh koo-AY-stah meh-dee-chEE-nah (een-soo-lEE-nah)*
I'm pregnant.	**Sono incinta.** *sOH-noh een-chEEn-tah*
I feel better (worse).	**Mi sento meglio (peggio).** *mee sEHn-toh mEH-ly-ee-oh (pEH-jee-oh)*
Is it serious (contagious)?	**È serio (contagioso)?** *EH sEH-ree-oh (kohn-tah-jee-OH-soh)*
Do I have to go to the hospital?	**Devo andare in ospedale?** *dAY-voh ahn-dAH-reh een oh-speh-dAH-leh*
When can I continue my trip?	**Quando potrò continuare la mia gita?** *koo-AHn-doh poh-trOH kohn-tee-noo-AH-reh lah mEE-ah jEE-tah*

DOCTOR'S INSTRUCTIONS

Apra la boca.	Open your mouth.
Tiri fuori la lingua.	Stick out your tongue.
Tossisca.	Cough.
Respiri profondamente.	Breathe deeply.
Si spogli.	Take off your clothing.
Si sdrai.	Lie down.

Si alzi.	Stand up.
Si vesta.	Get dressed.

FOLLOWING UP

Are you giving me a prescription?

Mi darà una ricetta? *mee dah-rAH oo-nah ree-chEHt-tah*

How often must I take this medicine (these pills)?

Quante volte devo prendere questa medicina (queste pillole)? *koo-AHn-teh vOHl-teh dAY-voh prAYn-deh-reh koo-AYs-tah meh-dee-chEE-nah (koo-AYs-teh pEEl-loh-leh)*

(How long) do I have to stay in bed?

(Quanto) devo rimanere a letto? *(koo-AHn-toh) dAY-voh ree-mah-nAY-reh ah lEHt-toh*

Thank you (for everything) doctor.

Grazie (di tutto), dottore. *grAH-tsee-eh (dee tOOt-toh) doht-tOH-reh*

How much do I owe you for your services?

Quanto le devo per la visita? *koo-AHn-toh leh dAY-voh pehr lah vEE-see-tah*

I have medical insurance.

Ho l'assicurazione (l'assistenza) medica. *oh lahs-see-koo-rah-tsee-OH-neh (lahs-sees-stEHn-tsah) mEH-dee-kah*

IN THE HOSPITAL (ACCIDENTS)

Help!	**Aiuto!** *ah-ee-OO-toh*
Get a doctor, quick!	**Chiamate un medico, subito!** *key-ah-mAH-teh oon mEH-dee-koh sOO-bee-toh*
Call an ambulance!	**Chiamate un'ambulanza!** *key-ah-mAH-teh oo-nahm-boo-lAHn-tsah*
Take him to the hospital.	**Portatelo in ospedale.** *pohr-tAH-teh-loh een oh-speh-dAH-leh*
I've fallen.	**Sono caduto(a).** *sOH-noh kah-dOO-toh(ah)*

She was run over.	**È stata investita.** *EH stAH-tah een-veh-stEE-tah*
I think I've had a heart attack.	**Credo che ho avuto un collasso cardiaco.** *krEH-do kay oh ah-vOO-toh oon kohl-lAHs-soh kahr-dEE-ah-koh*
I burned myself.	**Mi sono ustionato(a).** *mee sOH-noh oo-stee-oh-nAH-toh(ah)*
I cut myself.	**Mi sono tagliato.** *mee sOH-noh tah-ly-ee-AH-toh*
I'm bleeding.	**Sto sanguinando.** *stOH sahn-goo-ee-nAHn-doh*
He's lost a lot of blood.	**Ha perduto molto sangue.** *ah pehr-dOO-toh mOHl-toh sAHn-goo-eh*
I think the bone is broken (dislocated).	**Penso che mi si sia fratturato (lussato) l'osso.** *pEHn-soh kay mee see sEE-ah fraht-too-rAH-toh (loos-sAH-toh) lOHs-soh*
The leg is swollen.	**La gamba è gonfia.** *lah gAHm-bah EH gOHn-fee-ah*
The wrist is sprained (twisted).	**Mi si è slogato (storto) il polso.** *mee see-EH sloh-gAH-toh (stOHr-toh) eel pOHl-soh*
The ankle is sprained (twisted).	**Mi si è slogata (storta) la caviglia.** *mee see-EH sloh-gAH-tah (stOHr-tah) lah kah-vEE-ly-ee-ah*
I can't move my elbow (knee).	**Non posso muovere il gomito (il ginocchio).** *nohn pOHs-soh moo-OH-veh-reh eel gOH-mee-toh (eel jee-nOHk-key-oh)*

AT THE DENTIST

Can you recommend a dentist?	**Può raccomandarmi un dentista?** *poo-OH rahk-koh-mahn-dAHr-mee oon dehn-tEE-stah*

I have a toothache that's driving me crazy.	**Ho un mal di denti che mi fa impazzire.** *oh oon mAHl dee dEHn-tee kay mee fah eem-pah-tsEE-reh*
I've lost a filling.	**Ho perduto l'otturazione.** *oh payr-dOO-toh loht-too-rah-tsee-OH-neh*
I'v : a broken tooth.	**Mi son rotto un dente.** *mee sOHn rOHt-toh oon dEHn-teh*
My gums hurt me.	**Mi fanno male le gengive.** *mee fAHn-noh mAH-leh leh jehn-jEE-veh*
Is there an infection?	**C'è un'infezione?** *chEH oo-neen-feh-tsee-OH-neh*
Will you have to extract the tooth?	**Deve estrarre il dente?** *dAY-veh ehs-trAHr-reh eel dEHn-teh*
I'd prefer you filled it ____.	**Preferisco farlo otturare ____.** *preh-feh-rIH-skoh fAHr-loh oht-too-rAH-reh*
▪ with amalgam	**con l'algama** *kOHn lAHl-gah-mah*
▪ with gold	**con oro** *kOHn OH-roh*
▪ with silver	**con argento** *kOHn ahr-jEHn-toh*
▪ for now temporarily	**provvisoriamente** *prohv-vee-soh-ree-ah-mEHn-teh*
Can you fix ____?	**Può riparare ____?** *poo-OH ree-pah-rAH-reh*
▪ this bridge	**questo ponte** *koo-AY-stoh pOHn-teh*
▪ this crown	**questa corona** *koo-AY-stah koh-rOH-nah*
▪ these dentures	**questi denti finti** *koo-AY-stee dEHn-tee fEEn-tee*
When should I come back?	**Quando dovrei ritornare?** *koo-AHn-doh doh-vrEH-ee ree-tohr-nAH-reh*

| How much do I owe you for your services? | **Quanto le devo per la visita?** *koo-AHn-toh leh dAY-voh pehr lah vEE-see-tah* |

WITH THE OPTICIAN

Can you repair these glasses (for me)?	**Può aggiustar(mi) questi occhiali?** *poo-OH ah-jee-oo-stAHr-(mee) koo-AY-stee oh-key-AH-lee*
I've broken a lens (the frame).	**Mi si è rotta una lente (la montatura).** *mee see-EH rOHt-tah OO-nah lEHn-teh (lah mohn-tah-tOO-rah)*
Can you put in a new lens?	**Può metterci una lente nuova?** *poo-OH mAYt-tehr-chee OO-nah lEHn-teh noo-OH-vah*
I do not have a prescription.	**Non ho la ricetta medica.** *nohn OH lah ree-chEHt-tah mEH-dee-kah*
Can you tighten the screw?	**Può stringere la vite?** *poo-OH strEEn-jeh-rEH lah vEE-teh*
I need the glasses as soon as possible.	**Ho bisogno degli occhiali al più presto possibile.** *oh bee-sOH-ny-ee-oh dAY-ly-ee oh-key-AH-lee ahl pee-OO prEH-stoh pohs-sEE-bee-leh*
I don't have any others.	**Non ne ho altri.** *nohn nay-OH AHl-tree*
I have lost a contact lens.	**Ho perduto una lente a contatto.** *oh pehr-dOO-toh OO-nah lEHn-teh ah kohn-tAHt-toh*
Can you replace it quickly?	**Può darmene un'altra subito?** *poo-OH dAHr-meh-neh oo-nAHl-trah sOO-bee-toh*

COMMUNICATIONS

POST OFFICE

I want to mail a letter.	**Voglio spedire una lettera.** *vOH-ly-ee-oh speh-dEE-reh OO-nah lAYt-teh-rah*
Where's the post office?	**Dov'è l'ufficio postale?** *doh-vEH loof-fEE-chee-oh poh-stAH-leh*
Where's a letter box?	**Dov'è una cassetta postale?** *doh-vEH OO-nah kas-sAYt-tah poh-stAH-leh*
What is the postage on ____ to the United States (Canada, England, Australia)?	**Qual è l'affrancatura per ____ per gli Stati Uniti (Canada, Inghilterra, Australia)?** *koo-ah-lEH lahf-frahn-kah-tOO-rah pehr pehr ly-ee stAH-tee oo-nEE-tee (kah-nah-dAH, een-gheel-tEHr-rah, ahoo-strAH lee-ah)*
■ a letter	**una lettera** *OO-nah lAYt-teh-rah*
■ an air-mail letter	**una lettera via aerea** *oo-nah layt-teh-rah vEE-ah ah-EH-reh-ah*
■ an insured letter	**una lettera assicurata** *OO-nah lAYt-teh-rah ahs-see-koo-rAH-tah*
■ a registered letter	**una lettera raccomandata** *OO-nah lAYt-teh-rah rahk-koh-mahn-dAH-tah*
■ a special delivery letter	**una lettera espresso** *OO-nah lAYt-teh-rah ehs-prEHs-soh*
■ a package	**un pacco** *oon pAHk-koh*
■ a postcard	**una cartolina postale** *OO-nah kahr-toh-lEE-nah poh-stAH-leh*
When will it arrive?	**Quando arriverà?** *koo-AHn-doh ahr-ree-veh-rAH*

Which is the _____ window?	**Qual è lo sportello per _____?** *koo-ah-lEH loh spohr-tEHl-loh pehr*
general delivery	**il fermo posta** *eel fAYr-moh pOH-stah*
money order	**i vaglia postali** *ee vAH-ly-ee-ah poh-stAH-lee*
stamp	**i francobolli** *ee frahn-koh-bOHl-lee*
Are there any letters for me? My name is _____.	**Ci sono lettere per me? Il mio nome è _____.** *chee sOH-noh lAYt-teh-reh pehr mAY? eel mEE-oh nOH-meh EH*
I'd like _____.	**Vorrei _____.** *vohr-rEH-ee*
10 post cards	**dieci cartoline postali** *dee-EH-chee kahr-toh-lEE-neh poh-stAH-lee*
5 (air mail) stamps	**cinque francobolli (via aerea)** *chEEn-koo-eh frahn-koh-bOHl-lee (vEE-ah ah-EH-reh-ah)*
Do I fill out a customs receipt?	**Devo compilare una ricevuta?** *dAY-voh kohm-pee-lAH-reh oo-nah ree-cheh-vOO-tah*

TELEGRAMS

How late is the telegraph window open (till what time?)	**L'ufficio Poste e Telegrafi sta aperto fino a tardi (fino a che ora)?** *loof-fEE-chee-oh pOHs-teh ay teh-lEH-grah-fee stah ah-pEHr-toh fEE-noh ah tAHr-dee (fEE-noh ah kay OH-rah)*
I'd like to send a telegram to _____.	**Vorrei spedire un telegramma a _____.** *vohr-rEH-ee speh-dEE-reh oon teh-leh-grAHm-mah ah*
How much is it per word?	**Quanto costa per parola?** *koo-AHn-toh kOH-stah pehr pah-rOH-lah*

I want to send it collect.	**Voglio spedirlo(la) a carico del destinatario.** *vOH-ly-ee-oh speh-dEEr-loh(lah) ah kAH-ree-koh dayl deh-stee-nah-tAH-ree-oh*
When will it arrive?	**Quando sarà recapitato(a)?** *koo-AHn-doh sah-rAH reh-kah-pee-tAH-toh(ah)*

TELEPHONES

Where is ____?	**Dov'è ____?** *doh-vEH*
a public telephone	**un telefono pubblico?** *oon teh-lEH-foh-noh pOOb-blee-koh*
a telephone booth	**una cabina telefonica?** *OO-nah kah-bEE-nah teh-leh-fOH-nee-kah*
a telephone directory	**un elenco telefonico?** *oon eh-lEHn-koh teh-leh-fOH-nee-koh*
May I use your phone?	**Posso usare il suo telefono?** *pOHs-soh oo-sAH-reh eel sOO-oh teh-lEH-foh-noh*
Can I call direct?	**Posso telefonare direttamente?** *pOHs-soh teh-leh-foh-nAH-reh dee-reht-tah-mEHn-teh*
I want to reverse the charges.	**Desidero fare una riversibile.** *deh-sEE-deh-roh fAH-reh oo-nah ree-vehr-sEE-bee-leh*
Do I need tokens for the phone?	**Occorrono i gettoni per il telefono?** *ohk-kOHr-roh-noh ee jeht-tOH-nee pehr eel teh-lEH-foh-noh*
I want to make a ____ to ____.	**Vorrei fare una ____ a ____.** *vohr-rEH-ee fAH-reh OO-nah ____ ah ____.*
local call	**telefonata urbana** *teh-leh-foh-nAH-tah oor-bAH-nah*

▧ long-distance call	**una telefonata in teleselezione (interurbana, internazionale)** *OO-nah teh-leh-foh-nAH-tah een teh-leh-seh-leh-tsee-OH-neh (een-tehr-oor-bAH-nah, een-tehr-nah-tsee-oh-nAH-leh)*
▧ person-to-person call	**una telefonata diretta con preavviso** *OO-nah teh-leh-foh-nAH-tah dee-rEHt-tah kohn preh-ahv-vEE-soh*
How do I get the operator?	**Come si ottiene il centralino?** *kOH-meh see oht-tee-EH-neh eel chehn-trah-lEE-noh*
Operator, can you give me _____?	**Signorina (signore, centralino), può darmi _____?** *see-ny-oh-rEE-nah (see-ny-OH-reh, chehn-trah-lEE-noh), poo-OH dAHr-mee*
▧ number 23 345	**il ventitrè trecentoquarantacinque** *eel vayn-tee-trEH treh-chEHn-toh-koo-ah-rahn-tah-chEEn-koo-eh*
▧ extension 19	**interno diciannove** *een-tEHr-noh dee-chee-ahn-nOH-veh*
▧ area code	**prefisso numero** *preh-fEEs-soh nOO-meh-roh*
▧ country code	**prefisso internazionale** *preh-fEEs-soh een-tehr-nah-tzee-oh-nAH-leh*
▧ city code	**prefisso interurbano** *preh-fEEs-soh een-tehr-oor-bAH-noh*
My number is _____.	**Il mio numero è _____.** *eel mEE-oh nOO-meh-roh EH*
May I speak to _____?	**Potrei parlare con _____?** *poh-trEH-ee pahr-lAH-reh kohn*
Speaking.	**Sono io.** *sOH-noh EE-oh*
Hello.	**Pronto.** *prOHn-toh*
Who is it?	**Chi è?** *key EH*

PROBLEMS ON THE LINE

I can't hear.	**Non si sente bene.** *nOHn see sEHn-teh bEH-neh*
Speak louder (please).	**Parli più forte (per favore).** *pAHr-lee pee-OO fOHr-teh (pehr fah-vOH-reh)*
Don't hang up.	**Non appenda il ricevitore.** *nohn ahp-pEHn-dah eel ree-cheh-vee-tOH-reh*
This is ____.	**Parla ____.** *pAHr-lah*
Operator, there is no answer (they don't answer).	**Centralino, non risponde nessuno.** *chehn-trah-lEE-noh nohn ree-spOHn-deh nehs-sOO-noh*
The line is busy.	**La linea è occupata.** *lah lEE-neh-ah EH ohk-koo-pAH-tah*
You gave me (that was) a wrong number.	**Mi ha dato (era) un numero sbagliato.** *mee ah dAH-toh (EH-rah) oon nOO-meh-roh sbah-ly-ee-AH-toh*
I was cut off.	**È caduta la linea.** *EH kah-dOO-tah lah lEE-neh-ah*
Please dial it again.	**Per favore, rifaccia il numero.** *pehr fah-vOH-reh ree-fAH-chee-ah eel nOO-meh-roh*
I want to leave a message.	**Voglio lasciare un (messaggio) appunto.** *vOH-ly-ee-oh lah-shee-AH-reh oon (mehs-sAH-jee-oh) ahp-pOOn-toh*

PAYING UP

How much do I have to pay?	**Quanto devo pagare?** *koo-AHn-toh dEH-voh pah-gAH-reh*
How many clicks did I have?	**Quanti scatti sono?** *koo-AHn-tee skAHt-tee sOH-noh*

DRIVING A CAR

CAR RENTALS

Where can I rent ____?	**Dove posso noleggiare ____?** *dOH-veh pOHs-soh noh-leh-jee-AH-reh*
a car	**una macchina** *OO-nah mAHk-kee-nah*
a motorcycle	**una motocicletta** *OO-nah moh-toh-chEEk-klAYt-tah*
a motorscooter	**una vespa (una lambretta)** *OO-nah vEH-spah (OO-nah lahm-brAYt-tah)*
a moped	**un motorino** *oon moh-toh-rEE-noh*
a bicycle	**una bicicletta** *OO-na bee-chee-klAYt-tah*
I want (I'd like) ____.	**Voglio (Vorrei) ____.** *vOH-ly-ee-oh (vohr-rEH-ee)*
a small car	**una macchina piccola** *OO-nah mAHk-kee-nah pEE-koh-lah*
a large car	**una macchina grande** *OO-nah mAHk-kee-nah grAHn-deh*
a sport car	**una macchina sportiva** *OO-nah mAHk-kee-nah spohr-tEE-vah*
I prefer automatic transmission.	**Preferisco il cambio automatico.** *preh-feh-rEE-skoh eel kAHm-bee-oh ah-oo-toh-mAH-tee-koh*
How much does it cost ____?	**Quanto costa ____?** *koo-AHn-toh kOH-stah*
per day	**al giorno** *ahl jee-OHr-noh*
per week	**alla settimana** *AHl-lah seht-tee-mAH-nah*
per kilometer	**per chilometro** *pehr key-lOH-meh-troh*

for unlimited mileage	**a chilometraggio illimitato** *ah key-loh-meh-trAH-jee-oh eel-lee-mee-tAH-toh*
How much is the (complete) insurance?	**Quant'è l'assicurazione (completa)?** *koo-ahn-tEH lahs-see-koo-rah-tsee-OH-neh (kohm-plEH-tah)*
Is gas included?	**È inclusa la benzina?** *EH een-klOO-sah lah behn-tsEE-nah*
Do you accept credit cards?	**Accetta (no) carte di credito?** *ah-chEHt-tah(noh) kAHr-teh dee krEH-dee-toh*
Here's my (international) driver's license.	**Ecco la mia patente (internazionale) di guida.** *EHk-koh lah mEE-ah pah-tEHn-teh (een-tehr-nah-tsee-oh-nAH-leh) dee goo-EE-dah*
Do I have to leave a deposit?	**Devo lasciare un acconto (un deposito)?** *dAY-voh lah-shee-AH-reh oon ahk-kOHn-toh (oon day-pOH-see-toh)*
Is there a drop-off charge?	**C'è un supplemento per la consegna dell'auto?** *chEH oon soop-pleh-mEHn-toh pehr lah kohn-seh-ny-ee-ah dayl-lAH-oo-toh*
I want to rent the car here and leave it in Turin.	**Desidero noleggiare l'auto qui e consegnarla a Torino.** *day-sEE-deh-roh noh-lay-jee-AH-reh lAH-oo-toh koo-EE ay kohn-say-ny-ee-AHr-lah ah toh-rEE-noh*
What kind of gasoline does it take?	**Che tipo di carburante usa?** *kay tEE-poh dee kahr-boo-rAHn-teh OO-sah*

ON THE ROAD

Excuse me. Can you tell me ____?	**Mi scusi. Può dirmi ____?** *mee skOO-see poo-OH dEEr-mee*
which way is it to ____?	**qual'è la via per ____?** *koo-ah-lEH lah vEE-ah pehr*

how I get to ____?	**come potrei raggiungere ____?** *kOH-meh poh-trEH-ee rah-jee-OOn-jeh-reh*
I think we're lost.	**Penso che ci siamo perduti(e).** *pEHn-soh kay chee see-AH-moh pehr-dOO-tee(eh)*
Is this the road (way) to ____?	**È questa la strada (via) per ____?** *EH koo-AYs-tah lah strAH-dah (vEE-ah) pehr*
Where does this road go?	**Dove porta questa strada?** *dOH-veh pOHr-tah koo-AYs-tah strAH-dah*
How far is it from here to the next town?	**Quanto dista da qui la prossima città?** *koo-AHn-toh dEE-stah dah koo-EE lah prOHs-see-mah cheet-tAH*
How far away is ____?	**Quanto dista ____?** *koo-AHn-toh dEE-stah*
Do you have a road map?	**Ha una cartina stradale?** *AH OO-nah kahr-tEE-nah strah-dAH-leh*
Can you show it to me on the map?	**Può indicarmelo sulla cartina?** *poo-OH een-dee-kAHr-meh-loh sOOl-lah kahr-tEE-nah*
Is it a good road?	**È buona la strada?** *EH boo-OH-nah lah strAH-dah*
Is this the shortest way?	**È questa la via più corta?** *EH koo-AY-stah lah vEE-ah pee-OO kOHr-tah*
Are there any detours?	**Ci sono deviazioni?** *chee sOH-noh day-vee-ah-tsee-OH-nee*
Do I go straight?	**Posso proseguire diritto?** *pOHs-soh proh-seh-goo-EE-reh dee-rEEt-toh*
Turn to the right (to the left).	**Giri a destra (a sinistra).** *jEE-ree ah dEH-strah (ah see-nEE-strah)*

No U-turn

No passing

Border crossing

Traffic signal ahead

Speed limit

Traffic circle (roundabout) ahead

Minimum speed limit

All traffic turns left

End of no passing zone

One-way street

Detour

Danger ahead

Entrance to expressway

Expressway ends

Guarded railroad crossing

Yield

Stop

Right of way

Dangerous intersection ahead

Gasoline (petrol) ahead

Parking

No vehicles allowed

Dangerous curve

Pedestrian crossing

Oncoming traffic has right of way

No bicycles allowed

No parking allowed

No entry

No left turn

AT THE SERVICE STATION

Where is there a gas (petrol) station?	**Dov'è una stazione di servizio?** *doh-vEH OO-nah stah-tsee-OH-neh dee sayr-vEE-tsee-oh*
Give me 15 (25) liters.	**Mi dia quindici (venticinque) litri.** *mee dEE-ah koo-EEn-dee-chee (vayn-tee-chEEn-koo-eh) lEE-tree*
Fill'er up with _____.	**Faccia il pieno di _____.** *fAH-chee-ah eel pee-AY-noh dee*
diesel	**diesel** *dEE-eh-sehl*
regular (standard)	**normale** *nohr-mAH-leh*
super (premium)	**super** *sOO-pehr*
Please check _____.	**Per favore mi controlli _____.** *pehr fah-vOH-reh mee kohn-trOHl-lee*
the battery	**la batteria** *lah baht-teh-rEE-ah*
the carburetor	**il carburatore** *eel kahr-boo-rah-tOH-reh*
the oil	**l'olio** *lOH-lee-oh*
the spark plugs	**le candele** *leh kahn-dAY-leh*
the tires	**i pneumatici (le gomme)** *ee pnay-oo-mAH-tee-chee (leh gOHm-meh)*
the tire pressure	**la pressione delle gomme** *lah prehs-see-OH-neh dAYl-leh gOHm-meh*
the antifreeze	**l'acqua** *lAH-koo-ah*
Change the oil (please).	**Mi cambi l'olio (per favore).** *mee kAHm-bee lOH-lee-oh (pehr fah-vOH-reh)*
Lubricate the car (please).	**Mi lubrifichi la macchina (per favore).** *mee loo-brEE-fee-key lah mAHk-kee-nah (pehr fah-vOH-reh)*

Charge the battery.	**Mi carichi la batteria.** *mee kAH-ree-key lah baht-teh-rEE-ah*
Change this tire.	**Mi cambi questa ruota.** *mee kAHm-bee koo-AY-stah roo-OH-tah*
Wash the car.	**Mi faccia il lavaggio alla macchina.** *mee fAH-chee-ah eel lah-vAH-jee-oh AHl-lah mAHk-kee-nah*
Where are the rest rooms?	**Dove sono i gabinetti?** *dOH-veh sOH-noh ee gah-bee-nAYt-tee*

ACCIDENTS AND REPAIRS

My car has broken down.	**Mi si è guastata la macchina.** *mee see-EH goo-ah-stAH-tah lah mAHk-kee-nah*
It overheats.	**Si surriscalda.** *see soor-ree-skAHl-dah*
It doesn't start.	**Non si avvia.** *nohn see ahv-vEE-ah*
I have a flat tire.	**Ho una gomma bucata.** *oh OO-nah gOHm-mah boo-kAH-tah*
The radiator is leaking.	**Il radiatore perde acqua.** *eel rah-dee-ah-tOH-reh pEHr-deh AH-koo-ah*
The battery is dead.	**La batteria è scarica.** *lah baht-teh-rEE-ah EH skAH-ree-kah*
The keys are locked inside the car.	**Le chiavi sono rimaste chiuse in macchina.** *leh key-AH-vee sOH-noh ree-mAH-steh key-OO-seh een mAHk-kee-nah*
Is there a garage near here?	**C'è un'autorimessa qui vicino?** *chEH oon-ah-oo-toh-ree-mEHs-sah koo-EE vee-chEE-noh*
I need a mechanic (tow truck).	**Ho bisogno di un meccanico (carroattrezzi).** *oh bee-sOH-ny-ee-oh dee oon mehk-kAH-nee-koh (kAHr-roh-aht-trAY-tsee)*

Can you give me a push?	**Può darmi una spinta?** *poo-OH dAHr-mee OO-nah spEEn-tah*
I don't have any tools.	**Non ho gli attrezzi.** *nohn-OH ly-ee aht-trAY-tsee*
Can you lend me _____?	**Può prestarmi _____?** *poo-OH preh-stAHr-mee*
a flashlight	**una lampadina tascabile** *OO-nah lahm-pah-dEE-nah tah-skAH-bee-leh*
a hammer	**un martello** *oon mahr-tEHl-loh*
a jack	**un cricco** *oon krEEk-koh*
a monkey wrench	**una chiave inglese** *OO-nah key-AH-veh een-glAY-seh*
pliers	**delle pinze** *dAYl-leh pEEn-tseh*
a screwdriver	**un cacciavite** *oon kah-chee-ah-vEE-teh*
I need _____.	**Ho bisogno di _____.** *oh bee-sOH-ny-ee-oh dee*
a bulb	**una lampadina** *OO-nah lahm-pah-dEE-nah*
a filter	**un filtro** *oon fEEl-troh*
a fuse	**un fusibile** *oon foo-sEE-bee-leh*
Can you fix the car?	**Può ripararmi la macchina?** *poo-OH ree-pah-rAHr-mee lah mAHk-kee-nah*
Can you repair it temporarily?	**Può farmi una riparazione provvisoria?** *poo-OH fAHr-mee OO-nah ree-pah-rah-tsee-OH-neh prohv-vee-sOH-ree-ah*
Do you have the part?	**Ha il pezzo di recambio?** *ah eel pEH-tsoh dee ree-kAHm-bee-oh*
I think there's something wrong with _____.	**Penso che ci sia un guasto _____.** *pEHn-soh kay chee sEE-ah oon goo-AH-stoh*
the directional signal	**alla freccia** *AHl-lah frAY-chee-ah*

the door handle	**alla maniglia della porta** *AHl-lah mah-nEE-ly-ee-ah dAYl-la pOHr-tah*
the electrical system	**all'impianto elettrico** *ahl-leem-pee-AHn-toh eh-lEHt-tree-koh*
the fan	**alla ventola** *AHl-lah vEHn-toh-lah*
the fan belt	**alla cinghia del ventilatore** *AHl-lah chEEn-ghee-ah dayl vehn-tee-lah-tOH-reh*
the fuel pump	**alla pompa della benzina** *AHl-lah pOHm-pah dAHl-lah behn-tsEE-nah*
the gear shift	**al cambio** *ahl kAHm-bee-oh*
the headlights	**agli abbaglianti** *AH-ly-ee ahb-bah-ly-ee-AHn-tee*
the horn	**al clacson** *ahl klAH-ksohn*
the ignition	**all'accensione** *ahl-lah-chehn-see-OH-neh*
the radio	**alla radio** *AHl-lah rAH-dee-oh*
the starter	**al motorino d'avviamento** *ahl moh-toh-rEE-noh dahv-vee-ah-mEHn-toh*
the steering wheel	**al volante** *ahl voh-lAHn-teh*
the tail light	**al fanalino posteriore** *ahl fah-nah-lEE-noh poh-steh-ree-OH-reh*
the transmission	**alla trasmissione** *AHl-lah trah-smees-see-OH-neh*
the water pump	**alla pompa dell'acqua** *AHl-lah pOHm-pah dayl-AH-koo-ah*
the windshield (windscreen) wiper	**al tergicristallo** *ahl tehr-jee-kree-stAHl-loh*
Can you take a look at (check out) ____?	**Può dare un'occhiata (una controllata) ____?** *poo-OH dAH-reh oo-noh-key-AH-tah (OO-nah kohn-trohl-lAH-tah)*
the brakes	**ai freni** *ah-ee frAY-nee*

the exhaust system	**al tubo di scappamento** *ahl tOO-boh dee skahp-pah-mEHn-toh*
the fender	**al parafango** *ahl pah-rah-fAHn-goh*
the gas tank	**al serbatoio (della benzina)** *ahl sehr-bah-tOH-ee-oh dAYl-lah behn-tsEE-nah*
the hood	**al cofano** *ahl kOH-fah-noh*
the trunk (boot)	**al portabagagli** *ahl pohr-tah-bah-gAH-ly-ee*
What's the matter?	**Che cosa c'è che non va?** *kay kOH-sah chEH kay nohn vAH*
Is it possible to (can you) fix it today?	**È possibile (può) aggiustarlo oggi?** *EH pohs-sEE-bee-leh (poo-OH) ah-jee-oo-stAHr-loh OH-jee*
How long will it take?	**Quanto tempo ci vorrà?** *koo-AHn-toh tEHm-poh chee vohr-rAH*
How much do I owe you?	**Quanto le devo?** *koo-AHn-toh leh dAY-voh*

GENERAL INFORMATION

TELLING TIME

What time is it?	**Che ora è?** *kay OH-rah EH*

When telling time in Italian, *it is* is expressed by **è** for 1:00, noon, and midnight; **sono** is used for all other numbers.

It's 1:00.	**È l'una.** *eh lOO-nah*
It's 12 o'clock (noon).	**È mezzogiorno.** *eh meh-tsoh-jee-OHr-noh*
It's midnight.	**È mezzanotte.** *eh meh-tsah-nOHt-teh*
It's early (late).	**È presto (tardi).** *eh prEH-stoh (tAHr-dee)*

It's 2:00. **Sono le due.** *sOH-noh leh dOO-eh*

It's 3:00, etc. **Sono le tre.** *sOH-noh leh trAY*

The number of minutes after the hour is expressed by adding **e** ("and"), followed by the number of minutes.

It's 4:10. **Sono le quattro e dieci.** *sOH-noh leh koo-AHt-roh ay dee-EH-chee*

It's 5:20. **Sono le cinque e venti.** *sOH-noh leh chEEn-koo-eh ay vAYn-tee*

Fifteen minutes after the hour and half past the hour are expressed by placing **e un quarto** and **e mezzo** after the hour.

It's 6:15. **Sono le sei e un quarto.** *sOH-noh leh sEH-ee ay oon koo-AHr-toh*

It's 7:30. **Sono le sette e mezzo.** *sOH-noh leh sEHt-teh ay mEH-tsoh*

After passing the half-hour point on the clock, time is expressed in Italian by *subtracting* the number of minutes to the *next* hour.

It's 7:40. **Sono le otto meno venti.** *sOH-noh leh OHt-toh mEH-noh vayn-tee*

It's 8:50. **Sono le nove meno dieci.** *sOH-noh leh nOH-veh mAY-noh dee-EH-chee*

At what time? **A che ora?** *ah kay OH-rah*

At 1:00. **All'una.** *ahl-lOO-nah*

At 2:00 (3:00, etc.). **Alle due (tre, . . .).** *AHl-leh dOO-eh (trAY)*

A.M. (in the morning) **del mattino** *dAYl maht-tEE-noh*

P.M. (in the afternoon) **del pomeriggio** *dAYl poh-meh-rEE-jee-oh*

At night. **Della notte.** *dAYl-lah nOHt-teh*

Official time is based on the 24-hour clock. You will find train schedules and other such times expressed in terms of a point within a 24-hour sequence.

The train leaves at 15.30.	**Il treno parte alle quindici a tenta.**	*eel trEH-noh pAHr-teh ahl-leh koo-EEn-dee-chee ay treHn-tah*
The time is now 21.15.	**Ora sono le ventuno e quindici.**	*OH-rah sOH-noh leh vayn-too-noh ay koo-EEn-dee-chee.*

DAYS OF THE WEEK

What day is it today?	**Che giorno è oggi?**	*kAY jee-OHr-noh EH OH-jee*

The days of the week are *not* capitalized in Italian.

Today is ____.	**Oggi è ____.**	*OH-jee EH*
▪ Monday	**lunedí**	*loo-neh-dEE*
▪ Tuesday	**martedí**	*mahr-teh-dEE*
▪ Wednesday	**mercoledí**	*mehr-koh-leh-dEE*
▪ Thursday	**giovedí**	*jee-oh-veh-dEE*
▪ Friday	**venerdí**	*veh-nehr-dEE*
▪ Saturday	**sabato**	*sAH-bah-toh*
▪ Sunday	**domenica**	*doh-mAY-nee-kah*

yesterday	**ieri**	*ee-EH-ree*
tomorrow	**domani**	*doh-mAH-nee*
the day after to-morrow	**dopodomani**	*doh-poh-doh-mAH-nee*
last week	**la settimana passata**	*lah seht-tee-mAH-nah pahs-sAH-tah*
next week	**la settimana prossima**	*lah seht-tee-mAH-nah prOHs-see-mah*
tonight	**questa notte (stanotte)**	*koo-AY-stah nOHt-teh (stah-nOHt-teh)*
last night	**la notte passata**	*lah nOHt-teh pahs-sAH-tah*

MONTHS OF THE YEAR

The months of the year are *not* capitalized in Italian.

January	**gennaio**	*jehn-nAH-ee-oh*
February	**febbraio**	*fehb-brAH-ee-oh*
March	**marzo**	*mAHr-tsoh*
April	**aprile**	*ah-prEE-leh*
May	**maggio**	*mAH-jee-oh*
June	**giugno**	*jee-OO-ny-ee-oh*
July	**luglio**	*lOO-ly-ee-oh*
August	**agosto**	*ah-gOH-stoh*

September	**settembre**	*seht-tEHm-breh*
October	**ottobre**	*oht-tOH-breh*
November	**novembre**	*noh-vEHm-breh*
December	**dicembre**	*dee-chEHm-breh*
What's today's date?	**Che data è oggi?**	*kay dAH-ta EH OH-jee*

The first of the month is *il primo* (an ordinal number). All other dates are expressed with *cardinal* numbers.

Today is August *first.*	**Oggi è il primo di agosto.** *OH-jee EH eel prEE-moh dee ah-gOH-stoh*
▧ second	**il due** *eel dOO-eh*
▧ fourth	**il quattro** *eel koo-AHt-troh*
▧ 25th	**il venticinque** *eel vayn-tee-chEEn-koo-eh*
This month	**Questo mese** *koo-AY-stoh mAY-seh*
Last month	**Il mese scorso** *eel mAY-seh skOHr-soh*
Next month	**Il mese prossimo** *eel mAY-seh prOHs-see-moh*
Last year	**L'anno scorso** *lAHn-noh skOHr-soh*
Next year	**L'anno prossimo** *lAHn-noh prOHs-see-moh*
May 1, 1876	**Il primo maggio, mille ottocento settanta sei** *EEl prEE-moh mAH-jee-oh mEEl-leh oht-toh-chEHn-toh seht-tAHn-tah sEH-ee*
July 4, 1984	**Il quattro luglio, mille novecento ottanta quattro** *eel koo-AHt-troh lOO-ly-ee-oh mEEl-leh noh-veh-chEHn-toh oht-tAHn-tah koo-AHt-troh*

THE FOUR SEASONS

Spring	**la primavera**	*lah pree-mah-vEH-rah*
Summer	**l'estate**	*leh-stAH-teh*
Fall	**l'autunno**	*lah-oo-tOOn-noh*
Winter	**l'inverno**	*leen-vEHr-noh*

THE WEATHER

How is the weather today?	**Che tempo fa oggi?**	*kay tEHm-poh fAH OH-jee*
It's good (bad) weather.	**Fa bel (cattivo) tempo.**	*fah behl (kaht-tEE-voh) tEHm-poh*
It's hot.	**Fa caldo.**	*fah kAHl-doh*
cold	**freddo**	*frAYd-doh*
cool	**fresco**	*frAY-skoh*
It's windy.	**Tira vento.**	*tEE-rah vEHn-toh*
It's sunny.	**C'è il sole.**	*chEH eel sOH-leh*
It's raining.	**Piove.**	*pee-OH-veh*
It's snowing.	**Nevica.**	*nAY-vee-kah*
It's drizzling.	**Pioviggina.**	*pee-oh-vEE-jee-nah*

IMPORTANT SIGNS

Acqua (non)potabile	(Not) potable water
Alt	Stop
Aperto	Open
Ascensore	Elevator (Lift)
Attenzione	Caution, watch out
Avanti	Enter (come in, go, walk [at the lights])
Caldo or **"C"**	Hot
Cassa	Cashier
Chiuso	Closed
Divieto di sosta	No parking
Divieto di transito	No entrance, keep out
Freddo or **"F"**	Cold
Gabinetti (WC)	Toilets
Ingresso	Entrance
Libero	Vacant
Non calpestare le aiuole	Keep off the grass
Non ostruire l'ingresso	Don't block entrance
Non toccare	Hands off, don't touch
Occupato	Occupied
Pericolo	Danger
Riservato	Reserved
Si affitta (si loca)	For rent

Si vende	For sale
Signora	Women's room
Signore	Men's room
Spingere	Push
Strada privata	Private road
Tirare	Pull
Uscita	Exit
Vietato fumare	No smoking
Vietato nuotare	No bathing
Vietato sputare	No spitting

COMMON ABBREVIATIONS

AA	Azienda Autonoma di Soggiorno e Turismo	Local Tourist Information Center
ACI	Automobile Club d'Italia	Automobile Club of Italy
Cap.	Capoluogo	Province
C.P.	Casella Postale	Post Office Box
CAP	Codice Postale	Zip Code
ENIT	Ente Nazionale per il Turismo	Italian State Tourist Office
EPT	Ente Provinciale per il Turismo	Provincial Tourist Information Center
F.lli	Brothers	Inc.
FS	Ferrovie dello Stato	Italian State Railways
IVA	Imposte sul Valore Aggiunto	Italian State Tax
L.	Lire	Italian currency
N., n°	Numero	Number

Pro Loco	Ente Locale per il Turismo	Local Tourist Information Office
Prov.	Provincia	Province
P.za	Piazza	(City) Square
S.	San, Santo(a)	Saint
S.A.	Società Anonima	Inc.
Sig.	Signor	Mr.
Sig.na	Signorina	Miss
Sig.ra	Signora	Mrs.
TCI	Touring Club Italiano	Italian Touring Club
v.	Via	Street
v.le	Viale	Boulevard

SPANISH

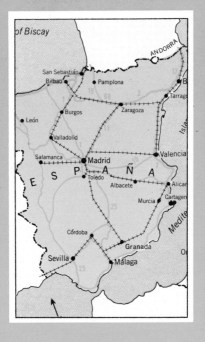

QUICK PRONUNCIATION GUIDE

SPANISH LETTER(S)	SOUND IN ENGLISH	EXAMPLES
VOWELS		
a	ah (y<u>a</u>cht)	taco *(TAH-koh)*
e	ay (d<u>a</u>y)	mesa *(MAY-sah)*
	eh (p<u>e</u>t)	perro *(PEH-roh)*
i	ee (m<u>ee</u>t)	libro *(LEE-broh)*
o	oh (<u>o</u>pen)	foto *(FOH-toh)*
u	oo (t<u>oo</u>th)	mucho *(MOO-choh)*
COMMON VOWEL COMBINATIONS (DIPHTHONGS)		
au	ow (c<u>ow</u>)	causa *(COW-sah)*
		auto *(OW-toh)*
ei	ay (d<u>a</u>y)	aceite *(ah-SAY-tay)*
ai	y (t<u>y</u>pe)	baile *(BY-lay)*
ie	yeh (y<u>et</u>)	abierto *(ah-BYEHR-toh)*
ue	weh (w<u>et</u>)	bueno *(BWEH-noh)*
CONSONANTS		
c (before *a, o, u*)	hard k sound (<u>c</u>at)	campo *(KAHM-poh)* cosa *(KOH-sah)* Cuba *(KOO-bah)*
c (before *e, i*)	soft s sound (<u>c</u>ent)	central *(sehn-TRAHL)* cinco *(SEEN-koh)*
cc	hard and soft cc (ks sound) (a<u>cc</u>ept)	acción *(ahk-see-OHN)*
ch	hard ch sound (<u>ch</u>air)	muchacho *(moo-CHAH-choh)*
g (before *a, o, u*)	hard g (<u>g</u>o)	gafas *(GAH-fahs)* goma *(GOH-mah)*
g (before *e, i*)	breathy h (<u>h</u>ot)	general *(hehn-eh-RAHL)*

SPANISH LETTER(S)	SOUND IN ENGLISH	EXAMPLES
h	always silent	hasta (AHS-tah)
j	breathy as in h sound (hot)	José (ho-SAY)
l	English l sound (lamp)	lámpara (LAHM-pahr-ah)
ll	as in English y (yes)	pollo (POH-yoh)
n	English n (no)	naranja (nah-RAHN-ha)
ñ	English ny (can-yon)	señorita (seh-nyoh-REE-tah)
qu	English k (keep)	que (kay)
r	trilled once	caro (KAH-roh)
rr (or r at beginning of word)	trilled strongly (operator saying three)	rico (RREE-koh) perro (PEH-rroh)
s	English s (see)	rosa (ROH-sah)
v	Approximately as in English b (book)	primavera (pree-mah-BEHR-ah)
x	English s, ks (sign, socks)	extra (ES-trah) examinar (ek-sah-mee-NAHR)
y	English y (yes) (by itself y = i)	yo (yoh) y (ee)
z	English s	zapato (sah-PAH-toh)

The above pronunciations apply to the Spanish that is spoken in Central and South America, and that is also spoken in parts of southern Spain. The remaining areas of Spain use the Castilian pronunciation:

SPANISH LETTER(S)	SOUND IN ENGLISH	EXAMPLES
ll	ly sound as in million	llamo (LYAH-moh)
c (before e or i) ⎫ z ⎭	a th sound instead of an s sound	gracias (GRAH-thee-ahs) lápiz (LAH-peeth)

THE BASICS FOR GETTING BY

MOST FREQUENTLY USED EXPRESSIONS

Hello!	**¡Hola!**	*OH-lah*
Yes	**Sí**	*see*
No	**No**	*noh*
Maybe	**Quizás**	*kee-SAHS*
Please	**Por favor**	*pohr-fah-BOHR*
Thank you (very much)	**(Muchas) gracias**	*(MOO-chahs) GRAH-see-ahs*
You're welcome	**De nada**	*day-NAH-dah*
Excuse me		
▪ (having disturbed or bumped into someone)	**Perdón**	*pehr-DOHN*
▪ (leaving a group or walking in front of a person)	**con permiso**	*kohn pehr-MEE-soh*
▪ (getting one's attention)	**por favor**	*pohr fah-BOHR*
I'm sorry	**Lo siento**	*loh see-EHN-toh*
Just a second	**Un momento**	*oon moh-MEN-toh*
That's all right, okay	**Está bien**	*eh-STAH bee-ehn*
It doesn't matter	**No importa**	*noh eem-PORT-ah*
Good morning	**Buenos días**	*bway-nohs DEE-ahs*

Good afternoon	**Buenas tardes**	*bway-nahs TAHR-dehs*
Good evening (night)	**Buenas noches**	*bway-nahs NOH-chehs*
Sir	**Señor**	*seh-NYOHR*
Madame	**Señora**	*seh-NYOHR-ah*
Miss	**Señorita**	*seh-nyohr-EE-tah*
Good-bye	**Adiós**	*ah-DYOHS*
See you later (so long)	**Hasta la vista (hasta luego)**	*AH-stah lah BEE-stah (AH-stah loo-AY-goh)*
See you tomorrow	**Hasta mañana**	*AH-stah mah-NYAH-nah*
Do you speak English?	**¿Habla usted inglés?** *ah-blah oos-TEHD een-GLAYS*	
I speak (a little) Spanish.	**Hablo español (un poco).** *AH-bloh ehs-pah-NYOHL (oon POH-koh)*	
I don't speak Spanish.	**No hablo español.** *noh AH-bloh ehs-pah-NYOHL*	
Is there anyone here who speaks English?	**¿Hay alguien aquí que hable inglés?** *AH-ee AHL-ghee-EHN ah-KEE kay AH-blay een-GLAYS*	
Do you understand?	**¿Comprende usted?** *kohm-PREHN-day oos-tehd*	
I understand.	**Yo comprendo.** *yoh kohm-PREHN-doh*	
I don't understand.	**No comprendo.** *noh kohm-PREHN-doh*	
What does this mean?	**¿Qué quiere decir ésto?** *kay kee-YEH-ray day-SEER ehs-toh*	
What? What did you say?	**¿Cómo?** *KOH-moh*	

How do you say ____ in Spanish?	**¿Cómo se dice ____ en español?** *KOH-moh say DEE-say ____ ehn ehs-NYOHL*
What do you call this (that) in Spanish?	**¿Cómo se llama esto (eso) en español?** *KOH-moh say YAH-mah EHS-toh (EHS-oh) ehn ehs-pahn-YOHL*
Please speak slowly.	**Hable despacio, por favor.** *AH-blay dehs-PAH-see-oh pohr fah-BOHR*
Please repeat.	**Repita, por favor.** *ray-PEE-tah pohr fah-BOHR*
I'm American (English) (Australian) (Canadian).	**Soy norteamericano(a), (inglés, inglesa), (australiano, australiana), (canadiense).** *soy nohr-tay-ah-mehr-ee-KAH-noh (nah), (een-GLAYS, een-GLAY-sah), (ow-strahl-YAH-noh, nah), (kah-nah-DYEHN-say)*
My name is ____.	**Me llamo ____.** *may YAH-moh*
What's your name?	**¿Cómo se llama usted?** *KOH-moh say YAH-mah oos-TEHD*
How are you?	**¿Cómo está usted?** *KOH-moh ehs-TAH oos-TEHD*
How's everything?	**¿Qué tal?** *kay tahl*
Very well, thanks. And you?	**Muy bien, gracias. ¿Y usted?** *mwee bee-EHN GRAH-see-ahs ee oos-TEHD*
Where is ____?	**¿Dónde está ____?** *DOHN-day ehs-TAH*
▪ the bathroom	**el baño** *ehl BAH-nyoh*
▪ the dining room	**el comedor** *ehl koh-meh-DOHR*
▪ the entrance	**la entrada** *lah ehn-TRAH-dah*
▪ the exit	**la salida** *lah sahl-EE-dah*
▪ the telephone	**el teléfono** *ehl tehl-EHF-oh-noh*
I'm lost.	**Me he perdido.** *may heh pehr-DEE-doh*

We're lost.	**Nos hemos perdido.**	*nohs HEH-mohs pehr-DEE-doh*
Where are ____?	**¿Dónde están ____?**	*dohn-day ehs-TAHN*
I am looking for ____.	**Busco ____.**	*BOOS-koh*
▪ to the left	**a la izquierda**	*ah lah ees-kee-EHR-dah*
▪ to the right	**a la derecha**	*ah lah dehr-EH-chah*
▪ straight ahead	**derecho**	*deh-REH-choh*
I'm hungry.	**Tengo hambre.**	*TEHN-goh-AHM-bray*
I'm thirsty.	**Tengo sed.**	*tehn-goh SEHD*
I'm tired.	**Estoy cansado (m.) Estoy cansada (f.)**	*eh-stoy kahn-SAH-doh (dah)*
What's that?	**¿Qué es eso?**	*kay ehs EHS-oh*
What's up?	**¿Qué hay?**	*kay AH-ee*
I (don't) know.	**Yo (no) sé.**	*yoh (noh) say*

QUESTIONS

Where is (are) ____?	**¿Dónde está (están) ____?**	*DOHN-day eh-STAH (STAHN)*
When?	**¿Cuándo?**	*KWAHN-doh*
How?	**¿Cómo?**	*KOH-moh*
How much?	**¿Cuánto?**	*KWAHN-toh*
Who?	**¿Quién?**	*key-EN*
Why?	**¿Por qué?**	*pohr-KAY*
Which?	**¿Cuál?**	*kwal*
What?	**¿Qué?**	*kay*

PROBLEMS, PROBLEMS, PROBLEMS

Watch out!	**¡Cuidado!**	*kwee-DAH-doh*
Hurry up!	**¡Dése prisa!**	*day-say PREE-sah*
Look.	**¡Mire!**	*MEE-reh*
Listen!	**¡Escuche!**	*ehs-KOO-cheh*
Wait!	**¡Espere!**	*ehs-PEHR-eh*
Fire!	**¡Fuego!**	*FWAY-goh*

Leave me alone!	**¡Déjeme en paz!**	*DAY-heh-meh ehn PAHS*
Help, police!	**¡Socorro, policía!**	*soh-KOH-roh poh-lee-SEE-yah*
He has stolen ＿＿＿.	**Me ha robado ＿＿＿.**	*may ah roh-BAH-doh*
I have lost ＿＿＿.	**He perdido ＿＿＿.**	*ay pehr-DEE-doh*

▪ my car	**el coche**	*ehl KOH-chay*
▪ my passport	**el pasaporte**	*ehl pah-sah-POHR-tay*
▪ my purse	**la bolsa**	*lah BOHL-sah*
▪ my suitcase	**la maleta**	*lah mahl-EH-tah*
▪ my wallet	**la cartera**	*lah kahr-TEHR-ah*
▪ my watch	**el reloj**	*ehl ray-LOH*

I want to go ＿＿＿.	**Quiero ir ＿＿＿.**	*kee-YEHR-oh eer*
▪ to the American (British) (Australian) (Canadian) Consulate	**al consulado norteamericano, inglés, australiano, canadiense**	*ahl kohn-soo-LAH-doh nohr-tay-ah-mehr-ee-KAH-noh, een-GLAYS, ow-strahl-YAH-noh, kah-nah-DYEHN-say*
▪ to the police station	**al cuartel de policía**	*ahl kwahr-TEHL day poh-lee-SEE-ah*

I need help, quick.	**Necesito ayuda, pronto.**	*nehs-ehs-EE-toh ah-YOO-dah PROHN-toh*
Can you help me, please?	**¿Puede usted ayudarme, por favor?**	*pweh-day oos-TEHD ah-yoo-DAHR-may pohr fah-BOHR*
Does anyone here speak English	**¿Hay alguien aquí que hable inglés?**	*AH-ee AHL-ghee-yehn ah-KEE kay AH-blay een-GLEHS*
I need an interpreter.	**Necesito un intérprete.**	*neh-seh-SEE-toh oon een-TEHR-preh-tay*

NUMBERS

CARDINAL NUMBERS

0	**cero**	*SEHR-oh*
1	**uno**	*OO-noh*
2	**dos**	*dohs*
3	**tres**	*trehs*
4	**cuatro**	*KWAH-troh*
5	**cinco**	*SEEN-koh*
6	**seis**	*sayss*
7	**siete**	*SYEH-tay*
8	**ocho**	*OH-choh*
9	**nueve**	*NWEH-bay*
10	**diez**	*dyess*
11	**once**	*OHN-say*
12	**doce**	*DOH-say*
13	**trece**	*TREH-say*
14	**catorce**	*kah-TOHR-say*
15	**quince**	*KEEN-say*

16	**diez y seis (dieciséis)**	*dyeh-see-SAYSS*
17	**diez y siete (diecisiete)**	*dyeh-see-SYEH-tay*
18	**diez y ocho (dieciocho)**	*dyeh-see-OH-choh*
19	**diez y nueve (diecinueve)**	*dyeh-see-NWEH-bay*
20	**veinte**	*BAYN-tay*
21	**veintiuno**	*bayn-tee-OO-noh*
22	**veintidós**	*bayn-tee-DOHS*
23	**veintitrés**	*bayn-tee-TREHS*
24	**veinticuatro**	*bayn-tee-KWAH-troh*
25	**veinticinco**	*bayn-tee-SEEN-koh*
26	**veintiséis**	*bayn-tee-SAYSS*
27	**veintisiete**	*bayn-tee-SYEH-tay*
28	**veintiocho**	*bayn-tee-OH-choh*
29	**veintinueve**	*bayn-tee-NWEH-bay*
30	**treinta**	*TRAYN-tah*
40	**cuarenta**	*kwahr-EHN-tah*
50	**cincuenta**	*seen-KWEHN-tah*
60	**sesenta**	*seh-SEHN-tah*
70	**setenta**	*seh-TEHN-tah*
80	**ochenta**	*oh-CHEHN-tah*
90	**noventa**	*noh-BEHN-tah*
100	**cien(to)**	*syehn(toh)*
101	**ciento uno**	*SYEHN-toh OO-noh*

▪ 102	**ciento dos**	*SYEHN-toh DOHS*
200	**doscientos (as)**	*dohs-SYEHN-tohs (tahs)*
300	**trescientos (as)**	*trehs-SYEHN-tohs (tahs)*
400	**cuatrocientos (as)**	*kwah-troh-SYEHN-tohs (tahs)*
500	**quinientos (as)**	*kee-NYEHN-tohs (tahs)*
600	**seiscientos (as)**	*sayss-SYEHN-tohs (tahs)*
700	**setecientos (as)**	*seh-teh-SYEHN-tohs (tahs)*
800	**ochocientos (as)**	*oh-choh-SYEHN-tohs (tahs)*
900	**novecientos (as)**	*noh-beh-SYEHN-tohs (tahs)*
1.000	**mil**	*meel*
2.000	**dos mil**	*dohs meel*
1.000.000	**un millón**	*oon mee-YOHN*
2.000.000	**dos millones**	*dohs mee-YOHN-ays*

ORDINAL NUMBERS

1°	**primero (primer, -a)**	*pree-MEH-roh*
2°	**segundo (a)**	*seh-GOON-doh (dah)*
3°	**tercero (tercer, -a)**	*tehr-SEH-roh*
4°	**cuarto (a)**	*KWAHR-toh (tah)*
5°	**quinto (a)**	*KEEN-toh (tah)*
6°	**sexto (a)**	*SEHS-toh (tah)*
7°	**séptimo (a)**	*SEHT-tee-moh (mah)*
8°	**octavo (a)**	*ohk-TAH-boh (bah)*

9°	**noveno (a)**	*noh-BAY-noh (nah)*
10°	**décimo (a)**	*DEH-see-moh (mah)*
last	**último (a)**	*OOL-tee-moh (mah)*
once	**una vez**	*OO-nah-behs*
twice	**dos veces**	*dohs BEH-sehs*
three times	**tres veces**	*trehs BEH-sehs*

FRACTIONS

half of ___.	**la mitad de ___.**	*lah mee-TAHD day*
■ half (of) the money	**la mitad del dinero**	*lah mee-TAHD del dee-NEH-row*
half a ___.	**medio ___.**	*MEH-dyoh*
■ half a kilo	**medio kilo**	*MEH-dyoh KEE-loh*
a fourth (quarter)	**un cuarto**	*oon KWAHR-toh*

WHEN YOU ARRIVE

PASSPORT AND CUSTOMS

My name is ___.	**Me llamo ___.** *may YAH-moh*
I'm American (British) (Australian) (Canadian).	**Soy norteamericano (a) (inglés, a) (australiano, a) (canadiense).** *soy nohr-tay-ah-mehr-ee-KAH-noh (nah) (een-GLAYS, ah) (ow-strahl-YAH-noh, nah) (kah-nah-DYEHN-say)*
My address is ___.	**Mi dirección es ___.** *mee dee-rehk-SYOHN ehs*
I'm staying at ___.	**Estoy en el hotel ___.** *ehs-TOY ehn ehl oh-TEHL*

Here is (are) _____.	**Aquí tiene _____.** *ah-KEE TYEHN-ay*
my documents	**mis documentos** *mees doh-koo-MEHN-tohs*
my passport	**mi pasaporte** *mee pah-sah-POHR-tay*
my tourist card	**mi tarjeta de turista** *mee tahr-HAY-tah day toor-EES-tah*
I'm _____.	**Estoy _____.** *ehs-TOY*
on a business trip	**en un viaje de negocios** *ehn oon bee-AH-hay day neh-GOH-see-ohs*
on vacation	**de vacaciones** *day bah-kah-SYOHN-ays*
visiting relatives	**visitando a mis familiares** *bee-see-TAHN-doh ah mees fah-meel-YAHR-ays*
just passing through	**solamente de paso** *soh-loh-MEHN-tay day PAH-soh*
I'll be staying here _____.	**Me quedaré aquí _____.** *may kay-dahr-AY ah-KEE*
a few days	**unos días** *OON-ohs DEE-ahs*
a few weeks	**unas semanas** *OON-ahs seh-MAH-nahs*
a week	**una semana** *OON-ah seh-MAH-nah*
a month	**un mes** *oon mehs*
These are my bags.	**Estas son mis maletas.** *EHS-tahs sohn mees mah-LAY-tahs*
I have nothing to declare.	**No tengo nada que declarar.** *noh tehn-goh NAH-dah kay day-klahr-AHR*
I only have _____.	**Sólo tengo _____.** *SOH-loh tehn-goh*
a carton of cigarettes	**un cartón de cigarrillos** *oon kahr-TOHN day see-gahr-EE-yohs*

■ a bottle of whisky	**una botella de whisky** *OON-nah boh-TEH-yah day WEE-skee*
What's the problem?	**¿Hay algun problema?** *AH-ee ahl-GOON proh-BLAY-mah*
They're gifts (for my personal use).	**Son regalos (para mi uso personal).** *sohn ray-GAH-lohs (pah-rah mee OO-soh pehr-sohn-AHL)*
Do I have to pay duty?	**¿Tengo que pagar impuestos?** *ten-goh kay pah-GAHR eem-PWEHS-tohs*
May I close my bag now?	**¿Puedo cerrar la maleta ahora?** *pweh-doh sehr-AHR lah mah-LEH-tah ah-OHR-ah*

BAGGAGE AND PORTERS

Where can I find a baggage cart?	**¿Dónde está un carrito para male- tas?** *DOHN-day eh-STAH oon kahr-REE-toh pah-rah mah-LET-tahs*
I need a porter!	**¡Necesito un maletero!** *neh-seh-SEE-toh oon mah-leh-TEH-roh*
These are our (my) bags.	**Estas son nuestras (mis) maletas.** *EHS-tahs sohn NWEHS-trahs (mees) mah-LEH-tahs*
■ that big (little) one	**esa grande (pequeña)** *eh-sah GRAHN-day (peh-KAYN-yah)*
■ these two black (green) ones	**estas dos negras (verdes)** *EHS-tahs dos NEH-grahs (BEHR-days)*
Put them here (there).	**Póngalas aquí (allí).** *POHN-gah-lahs ah-KEE (ah-YEE)*
Be careful with that one!	**¡Cuidado con ésa!** *kwee-DAH-doh kohn EH-sah*
I'll carry this one myself.	**Yo me llevo ésta.** *yoh may YEH-boh EHS-tah*

I'm missing a suit-case.	**Me falta una maleta.** *may FAHL-tah oo-nah mah-LEH-tah*
How much do I owe you?	**¿Cuánto le debo?** *KWAHN-toh lay DEHB-oh*
Thank you (very much). This is for you.	**(Muchas) gracias. Esto es para usted.** *(moo-chahs) GRAHS-yahs EHS-toh ehs pah-rah oos-TEHD*

MONEY MATTERS

EXCHANGING MONEY

Where is the curren-cy exchange (bank)?	**¿Dónde hay un banco para cam-biar moneda extranjera?** *DOHN-day AH-ee oon BAHN-koh pah-rah kahm-bee-AHR moh-NAY-dah ehs-trahn-HEHR-ah*
I wish to change ____.	**Quiero cambiar ____.** *kee-YEHR-oh kahm-bee-YAHR*
▪ money	**dinero** *dee-NEHR-oh*
▪ dollars (pounds)	**dólares (libras)** *DOH-lahr-ays (LEE-brahs)*
▪ travelers checks	**cheques de viajero** *CHEH-kays day bee-ah-HAIR-oh*
Can I cash a per-sonal check?	**¿Puedo cambiar un cheque personal?** *PWEH-doh kahm-bee-YAHR oon CHEH-kay pehr-sohn-AHL*
At what time do they open (close)?	**¿A qué hora abren (cierran)?** *ah kay ohra AH-brehn (SYEHR-ahn)*
Where is the cashier's window?	**¿Dónde está la caja, por favor?** *DOHN-day eh-STAH lah KAH-hah pohr fah-BOHR*

What's the current exchange rate for dollars (pounds)?	**¿A cómo está el cambio hoy del dólar (de la libra)?** *ah KOH-moh ehs-TAH ehl KAHM-bee-oh oy del DOH-lahr (day lah LEE-brah)*
What commission do you charge?	**¿Cuál es el interés que Vds. cobran?** *kwahl ehs ehl een-tehr-AYS kay oos-TEHD-ays KOH-brahn*
I'd like to cash this check.	**Quisiera cobrar este cheque.** *kee-SYEHR-ah koh-BRAHR EHS-teh CHEH-kay*
Where do I sign?	**¿Dónde debo firmar?** *DOHN-day DEH-boh feer-MAHR*
I'd like the money ____.	**Quisiera el dinero ____.** *kee-SYEHR-ah ehl dee-NEHR-oh*

■ in (large) bills   **en billetes (grandes)** *ehn bee-YEH-tehs (GRAHN-days)*

■ in small change   **en suelto** *ehn SWEHL-toh*

Give me two twenty-peso bills.	**Déme dos billetes de a veinte pesos.** *DEH-may dohs bee-YEH-tays day ah BAYN-tay PAY-sohs*
fifty-peso bills	**cincuenta** *seen-KWEHN-tah*
one hundred-peseta bills	**cien** *see-YEHN*

AT THE HOTEL

CHECKING IN

| I'd like a single (double) room for tonight. | **Quisiera una habitación con una sola cama (con dos camas) para esta noche.** *kee-SYEHR-ah OO-nah ah-bee-tah-SYOHN kohn OO-nah SOH-lah KAH-mah (kohn dohs KAH-mahs) pah-rah EHS-tah NOH-chay* |

How much is the room ____?	**¿Cuánto cuesta el cuarto ____?** *KWAHN-toh KWEHS-tah ehl KWAHR-toh*
with a shower	**con ducha** *kohn DOO-chah*
with a private bath	**con baño privado** *kohn BAHN-yoh pree-BAH-doh*
with a balcony	**con balcón** *kohn bahl-KOHN*
facing the ocean	**con vista al mar** *kohn bees-tah ahl mahr*
facing (away from) the street	**que dé a la calle** *kay day ah lah KAH-yeh*
facing the court-yard	**que dé al patio** *kay day ahl PAH-tee-oh*
in the back	**al fondo** *ahl FOHN-doh*
Does it have ____?	**¿Tiene ____?** *tee-YEH-neh*
air-conditioning	**aire acondicionado** *AH-ee-ray ah-kohn-dee-syohn-AH-doh*
hot water	**agua caliente** *ah-guah kahl-YEN-tay*
television	**televisión** *teh-lay-bee-SYOHN*
I (don't) have a res-ervation.	**(No) tengo reserva.** *(noh) ten-goh reh-SEHR-bah*
Could you call anoth-er hotel to see if they have some-thing?	**¿Podría llamar a otro hotel para ver si tienen algo?** *poh-DREE-ah yah-MAHR ah OH-troh o-TEL pah-rah behr see tee-yen-ehn AHL-goh*
May I see the room?	**¿Podría ver la habitación?** *poh-DREE-ah behr lah ah-bee-tah-SYOHN*
I (don't) like it.	**(No) me gusta.** *(noh) may GOOS-tah*
Do you have some-thing ____?	**¿Hay algo ____?** *AH-ee ahl-goh*
better	**mejor** *may-HOHR*

▪ larger	**más grande** *mahs GRAHN-day*
▪ smaller	**más pequeño** *mahs peh-KAYN-yo*
▪ cheaper	**más barato** *mahs bah-RAH-toh*
▪ quieter	**donde no se oigan ruidos** *DOHN-day noh say OY-gahn RWEE-dohs*
What floor is it on?	**¿En qué piso está?** *ehn kay PEE-soh ehs-TAH*
Is there an elevator (lift)?	**¿Hay ascensor?** *AH-ee ah-sen-SOHR*
Is everything included?	**¿Está todo incluído?** *eh-STAH toh-doh een-kloo-EE-doh*
How much is the room with _____?	**¿Cuánto cobra usted por la habitación _____?** *KWAHN-toh KOH-brah oos-TEHD pohr lah ah-bee-tah-SYOHN kohn*
▪ the American plan (2 meals a day)	**con media pensión** *kohn MEH-dee-yah pen-SYOHN*
▪ bed and breakfast	**con desayuno** *kohn dehs-ah-YOO-noh*
▪ no meals	**sin la comida** *seen lah koh-MEE-dah*
The room is very nice. I'll take it.	**La habitación es muy bonita. Me quedo con ella.** *lah ah-bee-tah-SYOHN ehs mwee boh-NEE-tah may KAY-doh kohn EH-ya*
We'll be staying _____.	**Nos quedamos _____.** *nohs kay-DAH-mohs*
▪ one night	**una noche** *OO-nah NOH-chay*
▪ a few nights	**unas noches** *OO-nahs NOH-chayes*
▪ one week	**una semana** *OO-nah seh-MAH-nah*
How much do you charge for children?	**¿Cuánto cobra por los niños?** *kwahn-toh KOH-brah pohr lohs NEEN-yohs*

Could you put another bed in the room?	**¿Podría poner otra cama en la habitación?** *poh-DREE-ah poh-NEHR oh-trah KAH-mah ehn lah ah-bee-tah-SYOHN*
Is there a charge? How much?	**¿Hay que pagar más? ¿Cuánto?** *AH-ee kay pah-GAHR mahs? KWAHN-toh*

OTHER ACCOMMODATIONS

I'm looking for _____.	**Busco _____.** *BOOS-koh*
▪ a boardinghouse	**una pensión (una casa de huéspedes)** *OO-nah pen-SYOHN (oo-nah kah-sah day WES-pehd-ays)*
▪ a private house	**una casa particular** *OO-na kah-sah pahr-teek-oo-LAHR*
I want to rent an apartment.	**Quiero alquilar un apartamento.** *kee-YEHR-oh ahl-kee-LAHR oon ah-pahr-tah-MEHN-toh*
I need a living room, bedroom, and kitchen.	**Necesito un salón, un dormitorio, y una cocina.** *neh-seh-SEE-toh oon sah-LOHN, oon dohr-mee-TOHR-ee-oh ee oo-nah koh-SEE-nah*
Do you have a furnished room?	**¿Tiene un cuarto amueblado?** *tee-YEN-ay oon KWAHR-toh ah-mway-BLAH-doh*
How much is the rent?	**¿Cuánto es el alquiler?** *KWAHN-toh ehs ehl ahl-kee-LEHR*
I'll be staying here for _____.	**Me quedaré aquí _____.** *may kay-dahr-AY ah-KEE*
▪ two weeks	**dos semanas** *dohs seh-MAH-nahs*
▪ one month	**un mes** *oon mehs*
▪ the whole summer	**todo el verano** *toh-doh ehl behr-AH-noh*

I want a place that's ___.	**Quiero un sitio** ___. *kee-yehr-oh oon SEE- tee-yo*
centrally located	**en el centro de la ciudad** *ehn ehl SEHN-troh day lah syoo-DAHD*
near public transportation	**cerca del transporte público** *SEHR-kah del trahns-POHR-tay POOB-lee-koh*
Is there a youth hostel around here?	**¿Hay un albergue juvenil por aquí?** *AH-ee oon ahl-BEHR-gay hoo-ben-EEL pohr ah-KEE*

ORDERING BREAKFAST

We'll have breakfast in the room.	**Queremos desayunarnos en nuestra habitación.** *keh-RAY-mohs dehs-ah-yoo-NAHR-nohs ehn NWEHS-trah ah-bee-tah-SYOHN*
Please send up ___.	**Haga el favor de mandarnos** ___. *AH- gah ehl fah-BOHR day mahn-DAHR- nohs*
one (two) coffee(s)	**una taza (dos tazas) de café** *oo-nah TAH-sah (dohs TAH-sahs) day kah-FAY*
tea	**una taza de té** *oo-nah TAH-sah day tay*
hot chocolate	**una taza de chocolate** *oo-nah TAH-sah day cho-koh-LAH-tay*
a sweet roll	**un pan dulce** *oon pahn DOOL-say*
fruit (juice)	**un jugo (de fruta)** *oon HOO-goh day FROO-tah*
I'll eat breakfast downstairs.	**Voy a desayunarme abajo.** *boy ah dehs-ah-yoo-NAHR-may ah-BAH-ho*

We'd both like ____.	**Quisieramos** ____.	*kee-SYEHR-ah-mohs*
bacon and eggs	**huevos con tocino**	*WEH-bohs kohn toh-SEE-noh*
scrambled (fried, boiled) eggs	**huevos revueltos (fritos, pasados por agua)**	*WEH-bohs ray-BWEHL-tohs (FREE-tohs, pah-SAH-dohs pohr AH-gwah)*
toast	**pan tostado**	*pahn tohs-TAH-doh*
jam (marmalade)	**mermelada**	*mehr-may-LAH-dah*
Please don't make it too spicy.	**No lo haga muy picante.**	*noh loh AH-gah mwee pee-KAHN-tay*

HOTEL SERVICES

Where is ____?	**¿Dónde está ____?**	*dohn-day ehs-TAH*
the dining room	**el comedor**	*ehl koh-meh-DOHR*
the bathroom	**el baño**	*ehl BAHN-yo*
the elevator (lift)	**el ascensor**	*ehl ah-sen-SOHR*
the phone	**el teléfono**	*ehl tel-EF-oh-no*
What is my room number?	**¿Cuál es el número de mi cuarto?**	*kwahl ehs ehl NOO-mehr-oh day mee KWAHR-toh*
May I please have my key?	**Mi llave, por favor.**	*mee YAH-bay pohr fah-BOHR*
I've lost my key.	**He perdido mi llave.**	*eh pehr-DEE-doh mee YAH-bay*
I need ____.	**Necesito ____.**	*neh-seh-SEE-toh*
a bellhop	**un botones**	*oon boh-TOH-nays*
a chambermaid	**una camarera**	*oo-nah kah-mah-REHR-ah*

Please send ___ to my room.	**Haga el favor de mandar ___ a mi habitación.** *AH-gah ehl fah-BOHR day mah-DAHR ___ ah mee ah-bee-tah-SYOHN*
a towel	**una toalla** *oo-nah toh-AH-yah*
a bar of soap	**una pastilla de jabón** *oo-nah pahs-TEE-yah day hah-BOHN*
some hangers	**unas perchas** *oo-nahs PEHR-chahs*
a pillow	**una almohada** *oo-nah ahl-moh-AH-dah*
a blanket	**una manta** *oo-nah MAHN-tah*
some ice cubes	**cubitos de hielo** *koo-BEE-tohs day YEH-loh*
some ice water	**agua helada** *ah-guah eh-LAH-dah*
a bottle of mineral water	**una botella de agua mineral** *oo-nah boh-TEH-yah day AH-guah mee nehr-AHL*
an ashtray	**un cenicero** *oon sen-ee-SEHR-oh*
toilet paper	**papel higiénico** *pah-PEHL ee-HYEHN-ee-koh*
a reading lamp	**una lámpara para leer** *oo-nah LAHM-pahr-ah pah-rah lay-EHR*
an electric adaptor	**un adaptador eléctrico** *oon ah-dahp-tah-DOHR eh-LEK-tree-koh*
Who is it?	**¿Quién es?** *kee-EHN ehs*
Just a minute.	**Un momento.** *oon moh-MEN-toh*
Come in.	**Adelante.** *ah-del-AHN-tay*
Put it on the table.	**Póngalo en la mesa.** *POHN-gah-loh ehn lah MAY-sah*
Please wake me tomorrow at ___.	**¿Puede despertarme mañana a ___?** *PWEH-day dehs-pehr-TAHR-may mahn-YAH-nah ah*

There is no ___.	**No hay ___.** *noh AH-ee*
running water	**agua corriente** *AH-gwah kohr-YEN-tay*
hot water	**agua caliente** *AH-gwah kahl-YEN-tay*
electricity	**electricidad** *eh-lek-tree-see-DAHD*
The ___ doesn't work.	**No funciona ___.** *noh foon-SYOHN-ah*
air-conditioning	**el aire acondicionado** *ehl AH-ee-ray ah-kohn-dees-yohn-AH-doh*
fan	**el ventilador** *ehl ben-tee-lah-DOHR*
faucet	**el grifo** *ehl GREE-foh*
lamp	**la lámpara** *lah LAHM-pah-rah*
light	**la luz** *lah loos*
radio	**la radio** *lah RAH-dee-oh*
electric socket	**el enchufe** *ehl ehn-CHOO-fay*
light switch	**el interruptor** *ehl een-tehr-oop-TOHR*
television	**el televisor** *ehl tel-eh-bee-SOHR*
Can you fix it ___?	**¿Puede arreglarlo ___?** *PWEH-day ah-ray-GLAHR-loh*
now	**ahora** *ah-OH-rah*
as soon as possible	**lo más pronto posible** *loh mahs PROHN-toh poh-SEE-blay*
Are there any ___ for me?	**¿Hay ___ para mí?** *AH-ee ___ pah-rah MEE*
letters	**cartas** *KAHR-tahs*
messages	**recados** *ray-KAH-dohs*
packages	**paquetes** *pah-KEH-tays*
post cards	**postales** *pohs-TAH-lays*

Did anyone call for me?	**¿Preguntó alguien por mí?** *preh-goon-TOH AHL-ghee-ehn pohr MEE*
I'd like to leave this in your safe.	**Quisiera dejar esto en su caja fuerte.** *kee-SYEHR-ah day-HAHR EHS-toh ehn soo KAH-ha FWEHR-tay*
Will you make this call for me?	**¿Podría usted hacerme esta llamada?** *poh-DREE-ah oos-TEHD ah-SEHR-may EHS-tah yah-MAH-dah*

CHECKING OUT

I'd like the bill, please.	**Quisiera la cuenta, por favor.** *kee-SYEHR-ah lah KWEHN-tah pohr fah-BOHR*
I'll be checking out today (tomorrow).	**Pienso marcharme hoy (mañana).** *PYEHN-soh mahr-CHAR-may oy (mahn-YA-nah)*
Please send someone up for our baggage.	**Haga el favor de mandar a alguien para recoger nuestro equipaje.** *AH-gah ehl fah-BOHR day mahn-DAHR ah AHL-ghy-ehn pah-rah ray-koh-HEHR NWEHS-troh AY-kee-PAH-hay*

GETTING AROUND TOWN

THE BUS

Where is the bus stop (terminal)?	**¿Dónde está la parada (la terminal) de autobús?** *DOHN-day ehs-TAH lah pah-RAH-dah (lah tehr-mee-NAHL) day AH-oo-toh-BOOS*

Which bus do I take to get to ____?	**¿Qué autobús hay que tomar para ir a ____?** *kay AH-oo-toh-BOOS AH-ee kay toh-MAHR PAH-rah eer ah ____?*
Do I need exact change?	**¿Necesito tener cambio exacto?** *neh-seh-SEE-toh ten-EHR KAHM-bee-oh ehk-SAHK-toh*
In which direction do I have to go?	**¿Qué rumbo tengo que tomar?** *kay ROOM-boh ten-goh kay toh-MAHR*
How often do the buses run?	**¿Con qué frecuencia salen los autobuses?** *kohn kay freh-KWEHN-see-ah sah-lehn lohs AH-oo-toh-BOOS-ehs*
Do you go to ____?	**¿Va usted a ____?** *bah oos-TEHD ah*
Is it far from here?	**¿Está lejos de aquí?** *eh-STAH LAY-hos day ah-KEE*
How many stops are there?	**¿Cuántas paradas hay?** *KWAHN-tahs pah-RAH-dahs AH-ee*
Do I have to change?	**¿Tengo que cambiar?** *TEN-goh kay kahm-bee-AHR*
How much is the fare?	**¿Cuánto es el billete?** *KWAHN-toh ehs ehl bee-YEH-tay*
Where do I have to get off?	**¿Dónde tengo que bajarme?** *DOHN-day ten-goh kay bah-HAHR-may*
Please tell me where to get off.	**¿Dígame, por favor, dónde debo bajarme?** *DEE-gah-may, pohr fa-BOHR DOHN-day deh-boh bah-HAHR-may*

THE SUBWAY (UNDERGROUND)

Is there a subway (underground) in this city?	**¿Hay un metro en esta ciudad?** *AH-ee oon MEHT-roh ehn EHS-tah syoo-DAHD*

Where is the closest subway (underground) station?	**¿Dónde hay la estación más cercana?** *DOHN-day AH-ee lah ehs-tah-SYOHN mahs sehr-KAH-nah*
How much is the fare?	**¿Cuánto es la tarifa?** *KWAHN-toh ehs lah tah-REE-fah*
Where can I buy a token (a ticket)?	**¿Dónde puedo comprar una ficha (un billete)?** *DOHN-day PWEH-doh kohm-PRAHR oo-nah FEE-chah (oon bee-YEH-teh)*
Which is the line that goes to ____?	**¿Cuál es la línea que va a ____?** *kwahl ehs lah LEEN-eh-ah kay bah ah*
Does this train go to ____?	**¿Va este tren a ____?** *bah ehs-teh trehn ah*
Do you have a map showing the stops?	**¿Tiene un mapa que indique las paradas?** *TYEH-nay oon MAH-pah kay een-DEE-kay lahs pahr-AH-dahs*
How many more stops?	**¿Cuántas paradas más?** *KWAHN-tahs pah-RAH-dahs mahs?*
What's the next station?	**¿Cuál es la próxima estación?** *kwahl ehs lah PROHK-see-mah ehs-tah-SYOHN*
Where should I get off?	**¿Dónde debo bajarme?** *DOHN-day deh-boh bah-HAHR-may*
Do I have to change?	**¿Tengo que hacer trasbordo?** *ten-goh kay ah-SEHR trahs-BOHRD-oh*
Please tell me when we get there.	**Haga el favor de avisarme cuando lleguemos.** *AH-gah ehl fah-BOHR day ah-bee-SAHR-may kwahn-doh yeh-GAY-mohs*

TAXIS

Is there a taxi stand near here?	**¿Hay una parada de taxis por aquí?** *AH-ee oo-nah pah-RAH-dah day TAHK-sees pohr ah-KEE*

Please get me a taxi.	**Puede usted conseguirme un taxi, por favor.** *PWEH-day oos-TEHD kohn-say-GHEER-may oon TAHK-si pohr fah-BOHR*
Where can I get a taxi?	**¿Dónde puedo coger un taxi?** *DOHN-day PWEH-doh koh-HAIR oon TAHK-see*
Taxi! Are you free (available)?	**¡Taxi! ¿Está libre?** *TAHK-see ehs-TAH LEE-bray*
Take me (I want to go) ____.	**Lléveme (Quiero ir) ____.** *YEHV-eh-may (kee-EHR-oh eer)*
▦ to the airport	**al aeropuerto** *ahl ah-ehr-oh-PWEHR-toh*
▦ to this address	**a esta dirección** *ah ehs-tah dee-rehk-SYOHN*
▦ to the hotel	**al hotel** *ahl o-TEL*
▦ to the station	**a la estación** *ah lah ehs-tah-SYOHN*
▦ to ____ street	**a la calle ____** *ah lah KAH-yeh*
Do you know where it is?	**¿Sabe dónde está?** *sah-bay DOHN-day ehs-TAH*
How much is it to ____?	**¿Cuánto cuesta hasta ____?** *KWAHN-toh KWEHS-tah AHS-tah*
Faster! I'm in a hurry.	**¡Más rápido, tengo prisa!** *mahs RAH-pee-doh, ten-goh PREE-sah*
Please drive slower.	**Por favor, conduzca más despacio.** *pohr fah-BOHR kohn-DOOS-kah mahs dehs-PAH-see-oh*
Stop here ____.	**Pare aquí ____.** *PAH-ray ah-KEE*
▦ at the corner	**en la esquina** *ehn lah ehs-KEE-nah*
▦ at the next block	**en la otra calle** *ehn lah OH-trah KAH-yeh*

Wait for me. I'll be right back.	**Espéreme. Vuelvo pronto.** *ehs-PEHR-eh-may BWEHL-boh PROHN-toh*
I think you are going the wrong way.	**Creo que me está llevando por una dirección equivocada.** *KRAY-oh kay may ehs-TAH yeh-BAHN-doh pohr oo-nah dee-rek-SYOHN eh-kee-boh-KAH-dah*
How much do I owe you?	**¿Cuánto le debo?** *KWAHN-toh lay DEHB-oh*
This is for you.	**Esto es para usted.** *ehs-toh ehs PAH-rah oos-TEHD*

SIGHTSEEING AND TOURS

Where is the Tourist Information Office?	**¿Dónde está la oficina de turismo?** *DOHN-day ehs-TAH lah of-fee-SEEN-ah day toor-EES-moh*
I need a(n) (English-speaking) guide.	**Necesito un guía (de habla ingle-sa).** *neh-seh-SEE-toh oon GHEE-ah (day AH-blah een-GLAY-sah)*
How much does he charge ____?	**¿Cuánto cobra ____?** *KWAHN-toh KOH-brah*
▮ per hour	**por hora** *pohr OHR-ah*
▮ per day	**por día** *pohr DEE-ah*
There are two (four, six) of us.	**Somos dos (cuatro, seis).** *soh-mohs dohs (KWAHT-roh, sayss)*
Where can I buy a guide book (map)?	**¿Dónde puedo comprar una guía (un mapa)?** *DOHN-day PWEH-doh kohm-PRAHR oo-nah GHEE-ah (oon MAH-pah)*
What are the main attractions?	**¿Cuáles son los puntos principales de interés?** *KWAHL-ehs sohn lohs poon-tohs preen-see-PAHL-ays day een-tehr-AYS*

What are things of interest here?	**¿Qué cosas interesantes hay aquí?** *kay KOH-sahs een-tehr-ehs-AHN-tays AH-ee ah-KEE*
Are there trips through the city?	**¿Hay excursiones por la ciudad?** *AH-ee ehs-koor-SYOHN-ehs pohr lah see-oo-DAHD*
When does the tour begin?	**¿Cuando empieza la excursión?** *KWAHN-doh ehm-PYEH-sah lah ehs-koor-SOYHN*
How long is the tour?	**¿Cuánto tiempo dura?** *KWAHN-toh TYEHM-poh DOOR-ah*
Where do they leave from?	**¿De dónde salen?** *day DOHN-day SAHL-ehn*
We want to see _____.	**Queremos ver _____.** *kehr-EHM-ohs behr*
▪ the botanical garden	**el jardín botánico** *ehl har-DEEN boh-TAHN-ee-koh*
▪ the bullring	**la plaza de toros** *lah plah-sah day TOHR-ohs*
▪ the business center	**el centro comercial** *ehl SEN-troh koh-mehr-SYAHL*
▪ the castle	**el castillo** *ehl kahs-TEE-yoh*
▪ the cathedral	**la catedral** *lah kah-tay-DRAHL*
▪ the church	**la iglesia** *lah eeg-LEHS-ee-ah*
▪ the concert hall	**la sala de conciertos** *lah SAH-lah day kohn-see-EHR-tohs*
▪ the downtown area	**el centro de la ciudad** *ehl SEN-troh day lah see-oo-DAHD*
▪ the fountains	**las fuentes** *lahs FWEHN-tays*
▪ the library	**la biblioteca** *lah beeb-lee-oh-TAY-kah*
▪ the main park	**el parque central** *ehl pahr-kay sen-TRAHL*

the main square	**la plaza mayor** *lah plah-sah my-YOR*
the market	**el mercado** *ehl mehr-KAH-doh*
the mosque	**la mezquita** *lah mehs-KEE-tah*
the museum (of fine arts)	**el museo (de bellas artes)** *ehl moo-SAY-oh (day bel-yahs AHR-tays)*
a nightclub	**una sala de fiestas** *oo-nah SAHL-ah day fee-ES-tahs*
the old part of town	**la ciudad vieja** *lah see-oo-DAHD BYEH-ha*
the opera	**la ópera** *lah OH-pehr-ah*
the palace	**el palacio** *ehl pah-LAH-see-oh*
the stadium	**el estadio** *ehl ehs-TAHD-ee-oh*
the synagogue	**la sinagoga** *lah seen-ah-GOH-gah*
the university	**la universidad** *lah oon-ee-behr-see-DAHD*
the zoo	**el parque zoológico** *ehl pahr-kay soh-oh-LOH-hee-koh*
Is it all right to go in now?	**¿Se puede entrar ahora?** *say PWEH-day ehn-TRAHR ah-OHR-ah*
Is it open (closed)?	**¿Está abierto (cerrado)?** *ehs-TAH ah-bee-YEHR-toh (sehr-AH-doh)*
At what time does it open (close)?	**¿A qué hora se abre (cierra)?** *ah kay OHR-ah say AH-bray (see-YEHR-ah)*
What's the admission price?	**¿Cuánto es la entrada?** *KWAHN-toh ehs lah ehn-TRAH-dah*
How much do children pay?	**¿Cuánto pagan los niños?** *KWAHN-toh pah-GAHN lohs NEEN-yohs*
Can they go in free? Until what age?	**¿Pueden entrar gratis? ¿Hasta qué edad?** *PWEH-dehn ehn-TRAHR GRAH-tees ah-stah kay eh-DAHD?*

Is it all right to take pictures?	**¿Se puede sacar fotos?** *say PWEH-deh sah-KAHR FOH-tohs*
How much extra does it cost to take pictures?	**¿Hay que pagar para poder sacar fotos?** *AH-ee kay pah-GAHR pah-rah poh-DEHR sah-KAHR FOH-tohs*
I do (not) use a flash attachment.	**(No) uso flash (luz instantánea).** *(noh) oo-soh flahsh (loos een-stahn-TAHN-ay-ah*

PLANNING A TRIP

AIR SERVICES

When is there a flight to ___?	**¿Cuándo hay un vuelo a ___?** *KWAHN-doh AH-ee oon BWEHL-oh ah*
I would like a ___ ticket.	**Quisiera un billete ___.** *kee-see-YEHR-ah oon bee-YEH-tay*
▪ round trip	**de ida y vuelta** *day EE-dah ee BWEHL-tah*
▪ one way	**de ida** *day EE-dah*
▪ tourist class	**en clase turista** *ehn KLAH-say toor-EES-tah*
▪ first class	**en primera clase** *ehn pree-MEHR-ah KLAH-say*
I would like a seat ___.	**Quisiera un asiento ___.** *kee-see-YEHR-ah oon ah-SYEHN-toh*
▪ in the smoking section	**en la sección de fumadores** *ehn lah sehk-SYOHN day foo-mah-DOHR-ehs*
▪ in the nonsmoking section	**en la sección de no fumadores** *ehn lah sehk-SYOHN day noh foo-mah-DOHR-ehs*

■ next to the window   **de ventanilla** *day behn-tah-NEE-yah*

■ on the aisle   **de pasillo** *day pah-SEE-yoh*

What is the fare?   **¿Cuál es la tarifa?** *kwahl ehs lah tah-REE-fah*

Are meals served?   **¿Se sirven comidas?** *say seer-behn koh-MEE-dahs*

When does the plane leave (arrive)?   **¿A qué hora sale (llega) el avión?** *ah kay oh-ra SAH-lay (YEH-gah) ehl ah-BYOHN*

When must I be at the airport?   **¿Cuándo debo estar en el aeropuerto?** *KWAHN-doh deh-boh ehs-TAHR en ehl ah-ehr-oh-PWEHR-toh*

What is my flight number?   **¿Cuál es el número del vuelo?** *kwahl ehs ehl NOO-mehr-oh dehl BWEH-loh*

What gate do we leave from?   **¿De qué puerta se sale?** *day kay PWEHR-tah say sah-lay*

I want to confirm (cancel) my reservation for flight ____.   **Quiero confirmar (cancelar) mi reservación para el vuelo ____.** *kee-YEHR-oh kohn-feer-MAHR (kahn-say-LAHR) mee reh-sehr-bah-SYOHN pah-rah ehl BWEH-loh*

I'd like to check my bags.   **Quisiera facturar mis maletas.** *kee-SYEHR-ah fahk-too-RAHR mees mah-LEH-tahs*

I have only carry-on baggage.   **Tengo solo equipaje de mano.** *TEN-goh so-loh ay-kee-PAH-hay day MAH-noh*

Can you pass my film (camera) through by hand?   **¿Podría inspeccionar el film (la cámara) a mano?** *poh-DREE-ah een-spek-syohn-AHR ehl feelm (lah KAH-mahr-ah) ah MAHN-oh*

TRAIN SERVICE

A first (second) class ticket to _____ please.	**Un billete de primera (segunda) clase a _____ por favor.** *oon bee-YEH-teh day pree-MEHR-ah (say-GOON-dah) KLAH-say ah _____ pohr fah-BOHR*
▪ a half price ticket	**un medio billete** *oon MEH-dee-oh bee-YEH-teh*
▪ a round trip ticket	**un billete de ida y vuelta** *oon bee-YEH-teh day EE-dah ee BWEHL-tah*
▪ a one way ticket	**un billete de ida** *oon bee-YEH-teh day EE-dah*
I'd like a (no) smoking compartment.	**Quisiera un departamento para (no) fumadores.** *kee-SYEHR-ah oon day-pahr-tah-MEHN-toh pah-rah (noh) foo-mah-DOHR-ays*
When does the train arrive (leave)?	**¿Cuándo llega (sale) el tren?** *kwahn-doh YEH-gah (SAH-lay) ehl trehn*
From (at) what platform does it leave (arrive)?	**¿De (A) qué andén sale (llega)?** *day (ah) kay ahn-DEHN SAH-lay (YEH-gah)*
Does this train stop at _____?	**¿Para este tren en _____?** *PAH-rah ehs-tay trehn ehn*
Is the train late?	**¿Tiene retraso el tren?** *tee-YEH-nay ray-TRAH-soh ehl trehn*
How long does it stop?	**¿Cuánto tiempo para?** *kwahn-toh tee-EHM-poh PAH-rah*
Is there time to get a bite?	**¿Hay tiempo para tomar un bocado?** *ahy tee-EHM-poh PAH-rah toh-MAHR oon boh-KAH-doh*
Do we have to stand in line?	**¿Tenemos que hacer cola?** *tehn-EH-mohs kay ah-SEHR KOH-lah*

Passengers, all aboard!	!Señores pasajeros, suban al tren! *sehn-YOHR-ays pah-sah-HEHR-ohs soo-bahn ahl trehn*
Is there a dining car (sleeping car)?	¿Hay coche-comedor (coche-cama)? *ahy KOH-chay koh-may-DOHR (KOH-chay KAH-mah)*
Is it _____?	¿Es _____? *ehs*
■ a through train	un tren directo *oon trehn dee-REHK-toh*
■ a local	un tren local (ómnibus, ordinario) *oon trehn loh-KAHL (OHM-nee-boos, ohr-dee-NAH-ree-oh)*
■ an express	un expreso (rápido) *oon eks-PREHS-oh (RAH-pee-doh)*
Do I have to change trains?	¿Tengo que trasbordar? *TEHN-goh kay trahs-bohr-DAHR*
Is this seat taken?	¿Está ocupado este asiento? *ehs-TAH oh-koo-PAH-doh EHS-tay ah-SYEHN-toh*
Where are we now?	¿Dónde estamos ahora? *DOHN-day ehs-tah-mohs ah-OHR-ah*
Will we arrive on time (late)?	¿Llegaremos a tiempo (tarde)? *yeh-gahr-EH-mohs ah tee-EHM-poh (tahr-day)*
Can I check my bag through to _____?	¿Puedo facturar mi maleta hasta _____? *PWEH-doh fahk-toor-AHR mee mah-LEH-tah AHS-tah*
Excuse me, but you are in my seat.	Perdón, creo que está ocupando mi asiento. *pehr-DOHN, KRAY-oh key ehs-TAH oh-koo-PAHN-doh mee ah-SYEHN-toh*

SHIPBOARD TRAVEL

Where is the dock?	**¿Dónde está el muelle?** *DOHN-day ehs-TAH ehl MWEH-yeh*
When does the next boat leave for _____?	**¿Cuándo sale el próximo barco para _____?** *KWAHN-doh SAH-lay ehl PROHKS-ee-moh BAHR-koh pah-rah*
How long does the crossing take?	**¿Cuánto dura la travesía?** *KWAHN-toh doo-rah lah trah-beh-SEE-ah*
Do we stop at any other ports?	**¿Hacemos escala en algunos puertos?** *ah-SAY-mohs ehs-KAH-lah ehn ahl-GOO-nohs PWEHR-tohs*
How long will we remain in the port?	**¿Cuánto tiempo permaneceremos en el puerto?** *KWAHN-toh tee-EHM-poh pehr-mah-neh-sehr-EH-mohs ehn ehl PWEHR-toh*
When do we land?	**¿Cuándo desembarcamos?** *KWAHN-doh dehs-ehm-bahr-KAH-mohs*
At what time do we have to be back on board?	**¿A qué hora debemos volver a bordo?** *ah kay OHR-ah deh-BAY-mohs bohl-BEHR ah BOHR-doh*
I'd like a _____ ticket.	**Quisiera un pasaje _____.** *kee-SYEHR-ah oon pah-SAH-hay*
first class	**de primera clase** *day pree-MEHR-ah KLAH-say*
tourist class	**de clase turista** *day KLAH-say toor-EES-tah*
cabin	**para un camarote** *PAH-rah oon kah-mah-ROH-tay*
I don't feel well.	**No me siento bien.** *noh may SYEHN-toh byehn*

| Can you give me something for sea sickness? | **¿Puede usted darme algo contra el mareo?** *PWEH-day oos-TEHD DAHR-may AHL-goh KOHN-trah ehl mah-RAY-oh* |

ENTERTAINMENT AND DIVERSIONS

MOVIES, THEATER, CONCERTS, OPERA, BALLET

Let's go to the ____.	**Vamos al ____.** *BAH-mohs ahl*
movies (cinema)	**cine** *SEE-nay*
theater	**teatro** *tay-AH-troh*
What are they showing today?	**¿Qué ponen hoy?** *kay POH-nehn oy*
Is it a ____?	**¿Es ____?** *ehs*
mystery	**un misterio** *oon mee-STEHR-ee-oh*
comedy	**una comedia** *OO-nah koh-MEH-dee-ah*
drama	**un drama** *oon DRAH-mah*
musical	**una obra musical** *OO-nah OH-brah moo-see-KAHL*
romance	**una obra romántica** *OO-nah OH-brah roh-MAHN-tee-kah*
Western	**una película del Oeste** *OO-nah pehl-EE-koo-lah del OWEST-ay*
war film	**una película de guerra** *OO-nah pehl-EE-koo-lah day GHEHR-ah*
science fiction film	**una película de ciencia ficción** *oo-nah pehl-EE-koo-lah day see-EHN-see-ah feek-SYOHN*

cartoon	**una película de dibujos animados** *oo-nah pehl-EE-koo-lah day dee-BOO-hohs ah-nee-MAH-dohs*
Is it in English?	**¿Es hablada en inglés?** *ehs ah-BLAH-dah ehn een-GLAYSS*
Has it been dubbed?	**¿Ha sido doblada?** *ah SEE-doh doh-BLAH-dah*
Where is the box office?	**¿Dónde está la taquilla?** *DOHN-day ehs-TAH lah tah-KEE-yah*
What time does the (first) show begin?	**¿A qué hora empieza la (primera) función?** *ah kay OHR-ah ehm-PYEH-sah lah (pree-MEHR-ah) foon-SYOHN*
What time does the (last) show end?	**¿A qué hora termina la (última) función?** *ah kay OHR-ah tehr-MEEN-ah lah (OOL-tee-mah) foon-SYOHN*
I want a seat near the middle (front, rear).	**Quisiera un asiento en el centro (al frente, atrás).** *kee SYEHR-ah oon ah-SYEHN-toh ehn ehl SEHN-troh (ahl FREHN-tay, ah-TRAHS)*
Can I check my coat?	**¿Puedo dejar mi abrigo?** *PWEH-doh day-HAHR mee ah-BREE-goh*
I need two tickets for tonight.	**Necesito dos entradas para esta noche.** *neh-seh-SEE-toh dohs ehn-TRAH-dahs pah-rah ehs-tah NOH-chay*
orchestra	**de platea** *dey plah-TAY-ah*
balcony	**de galería** *day gahl-ehr-EE-ah*
mezzanine	**de anfiteatro** *day ahn-fee-tay-AH-troh*
We would like to attend ___.	**Quisiéramos asistir a ___.** *kee-SYEHR-ah-mohs ah-sees-TEER ah*
a ballet	**un ballet** *oon bah-LEH*
a concert	**un concierto** *oon kohn-SYEHR-toh*
an opera	**una ópera** *oo-nah OH-pehr-ah*

What are they playing (singing)?	**¿Qué están interpretando?** *kay ehs-TAHN een-tehr-pray-TAHN-doh*
Who is the conductor?	**¿Quién es el director?** *kee-YEHN ehs ehl dee-rehk-TOHR*
I prefer ____.	**Prefiero ____.** *preh-fee-YEHR-oh*
■ classical music	**la música clásica** *lah MOO-see-kah KLAH-see-kah*
■ popular music	**la música popular** *lah MOO-see-kah poh-poo-LAHR*
■ folk dance	**el ballet folklórico** *ehl bah-LEH foh-KLOHR-ee-koh*
■ ballet	**el ballet** *ehl bah-LEH*
Are there any seats for tonight's performance?	**¿Hay localidades para la representación de esta noche?** *AH-ee loh-kahl-ee-DAHD-ays pah-rah lah rep-reh-sen-tah-SYOHN day ehs-tah NOH-chay*
When does the season begin (end)?	**¿Cuándo empieza (termina) la temporada?** *KWAHN-doh ehm-PYEH-sah (tehr-MEEN-ah) lah tem-pohr-AH-dah*
Should I get the tickets in advance?	**¿Debo sacar las entradas de antemano?** *deh-boh sah-KAHR lahs ehn-TRAH-dahs day ahn-tay-MAH-noh*
Do I have to dress formally?	**¿Tengo que ir de etiqueta?** *TEN-goh kay eer day eh-tee-KEH-tah*
How much are the front row seats?	**¿Cuánto valen los asientos delanteros?** *KWAHN-toh bah-lehn lohs ahs-YEHN-tohs day-lahn-TEHR-ohs*
What are the least expensive seats?	**¿Cuáles son los asientos más baratos?** *KWAHL-ays sohn lohs ahs-YEHN-tohs mahs bah-RAH-tohs*
May I buy a program?	**¿Puedo comprar un programa?** *PWEH-doh kohm-PRAHR oon pro-GRAHM-ah*

What opera (ballet) are they performing?	**¿Qué ópera (ballet) ponen?** *kay OH-pehr-ah (bah-LEH) POH-nen*
Who's singing (tenor, soprano, baritone, contralto)?	**¿Quién canta (tenor, soprano, barítono, contralto)?** *kee-YEHN KAHN-tah (ten-OHR, soh-PRAH-noh, barítono, kohn-TRAHL-toh)*

NIGHTCLUBS, DANCING

Let's go to a night-club.	**Vamos a un cabaret.** *BAH-mohs ah oon kah-bah-REH*
Is a reservation necessary?	**¿Hace falta una reserva?** *ah-say FAHL-tah oo-nah reh-SEHR-bah*
Is it customary to dine there as well?	**¿Se puede comer allá también?** *say PWEH-day koh-MEHR ah-YAH tahm-BYEHN*
Is there a good discotheque here?	**¿Hay aquí una buena discoteca?** *AH-ee ah-KEE oo-nah BWEH-nah dees-koh-TAY-kah*
Is there dancing at the hotel?	**¿Hay un baile en el hotel?** *AH-ee oon BAH-ee-lay ehn ehl oh-TEL*
We'd like a table near the dance floor.	**Quisiéramos una mesa cerca de la pista.** *kee-SYEHR-ah-mohs oo-nah MAY-sah sehr-kah day lah PEES-tah*
Is there a minimum (cover charge)?	**¿Hay un mínimo?** *AH-ee oon MEE-nee-moh*
Where is the checkroom?	**¿Dónde está el guardarropa?** *DOHN-day eh-STAH ehl gwahr-dah-ROH-pah*
At what time does the floor show go on?	**¿A qué hora empieza el espectáculo?** *ah kay OH-rah ehm-pee-EH-sah ehl ehs-peh-TAH-kool-oh*

SPECTATOR SPORTS

THE BULLFIGHT

el matador	kills the bull with his espada (sword).
el banderillero	thrusts three sets of long darts (banderillas) into the bull's neck to enfuriate him.
el picador	bullfighter mounted on a horse who weakens the bull with his lance (pica).
la cuadrilla	a team of helpers for the torero, who confuse and tire the bull with their capes (capas).
el monosabio	assistant who does various jobs in the redondel (bullring).

Is there a bullfight this afternoon? (every Sunday)?	**¿Hay una corrida de toros esta tarde (todos los domingos)?** *AH-ee oo-nah koh-REE-dah day TOH-rohs ehs-tah TAHR-day (toh-dohs lohs doh-MEEN-gohs)*
Take me to the bullring.	**Lléveme a la Plaza de Toros.** *YEH-bay-may ah lah PLAH-sah day TOHR-ohs*
I'd like a seat in the shade (in the sun).	**Quisiera un sitio a la sombra (al sol).** *kees-YEH-rah oon SEE-tee-oh ah lah SOHM-brah (ahl sohl)*
When does the parade of the bullfighters begin?	**¿Cuándo empieza el desfile de la cuadrilla?** *KWAHN-doh ehm-PYEH-sah ehl dehs-FEEL-ay day lah kwahd-REE-yah*
When does the first bull appear?	**¿Cuándo sale el primer toro?** *KWAHN-doh sah-lay ehl pree-MEHR TOH-roh*

How well that bull-fighter works!	**¡Qué bien torea aquel matador!** *kay bee-EHN toh-RAY-ah ah-kehl mah-tah-DOHR*
Bravo!	**¡Olé!** *oh-LAY*

SOCCER

I'd like to watch a soccer match.	**Quisiera ver un partido de fútbol.** *kee-SYEHR-ah behr oon pahr-TEE-doh day FOOT-bohl*
Where's the stadium?	**¿Dónde está el estadio?** *DOHN-day ehs-TAH ehl ehs-TAH-dee-oh*
When does the first half begin?	**¿Cuándo empieza el primer tiempo?** *KWAHN-doh ehm-pee-EH-sah ehl pree-MEHR tee-EM-poh*
What teams are going to play?	**¿Qué equipos van a jugar?** *kay eh-kee-pohs bahn ah hoo-GAHR*
Who is playing ____?	**¿Quién es ____?** *kee-YEHN ehs*

■ center   **el centro** *ehl SEN-troh*

■ fullback   **el defensa** *ehl day-FEN-sah*

■ halfback   **el medio** *ehl MED-ee-oh*

■ wing   **el ala** *ehl AH-lah*

What was the score?	**¿Cuál fue la anotación?** *kwahl fway lah ah-noh-tah-SYOHN*

JAI ALAI

Are you a jai alai fan?	**¿Es usted aficionado a la pelota?** *ehs oos-TEHD ah-fee-syohn-AH-doh ah lah pel-OH-tah*
I'd like to see a jai alai match.	**Me gustaría ver un partido de pelota.** *may goos-tahr-EE-ah behr oon par-TEE-doh day pel-OH-tah*

Where can I get tickets?	**¿Dónde puedo conseguir billetes?** *DOHN-day pweh-doh kohn-seh-GEER bee-YEH-tays*
Where is the jai alai court?	**¿Dónde está el frontón?** *DOHN-day ehs-TAH ehl frohn-TOHN*
Who are the players?	**¿Quiénes son los jugadores?** *kee-YEHN-ehs sohn lohs hoo-gah-DOHR-ays*
Each team has a forward and a back.	**Cada equipo teine un delantero y un zaguero.** *kah-dah eh-kee-poh tee-EHN-ay oon day-lahn-TEHR-oh ee oon sah-GHER-oh*
Where do I place my bet?	**¿Dónde hago la apuesta?** *DOHN-day ah-goh lah ah-PWEH-stah*
■ at that window	**en esa ventanilla** *ehn EH-sah ben-tah-NEE-yah*

HORSE RACING

Is there a race track here?	**¿Hay un hipódromo aquí?** *AH-ee oon ee-POH-droh-moh ah-KEE*
I want to see the races.	**Quiero ver las carreras de caballos.** *kee-EHR-oh behr lahs kahr-EHR-ahs day kah-BAH-yohs*

ACTIVE SPORTS

Do you play tennis?	**¿Sabe usted jugar al tenis?** *SAH-bay oos-TEHD hoo-GAHR ahl TEN-ees*
I (don't) play very well.	**(No) juego muy bien.** *(noh) hoo-AY-goh mwee bee-EHN*
Do you play singles (doubles)?	**¿Juega usted solo (en pareja)?** *HWAY-gah oos-TEHD SOH-loh (ehn pahr-AY-hah)*

Do you know where there is a court?	**¿Sabe usted dónde hay una cancha?** *SAH-bay oos-TEHD DOHN-day AH-ee oo-nah KAHN-chah*
Is it a private club? I'm not a member.	**¿Es un club privado? No soy socio.** *ehs oon kloob pree-BAH-do noh soy SOH-see-oh*
Can I rent a racquet?	**¿Se puede alquilar una raqueta?** *say PWEH-day ahl-kee-LAHR oo-nah rah-KAY-tah*
How much do they charge per hour (per day)?	**¿Cuánto cobran por hora (por día)?** *KWAHN-toh KOH-brahn pohr OH-rah (pohr DEE-ah)?*
Do you sell balls for a hard (soft) surface?	**¿Vende pelotas para una superficie dura (blanda)?** *BEN-day peh-LOH-tahs pah-rah oo-nah soo-pehr-FEE-syeh DOO-rah (BLAHN-dah)*
I serve (You serve) first.	**Yo saco (Usted saca) primero.** *yoh SAH-koh (oos-TEHD SAH-kah) pree-MEHR-oh*
Where is a safe place to run (to jog)?	**¿Dónde hay un sitio seguro para correr?** *DOHN-day AH-ee oon SEE-tee-oh seh-GOOR-oh pah-rah kohr-EHR*
Where is there a health club (spa)?	**¿Dónde hay un gimnasio (balneario)?** *DOHN-day AH-ee oon heem-NAH-see-oh (bahl-nay-AHR-ee-oh)*

AT THE BEACH/POOL

Let's go to the beach (to the pool).	**Vamos a la playa (piscina).** *BAH-mohs ah lah PLAH-ee-ah (pee-SEEN-ah)*
Which bus will take us to the beach?	**¿Qué autobús nos lleva a la playa?** *kay AH-oo-toh-BOOS nohs yeh-bah ah lah PLAH-ee-ah*

Is there an indoor pool (outdoor) in the hotel?	**¿Hay una piscina cubierta (al aire libre) en el hotel?** *AH-ee oo-nah pee-SEE-nah (_____) ehn ehl oh-TEL*
I (don't) know how to swim well.	**(No) sé nadar bien.** *(noh) say nah-DAHR bee-EHN*
I just want to stretch out in the sand.	**Sólo quiero estirarme en la arena.** *SOH-loh kee-YEHR-oh ehs-tee-RAHR-may ehn lah ah-RAY-nah*
Is it safe to swim here?	**¿Se puede nadar aquí sin peligro?** *Say PWEH-day nah-DAHR ah-KEE seen peh-LEE-groh*
Is it dangerous for children?	**¿Hay peligro para los niños?** *AH-ee pel-EE-groh pah-rah lohs NEEN-yohs*
Is there a lifeguard?	**¿Hay salvavidas?** *AH-ee sahl-bah-BEE-dahs*
Where can I get _____?	**¿Dónde puedo conseguir _____?** *DOHN-day PWEH-doh kohn-seh-GHEER*
▪ an air mattress	**un colchón flotante** *oon kohl-CHOHN floh-tahn-tay*
▪ a beach ball	**una pelota de playa** *oo-nah pel-OH-tah day PLAH-ee-ah*
▪ a beach chair	**un sillón de playa** *oon see-YOHN day PLAH-ee-ah*
▪ a beach towel	**una toalla de playa** *oo-nah toh-AH-yah day PLAH-ee-yah*
▪ a beach umbrella	**una sombrilla playera** *oo-nah sohm-BREE-yah plah-YEHR-ah*
▪ diving equipment	**equipo de buceo** *eh-KEE-poh day boo-SAY-oh*
▪ a surfboard	**una plancha de deslizamiento, un acuaplano** *OO-nah PLAHN-chah day dehs-lees-ah-mee-EHN-toh, oon ah-kwah-PLAH-noh*

■ water skis   **esquís acuáticos** *ehs-KEES ah-KWAHT-ee-kohs*

ON THE SLOPES

Which ski area do you recommend?	**¿Qué sitio de esquiar recomienda usted?** *kay SEE-tee-oh day ehs-kee-AHR ray-koh-MYEHN-dah oos-TEHD*
I am a novice (intermediate, expert) skier.	**Soy principiante (intermedio, experto).** *soy preen-seep-YAHN-tay (een-tehr-MEHD-ee-oh, ehs-PEHR-toh)*
Is there enough snow at this time of year?	**¿Hay bastante nieve durante esta temporada?** *AH-ee bahs-TAHN-tay nee-EHB-ay door-ahn-tay ehs-tah temp-ohr-AH-dah*
How would I get to that place?	**¿Por dónde se va a ese sitio?** *pohr DOHN-day say bah ah eh-say SEE-tee-oh*
Can I rent _____ there?	**¿Puedo alquilar _____?** *PWEH-doh ahl-kee-lahr*

■ equipment   **equipo** *eh-KEEP-oh*

■ poles   **palos** *PAH-lohs*

■ skis   **esquís** *ehs-KEES*

■ ski boots   **botas de esquiar** *boh-tahs day ehs-kee-ahr*

Do they have ski lifts?	**¿Tienen funicular?** *TYEHN-eh foo-nee-koo-LAHR*
How much does the lift cost?	**¿Cuánto cobran?** *KWAHN-toh KOH-brahn*
Do they give lessons?	**¿Dan lecciones?** *dahn lek-SYOHN-ays*
Where can I stay at the summit?	**¿Dónde puedo alojarme en la cumbre?** *DOHN-day PWEH-doh ah-loh-HAHR-may ehn lah KOOM-bray*

ON THE LINKS

Is there a golf course?	**¿Hay un campo de golf?** *AH-ee oon KAHM-poh day gohlf*
Can one rent clubs?	**¿Se puede alquilar los palos?** *say PWEH-day ahl-kee-LAHR lohs PAH-lohs*

CAMPING

Is there a camping area near here?	**¿Hay un camping cerca de aquí?** *AH-ee oon KAHM-peeng sehr-kah day ah-KEE*
Do we pick our own site?	**¿Escogemos nuestro propio sitio?** *ehs-koh-HAY-mohs NWEHS-troh PROH-pee-oh SEE-tee-oh*
We only have a tent.	**Tenemos solo una tienda.** *ten-AY-mohs SOH-loh oo-nah TYEHN-dah*
Can we camp for one night only?	**¿Se puede acampar por una noche sola?** *say PWEH-day ah-kahm-pahr pohr oo-nah noh-chay SOH-lah*
Can we park our trailer (our caravan)?	**¿Podemos estacionar nuestro coche-vivienda (nuestra cara-vana)?** *poh-DAY-mos eh-stah-syohn-AHR-nwehs-troh KOH-chay bee-bee-EHN-dah (NWEHS-trah kahr-ah-BAHN-ah)*
Is (are) there ____?	**¿Hay ____?** *AH-ee*
▇ drinking water	**agua potable** *AH-gwah poh-TAH-blay*
▇ showers	**duchas** *DOO-chahs*
▇ fireplaces	**hogueras** *oh-GEHR-ahs*
▇ picnic tables	**mesas de camping** *may-sahs day KAHM-peeng*

flush toilets	**servicios** *sehr-BEE-see-ohs*
electricity	**electricidad** *eh-lek-tree-see-DAHD*
a children's play-ground	**un parque infantil** *oon PAHR-kay een-fahn-TEEL*
a grocery store	**una tienda de comestibles** *oo-nah tee-EHN-dah day koh-mes-TEE-blays*

| How much do they charge per person (per car)? | **¿Cuánto cobran por persona (por coche)?** *KWAHN-toh KOH-brahn pohr pehr-SOHN-ah (pohr koh-chay)* |
| We intend staying ____ days (weeks). | **Pensamos quedarnos ____ días (semanas).** *pen-SAH-mohs kay-DAHR-nohs ____ DEE-ahs (seh-MAHN-ahs)* |

FOOD AND DRINK

IN SPAIN

café	small place which serves alcoholic and nonalcoholic drinks, plus simple snacks; very casual
cafetería	not a self-service restaurant, as the name implies in English, but a cafe-type place specializing in informal food such as sandwiches, snacks, sweets, aperitifs, coffee, and tea
bar (tasca, taberna)	similar to a pub or bar in the U.S., in which drinks and small snacks (**ta-pas** or **pinchos**) are served
fonda (hostería, venta, posada)	small, informal inn which usually specializes in regional dishes
merendero (chirin-guito)	outdoor stall (usually at the beaches or piers) selling seafood, soft drinks, and ice cream

restaurante	traditional restaurant, varying in the extensiveness of their menu, usually offering a blending of regional specialties and more broad-based dishes; often also offers a tourist menu

IN LATIN AMERICA

bar	serves drinks and **botanas** (snacks)
cantina	men's bar, usually also serving snacks; this is a place for the neighborhood men to gather
hacienda	a ranch-style restaurant, usually with a garden and dining out-of-doors; gracious, usually with regional specialties
hostería (fonda, posada)	a casual restaurant, usually with regional specialties
restaurante	varying from the most casual, neighborhood place to a fancy establishment catering to tourists

EATING OUT

Do you know a good restaurant?	**¿Conoce usted un buen restaurante?** *koh-NOH-say oos-TEHD oon bwehn rehs-tah-oo-RAHN-tay*
Is it very expensive?	**¿Es muy caro?** *ehs mwee KAH-roh*
Do you know a restaurant that serves native dishes?	**¿Conoce usted un restaurante típico?** *koh-NOH-say oos-TEHD oon rehs-tah-oo-RAHN-tay TEE-pee-koh*
Waiter!	**¡Camarero!** *kah-mah-REHR-oh*
Miss!	**¡Señorita!** *sen-yohr-EE-tah*

A table for two, please.	**Una mesa para dos, por favor.** *oo-nah MAY-sah pah-rah dohs pohr fa-BOHR*
▪ in the corner	**en el rincón** *ehn ehl reen-KOHN*
▪ near the window	**cerca de la ventana** *sehr-kah day lah ben-TAHN-ah*
▪ on the terrace	**en la terraza** *ehn lah teh-RAH-sah*
I would like to make a reservation _____.	**Quisiera hacer una reserva _____.** *kee-see-EHR-ah ah-SEHR oo-nah ray-SEHR-bah*
▪ for tonight	**para esta noche** *pah-rah ehs-tah NOH-chay*
▪ for tomorrow evening	**para mañana por la noche** *pah-rah mahn-YAH-nah pohr lah NOH-chay*
▪ for two (four) persons	**para dos (cuatro) personas** *pah-rah dohs (KWAH-troh) pehr-SOHN-ahs*
▪ for 9 p.m.	**para las nueve** *pah-rah las NWEH-bay*
▪ for 9:30	**para las nueve y media** *pah-rah lahs NWEH-bay ee MEHD-yah*
We'd like to have lunch now.	**Queremos almorzar ahora.** *kehr-AY-mohs ahl-mohr-SAHR ah-OHR-ah*
The menu, please.	**La carta, por favor.** *lah KAHR-tah pohr fa-BOHR*
I'd like the set menu.	**Quisiera el menú del día.** *kee-see-YEHR-ah ehl men-OO del DEE-ah*
What's today's special?	**¿Cuál es el plato del día de hoy?** *KWAHL ehs ehl PLAH-toh del DEE-ah day oy*
What do you recommend?	**¿Qué recomienda usted?** *KAY reh-koh-mee-EHN-dah oos-TEHD*

What's the house specialty?	**¿Cuál es la especialidad de la casa?** *KWAHL ehs lah ehs-peh-see-ah-lee-DAHD day lah KAH-sah*
Do you serve children's portions?	**¿Hay platos especiales para niños?** *AH-ee PLAH-tohs ehs-peh-see-AHL-ays pah-rah NEEN-yohs*
I'm (not) very hungry.	**(No) tengo mucha hambre.** *(noh) TEN-goh moo-chah AHM-bray*
Are the portions small (large?)	**¿Son pequeños (grandes) las porciones?** *sohn peh-KAYN-yohs (GRAHN-days) lahs pohr-SYOHN-ays*
To begin with, please bring us ____.	**Para empezar, tráiganos ____ por favor.** *pahr-rah ehm-peh-SAHR, TRAH ee-gah-nohs ____ pohr fa-BOHR*
■ an aperitif	**un aperitivo** *oon ah-pehr-ee-TEE-boh*
■ a cocktail	**un coctel** *oon cohk-TEHL*
■ some white (red) wine	**un vino blanco (tinto)** *oon BEE-noh BLAHN-koh (TEEN-toh)*
■ some ice water	**agua helada** *AH-gwah eh-LAH-dah*
■ a bottle of mineral water, with (without) gas	**una botella de agua mineral, con (sin) gas** *oo-nah boh-TEH-yah day AH-gwah mee-nehr-AHL, kohn (seen) gahs*
■ a beer	**una cerveza** *oo-nah sehr-BEH-sah*
I'd like (to order now).	**Me gustaría (ordenar ahora).** *may goos-tahr-EE-ah (ohr-den-AHR-ah ah-OHR-ah)*
Do you have a house wine?	**¿Tiene un vino de la casa?** *tee-YEHN-ay oon BEE-noh day lah KAH-SAH*
Is it dry (mellow, sweet?)	**¿Es seco (suave, dulce)?** *ehs SAY-koh (SWAH-bay, DOOL-say)*

Please also bring us ____.	**Tráiganos también ____.** *TRAH-ee-gah-nohs tahm-BYEHN*
a roll	**un panecillo** *oon pah-neh-SEE-yoh*
bread	**pan** *pahn*
bread and butter	**pan y mantequilla** *pahn ee mahn-tay-KEE-yah*
tortillas (Mexico)	**tortillas** *tohr-TEE-yahs*
Waiter, we need ____.	**Camerero, necesitamos ____.** *kah-mah-REH-roh, neh-seh-see-TAH-mohs*
a knife	**un cuchillo** *oon koo-CHEE-yoh*
a fork	**un tenedor** *oon ten-eh-DOHR*
a spoon	**una cuchara** *oo-nah koo-CHAHR-ah*
a teaspoon	**una cucharita** *oo-nah koo-chahr-EE-tah*
a soup spoon	**una cuchara de sopa** *oo-nah koo-CHAH-rah day SOH-pah*
a glass	**un vaso** *oon BAH-soh*
a cup	**una taza** *oo-nah TAH-sah*
a saucer	**un platillo** *oon plah-TEE-yoh*
a plate	**un plato** *oon PLAH-toh*
a napkin	**una servilleta** *oo-nah sehr-bee-YEH-tah*
a toothpick	**un palillo** *oon pahl-EE-yoh*

APPETIZERS (STARTERS)

alcachofas	artichokes
almejas	clams
anguilas ahumadas	smoked eels

calamares	squid
caracoles	snails
champiñones	mushrooms
chorizo	spicy sausage, usually pork
cigales	crayfish
gambas (Spain only)	shrimp
huevos	eggs
jamón serrano (Spain only)	cured ham
melón	melon
moluscos	mussels
ostras (ostiones)	oysters
quisquillas (Spain only)	small shrimp
sardinas	sardines

And in Latin America, there would be some of the following.

camarones	shrimp
guacamole	puréed avocado spread
tostadas	tortilla chips with various pepper and cheese toppings

SOUPS

gazpacho	a highly variable purée of fresh, uncooked vegetables, including cucumbers, peppers, onions, and tomatoes; served cold
potaje madrileño	a thick soup of puréed chick peas, cod, and spinach
sopa de ajo	garlic soup
sopa de cebolla	onion soup
sopa de fideos	noodle soup
sopa de mariscos	seafood soup
sopa de gambas	shrimp soup
sopa de albóndigas	soup with meatballs
sopa de pescado	fish soup
sopa de verduras	soup made from puréed greens and vegetables

In Latin America, particularly Mexico, you are also likely to find:

cazuela	a spicy soup-stew, simmered for a long time in an earthenware pot; can be fish, vegetables, or meat
pozole	a hearty pork and hominy stew
sopa de aguacate	creamed avocado soup
sopa de huitlacoche	black corn soup made from the fungus that grows on corn cobs

ENTREES (MEAT AND FISH DISHES)

carne de	*KAHR-nay day*	meat of
■**buey**	*bway*	beef
■**cabrito**	*kah-BREE-toh*	goat (kid)
■**carnero**	*kahr-NEHR-oh*	mutton
■**cerdo**	*SEHR-doh*	pork
■**cordero**	*kohr-DEHR-oh*	lamb
■**ternera**	*tehr-NEHR-ah*	veal
■**vaca, res**	*BAH-kah, rehs*	beef
albóndigas	*ahl-BOHN-dee-gahs*	meatballs
bistec	*bees-TEHK*	beef steak
carne picada	*kahr-nay pee-KAH-dah*	ground (minced) meat
chuletas	*choo-LEH-tahs*	chops
churrasco	*choo-RAHS-koh*	charcoal-grilled steak
cocido	*koh-SEE-doh*	stew
costilla	*kohs-TEE-yah*	cutlet

corazón	*koh-rah-SOHN*	heart
criadillas	*kree-ah-DEE-yahs*	sweetbreads
filete	*fee-LEH-tay*	filet
hígado	*EE-gah-doh*	liver
jamón	*ha-MOHN*	ham
lechón	*leh-CHOHN*	suckling pig
lengua	*LEN-gwah*	tongue
morcilla	*mohr-SEE-yah*	blood sausage
rabo de buey	*RAH-boh day BWAY*	oxtails
riñones	*reen-YOH-nays*	kidneys
salchichas	*sahl-CHEE-chahs*	sausages
sesos	*SAY-sohs*	brains
solomillo	*soh-loh-MEE-yoh*	pork tenderloin steak
tocino	*toh-SEE-noh*	bacon
tripas	*TREE-pahs*	tripe
almejas	*ahl-MAY-has*	clams
anchoas	*ahn-CHOH-ahs*	anchovies
anguilas	*ahn-GHEE-lahs*	eels
arenque, ahumado	*ah-REHN-kay, ah-oo-MAH-doh*	herring, smoked
atún	*ah-TOON*	tuna
bacalao	*bah-kah-LAH-oh*	codfish
besugo	*beh-SOO-goh*	sea bream
boquerones	*boh-keh-ROH-nehs*	whitebait
caballa	*kah-BAH-yah*	mackerel

calamares	*kahl-ah-MAHR-ayss*	squid
camarones	*kah-mah-ROH-nayss*	shrimp
cangrejos	*kahn-GRAY-hohs*	crabs
caracoles	*kahr-ah-KOH-layss*	snails
cigalas	*see-GAH-lahs*	large crayfish
congrio	*KOHN-gree-oh*	conger eel
gambas	*GAHM-bahs*	large shrimp
lampresas	*lahm-PRAY-sahs*	lamprey
langosta	*lahn-GOH-stah*	spiny lobster
langostino	*lahn-gohs-TEE-noh*	small crayfish
lenguado	*len-GWAH-doh*	flounder, sole
mejillones	*meh-hee-YOH-nayss*	mussels
mújol	*MOO-hohl*	mullet
merluza	*mehr-LOOS-ah*	bass, hake
pescadilla	*pehs-kah-DEE-yah*	whiting
pulpo	*POOL-poh*	octopus
quesquillas	*kehs-KEE-yahs*	shrimp
rape	*RAH-pay*	monkfish, angler-fish
salmón	*sahl-MOHN*	salmon
sardinas	*sahr-DEE-nahs*	sardines
trucha	*TROO-chah*	trout
capón	*kah-POHN*	capon
codorniz	*koh-dohr-NEES*	quail
conejo	*kohn-AY-hoh*	rabbit

faisán	*fah-ee-SAHN*	pheasant
ganso	*GAHN-soh*	goose
pato	*PAH-toh*	duck
pavo	*PAH-boh*	turkey
perdiz	*pehr-DEES*	partridge
pichón	*pee-CHOHN*	squab
pollo	*POH-yoh*	chicken
venado	*beh-NAH-doh*	venison
Is the meat ____?	**¿Es carne ____?**	*ehs KAHR-nay*
■ baked	**al horno**	*ahl-OHR-noh*
■ boiled	**guisada**	*ghee-SAH-dah*
■ braised (stewed)	**estofada**	*ehs-toh-FAH-dah*
■ broiled	**a la parrilla**	*ah lah pahr-EE-yah*
■ roasted	**asada**	*ah-SAH-dah*
■ poached	**escalfada**	*ehs-KAHL-fah-dah*
I like the meat ____.	**Me gustaría la carne ____.**	*may goos-tah-REE-ah lah KAHR-nay*
■ well done	**bien hecha**	*bee-EHN EH-chah*
■ medium	**término medio**	*TEHR-mee-noh MED-yoh*
■ rare	**poco hecha**	*POH-koh EH-chah*
■ tender	**tierna**	*tee-EHR-nah*

RICE DISHES

a la campesina	with ham, chicken, sausage, and small game birds

a la catalana	with sausages, pork, squid, chilies, and peas, or with chicken, snails, beans, and artichokes
alicantina	with rabbit, mussels, and shrimp
bruta	with pork, chicken, and whitefish
de mariscos	with crayfish, anglerfish, and other seafood
valenciana	with chicken, seafood, peas, and to-matoes—the most well-known version

TORTILLA-BASED DISHES

chalupas	tortillas that have been curled at the edges and filled with a ground pork filling, sauced with a green chili sauce
chilaquiles	layers of tortillas, alternated with beans, meat, chicken, and cheese, then baked
enchiladas	tortillas that have been fried, then rolled up and baked in a sauce
flautas	sort of a tortilla sandwich that is then rolled and deep-fried
quesadillas	tortillas that are stuffed with cheese and deep-fried
tacos	a tortilla with any of several fillings, usually eaten as a snack

VEGETABLES

alcachofas	*ahl-kah-CHOH-fahs*	artichokes
apio	*AH-pee-oh*	celery
berenjena	*behr-ehn-HAY-nah*	eggplant (aubergine)
calabacín	*kah-lah-bah-SEEN*	zucchini
cebollas	*seh-BOH-yahs*	onions

col	*kohl*	cabbage
coliflor	*kohl-ee-FLOHR*	cauliflower
espinacas	*eh-spee-NAH-kahs*	spinach
espárragos	*ehs-PAHR-ah-gohs*	asparagus
champiñones	*chahm-peen-YOH-nays*	mushrooms
garbanzos	*gahr-BAHN-sohs*	chickpeas
guisantes	*ghee-SAHN-tays*	peas
judías	*hoo-DEE-ahs*	green beans
papas, patatas	*PAH-pahs, pah-TAH-tahs*	potatoes
■ **papas fritas**	*PAH-pahs FREE-tahs*	french fries
pimiento	*pee-MYEHN-toh*	pepper
puerros	*PWEHR-ohs*	leeks
maíz	*mah-EES*	corn
tomate	*toh-MAH-tay*	tomato
zanahorias	*sah-nah-OHR-ee-ahs*	carrots

In parts of Latin America you are likely also to see the following on a menu.

chile	*CHEE-lay*	chili peppers, of any variety
frijoles	*free-HOH-lays*	beans, usually kidney or pinto
huitlacoche	*WEET-lah-koh-chay*	corn fungus
nopalito	*noh-pah-LEE-toh*	prickly pear cactus
yuca	*YOO-kah*	root vegetable, from yucca plant

SEASONINGS AND CONDIMENTS

In Latin America, foods tend to be more heavily spiced, especially in Mexico. Here are some terms you might encounter on menus, describing the dish in terms of its major flavoring.

achiote	*ah-chee-OH-tay*	annatto
albahaca	*ahl-bah-AH-kay*	basil
azafrán	*ah-sah-FRAHN*	saffron
cilantro	*see-LAHN-troh*	coriander
orégano	*oh-REH-ga-noh*	oregano
romero	*roh-MEHR-oh*	rosemary

Descriptions of the different types of chilies could fill an entire book. Here we will mention a few of the major ones likely to be seen on menus.

ancho	mild to hot, with mild most common
chipotle	medium hot to hot, with a smokey flavor
jalapeño	hot, with a meaty flavor
pasilla	mild to medium hot, with a rich sweet flavor
pequín	hot
pimiento	sweet bell pepper
poblano	mild to hot, with a rich flavor
serrano	hot to very hot, with a bright flavor

And in sauces, you'll find:

salsa cruda	an uncooked tomato sauce, often served as a dip or table seasoning
salsa de tomatillo	delicate sauce made from Mexican green tomatoes (a husk tomato unlike the regular red tomato)
salsa de perejil	parsley sauce
ají de queso	cheese sauce

adobo	sauce made with ancho and pasilla chilies, sesame seeds, nuts, and spices
mole	a sauce of varying ingredients, made from chilies, sesame seeds, cocoa, and spices
pipián	sauce made from pumpkin seeds, chilies, coriander, and bread crumbs
verde	sauce of green chilies and green tomatoes

DESSERTS—SWEETS

arroz con leche	*ah-ROHS kohn LEH-chay*	rice pudding
crema catalana or flan	*krem-ah kah-tah-LAN-nah or flahn*	caramel custard
galletas	*gah-YEH-tahs*	cookies (biscuits)
helado	*ay-LAH-doh*	ice cream
■ **de chocolate**	*day cho-koh-LAH-tay*	chocolate
■ **de pistacho**	*day pees-TAH-choh*	pistachio
■ **de vainilla**	*day bah-ee-NEE-yah*	vanilla
■ **de nueces**	*day NWEH-says*	walnut
■ **de fresa**	*day FRAY-sah*	strawberry
mazapán	*mah-sah-PAHN*	marzipan
merengue	*meh-REHN-gay*	meringue
natilla	*nah-TEE-yah*	cream pudding
pastel	*pahs-TEHL*	pastry
tarta	*TAHR-tah*	tart, usually fruit

FRUITS AND NUTS

What kind of fruit do you have?	**¿Qué frutas tiene?**	*kay FROO-tahs tee-YEHN-ay*
albaricoque	*ahl-bahr-ee-KOH-kay*	apricot
cereza	*sehr-AY-sah*	cherry
ciruela	*seer-WEH-lah*	plum
coco	*KOH-koh*	coconut
dátil	*DAH-teel*	date
frambuesa	*frahm-BWEH-sah*	raspberry
fresa	*FRAY-sah*	strawberry
higo	*EE-goh*	fig
lima	*LEE-mah*	lime
limón	*lee-MOHN*	lemon
mandarina	*mahn-dahr-EE-nah*	tangerine
manzana	*mahn-SAH-nah*	apple
melocotón	*mel-oh-koh-TOHN*	peach
melón	*meh-LOHN*	melon
naranja	*nah-RAHN-hah*	orange
pera	*PEH-rah*	pear
piña	*PEEN-yah*	pineapple
pomelo	*poh-MEH-loh*	grapefruit
sandía	*sahn-DEE-ah*	watermelon
uva	*OO-bah*	grape

In Latin American countries you'll find many more exotic fruits, including:

banana, plátano	*bah-NAH-nah, PLAH-ta-noh*	banana, plantain (green banana)

guayaba	*gwah-ee-AH-bah*	guava
mango	*MAHN-goh*	mango
jicama	*hee-KAH-mah*	jicama
tuna	*TOO-nah*	prickly pear

For some common varieties of nuts:

almendras	*ahl-MEN-drahs*	almonds
castañas	*kahs-TAHN-yahs*	chestnuts
avellanas	*ah-bay-YAHN-ahs*	hazelnuts (filberts)
nueces	*NWEH-sayss*	walnuts

SPECIAL CIRCUMSTANCES

I don't want anything fried (salted).	**No quiero nada frito (salado).** *noh kee-YEHR-oh nah-dah FREE-toh (sah-LAH-doh)*	
Do you have anything that is not spicy?	**¿Tiene algo que no sea picante?** *tee-YEHN-ay AHL-goh kay noh SAY-ah pee-KAHN-tay*	
I cannot eat anything made with _____.	**No puedo comer nada hecho con _____.** *No PWEH-doh koh-MEHR NAH-dah AY-choh kohn*	
Do you have any dishes without meat?	**¿Tiene platos sin carne?** *tee-YEHN-ay PLAH-tohs seen KAHR-nay*	

BEVERAGES

Waiter, please bring me _____.	**Camarero, tráiganos por favor _____.**	*kah-mah-REHR-oh, TRAH-ee-gah-nohs pohr fah-BOHR*
coffee	**café**	*kah-FAY*
■ black coffee	**café solo**	*kah-FAY SOH-loh*

■ with cream	**café con crema**	*kah-FAY kohn KRAY-mah*
■ with milk (regular or American)	**un cortado**	*oon kohr-TAH-doh*
■ espresso	**un exprés (un expreso)**	*oon ehs-PRESS (oon ehs-PRESS-oh)*
■ half coffee/half milk (drunk in morning)	**café con leche**	*kah-FAY kohn LEH-chay*
■ iced coffee	**café helado**	*kah-FAY eh-LAH-doh*
tea	**té**	*tay*
■ with milk	**con leche**	*kohn LEH-chay*
■ with lemon	**con limón**	*kohn lee-MOHN*
■ with sugar	**con azúcar**	*kohn ah-SOO-kahr*
■ iced tea	**té helado**	*tay eh-LAH-doh*
chocolate (hot)	**chocolate**	*choh-koh-LAH-tay*
water	**agua**	*AH-gwah*
■ cold	**agua fría**	*AH-gwah FREE-ah*
■ ice	**agua helada**	*AH-gwah ay-LAH-dah*
■ mineral, with gas (without gas)	**agua mineral, con gas (sin gas)**	*AH-gwah mee-nehr-AHL, kohn gahs (seen gahs)*
cider	**una sidra**	*oo-nah SEE-drah*
juice	**un jugo**	*oon HOO-goh*
lemonade	**una limonada**	*oo-nah lee-moh-NAH-dah*

milk	**la leche**	*lah LEH-chay*
■ malted milk	**una leche malteada**	*oo-nah LEH-chay mahl-tay-AH-dah*
■ milk shake	**un batido de leche**	*oon bah-TEE-doh day LEH-chay*
orangeade	**una naranjada**	*oo-nah nahr-ahn-HAH-dah*
punch	**un ponche**	*oon POHN-chay*
soda	**una gaseosa**	*oo-nah gah-say-OH-sah*
tonic water	**un tónico**	*oon TOH-nee-koh*

The check, please.	**La cuenta, por favor.** *lah KWEHN-tah pohr fah-BOHR*
Separate checks.	**Cuentas separadas.** *KWEHN-tahs sep-ahr-AH-dahs*
Is the service (tip) included?	**¿Está incluída la propina?** *ehs-TAH een-kloo-EE-dah lah proh-PEE-nah*
I haven't ordered this.	**No he pedido ésto.** *noh ay ped-EE-doh EHS-toh*
I don't think the bill is right.	**Me parece que hay un error en la cuenta.** *may pah-RAY-say kay AH-ee oon ehr-OHR ehn lah KWEHN-tah*
This is for you.	**Esto es para usted.** *EHS-toh ehs pah-rah oos-TEHD*
We're in a hurry.	**Tenemos prisa.** *ten-EH-mohs PREE-sah*

DRINKS AND SNACKS

TAPAS (BAR SNACKS)

aceitunas	olives

alcachofas a la vi-nagreta	artichokes with vinaigrette dressing
almejas en salsa de ajo	clams in a garlic sauce
angulas	fried baby eels
calamares a la ro-mana	batter-fried squid strips
caracoles en salsa	snails in a tomato sauce
chorizo al diablo	sausage, especially spicy
entremesas varia-dos	platter of assorted snacks
gambas a la plancha	grilled shrimp
huevos rellenos	stuffed hard-cooked eggs
palitos de queso	cheese straws
pan con jamón	toast slices with ham
pinchitos	kebabs
salchichón	salami

WINES

I would like ____.	**Quisiera ____.** *kee-SYEHR-ah*
▪ a glass of wine	**una vaso de vino** *oon BAH-soh day BEE-noh*
▪ a bottle of wine	**una botella de vino** *oo-nah boh-TEH-yah day BEE-noh*
Is it ____?	**¿Es ____?** *ehs*
▪ red	**tinto** *TEEN-toh*
▪ white	**blanco** *BLAHN-koh*
▪ rosé	**rosado** *roh-SAH-doh*
light	**ligero** *lee-GEH-roh*
sparkling	**espumoso** *ehs-poo-MOH-soh*

| dry | **seco** *SAY-koh* |
| sweet | **dulce** *DOOL-say* |

LATIN AMERICAN DRINKS

cuba libre	rum, lime juice, and Coca Cola
margarita	tequila, lime juice, and salt
piña colada	coconut cream, pineapple juice, and rum
ponche	fruit juice and rum or tequila
pulque	the fermented juice of the agave (maguey) plant, often with flavorings added such as herbs, pineapple, celery; available in special pulque bars
tequila sunrise	orange juice, grenadine, tequila

FOOD SPECIALTIES OF SPAIN

There are no hard-and-fast rules for Spanish cooking. Seasonings and ingredients will vary from region to region, depending on what's available and what the background is of the people. In Basque country, the helpings are large and the food is heavy with seafood: fried cod, fried eels, squid, and sea bream. Along the Cantabrian coast are excellent cheeses and exquisite sardines. **Sopa montañesa** (a regional soup) is famous, as are **caracoles a la santona** (snails) and **tortilla a la montañesa,** the regional omelet. In Asturias, have a good plate of **fabada,** the beans and blood sausage stew. Tripe is also good. In Galicia, the **pote gallego** (hot pot) is tasty, as is **merluza a la gallega** (hake). Santiago clams, spider crabs, and rock barnacle (**centollos** and **percebes**), are succulent.

Along the eastern coast, in Catalonia, you'll sample **escudella i carn d'olla,** a vegetable and meat stew, or **butifarra con judías,** pork sausage with beans. **Habas estofadas** is stewed broad beans. Toward Valencia is the land of **paella,** the famous saffron-tinted rice which is mixed with a variety of seafood and meats. If you travel to the Balearic Islands, sample **sopas mallorqinas** (soups), sausages, sardine omelet, or Ibiza-style lobster.

Castilian cuisine is famous for a chickpea and blood sausage stew (**cocido a la madrileña**). In Segovia and Sepúlveda you should eat the lamb and suckling pig. **Chorizo** and smoked ham (**jamón serrano**) are world famous. In Toledo, enjoy the **huevos a caballo,** stewed partridge, and marzipan.

Andalusian food is famous for **gazpacho,** a cold spicy soup of raw tomatoes, peppers, cucumber, and other ingredients depending on the cook. Also here try the mixed fried fishes.

Some other specialties include the following:

bacalao a la vizcaína	salt cod stewed with olive oil, peppers, tomatoes and onions
calamares en su tinta	baby squid cooked in its own ink
callos a la andaluza	tripe stew, with sausages, vegetables and seasonings
camarones en salsa verde	shrimps in a green sauce
capón relleno a la catalana	roasted capon stuffed with meat and nuts
carnero verde	stewed lamb with herbs and pignolis
cocido madrileño	mixed meat stew with chickpeas and vegetables
criadillas fritas	fried testicles
empanadas	deep-fried pies filled with meat and vegetables
fabada asturiana	spicy mixture of white beans, pork, and sausages
gallina en pepitoría	chicken dish with nuts, rice, garlic, and herbs
langosta a la barcelonesa	spiny lobster sauteed with chicken and tomatoes, garnished with almonds
lenguado a la andaluza	stuffed flounder or sole with a vegetable sauce
liebre estofada	hare and green beans, cooked in a tart liquid
marmitako	Basque tuna stew

pescado a la sal	a white fish, packed in salt and roasted
pisto manchego	vegetable stew of tomatoes, peppers, onions, eggplant, and zucchini
sesos en caldereta	calves brains, simmered in wine
zarzuela	fish stew; varies greatly depending on region but usually similar to a bouillabaisse

SOME MEXICAN SPECIALTIES

In the vicinity of Mexico City, the food is fairly sophisticated, with a variety of ingredients appearing in dishes made with chicken, seafood, and various types of meat. Perhaps most famous is the **mole poblano,** in which turkey is served with a dark brown sauce that contains a variety of spices, ground poblano chilies, and a hint of chocolate.

Along the Mexican coast around Acapulco, as well as along the Gulf Coast, the dishes are mostly made with fresh ingredients, including seafood and fruit. In the Yucatán, the dishes reflect very strongly the ancient Mayan culture, with **pollo pibil,** a chicken dish that is colored with annato, rolled in banana leaves, and steamed in a pit.

Wherever you are, ask for the local specialties. You are apt to sample one of the following.

amarillito	chicken or pork stew with green tomatoes, pumpkin, and chilies
carne asada	marinated pieces of beef that have been grilled
ceviche acapulqueño	raw fish or shellfish marinated in lime juice
chile relleno	stuffed chile (usually with cheese), that is coated with a light batter and fried
cochinita pibil	a suckling pig stuffed with fruits, chilies, and spices, then wrapped and baked in a pit

coloradito	chicken stew made with ancho chilies, tomatoes, and red peppers
frijoles refritos	kidney or pinto beans that have been cooked then mashed and re-heated, often with chilies
guajolote relleno	turkey stuffed with fruit, nuts, and chilies and braised in wine
gorditas	bits of meat and cheese, fried and served with guacamole
guacamole	a purée of avocado, onion, garlic, and chilies, used as a condiment and a sauce for a variety of dishes
huachinango a la veracruzana	red snapper marinated in lime juice and baked with tomatoes, olives, capers, and chilies
jaibas en chilpachole	crabs cooked in a tomato sauce, flavored with the Mexican spice epazote
mancha manteles	a stew of chicken or pork, with a mixture of vegetables and in a sauce of nuts, green tomatoes, and chilies
muk-bil pollo	chicken pie with a cornmeal topping
papazul	rolled tortillas in a pumpkin sauce
panuchos	chicken dish baked with black beans and eggs
puchero	a stew made from a variety of meats, vegetables, fruits; served as a soup, then a main course
sopa de lima	a chicken soup laced with lime

SOUTH AND CENTRAL AMERICAN FOODS

Peru and Ecuador, and parts of Bolivia and Chile, have a heritage of Incan culture and so the food is a combination of Indian and Spanish. Here are some specialties of this region.

anticuchos	skewered chunks of marinated beef heart, served with a hot sauce
caldillo de congrio	conger eel in a stew
humitas	cornmeal bits flavored with onion, peppers, and spices
llapingachos	potato-cheese croquettes
papas a la huan-caína	potatoes in a spicy cheese sauce

Argentina, Uruguay, and Paraguay are countries that favor beef, so some of their notable dishes include **carbonada,** a stew of meat with vegetables served in a pumpkin shell. **Carne con cuero** is roasted beef (done in the skin), and **matambre** is a large steak stuffed with spinach, eggs, and carrots, then braised. The **parillada** is a type of English mixed grill, but just about every part of the animal is served. **Yerbe mate** is a tea drunk in this region made by steeping leaves from a holly bush.

Colombia and Venezuela are noted for their **arepas,** which are cornmeal buns filled with meat, chicken or cheese. **Buñuelos** are balls of fried cornmeal, dusted with powdered sugar. **Empanadas** are also popular here, and these pies are usually stuffed with meat, onions, and dried fruits. **Hallacas** is a seasoned mixture of meat stuffed into cornmeal dough and wrapped in banana leaves—sort of a tamale. For fish, the Colombians have **vindo de pescado,** a fish stew that is cooked on an outdoor grill.

Bolivia is well known for its roast suckling pig, as well as **picante de pollo,** a fried chicken that is rather spicy. **Lomo montado** is a steak topped with a fried egg.

The Central American countries reflect the tastes and dishes of the Spanish, but incorporate many tropical fruits in their food. Look for **gallo en sidra** (chicken in cider), tripe and vegetable stews, and a whole range of meat stews-soups.

FOODS OF THE CARIBBEAN

| asopao | a chicken and rice soup-stew with ham, peas, and peppers |

chicharrones	deep-fried pork cracklings
frituras de baca-lao (bacalaítos)	fish cakes that are fried in hot oil
mondongo	thick stew of beef tripe, potatoes, tomatoes, pumpkin, chickpeas and other tropical vegetables
moros y cristianos	black beans and rice
pasteles	a mixture of plaintain and seasonings, steamed in a banana leaf
picadillo	mixture of chopped meat with peppers, olives, raisins, and tomatoes
plátanos fritos	sliced, fried green bananas (plantains)
relleno de papa	potato dough stuffed with a mixture of meat, olives, and tomatoes
ropa vieja	literally "old clothes," this is shredded beef cooked with tomatoes and peppers
sancocho	a vegetable stew with potatoes, tomatoes, and tropical vegetables
yuca con mojo	stewed yucca root (cassava), in a garlic sauce

MEETING PEOPLE

SMALL TALK

My name is ____.	**Me llamo ____.**	*may YAH-mo*
Do you live here?	**¿Vive usted aquí?**	*BEE-bay oos-TEHD ah-KEE*
Where are you from?	**¿De dónde es usted?**	*day DOHN-day ehs oos-TEHD*

I am ____.	**Soy ____.** *soy*
■ from the United States	**de Estados Unidos** *day ehs-TAH-dohs oo-NEE-dohs*
■ from Canada	**del Canadá** *del cah-nah-DAH*
■ from England	**de Inglaterra** *day een-glah-TEHR-ah*
■ from Australia	**de Australia** *day ow-STRAHL-yah*
I like Spain (South America) very much.	**Me gusta mucho España (Sud América).** *may GOOS-tah MOO-choh ehs-PAHN-yah (sood ah-MEHR-ee-kah)*
I would like to go there.	**Me gustaría ir allá.** *may goos-tahr-EE-ah eer ah-YAH*
How long will you be staying?	**¿Cuánto tiempo va a quedarse?** *KWAHN-toh tee-EHM-poh bah ah kay-DAHR-say*
I'll stay for a few days (a week).	**Me quedaré unos días (una semana).** *may kay-dahr-AY oo-nohs DEE-ahs (oo-nah sehm-AHN-ah)*
What hotel are you at?	**¿En qué hotel está?** *ehn kay oh-TEL ehs-TAH*
What do you think of ____?	**¿Qué le parece ____?** *kay lay pah-REH-say*
I (don't) like it very much.	**(No) me gusta mucho.** *(noh) may GOOS-tah MOO-choh*
I think it's ____.	**Creo que es ____.** *KREH-oh kay ehs*
■ (very) beautiful	**(muy) bonito(a)** *(mwee) bohn-EE-toh(ah)*
■ interesting	**interesante** *een-tehr-ehs-AHN-tay*
■ magnificent	**magnífico(a)** *mahg-NEEF-ee-koh(kah)*
■ wonderful	**maravilloso(a)** *mahr-ah-bee-YOH-soh(sah)*

INTRODUCTIONS

May I introduce my ____?	**Le presento a mi ____?** *lay pray-SENT-oh ah mee*
▪ brother (sister)	**hermano(a)** *ehr-MAH-noh(nah)*
▪ father (mother)	**padre (papá) [madre (mamá)]** *PAH-dray (pah-PAH) MAH-dray (mah-MAH)*
▪ friend	**amigo(a)** *ah-MEE-goh(gah)*
▪ husband (wife)	**marido (esposa)** *mahr-EE-doh (ehs-POH-sah)*
▪ sweetheart	**novio(a)** *NOH-bee-oh(ah)*
▪ son (daughter)	**hijo(a)** *EE-hoh(hah)*
How do you do (Glad to meet you).	**Mucho gusto (en conocerle).** *MOO-choh GOOS-toh (ehn koh-noh-SEHR-lay)*
How do you do (The pleasure is mine).	**El gusto es mío.** *ehl GOOS-toh ehs MEE-oh*
I am a ____.	**Soy ____.** *soy*
▪ teacher	**maestro(a)** *mah-EHS-troh(trah)*
▪ doctor	**médico** *MED-ee-koh*
▪ lawyer	**abogado** *ah-boh-GAH-doh*
▪ businessperson	**persona de negocios** *pehr-SOHN-ah day neh-GOH-see-ohs*
▪ student	**estudiante** *ehs-too-DYAHN-tay*
Would you like a picture (snapshot)?	**¿Quiere una foto?** *kee-YEHR-ay oo-nah FOH-toh*
Stand here (there).	**Párese aquí (____).** *PAH-ray-say ah-KEE*
Don't move.	**No se mueva.** *noh say MWEH-bah*
Smile. That's it.	**Sonría. ¡Así es!** *sohn-REE-ah ah-SEE-ehs*

Will you take a picture of me (us)?	**¿(Nos)Me quiere sacar una foto?** *(nos)may kee-YEHR-ay sah-KAHR oo-nah FOH-toh*

DATING AND SOCIALIZING

May I have this dance?	**¿Quiere usted bailar?** *kee-YEHR-ay oos-TEHD bah-ee-LAHR*
Yes, of course.	**Sí, con mucho gusto.** *see kohn MOO-choh GOOS-toh*
Would you like a cigarette (drink)?	**¿Quiere fumar (tomar algo)?** *kee-YEHR-ay foo-MAHR (toh-MAHR AHL-goh)*
Do you have a light (a match)?	**¿Tiene fuego (un fósforo)?** *tee-YEH-nay FWAY-goh (oon FOHS-fohr-oh)*
Do you mind if I smoke?	**¿Le molesta que fume?** *lay moh-LEHS-tah kay FOO-may*
May I take you home?	**¿Me permite llevarle a casa?** *may pehr-MEE-tay yeh-BAHR-lay ah KAH-sah*
May I call you?	**¿Puedo llamarle?** *PWEH-doh yah-MAHR-lay*
Are you doing anything tomorrow?	**¿Está libre mañana?** *eh-STAH LEE-bray mahn-YAH-nah*
Are you free this evening?	**¿Está usted libre esta tarde?** *eh-STAH oos-TEHD LEE-bray ehs-tah TAHR-day*
Would you like to go ____ together?	**¿Quiere acompañarme a ____?** *kee-YEHR-ay ah-kohm-pahn-YAHR-may ah*
I'll wait for you in front of the hotel.	**Le espero delante del hotel.** *lay ehs-PEHR-oh del-AHN-tay del oh-TEL*

SAYING GOODBYE • 453

I'll pick you up at your house (hotel). **Le recogeré en su casa (hotel).** *lay ray-koh-hehr-AY ehn soo KAH-sah (oh-TEL)*

What is your telephone number? **¿Cuál es su número de teléfono?** *kwahl ehs soo NOO-mehr-oh day tel-EH-foh-noh*

Here's my telephone number (address). **Aquí tiene mi número de teléfono (mi dirección).** *ah-KEE tee-EH-nay mee NOO-mehr-oh day tel-EH-foh-noh (mee dee-rehk-SYOHN)*

Will you write to me? **¿Me escribirá?** *may ehs-kree-beer-AH*

I'm single (married). **Soy soltero, a (casado, a).** *soy sohl-TEHR-oh, ah (koh-SAH-doh, ah)*

Is your husband (wife) here? **¿Está aquí su esposo (esposa)?** *eh-STAH ah-KEE soo ehs-POH-soh (sah)*

I'm here with my family. **Estoy aquí con mi familia.** *ehs-TOY ah-KEE kohn mee fah-MEEL-yah*

Do you have any children? **¿Tiene usted hijos?** *tee-EH-nay oos-TEHD EE-hohs*

How many? **¿Cuántos?** *KWAHN-tohs*

SAYING GOOD-BYE

Nice to have met you. **Ha sido un verdadero gusto.** *ah SEED-oh oon behr-dah-DEHR-oh GOOS-toh*

The pleasure was mine. **El gusto ha sido mío.** *ehl GOOS-toh ah SEE-doh MEE-oh*

Regards to ____. **Saludos a ____ de mi parte.** *sah-LOO-dohs ah ____ day mee PAHR-tay*

Thanks for a wonderful evening.	**Gracias por su invitación. Ha sido una noche extraordinaria.** *GRAH-see-ahs pohr soo een-bee-tah-SYOHN. Ah see-doh oo-nah NOH-chay ehs-trah-ohr-dee-NAHR-ee-ah*
I must go home now.	**Tengo que marcharme ahora.** *TEN-goh kay mahr-CHAR-may ah-OH-rah*
You must come to visit us.	**Debe venir a visitarnos.** *DEH-bay ben-EER ah bee-see-TAHR-nohs*

SHOPPING

GOING SHOPPING

Where can I find _____?	**¿Dónde se puede encontrar _____?** *DOHN-day say pweh-day ehn-kohn-TRAHR*
▪ a bakery	**una panadería** *OO-nah pah-nah-dehr-EE-ah*
▪ a book store	**una librería** *OO-nah leeb-rehr-EE-ah*
▪ a butcher shop	**una carnicería** *OO-nah kahr-nee-sehr-EE-ah*
▪ a camera shop	**una tienda de fotografía** *OO-nah tee-EHN-dah day foh-toh-grah-FEE-ah*
▪ a candy store	**una confitería** *OO-nah kohn-fee-tehr-EE-ah*
▪ a clothing store	**una tienda de ropa** *OO-nah tee-YEHN-dah day ROH-pah*
▪ a delicatessen	**una tienda de ultramarinos** *OO-nah tee-YEHN-dah day ool-trah-mah-REE-nohs*

a department store	**un almacén** *oon ahl-mah-SEHN*
a pharmacy (chemist)	**una farmacia** *OO-nah fahr-MAH-see-ah*
a florist	**una florería** *OO-nah flohr-ehr-EE-ah*
a gift (souvenir) shop	**una tienda de regalos (recuerdos)** *OO-nah tee-YEHN-dah day ray-GAHL-ohs (ray-kwehr-dohs)*
a grocery store	**una tienda de comestibles** *OO-nah tee-YEHN-dah day koh-mehs-TEE-blays*
a hardware store (ironmonger)	**una ferretería** *OO-nah feh-reh-teh-REE-ah*
a jewelry store	**una joyería** *OO-nah hoy-ehr-EE-ah*
a liquor store	**una licorería** *OO-nah lee-kohr-ehr-EE-ah*
a newsstand	**un puesto de periódicos** *oon PWEHS-toh day peh-ree-OH-dee-kohs*
a record store	**una tienda de discos** *OO-nah tee-yehn-dah day DEES-kohs*
a shoe store	**una zapatería** *OO-nah sah-pah-tehr-EE-ah*
a supermarket	**un supermercado** *oon SOO-pehr-mehr-KAH-doh*
a tobacco shop	**un estanco** *oon ehs-TAHN-koh*
a toy store	**una juguetería** *OO-nah hoo-get-ehr-EE-ah*
Do you take credit cards?	**¿Acepta tarjetas de crédito?** *ah-SEP-tah tahr-HAY-tahs day KRED-ee-toh*
Can I pay with a traveler's check?	**¿Puedo pagar con un cheque de viajero?** *PWEH-doh pah-GAHR kohn oon CHEH-kay day bee-ah-HEHR-oh*

BOOKS

Is there a store that carries English-language books?	**¿Hay una tienda que lleve libros en inglés?** *AH-ee oo-nah TYEHN-dah kay YEH-bay LEE-brohs ehn een-GLAYS*
What is the best (biggest) bookstore here?	**¿Cuál es la mejor librería (la librería más grande) de aquí?** *kwahl ehs lah may-HOHR lee-brehr-EE-ah (lah lee-brehr-EE-ah mahs grahn-day) day ah-KEE*
I'm just looking.	**Estoy solo mirando.** *ehs-TOY SOH-loh meer-AHN-doh*
Do you have books (novels) in English?	**¿Tiene usted libros (novelas) en inglés?** *tee-EHN-eh oos-TEHD LEE-brohs (noh-BEL-ahs) ehn een-GLAYSS*
Do you have paperback copies?	**¿Tiene usted ejemplares en rústica?** *tee-EHN-ay oos-TEHD eh-hem-PLAHR-ays ehn ROOS-tee-kah*
I want a _____.	**Quiero _____.** *kee-EHR-oh*
guide book	**una guía** *oon-ah GHEE-ah*
map of this city	**un plano de esta ciudad** *oon PLAH-noh day ehs-tah see-oo-DAHD*
pocket dictionary	**un diccionario de bolsillo** *oon deek-syohn-AHR-ee-oh day bohl-SEE-yoh*
Spanish-English dictionary	**un diccionario español-inglés** *oon deek-syohn-AHR-ee-oh ehs-pahn-YOHL-een-GLAYSS*
I'll take these books.	**Me quedo con estos libros.** *may kay-doh kohn EHS-tohs LEE-brohs*
Will you wrap them, please?	**¿Quiere envolverlos, por favor?** *kee-YEHR-ay ehn-bohl-BEHR-lohs pohr fah-BOHR*

CLOTHING

Would you please show me ____?	**¿Quiere enseñarme ____, por favor?** *kee-YEHR-ay ehn-sehn-YAHR-may pohr fah-BOHR*
■a belt	**un cinturón** *oon seen-toor-OHN*
■a blouse	**una blusa** *oo-nah BLOO-sah*
■a bra	**un sostén** *oon soh-STEHN*
■a dress	**un vestido** *oon bes-tee-doh*
■an evening gown	**un traje de noche** *oon TRAH-hay day NOH-chay*
■leather (suede) gloves	**guantes de cuero (de gamuza)** *GWAHN-tays day KWEHR-oh (day gah-MOOS-ah)*
■handkerchiefs	**pañuelos** *pahn-yoo-EH-lohs*
■a hat	**un sombrero** *oon sohm-BREHR-oh*
■a jacket	**una chaqueta** *oo-nah chah-KAY-tah*
■an overcoat	**un abrigo** *oon ah-BREE-goh*
■pants	**pantalones** *pahn-tah-LOHN-ays*
■pantyhose	**pantimedias** *pahn-tee-MEHD-ee-ahs*
■a raincoat	**un impermeable** *oon eem-pehr-may-AH-blay*
■a robe	**una bata** *oo-nah BAH-tah*
■a shirt	**una camisa** *oo-nah kah-MEES-ah*
■(a pair of) shoes	**(un par de) zapatos** *(oon pahr day) sah-PAH-tohs*
■shorts (briefs)	**calzoncillos** *kahl-sohn-SEE-yohs*
Do you have something ____?	**¿Tiene algo ____?** *tee-EH-nay AHL-goh*

■ else	**más** *mahs*
■ larger	**más grande** *mahs grahn-day*
■ less expensive	**menos caro** *may-nohs KAHR-oh*
■ longer	**más largo** *mahs LAHR-goh*
■ of better quality	**de más alta calidad** *day mahs AHL-tah kahl-ee-DAHD*
■ shorter	**más corto** *mahs KOHR-toh*
■ smaller	**más pequeño** *mahs peh-KAYN-yoh*
I (don't) like the color.	**(No) me gusta este color.** *(noh) may GOOS-tah ehs-tay koh-LOHR*
Do you have it in _____?	**¿Tiene algo en _____?** *tee-EHN-ay ahl-goh ehn*
■ black	**negro** *NEH-groh*
■ blue	**azul** *ah-SOOL*
■ brown	**marrón, pardo** *mah-ROHN, PAHR-doh*
■ gray	**gris** *grees*
■ green	**verde** *BEHR-day*
■ orange	**anaranjado** *a-nah-rahn-HAH-do*
■ pink	**rosado** *roh-SAH-doh*
■ red	**rojo** *ROH-hoh*
■ white	**blanco** *BLAHN-koh*
■ yellow	**amarillo** *ah-mah-REE-yoh*
I want something in _____.	**Quiero algo en _____.** *kee-YEHR-oh AHL-goh ehn*
■ chiffon	**gasa** *GAH-sah*
■ corduroy	**pana** *PAH-nah*
■ cotton	**algodón** *ahl-goh-DOHN*

■denim	**dril de algodón, tela tejana** *dreel day ahl-goh-DOHN, TEH-la tay-HAH-nah*
■felt	**fieltro** *fee-EHL-troh*
■flannel	**franela** *frah-NEHL-ah*
■gabardine	**gabardina** *gah-bahr-DEEN-ah*
■lace	**encaje** *ehn-KAH-hay*
■leather	**cuero** *KWEHR-oh*
■linen	**hilo** *EE-loh*
■nylon	**nilón** *nee-LOHN*
■satin	**raso** *RAH-soh*
■silk	**seda** *SAY-dah*
■suede	**gamuza** *gah-MOO-sah*
■taffeta	**tafetán** *tah-fay-TAHN*
■terrycloth	**tela de toalla** *TEHL-ah-day toh-AH-yah*
■velvet	**terciopelo** *tehr-see-oh-PEHL-oh*
■wool	**lana** *LAH-nah*
■worsted	**estambre** *ehs-TAHM-bray*
■synthetic (polyester)	**sintético** *seen-TET-ee-koh*
I prefer _____.	**Prefiero** _____. *preh-FYEHR-oh*
■permanent press	**algo inarrugable** *AHL-goh een-ah-roo-GAH-blay*
■wash and wear	**algo que no necesita planchar** *AHL-goh kay noh neh-seh-SEE-tah plahn-CHAHR*
Can I try it on?	**¿Puedo probármelo?** *PWEHD-oh proh-BAHR-may-loh*

Can you alter it?	**¿Puede arreglarlo?** *PWEH-day ah-ray-GLAHR-loh*
Can I return the article?	**¿Puedo devolver el artículo?** *PWEH-doh day-bohl-BEHR ehl ahr-TEE-koo-loh*
Do you have something hand made?	**¿Tiene algo hecho a mano?** *tee-YEH-nay ahl-goh ay-choh ah mah-noh*
The zipper doesn't work.	**No funciona la cremallera.** *noh foon-SYOHN-ah lah kray-mah-YEH-rah*
It doesn't fit me.	**No me queda bien.** *noh may KAY-dah BYEHN*
It fits very well.	**Me queda muy bien.** *may KAY-dah mwee BYEHN*
I'll take it.	**Me lo llevo.** *may loh YEH-boh*
Will you wrap it?	**¿Quiere envolverlo?** *kee-YEHR-ay ehn-bohl-BEHR-loh*
I'd like to see the pair of shoes (boots) in the window.	**Quisiera ver el par de zapatos (botas) de la vitrina.** *kee-see-YEH-rah behr ehl pahr day sah-PAH-tohs (BOH-tahs) day lah bee-TREE-nah*
They're too narrow (wide).	**Son demasiado estrechos (anchos).** *sohn day-mahs-ee-AH-doh ehs-TRAY-chohs (AHN-chohs)*
I'll take them.	**Me los llevo.** *may lohs YEH-boh*
I also need shoelaces.	**También necesito cordones de zapato.** *tahm-BYEHN neh-say-SEE-toh kohr-DOHN-ays day sah-PAH-toh*
That's all I want for now.	**Eso es todo por ahora.** *eh-soh ehs TOH-doh pohr ah-OHR-ah*

FOODS AND HOUSEHOLD ITEMS

I'd like _____.   **Quisiera _____.** *kee-SYEHR-ah*

◻ a bar of soap   **una pastilla de jabón** *OO-nah pahs-TEE-yah day hah-BOHN*

◻ a bottle of juice   **una botella de jugo** *OO-nah boh-TEH-yah day HOO-goh*

◻ a box of cereal   **una caja de cereal** *OO-nah KAH-hah day sehr-ay-AHL*

◻ a can (tin) of tomato sauce   **una lata de salsa de tomate** *OO-nah LAH-tah day SAHL-sah day toh-MAH-tay*

◻ a dozen eggs   **una docena de huevos** *OO-nah doh-SAY-nah day WAY-bohs*

◻ a jar of coffee   **un pomo de café** *oon POH-moh day kah-FAY*

◻ a kilo of potatoes (2.2 lbs) **un kilo de papas (patatas)** *oon KEE-loh day PAH-pahs (pah-TAH-tahs)*

◻ a half-kilo of cherries   **medio kilo de cerezas** *MED-ee-oh KEE-loh day sehr-AY-sahs*

◻ a liter of milk   **un litro de leche** *oon LEE-troh day LEH-chay*

◻ a package of candies   **un paquete de dulces** *oon pah-KEH-tay day dool-sayss*

◻ 100 grams of cheese   **cien gramos de queso** *see-EHN GRAH-mohs day KAY-soh*

◻ a roll of toilet paper   **un rollo de papel higiénico** *oon ROH-yoh day pah-pel ee-hee-EHN-ee-koh*

What is this (that)?   **¿Qué es esto (eso)?** *kay ehs EHS-toh (EHS-oh)*

Is it fresh?	**¿Está fresco?** *ehs-TAH FRES-koh*
I'd like a kilo (about 2 pounds) of oranges.	**Quisiera un kilo de naranjas.** *kee-SYEHR-ah oon KEE-loh day nah-RAHN-hahs*
a half-kilo of butter	**medio kilo de mantequilla** *MED-ee-oh kee-loh day mahn-tay-KEE-yah*
200 grams (about $\frac{1}{2}$ pound) of cookies (cakes)	**doscientos gramos de galletas (pasteles)** *dohs-SYEHN-tohs GRAH-mohs day gah-YEH-tahs*
100 grams (about $\frac{1}{4}$ pound) of ham	**cien gramos de jamón** *SYEHN GRAH-mohs day hah-MOHN*

JEWELRY

I'd like to see _____.	**Quisiera ver _____.** *kee-SYEHR-ah-behr*
a bracelet	**un brazalete** *oon brah-sah-LAY-tay*
a brooch	**un broche** *oon BROH-chay*
a chain	**una cadena** *oo-nah kah-DAY-nah*
a charm	**un dije** *oon DEE-hay*
some earrings	**unos aretes (in Spain, pendientes)** *OO-nohs ah-REH-tays (pen-DYEHN-tays)*
a necklace	**un collar** *oon koh-YAHR*
a pin	**un alfiler** *oon ahl-fee-LEHR*
a ring	**un anillo (una sortija)** *oon ahn-EE-yoh (OO-nah sohr-TEE-hah)*
a rosary	**un rosario** *oon roh-SAHR-ee-oh*
a (wrist) watch	**un reloj (de pulsera)** *oon ray-LOH (day pool-SEHR-ah)*

Is this ____?	**¿Es esto ____?** *ehs EHS-toh*
gold	**oro** *OH-roh*
platinum	**platino** *plah-TEE-noh*
silver	**plata** *PLAH-tah*
stainless steel	**acero inoxidable** *ah-SEHR-oh een-ohks-ee-DAH-blay*
Is it solid or gold plated?	**¿Es macizo o dorado?** *ehs mah-SEE-soh oh dohr-AH-doh*
How many carats is it?	**¿De cuántos quilates es?** *day KWAHN-tohs kee-LAH-tays ehs*
What is that stone?	**¿Qué es esa piedra?** *kay ehs EHS-ah pee-YEHD-drah*
I want ____.	**Quiero ____.** *kee-YEHR-oh*
an amethyst	**una amatista** *oo-nah ah-mah-TEES-tah*
an aquamarine	**una aguamarina** *oo-nah ah-gwah-mah-REE-nah*
a diamond	**un diamante** *oon dee-ah-MAHN-tay*
an emerald	**una esmeralda** *oo-nah ehs-mehr-AHL-dah*
ivory	**marfil** *mahr-FEEL*
jade	**jade** *HAH-day*
onyx	**ónix** *OH-neeks*
pearls	**perlas** *PEHR-lahs*
a ruby	**un rubí** *oon roo-BEE*
a sapphire	**un zafiro** *oon sah-FEER-oh*
a topaz	**un topacio** *oon toh-PAH-see-oh*
turquoise	**turquesa** *toor-KAY-sah*
How much is it?	**¿Cuánto vale?** *KWAHN-toh BAH-lay*

NEWSPAPERS AND MAGAZINES

Do you carry English newspapers (magazines)?	**¿Tiene usted periódicos (revistas) en inglés?** *tee-YEHN-ay oos-TEHD peh-ree-OH-dee-kohs (ray-BEES-tahs) en een-GLAYSS*
I'd like to buy some (picture) post cards.	**Quisiera comprar postales (ilustradas).** *kee-SYEHR-ah kohm-PRAHR pohs-TAHL-ays (ee-loos-TRAH-dahs)*
Do you have stamps?	**¿Tiene sellos?** *tee-YEHN-ay SEH-yohs*
How much is that?	**¿Cuánto es?** *KWAHN-toh ehs*

PHOTOGRAPHIC SUPPLIES

Where is there a camera shop?	**¿Dónde hay una tienda de artículos fotográficos?** *DOHN-day AH-ee oo-nah tee-YEHN-dah day ahr-TEEK-oo-lohs foh-toh-GRAHF-ee-kohs*
Do you develop film here?	**¿Aquí revelan películas?** *ah-KEE ray-BEHL-ahn pel-EE-koo-lahs*
How much does it cost to develop a roll?	**¿Cuánto cuesta revelar un carrete?** *KWAHN-toh KWEHS-tah ray-behl-AHR oon kahr-reh-tay*
I want _____.	**Quiero _____.** *kee-YEHR-oh*
▇ one print of each	**una copia de cada uno** *oo-nah KOH-pee-ah day kah-dah OO-noh*
▇ an enlargement	**una ampliación** *oo-nah ahm-plee-ah-SYOHN*
with a glossy (matte) finish	**con acabado brillante (mate)** *kohn ah-kah-bah-doh bree-YAHN-tay (MAH-tay)*

I want a roll of color (black and white) film.	**Quiero un rollo de películas en colores (en blanco y negro).** *kee-YEHR-oh oon roh-yoh day pehl-EE-koo-lahs ehn koh-LOHR-ays (ehn BLAHN-koh ee NEH-groh)*
When can I pick up the pictures?	**¿Cuándo puedo recoger las fotos?** *KWAHN-doh PWEH-doh ray-koh-HEHR lahs FOH-tohs*
Do you sell cameras?	**¿Vende usted cámaras?** *ben-day oos-TEHD KAH-mah-rahs*
I want an inexpensive camera.	**Quiero una cámara barata.** *kee-YEHR-oh oo-nah KAH-mah-rah bah-RAH-tah*

RECORDS AND TAPES

Is there a record shop around here?	**¿Hay una tienda de discos por aquí?** *AH-ee oo-nah tee-yehn-dah day DEES-kohs pohr ah-kee*
Where is the _____ section?	**¿Dónde está la sección de _____?** *DOHN-day ehs-TAH lah sek-SYOHN day*
◼ classical music	**la música clásica** *lah MOO-see-kah KLAHS-ee-kah*
◼ folk music	**la musica folklórica** *lah MOO-see-kah fohl-KLOHR-ee-kah*
◼ latest hits	**los últimos éxitos** *lohs OOL-tee-mohs EHK-see-tohs*
◼ opera	**la ópera** *lah OH-pehr-ah*
◼ popular music	**la música popular** *lah MOO-see-kah poh-poo-LAHR*
◼ Spanish music	**la música española** *lah MOO-see-kah ehs-pahn-YOH-lah*
◼ Latin music	**la música latina** *lah MOO-see-kah lah-TEEN-ah*

SOUVENIRS, HANDICRAFTS

I'd like ____.	**Quisiera** ____. *kee-SYEHR-ah*
a pretty gift	**un regalo bonito** *oon ray-GAH-loh boh-NEE-toh*
a small gift	**un regalito** *oon ray-gah-LEE-toh*
a souvenir	**un recuerdo** *oon ray-KWEHR-doh*
It's for ____.	**Es para** ____. *ehs pah-rah*
I don't want to spend more than ____ dollars.	**No quiero gastar más de** ____ **dólares.** *noh kee-YEHR-oh gahs-TAHR mahs day* ____ *DOH-lahr-ays*
Could you suggest something?	**¿Podría usted sugerir algo?** *poh-DREE-ah oos-TEHD soo-hehr-EER AHL-goh*
Would you show me your selection of ____?	**¿Quiere enseñarme su surtido de** ____? *kee-YEHR-ay ehn-sen-YAHR-may soo soor-TEE-doh day*
blown glass	**vidrio soplado** *BEE-dree-oh soh-PLAH-doh*
carved objects	**objetos de madera tallada** *ohb-HET-ohs day mah-DEHR-ah tah-YAH-dah*
cut crystal	**vidrio tallado** *BEE-dree-oh tah-YAH-doh*
dolls	**muñecas** *moon-YEH-kahs*
earthenware (pottery)	**loza** *LOH-sah*
fans	**abanicos** *ah-bah-NEE-kohs*
jewelry	**joyas** *HOY-ahs*
lace	**encaje** *ehn-KAH-hay*

■ leathergoods **objetos de cuero** *ohb-HET-ohs day KWEHR-oh*

■ liqueurs **licores** *lee-KOHR-ays*

■ musical instruments **instrumentos musicales** *een-stroo-MEN-tohs moo-see-KAHL-ays*

■ perfumes **perfumes** *pehr-FOO-mays*

■ pictures **dibujos** *dee-BOO-hohs*

■ posters **carteles** *kahr-TEHL-ays*

■ religious articles **artículos religiosos** *ahr-TEE-koo-lohs ray-lee-hee-OH-sohs*

LITTLE TREASURES

Is this an antique?	**¿Es una antigüedad?** *ehs oo-nah ahn-tee-gway-DAHD*
How old is it?	**¿Cuántos años tiene?** *KWAHN-tohs anh-yohs tee-YEHN-ay*
Is it a reproduction?	**¿Es una reproducción?** *ehs oo-nah ray-proh-dook-SYOHN*
Tell me its history.	**¿Puede decirme algo de su historia?** *PWEH-day day-SEER-may AHL-go day soo ee-STOHR-ee-ah*
Is the artist well known?	**¿Es conocido el artista?** *ehs kohn-oh-SEE-doh ehl ahr-TEES-tah*
Where has he (she) exhibited?	**¿Dónde está exhibiendo?** *DOHN-day ehs-TAH eks-ee-BYEHN-doh*
What materials are used?	**¿De qué está hecho?** *day KAY ehs-TAH AY-choh*
What does this signify?	**¿Qué quiere decir esto?** *Kay KYEHR-ay day-SEER EHS-toh*
Is this hand-made?	**¿Está hecho a mano?** *eh-STAH AY-choh ah MAH-noh*

What is the name of the type of work?	**¿Cómo se llama este tipo de trabajo?** *KOH-moh say YAH-mah EHS-tay TEE-poh day trah-BAH-ho*
Is this a specialty of this region? this town?	**¿Es una especialidad de esta región? de este pueblo?** *ehs oo-nah ehs-pehs-yah-lee-DAHD day ehs-tah ray-HYOHN day ehs-tay PWEHB-loh*
What are the local specialties of _____?	**¿Cuáles son las especialidades locales de _____?** *KWAHL-ays sohn lahs ehs-pehs-yah-lee-DAHD-ays loh-KAHL-ays day*
Is this washable?	**¿Es lavable?** *ehs lah-bah-blay*
Will it shrink?	**¿Se encoge?** *say ehn-KOH-hay*
Should it be washed by hand?	**¿Debe lavarse a mano?** *DEH-bay lah-BAHR-say ah MAH-noh*
▪ in cold water	**¿en agua fría?** *ehn AH-gwah FREE-ah*
Can it go in the dryer?	**¿Se puede meter en la secadora?** *say PWEHD-ay meh-TEHR ehn lah seh-kah-DOHR-ah*
Can this go in the dishwasher?	**¿Se puede meter esto en el lavaplatos?** *say PWEH-day meh-TEHR ehs-toh ehn ehl lah-bah-PLAH-tohs*
Is it ovenproof?	**¿Está a prueba de horno?** *ehs-TAH ah PRWEH-bah day OR-noh*
Is this safe to use for cooking?	**¿Se puede usar sin peligro para cocinar?** *say PWEH-day oo-SAHR SEEN pe-LEE-groh pah-rah koh-see-NAHR*
What is the lead content?	**¿Qué contenido de plomo tiene?** *kay kohn-ten-EE-doh day PLOH-moh tee-YEHN-ay*
Did you make this yourself?	**¿Lo ha hecho usted?** *loh ah AY-choh oos-TEHD*

BARGAINING

Please, madam, how much is this?	**Por favor, señora, ¿Cuánto vale esto?** *pohr fah-BOHR sehn-YOHR-ah KWAHN-toh BAH-lay EHS-toh*
Oh, no, that is more than I can spend.	**Ay, no, eso es más de lo que puedo gastar.** *AH-ee noh EHS-oh ehs MAHS day loh kay PWEH-doh gahs-TAHR*
How about ____?	**¿Y si le doy ____?** *EE see lay doy*
No, that is too high. Would you take ____?	**No, eso es demasiado. ¿Aceptaría ____?** *noh EHS-oh ehs day-mahs-ee-AH-doh ah-sep-tahr-EE-ah*
But there seems to be a scratch (tear) here.	**Me parace que hay un arañazo (un roto) aquí.** *may pahr-ay-say kay AH-ee oon ah-rahn-YAH-soh ah-KEE*
Yes, that's fine. I'll take it.	**Así esta bien. Me lo llevo.** *ah-SEE ehs-TAH byehn may loh YEH-boh*
Thank you. Have a nice day.	**Gracias. Qué lo pase bien.** *GRAH-see-ahs kay loh PAH-say byehn*

STATIONERY ITEMS

I want to buy ____.	**Quiero comprar ____.** *kee-YEHR-oh kohm-PRAHR*
a ball-point pen	**un bolígrafo** *oon boh-lee-grah-foh*
a deck of cards	**una baraja** *oo-nah bahr-AH-hah*
envelopes	**sobres** *SOH-brays*
an eraser	**una goma de borrar** *oo-nah GOH-mah day bohr-AHR*
glue	**cola de pegar** *koh-lah day peh-GAHR*

▪ a notebook	**un cuaderno** *oon kwah-DEHR-noh*
▪ pencils	**lápices** *LAH-pee-sayss*
▪ a pencil sharpener	**un sacapuntas** *oon sah-kah-POON-tahs*
▪ a ruler	**una regla** *oo-nah REHG-lah*
▪ Scotch Tape	**cinta adhesiva** *SEEN-tah ahd-ehs-EE-bah*
▪ some string	**cuerda** *KWEHR-dah*
▪ typing paper	**papel de máquina** *pah-PEL day MAH-kee-nah*
▪ wrapping paper	**papel de envolver** *pah-PEL day ehn-bohl-BEHR*
▪ a writing pad	**un bloc de papel** *oon blohk day pah-PEL*

TOBACCO

A pack (carton) of cigarettes, please.	**Un paquete (cartón) de cigarrillos, por favor.** *oon pah-KAY-tay (kahr-TOHN) day see-gahr-EE-yohs pohr fah-BOHR*
▪ filtered	**con filtro** *kohn FEEL-troh*
▪ unfiltered	**sin filtro** *seen FEEL-troh*
▪ menthol	**de mentol** *day mehn-TOHL*
▪ king-size	**extra largos** *EHS-trah LAHR-gohs*
Are these cigarettes (very) strong (mild)?	**¿Son (muy) fuertes (suaves) estos cigarrillos?** *sohn (mwee) FWEHR-tays (SWAH-bays) ehs-tohs see-gahr-EE-yohs*

Do you have American cigarettes?	**¿Tiene usted cigarrillos norteamericanos?** *tee-YEHN-ay oos-TEHD see-gahr-EE-yohs nohr-tay-ah-mehr-ee-KAH-nohs*
What brands?	**¿De qué marcas?** *day kay MAHR-kahs*
Please give me a pack of matches also.	**Déme una caja de fósforos también.** *DAY-may oo-nah kah-hah day FOHS-for-ohs tahm-bee-EHN*
Do you sell _____?	**¿Vende usted _____?** *BEHN-day oo-STEHD*
a cigarette holder	**una boquilla** *oo-nah boh-KEE-yah*
cigars	**cigarros** *see-GAHR-rohs*
flints	**piedras de encendedor** *pee-EH-drahs day ehn-sen-day-DOHR*
lighter fluid	**líquido de encendedor** *LEE-kee-doh day ehn-sen-day-DOHR*
lighters	**encendedores** *ehn-sen-day-DOHR-ays*
pipes	**pipas** *PEE-pahs*
pipe tobacco	**tobaco de pipa** *tah-BAH-koh day PEE-pah*

TOILETRIES

Do you have _____?	**¿Tiene usted _____?** *tee-YEHN-ay oo-STEHD*
bobby pins	**horquillas** *ohr-KEE-yahs*
a brush	**un cepillo** *oon sep-EE-yoh*
cleansing cream	**crema limpiadora** *KRAY-mah leem-pee-ah-DOHR-ah*

a comb	**un peine** *oon PAY-nay*
a deodorant	**un desodorante** *oon dehs-oh-dohr-AHN-tay*
(disposable) diapers	**pañales (desechables)** *pahn-YAH-lays (dehs-ay-CHAH-blays)*
emery boards	**limas de cartón** *LEE-mahs day kahr-TOHN*
eye liner	**un lápiz de ojos** *oon LAH-pees day OH-hohs*
hair spray	**laca** *LAH-kah*
lipstick	**lápiz de labios** *LAH-pees day LAH-bee-ohs*
make-up	**maquillaje** *mah-kee-YAH-hay*
mascara	**rimel** *ree-MEHL*
a mirror	**un espejo** *oon ehs-PAY-ho*
mouthwash	**un lavado bucal** *oon lah-bah-doh boo-kahl*
nail clippers	**un cortauñas** *oon kohr-tah-OON-yahs*
a nail file	**una lima de uñas** *oo-nah lee-mah day OON-yahs*
nail polish	**esmalte de uñas** *ehs-MAHL-tay day OON-yahs*
nail polish remover	**un quita-esmalte** *oon kee-tah ehs-MAHL-tay*
a razor	**una navaja** *oo-nah nah-BAH-hah*
razor blades	**hojas de afeitar** *OH-hahs day ah-fay-TAHR*
sanitary napkins	**servilletas higiénicas** *sehr-bee-YEH-tahs ee-HYEHN-ee-kahs*

(cuticle) scissors	**tijeras (de cutículas)** *tee-HAIR-ahs (day koo-TEE-kool-ahs)*
shampoo	**champú** *chahm-POO*
shaving lotion	**loción de afeitar** *loh-SYOHN day ah-fay-TAHR*
soap	**jabón** *hah-BOHN*
a sponge	**una esponja** *oo-nah ehs-POHN-hah*
tampons	**tapones** *tah-POHN-ays*
tissues	**pañuelos de papel** *pahn-yoo-EH-lohs day pah-PEL*
toilet paper	**papel higiénico** *pah-PEL ee-hy-EHN-ee-koh*
a tooth brush	**un cepillo de dientes** *oon sep-EE-yoh day dee-YEHN-tays*
toothpaste	**pasta de dientes** *pah-stah day dee-YEHN-tays*
tweezers	**pinzas** *PEEN-sahs*

PERSONAL CARE AND SERVICES

AT THE BARBER

Where is there a good barber shop?	**¿Dónde hay una buena barbería?** *DOHN-day AH-ee oo-nah BWEH-nah bahr-behr-EE-ah*
Do I have to wait long?	**¿Tengo que esperar mucho?** *ten-goh kay ehs-pehr-AHR MOO-choh*
Am I next?	**¿Me toca a mí?** *may TOH-kay ah mee*

I want a shave.	**Quiero que me afeiten.** *kee-YEHR-oh kay may ah-FAY-tehn*
I want a haircut (razorcut).	**Quiero un corte de pelo (a navaja).** *kee-YEHR-oh oon KOHR-tay day PEH-loh (ah nah-BAH-hah)*
Short in back, long in front.	**Corto por detrás, largo por delante.** *KOHR-toh pohr day-TRAHS, lahr-goh pohr day-LAHN-tay*
Leave it long.	**Déjelo largo.** *DAY-hay-loh LAHR-goh*
I want it (very) short.	**Lo quiero (muy) corto.** *loh kee-YEHR-oh (mwee) KOHR-toh*
You can cut a little _____.	**Puede cortar un poquito _____.** *PWEH-day kohr-TAHR oon poh-KEE-toh*
▪ in back	**por detrás** *pohr day-TRAHS*
▪ in front	**por delante** *pohr day-LAHN-tay*
▪ off the top	**de arriba** *day ah-REE-bah*
▪ on the sides	**a los lados** *ah lohs LAH-dohs*
Cut a little bit more here.	**Córteme un poco más aquí.** *KOHR-tay-may oon POH-koh mahs ah-KEE*
That's enough.	**Eso es bastante.** *EH-soh ehs bah-STAHN-tay*
I (don't) want _____.	**(No) quiero _____.** *(noh) kee-YEHR-oh*
▪ shampoo	**champú** *chahm-POO*
▪ tonic	**tónico** *TOHN-ee-koh*
Use the scissors only.	**Use sólo las tijeras.** *oo-say soh-loh lahs tee-HAIR-ahs*
Please trim my _____.	**Recórteme _____ por favor.** *ray-KOHR-tay-may _____ pohr fah-BOHR*

■ beard   **la barba**   *lah bahr-bah*

■ moustache   **el bigote**   *ehl bee-GOH-tay*

■ sideburns   **las patillas**   *lahs pah-TEE-yahs*

I'd like to look at myself in the mirror.

Quisiera mirarme al espejo. *kee-SYEHR-ah meer-AHR-may ahl ehs-PAY-hoh*

How much do I owe you?

¿Cuánto le debo? *KWAHN-toh lay DEH-boh*

Is service included?

¿Está incluída la propina? *eh-STAH een-kloo-EE-dah lah proh-PEE-nah*

AT THE BEAUTY PARLOR

Is there a beauty parlor (hairdresser) near the hotel?

¿Hay un salón de belleza (una pe-luquería) cerca del hotel? *AH-ee oon sah-LOHN day beh-YEH-sah (OO-nah pel-oo-kehr-EE-ah) SEHR-kah del oh-TEL*

I'd like an appoint-ment for this after-noon (tomorrow).

Quisiera hacer una cita para esta tarde (mañana). *kee-SYEHR-ah ah-SEHR oo-nah SEE-tah pah-rah EHS-tah TAHR-day (mahn-YA-nah)*

Can you give me _____?

¿Puede darme _____? *PWEH-day DAHR-may*

■ a color rinse   **un enjuague de color**   *oon ehn-hoo-AH-gay day koh-LOHR*

■ a facial massage   **un masaje facial**   *oon mah-SAH-hay fah-see-AHL*

■ a haircut   **un corte de pelo**   *oon KOHR-tay day PEH-loh*

■ a manicure   **una manicura**   *oo-nah mah-nee-KOOR-ah*

■ a permanent	**una permanente** *oon-nah pehr-mah-NEN-tay*
■ a shampoo	**un champú** *oon chahm-POO*
■ a tint	**un tinte** *oon TEEN-tay*
■ a touch up	**un retoque** *oon ray-TOH-kay*
■ a wash and set	**un lavado y peinado** *oon lah-bah-doh ee pay-NAH-doh*
I'd like to see a color chart.	**Quisiera ver un muestrario.** *kee-SYEHR-ah behr oon mwehs-TRAHR-ee-oh*
I want _____.	**Quiero _____.** *kee-YEHR-oh*
■ auburn	**rojizo** *roh-HEE-soh*
■ (light) blond	**un rubio (claro)** *oon ROO-bee-oh (KLAHR-oh)*
■ brunette	**castaño** *kahs-TAHN-yo*
■ a darker color	**un color más oscuro** *oon koh-LOHR mahs oh-SKOOR-oh*
a lighter color	**un color más claro** *oon koh-LOHR mahs KLAH-roh*
the same color	**el mismo color** *ehl MEES-moh koh-LOHR*
Don't apply any hairspray.	**No me ponga laca.** *noh may POHN-gah lah-kah*
Not too much hairspray.	**Sólo un poco de laca.** *SOH-loh oon POH-koh day LAH-kah*
I want my hair _____.	**Quiero el pelo _____.** *kee-YEHR-oh ehl peh-loh*
■ with bangs	**con flequillo** *kohn fleh-KEE-yoh*
■ in a bun	**con un moño** *kohn oon MOHN-yoh*
■ in curls	**con bucles** *kohn boo-KLAYS*

| with waves | **con ondas** *kohn OHN-dahs* |

I'd like to look at myself in the mirror.
Quiero mirarme al espejo. *kee-YEHR-oh meer-AHR-may ahl ehs-PAY-hoh*

How much do I owe you?
¿Cuánto le debo? *KWAHN-toh lay DEH-boh*

Is service included?
¿Está incluída la propina? *es-TAH een-kloo-EE-dah lah proh-PEE-nah*

LAUNDRY AND DRY CLEANING

Where is the nearest laundry (dry cleaners)?
¿Dónde está la lavandería (la tintorería) más cercana? *DOHN-day ehs-TAH lah lah-bahn-deh-REE-ah (lah teen-TOHR-ehr-EE-ah) mahs sehr-KAH-nah*

I have a lot of (dirty) clothes to be ____.
Tengo mucha ropa (sucia) que ____. *ten-goh moo-chah ROH-pah (SOO-see-ah) kay*

(dry) cleaned	**limpiar (en seco)** *leem-pee-AHR (ehn SEH-koh)*
washed	**lavar** *lah-BAHR*
mended	**arreglar** *ah-ray-GLAHR*
ironed	**planchar** *plahn-CHAHR*

I need them for ____.
Las necesito para ____. *lahs neh-seh-SEE-toh PAH-rah*

tonight	**esta noche** *EHS-tah NOH-chay*
tomorrow	**mañana** *mahn-YAH-nah*
next week	**la semana próxima** *lah seh-MAH-nah PROHK-see-mah*
the day after tomorrow	**pasado mañana** *pah-SAH-doh mahn-YAH-nah*

When will you bring it back?	**¿Cuándo la traerá?** *kwahn-doh lah trah-ehr-AH*
When will it be ready?	**¿Cuándo estará lista?** *kwahn-doh ehs-tah-RAH lees-tah*
There's a button missing.	**Falta un botón.** *fahl-tah oon boh-TOHN*
Can you sew it on?	**¿Puede usted coserlo?** *pweh-deh oos-TEHD koh-SEHR-loh*
This isn't my laundry.	**Esta no es mi ropa.** *EHS-tah noh ehs mee ROH-pah*

SHOE REPAIRS

Can you fix these shoes (boots)?	**¿Puede arreglar estos zapatos (estas botas)?** *PWEH-day ah-ray-GLAHR ehs-tohs sah-PAH-tohs (ehs-tahs BOH-tahs)*
Put on (half) soles and rubber heels.	**Póngales (medias) suelas y tacones de goma.** *POHN-gah-lays (MED-ee-ahs) SWAY-lahs ee tah-KOHN-ays day GOH-mah*
When will they be ready?	**¿Para cuándo los tendrá?** *pah-rah KWAHN-doh lohs ten-DRAH*
I need them by Saturday (without fail).	**Los necesito para el sábado (sin falta).** *lohs nes-ehs-see-toh pah-rah ehl SAH-bah-doh (seen FAHL-tah)*

WATCH REPAIRS

Can you fix this watch (alarm clock) (for me)?	**¿(Me) puede arreglar este reloj (despertador)?** *(may) PWEH-day ah-ray-GLAHR EHS-tay ray-LOH (dehs-pehr-tah-dohr)*

Can you clean it?	**¿Puede usted limpiarlo?** *PWEH-day oos-TEHD leem-pee-AHR-loh*
I dropped it.	**Se me cayó.** *say may kah-YOH*
It's running slow (fast).	**Se atrasa (se adelanta).** *say ah-TRAH-sah (Say ah-deh-LAHN-tah)*
It's stopped.	**Está parado.** *ehs-TAH pah-RAH-doh*
I wind it everyday.	**Le doy cuerda todos los días.** *lay doy KWEHR-dah toh-dohs lohs DEE-ahs*
When will it be ready?	**¿Cuándo estará listo?** *KWAHN-doh ehs-tah-RAH LEES-toh*
May I have a receipt?	**¿Me puede dar un recibo?** *may PWEH-day dahr oon ray-SEE-boh*

CAMERA REPAIRS

Can you fix this camera?	**¿Puede usted arreglar esta cámara?** *PWEHD-eh oos-TEHD ah-ray-GLAHR ehs-tah KAH-mah-rah*
The film doesn't advance.	**El carrete no se mueve.** *ehl kah-REH-tay noh say MWEH-bay*
I think I need new batteries.	**Creo que necesito una nueva pila.** *KRAY-oh kay reh-seh-SEE-toh oo-nah NWEH-bah PEE-lah*
How much will the repair cost?	**¿Cuánto costará el arreglo?** *KWAHN-toh kohs-tah-RAH ehl ah-REG-loh*
When can I come and get it?	**¿Cuándo puedo venir a buscarla?** *KWAHN-doh PWEHD-oh ben-EER ah boos-KAHR-lah*
I need it as soon as possible.	**La necesito lo más pronto posible.** *lah neh-say-SEE-toh loh mahs PROHN-toh poh-SEE-blay*

MEDICAL CARE

THE PHARMACY (CHEMIST)

Where is the nearest (all-night) pharmacy (chemist)?	**¿Dónde está la farmacia (de guardia) más cercana?** *DOHN-day ehs-TAH lah fahr-MAH-see-ah (day GWAHR-dee-ah) mahs sehr-KAH-nah*
At what time does the pharmacy open (close)?	**¿A qué hora se abre (se cierra) la farmacia?** *ah kay OH-rah say AH-bray (say SYEHR-ah) lah fahr-MAH-see-ah*
I need something for _____.	**Necesito algo para _____.** *neh-seh-SEE-toh AHL-goh pah-rah*
▒ a cold	**un catarro** *oon kah-TAH-roh*
▒ constipation	**el estreñimiento (constipación estomacal)** *ehl ehs-trayn-yee-MYEHN-toh*
▒ a cough	**la tos** *lah-tohs*
▒ diarrhea	**la diarrea** *lah dee-ahr-RAY-ah*
▒ a fever	**la fiebre** *lah fee-YEHB-ray*
▒ hay fever	**la fiebre del heno** *lah fee-YEHB-ray del AY-noh*
▒ a headache	**un dolor de cabeza** *oon doh-LOHR day kah-BAY-sah*
▒ insomnia	**el insomnio** *ehl een-SOHM-nee-oh*
▒ nausea	**náuseas** *NAH-oo-say-ahs*
▒ sunburn	**la quemadura del sol** *lah kay-mah-DOOR-ah del SOHL*
▒ a toothache	**un dolor de muelas** *oon doh-LOHR day MWEH-lahs*
▒ an upset stomach	**la indigestión** *lah een-dee-hes-TYOHN*

I do not have a prescription.	**No tengo la receta.** *noh TEN-goh lah reh-SAY-tah*
May I have it right away?	**¿Me la puede dar en seguida?** *May lah PWEH-day DAHR ehn seh-GHEE-dah*
It's an emergency!	**¡Es urgente!** *ehs oor-HEN-tay*
How long will it take?	**¿Cuánto tiempo tardará?** *KWAHN-toh tee-YEHM-poh tahr-dahr-AH*
When can I come for it?	**¿Cuándo puedo venir a recogerla?** *KWAHN-doh PWEH-doh ben-EER ah ray-koh-HAIR-lah*
I would like _____.	**Quisiera _____.** *kee-see-YEHR-ah*
adhesive tape	**esparadrapo** *ehs-pah-rah-DRAH-poh*
alcohol	**alcohol** *ahl-koh-OHL*
an antacid	**un antiácido** *oon ahn-tee-AH-see-doh*
an antiseptic	**un antiséptico** *oon ahn-tee-SEP-tee-koh*
aspirins	**aspirinas** *ahs-peer-EE-nahs*
Band-Aids	**curitas** *koor-EE-tahs*
contraceptives	**contraceptivos** *kohn-trah-sep-TEE-bohs*
corn plasters	**callicidas** *kah-yee-SEE-dahs*
cotton	**algodón** *ahl-goh-DOHN*
cough drops	**pastillas para la tos** *PAHS-TEE-yahs pah-rah lah TOHS*
cough syrup	**jarabe para la tos** *hah-RAH-bay pah-rah lah TOHS*
ear drops	**gotas para los oídos** *goh-tahs pah-rah lohs oh-EE-dohs*
eye drops	**gotas para los ojos** *goh-tahs pah-rah lohs OH-hohs*

▣ iodine	**yodo** *YOH-doh*
▣ a (mild) laxative	**un laxante (ligero)** *oon lahk-SAHN-tay (lee-HEHR-oh)*
▣ milk of magnesia	**la leche de magnesia** *lah leh-chay day mahg-NAY-see-ah*
▣ prophylactics	**profilácticos** *pro-fee-LAHK-tee-kohs*
▣ sanitary napkins	**servilletas higiénicas** *sehr-bee-YEH-tahs ee-HYEHN-ee-kahs*
▣ suppositories	**supositorios** *soo-pohs-ee-TOHR-ee-ohs*
▣ talcum powder	**polvos de talco** *POHL-bohs day TAHL-koh*
▣ tampons	**tapones** *tah-POHN-ays*
▣ a thermometer	**un termómetro** *oon tehr-MOH-met-roh*
▣ tranquilizers	**un tranquilizante** *oon trahn-kee-lee-SAHN-tay*
▣ vitamins	**vitaminas** *bee-tah-MEE-nahs*

WITH THE DOCTOR

I don't feel well.	**No me siento bien.** *noh may SYEHN-toh BYEHN*
I need a doctor.	**Necesito un médico.** *neh-seh-SEE-toh oon MEH-dee-koh*
Do you know a doctor who speaks English?	**¿Conoce un médico que hable inglés?** *koh-NOH-say oon MEH-dee-koh kay ah-blay een-GLAYSS*
Where is his office (surgery)?	**¿Dónde está su consultorio?** *DOHN-day ehs-TAH soo kohn-sool-TOHR-ee-oh*

Will the doctor come to the hotel?	**¿Vendrá el medico al hotel?** *ben-DRAH ehl MED-ee-koh ahl oh-TEL*
I feel dizzy.	**Estoy mareado.** *ehs-TOY mahr-ay-AH-doh*
I feel weak.	**Me siento débil.** *may SYEHN-toh DAY-beel*
I (think I) have _____.	**(Creo que) tengo _____.** *KRAY-oh kay TEN-goh*
▪ an abscess	**un absceso** *oon ahb-SEHS-oh*
▪ a broken bone	**un hueso roto** *oon WAY-soh ROH-toh*
▪ a bruise	**una contusión** *oo-nah kohn-too-SYOHN*
▪ a burn	**una quemadura** *oo-nah kay-mah-DOOR-ah*
▪ something in my eye	**algo en el ojo** *AHL-goh ehn ehl OH-hoh*
▪ the chills	**escalofríos** *ehs-kah-loh-FREE-ohs*
▪ a chest (head) cold	**un catarro (resfriado)** *oon kah-TAHR-oh (res-free-AH-doh)*
▪ constipation	**el estreñimiento** *ehl ehs-trayn-yee-mee-YENT-oh*
▪ stomach cramps	**calambres** *kahl-AHM-brays*
▪ a cut	**una cortadura** *oo-nah kohr-tah-DOOR-ah*
▪ diarrhea	**la diarrea** *lah dee-ah-RAY-ah*
▪ a fever	**fiebre** *fee-YEHB-bray*
▪ a fracture	**una fractura** *oo-nah frahk-TOOR-ah*
▪ a headache	**un dolor de cabeza** *oon doh-lohr day kah-BAY-sah*

■ an infection	**una infección** *oo-nah een-fek-SYOHN*
■ a lump	**un bulto** *oon BOOL-toh*
■ a sore throat	**un dolor de garganta** *oon doh-lohr day gahr-GAHN-tah*
■ a stomach ache	**un dolor de estómago** *oon doh-lohr day ehs-TOH-mah-goh*
It hurts me here.	**Me duele aquí.** *may DWEH-lay ah-KEE*
My whole body hurts.	**Me duele todo el cuerpo.** *may DWEH-lay toh-doh ehl KWEHR-poh*
thumb	**el pulgar** *ehl pool-GAHR*
throat	**la garganta** *lah gahr-GAHN-tah*
toe	**el dedo del pie** *ehl DAY-doh del pee-YEH*
tooth	**el diente** *ehl dee-YEHN-tay*
wrist	**la muñeca** *lah moon-YEH-kah*
I've had this pain since yesterday.	**Tengo este dolor desde ayer.** *ten-goh ehs-tay doh-LOHR des-day ah-YEHR*

TELLING THE DOCTOR

There's a (no) history of asthma (diabetes) in my family.	**(No) hay incidencia de asma (diabetes) en mi familia.** *(noh) AH-ee een-see-DEN-see-ah day AHS-mah (dee-ah-BEH-tays) ehn mee fah-MEEL-yah.*
I'm (not) allergic to antibiotics (penicillin).	**(No) soy alérgico(a) a los antibióticos (penicilina).** *(noh) soy ah-LEHR-hee-koh (kah) ah lohs ahn-tee-bee-OH-tee-kohs (pen-ee-see-LEE-nah).*
I have a pain in my chest.	**Tengo dolor en el pecho.** *TEN-goh doh-LOHR ehn ehl PAY-choh*
I had a heart attack ____ year(s) ago.	**Tuve un ataque al corazón hace ____ año(s).** *TOO-bay oon ah-TAH-kay ahl kohr-ah-SOHN ah-say ____ ahn-yoh(s)*

I'm taking this medicine (insulin).	**Tomo esta medicina (insulina).** *toh-moh ehs-tah med-ee-SEE-nah (een-soo-LEE-nah)*
I'm pregnant.	**Estoy embarazada.** *ehs-toy ehm-bahr-ah-SAH-dah*
I feel better (worse).	**Me siento mejor (peor).** *may see-YEN-toh may-HOHR (pay-OHR)*
Is it serious (contagious)?	**¿Es grave (contagioso)?** *ehs GRAH-bay (kohn-tah-hee-OH-soh)*
Do I have to go to the hospital?	**¿Tengo que ir al hospital?** *ten-goh kay eer ahl ohs-pee-TAHL*
When can I continue my trip?	**¿Cuándo puedo continuar mi viaje?** *KWAHN-doh PWEH-doh kon-teen-oo-AHR mee bee-AH-hay*

DOCTOR'S INSTRUCTIONS

Abra la boca.	Open your mouth.
Saque la lengua.	Stick out your tongue.
Tosa.	Cough.
Respire fuerte.	Breathe deeply.
Quítese la ropa	Take off your clothing.
Acuéstese.	Lie down.
Levántese.	Stand up.
Vístase.	Get dressed.

FOLLOWING UP

Are you giving me a prescription?	**¿Va a darme una receta?** *bah ah DAHR-may oo-nah ray-SAY-tah?*
How often must I take this medicine (these pills)?	**¿Cuántas veces al día tengo que tomar esta medicina (estas píldoras)?** *KWAHN-tahs BEH-says ahl DEE-ah ten-goh kay toh-MAHR ehs-tah med-ee-SEE-nah (EHS-tahs PEEL-dohr-ahs)*

(How long) do I have to stay in bed?	**¿(Cuánto tiempo) tengo que quedarme en cama?** *(KWAHN-toh tee-YEHM-poh) ten-goh kay kay-DAHR-may ehn KAH-mah*
Thank you (for everything), doctor.	**Muchas gracias (por todo), doctor.** *MOO-chahs GRAH-see-ahs (pohr TOH-doh) dohk-TOHR*
How much do I owe you for your services?	**¿Cuánto le debo?** *KWAHN-toh lay DEHB-oh*

IN THE HOSPITAL (ACCIDENTS)

Help!	**¡Socorro!** *soh-KOH-roh*
Get a doctor, quick!	**¡Busque un médico, rápido!** *BOO-skay oon MED-ee-koh, RAH-pee-doh*
Call an ambulance!	**¡Llame una ambulancia!** *YAH-may oo-nah ahm-boo-LAHN-see-ah*
Take him to the hospital!	**¡al hospital!** *ahl ohs-pee-TAHL*
I've fallen.	**Me he caído.** *may ay kah-EE-doh*
I was knocked down (run over).	**Fui atropellado(a).** *fwee ah-troh-peh-YAH-doh*
I think I've had a heart attack.	**Creo que he tenido un ataque al corazón.** *KRAY-oh kay ay ten-EE-doh oon ah-TAH-kay ahl kohr-ah-SOHN*

AT THE DENTIST

Can you recommend a dentist?	**¿Puede recomendar un dentista?** *PWEH-day reh-koh-men-DAHR oon den-TEES-tah*
I have a toothache that's driving me crazy.	**Tengo un dolor de muela que me vuelve loco.** *ten-goh oon doh-LOHR day MWEH-lah kay may BWEHL-bay loh-koh*

I've lost a filling.	**Se me ha caído un empaste.** *say may ah kah-EE-doh oon ehm-PAHS-tay*
I've broken a tooth.	**Me rompí un diente.** *may rohm-PEE oon dee-EHN-tay*
My gums hurt me.	**Me duelen las encías.** *may DWEH-len lahs ehn-SEE-ahs*
Is there an infection?	**¿Hay una infección?** *AH-ee oo-nah een-fehk-SYOHN*
Will you have to extract the tooth?	**¿Tendrá que sacar la muela (el diente)?** *ten-DRAH kay sah-kahr lah MWEH-lah (ehl dee-EHN-tay)*
Can you fill it _____?	**¿Podría empastarlo _____?** *poh-DREE-ah ehm-pahs-TAHR-loh*
Can you fix _____?	**¿Puede usted reparar _____?** *PWEH-day oo-STEHD ray-pah-RAHR*
◼ this bridge	**este puente** *EHS-tay PWEHN-tay*
◼ this crown	**esta corona** *ehs-tah kohr-OH-nah*
◼ these dentures	**estos dientes postizos** *ehs-tohs dee-EHN-tays pohs-TEE-sohs*
When should I come back?	**¿Cuándo debo volver?** *KWAHN-doh DEH-boh bohl-BEHR*
How much do I owe you for your services?	**¿Cuánto le debo?** *KWAHN-toh lay DEH-boh*

WITH THE OPTICIAN

Can you repair these glasses (for me)?	**¿Puede usted arreglar(me) estas gafas?** *PWEH-day oos-TEHD ah-ray-GLAHR (may) ehs-tahs GAH-fahs*
I've broken a lens (the frame).	**Se me ha roto un cristal (la armadura).** *say may ah ROH-toh oon krees-TAHL (lah ahr-mah-DOOR-ah)*

Can you put in a new lens?	¿Puede usted ponerme un cristal nuevo? *PWEH-day oos-TEHD poh-NEHR-may oon krees-TAHL NWEH-boh*
I do not have a prescription.	No tengo receta. *noh TEN-goh ray-SAY-tah*
Can you tighten the screws?	¿Puede usted apretar los tornillitos? *PWEH-day oos-TEHD ah-pray-tahr lohs tohr-NEE-yee-tohs*
I need the glasses as soon as possible.	Necesito las gafas urgentemente. *neh-seh-SEE-toh lahs GAH-fahs oor-hen-tay-MEN-tay*
I don't have any others.	No tengo otras. *noh TEN-goh OH-trahs*
I've lost a contact lens.	Se me ha perdido una lente de contacto. *say may ah pehr-DEE-doh oo-nah LEN-tay day kohn-TAHK-toh*
Can you replace it quickly?	¿Puede reemplazarla rápidamente? *PWEH-day ray-ehm-plah-SAHR-lah rah-pee-dah-MEN-tay*

COMMUNICATIONS

POST OFFICE

I want to mail a letter.	Quiero echar una carta al correo. *kee-YEHR-oh ay-CHAHR OO-nah KAHR-tah ahl kohr-AY-oh*
Where's the post office?	¿Dónde está correos? *DOHN-day ehs-TAH kohr-AY-ohs*
Where's a letterbox?	¿Dónde hay un buzón? *DOHN-day AH-ee oon boo-SOHN*

What is the postage on ____ to the United States (Canada, England, Australia)?	**¿Cuánto es el franqueo de ____ a los Estados Unidos (al Canadá, a Inglaterra, a Australia)?** *KWAHN-toh ehs ehl frahn-KAY-oh day ____ ah lohs ehs-TAH-dohs oo-NEE-dohs (ahl kahn-ah-DAH, ah eeng-lah-TEHR-ah, ah ow-STRAHL-yah)*
▨ a letter	**una carta** *oo-nah KAHR-tah*
▨ an insured letter	**una carta asegurada** *oo-nah KAHR-tah ah-say-goor-AH-dah*
▨ a registered letter	**una carta certificada** *oo-nah KAHR-tah sehr-teef-ee-KAH-dah*
▨ a special delivery letter	**una carta urgente** *oo-nah KAHR-tah oor-HEN-tay*
▨ a package	**un paquete postal** *oon pah-kay-tay pohs-TAHL*
▨ a post card	**una postal** *oo-nah pohs-TAHL*
When will it arrive?	**¿Cuándo llegará?** *KWAHN-doh yeh-gahr-AH*
Which is the ____ window?	**¿Cuál es la ventanilla de ____?** *kwahl ehs lah ben-tah-NEE-yah day*
▨ general delivery	**la lista de correos** *lah LEES-tah day kohr-AY-ohs*
▨ money order	**los giros postales** *lohs HEER-ohs pohs-TAHL-ays*
▨ stamp	**los sellos** *lohs SEH-yohs*
Are there any letters for me? My name is ____.	**¿Hay cartas para mí? Me llamo ____.** *AH-ee KAHR-tahs pah-rah mee may YAH-moh*
I'd like ____.	**Quisiera ____.** *kee-see-YEHR-ah*
▨ 10 envelopes	**diez sobres** *dee-EHS SOH-brays*
▨ 6 postcards	**seis postales** *sayss pohs-TAHL-ays*
▨ 5 (air mail) stamps	**cinco sellos (aéreos)** *SEEN-koh SEH-yohs (ah-EHR-ay-ohs)*

TELEGRAMS

Where's the telegraph office?	**¿Dónde está el Correos y Telégrafos?** *DOHN-day ehs-TAH ehl kohr-AY-ohs ee tel-AY-grah-fohs*
How late is it open?	**¿Hasta cuándo está abierto?** *AH-stah KWAHN-doh ehs-TAH ah-bee-YEHR-toh*
I'd like to send a telegram (night letter) to ____.	**Quisiera mandar un telegrama (un cable nocturno) a ____.** *kee-see-YEHR-ah mahn-DAHR oon teh-lay-GRAH-mah (oon KAH-blay nohk-TOOR-noh) ah*
How much it is per word?	**¿Cuánto cuesta por palabra?** *KWAHN-toh KWEHS-tah pohr pah-LAH-brah*
I need to send a telex.	**Tengo que enviar un "telex."** *TEN-goh kay ehm-bee-AHR oon TEL-eks*
I want to send it collect.	**Quiero mandarlo con cobro revertido.** *kee-YEHR-oh mahn-DAHR-loh kohn KOH-broh reh-behr-TEE-doh*
When will it arrive?	**¿Cuándo llegará?** *KWAHN-doh yeh-gahr-AH*

TELEPHONES

Where is ____?	**Donde hay ____?** *DOHN-day AH-ee*
a public telephone	**un teléfono público** *oon tel-EHF-oh-noh POO-blee-koh*
a telephone booth	**una cabina telefónica** *oo-nah kah-BEE-nah tel-eh-FOHN-ee-kah*
a telephone directory	**una guía telefónica** *oo-nah GHEE-ah tel-eh-FOHN-ee-kah*

May I use your phone?	**¿Me permite usar su teléfono?** *may pehr-MEE-tay oo-sahr soo tel-EHF-oh-noh*
I want to make a ____.	**Quiero hacer una llamada ____.** *kee-YEHR-oh ah-sehr oo-nah yah-MAH-dah*
■ local	**local** *loh-kahl*
■ long distance	**a larga distancia** *ah LAHR-gah dees-TAHN-see-ah*
■ person to person	**personal** *pehr-SOHN-ahl*
■ collect	**a cobro revertido** *ah KOH-broh ray-behr-TEE-doh*
Can I call direct?	**¿Puedo marcar directamente?** *PWEH-doh mahr-KAHR dee-rehk-tah-MEN-tay*
Do I need tokens for the phone?	**¿Necesito fichas para el teléfono?** *neh-seh-SEE-toh fee-chahs pah-rah ehl tel-EHF-oh-no*
How do I get the operator?	**¿Cómo puedo conseguir la central?** *KOH-moh PWEH-doh kon-seh-GHEER lah sehn-TRAHL*
Operator, can you get me number ____?	**Señorita, quiere comunicarme con ____?** *sehn-yohr-EE-tah, kee-YEHR-ay koh-moo-nee-KAHR-may kohn*
My number is ____.	**Mi número es ____.** *mee NOO-mehr-oh ehs*
I can't hear.	**No oigo.** *noh OY-goh*
Speak louder, please.	**Hable más alto, por favor.** *AH-blay mahs AHL-toh pohr fah-BOHR*
Don't hang up. Hold the wire.	**No cuelgue.** *noh KWEHL-gay*
This is ____.	**Habla ____.** *AH-blah*

Operator, there's no answer (they don't answer).	**Señorita, no contestan.** *sen-yohr-EE-tah, noh kohn-TEST-ahn*
The line is busy.	**La línea está ocupada.** *lah LEE-nay-ah ehs-TAH oh-koo-PAH-dah*
You gave me (that was) a wrong number.	**Me ha dado (fue) un número equivocado.** *may ah DAH-doh (fway) oon NOO-mehr-oh ay-kee-boh-KAH-doh*
I was cut off.	**Me han cortado.** *may ahn kohr-TAH-doh*
Please dial it again.	**Llame otra vez, por favor.** *YAH-may OH-trah bes, pohr fah-BOHR*
I want to leave a message.	**Quiero dejar un recado.** *kee-YEHR-oh day-HAHR oon ray-KAH-doh*
How much do I have to pay?	**¿Cuanto tengo que pagar?** *KWAHN-toh TEN-goh kay pah-GAHR?*
Will you help me place a long-distance call?	**¿Podría ayudarme a hacer una llamada a larga distancia?** *poh-DREE-ah ah-yoDAHR-may ah-SEHR oo-nah yah-MAH-dah ah LAHR-gah dees-TAHN-see-ah*

DRIVING A CAR

CAR RENTALS

Where can I rent _____?	**¿Dónde puedo alquilar _____?** *dohn-day PWEH-doh ahl-kee-LAHR*
■ a car	**un coche** *oon KOH-chay*
■ a motorcycle	**una motocicleta** *oo-nah moh-toh-see-KLAY-tah*
■ a bicycle	**una bicicleta** *oo-nah bee-see-KLAY-tah*

CAR RENTALS • 493

I want a _____.	**Quiero _____.** *kee-EH-roh*
▪ small car	**un coche pequeño** *oon KOH-chay peh-KAYN-yoh*
▪ large car	**un coche grande** *oon KOH-chay GRAHN-day*
▪ sports car	**un coche deportivo** *oon KOH-chay day-pohr-TEE-boh*
I prefer automatic transmission.	**Prefiero el cambio automático.** *preh-fee-EHR-oh ehl KAHM-bee-oh AH-oo-toh-MAH-tee-koh*
How much does it cost _____?	**¿Cuánto cuesta _____?** *KWAHN-toh KWEHS-tah*
▪ per day	**por día** *pohr DEE-ah*
▪ per week	**por semana** *pohr seh-MAHN-ah*
▪ per kilometer	**por kilómetro** *pohr kee-LOH-meht-roh*
▪ for unlimited mile-age	**con kilometraje ilimitado** *kohn kee-loh-may-TRAH-hay ee-lee-mee-TAH-doh*
How much is the in-surance?	**¿Cuánto es el seguro?** *KWAHN-toh ehs ehl seh-GOOR-oh*
Is the gas included?	**¿Está incluída la gasolina?** *ehs-TAH een-kloo-EE-dah lah gahs-oh-LEEN-ah*
Do you accept credit cards?	**¿Acepta usted tarjetas de crédito?** *ah-sehp-tah oos-TEHD tahr-HAY-tahs day KREH-dee-toh*
Here's my driver's li-cense.	**Aquí tiene mi licencia de conducir.** *ah-KEE tee-EH-nay mee lee-SEN-see-ah day kohn-doo-SEER*
Do I have to leave a deposit?	**¿Tengo que dejar un depósito?** *ten-goh kay day-hahr oon day-POHS-ee-toh*

I want to rent the car here and leave it in ____.	**Quiero alquilar el coche aquí y dejarlo en ____.** *kee-YEHR-oh ahl-kee-LAHR ehl koh-chay ah-KEE ee day-HAHR-loh ehn*
What kind of gasoline does it take?	**Que tipo de gasolina necesita?** *kay TEE-poh day gah-so-LEE-nah neh-seh-SEE-tah*

ON THE ROAD

Excuse me, can you tell me ____?	**Por favor, ¿puede usted decirme ____?** *pohr fah-BOHR, pweh-day oos-TEHD day-SEER-may*
Which way is it to ____?	**¿Por dónde se va a ____?** *pohr DOHN-day say bah ah*
How do I get to ____?	**¿Cómo se va a ____?** *KOH-moh say bah ah*
I think we're lost.	**Creo que estamos perdidos.** *KRAY-oh kay ehs-TAH-mohs pehr-DEE-dohs*
Is this the way to ____?	**¿Es éste el camino a ____?** *ehs EHS-tay ehl kah-MEE-noh ah*
Is it a good road?	**¿Es buena la carretera?** *ehs BWAY-nah la kahr-ray-TEHR-ah*
Where does this highway go to?	**¿Adónde va esta carretera?** *ah DOHN-day bah ehs-tah kah-ray-TEHR-ah*
Is this the shortest way?	**¿Es éste el camino más corto?** *ehs EHS-tay ehl kah-MEE-noh mahs KOHR-toh*
Are there any detours?	**¿Hay desviaciones?** *AH-ee des-bee-ah-SYOHN-ays*
Do I go straight?	**¿Sigo derecho?** *see-goh deh-RAY-choh*
Do I turn to the right (to the left)?	**¿Doblo a la derecha (a la izquierda)?** *DOH-bloh ah lah deh-RAY-chah (ah lah ees-kee-YEHR-dah)*

How far is it from here to the next town?	**¿Cuánta distancia hay de aquí al primer pueblo?** *KWAHN-tah dees-TAHN-see-ah ah-ee day ah-KEE-ahl pree-MEHR PWEH-bloh*
How far away is _____?	**¿A qué distancia está _____?** *ah kay dees-TAHN-see-ah ehs-tah*
Do you have a road map?	**¿Tiene usted un mapa de carreteras?** *tee-yehn-ay-oos-TEHD oon MAH-pah day kahr-ray-TEHR-ahs*
Can you show it to me on the map?	**¿Puede indicármelo en el mapa?** *PWEH-day een-dee-KAHR-may-loh ehn ehl MAH-pah*

AT THE SERVICE STATION

Where is there a gas (petrol) station?	**¿Dónde hay una estación de gasolina?** *DOHN-day AH-ee oo-nah ehs-tah-SYOHN day gahs-oh-LEE-nah*
Fill it up with _____.	**Llénelo con _____.** *YAY-nay-loh kohn*
diesel	**diesel** *dee-EH-sel*
regular (90 octane)	**normal** *nohr-MAHL*
super (96 octane)	**super** *SOO-pehr*
extra (98 octane)	**extra** *EHS-trah*
Give me _____ liters.	**Déme _____ litros.** *day-may _____ LEE-trohs*
Please check _____.	**¿Quiere inspeccionar _____.** *kee-YEHR-ay eens-pehk-syohn-AHR*
the battery	**la batería** *lah bah-tehr-EE-ah*
the carburetor	**el carburador** *ehl kahr-boor-ah-DOHR*
the oil	**el aceite** *ehl ah-SAY-tay*
the spark plugs	**las bujías** *lahs boo-HEE-ahs*

the tires	**las llantas, las ruedas** *lahs YAHN-tahs, RWAY-dahs*
the tire pressure	**la presión de las llantas** *lah preh-SYOHN day lahs YAHN-tahs*
the antifreeze	**el agua del radiador** *ehl ah-GWAH del rah-dee-ah-DOHR*
Change the oil.	**Cambie el aceite.** *KAHM-bee-ay ehl ah-SAY-tay*
Lubricate the car.	**Engrase el coche.** *ehn-GRAH-say ehl KOH-chay*
Charge the battery.	**Cargue la batería.** *KAHR-gay lah bah-tehr-EE-ah*
Change the tire.	**Cambie esta llanta.** *KAHM-bee-ay ehs-tah YAHN-tah*

ACCIDENTS AND REPAIRS

My car has broken down.	**Mi coche se ha averiado.** *mee KOH-chay say AH ah-behr-ee-AH-doh*
It overheats.	**Se calienta demasiado.** *say kahl-YEN-tah day-mahs-ee-AH-doh*
It doesn't start.	**No arranca.** *noh ah-RAHN-kah*
I have a flat tire.	**Se me ha pinchado una rueda.** *say may ah peen-CHAH-doh oon-ah RWEH-dah*
Is there a garage (repair shop) near here?	**¿Hay un garage (taller) por aquí?** *AH-ee oon gah-RAH-hay (tah-YEHR) pohr ah-KEE*
I need a mechanic (tow truck).	**Necesito un mecánico (remolca-dor).** *neh-seh-SEE-toh oon meh-KAHN-ee-koh (ray-mohl-kah-DOHR)*

Can you _____? **¿Puede usted _____?** *PWEH-day oos-TEHD*

■ give me a push **empujarme** *ehm-poo-HAHR-may*

■ help me **ayudarme** *ah yoo DAHR may*

I don't have any tools. **No tengo herramientas.** *noh ten-goh ehr-ah-MYEHN-tahs*

Can you fix the car? **¿Puede usted arreglar el coche?** *PWEH-day oos-TEHD ah-ray-GLAHR ehl KOH-chay*

Can you repair it temporarily? **¿Puede repararlo temporalmente?** *PWEH-day ray-pahr-AHR-loh tem-pohr-AHL-men-tay*

Do you have the part? **¿Tiene la pieza?** *tee-EHN-ay lah pee-ay-sah*

I think there's something wrong with_____. **Creo que pasa algo con _____.** *KRAY-oh kay PAH-sah AHL-goh kohn*

■ the electrical system **el sistema eléctrico** *ehl sees-tay-mah eh-LEK-tree-koh*

■ the fan **el ventilador** *ehl ben-tee-lah-DOHR*

■ the fan belt **la correa de ventilador** *lah koh-ray-ah day ben-tee-lah-DOHR*

■ the fuel pump **la bomba de gasolina** *lah bohm-bah day gahs-oh-LEE-nah*

■ the gear shift **el cambio de velocidad** *ehl kahm-bee-oh day beh-lohs-ee-DAHD*

■ the headlight **el faro delantero** *ehl fah-ROH deh-lahn-TEHR-oh*

■ the horn **la bocina** *lah boh-SEEN-ah*

■ the ignition **el encendido** *ehl ehn-sen-DEE-doh*

■ the radio **la radio** *lah RAH-dee-oh*

■ the starter **el arranque** *ehl ah-RAHN-kay*

No U-turn

No passing

Border crossing

Traffic signal ahead

Speed limit

Traffic circle (roundabout) ahead

Minimum speed limit

All traffic turns left

End of no passing zone

One-way street

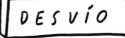

Detour

Danger ahead

Entrance to expressway

Expressway ends

Guarded railroad crossing

Yield

Stop

Right of way

Dangerous intersection
ahead

Gasoline (petrol) ahead

Parking

No vehicles allowed

Dangerous curve

Pedestrian crossing

Oncoming traffic
has right of way

No bicycles allowed

No parking allowed

No entry

No left turn

■ the steering wheel	**el volante**	*ehl boh-LAHN-tay*
■ the tail light	**el faro trasero**	*ehl fah-ROH trah-SEHR-oh*
■ the transmission	**la transmisión**	*lah trahns-mee-SYOHN*
■ the water pump	**la bomba de agua**	*lah BOHM-bah day AH-gwah*
■ the windshield (windscreen) wiper	**el limpiaparabrisas**	*ehl LEEM-pee-ah-pah-rah-BREE-sahs*
■ the brakes	**los frenos**	*lohs FRAY-nohs*
What's the matter?	**¿Qué pasa?**	*kay PAH-sah*
Would it be possible to fix it today?	**¿Sería posible arreglarlo hoy?**	*sehr-EE-ah poh-SEE-blay ah-ray-GLAHR-loh oy*
How long will it take?	**¿Cuánto tiempo tardará?**	*KWAHN-toh tee-EHM-poh tahr-dahr-AH*

GENERAL INFORMATION

TELLING TIME

What time is it?	**¿Qué hora es?**	*kay OH-rah ehs*

When telling time in Spanish, *It is* is expressed by **Es la** for 1:00 and **Son las** for all other numbers.

It's 1:00.	**Es la una.**	*ehs lah OO-nah*
It's 2:00.	**Son las dos.**	*sohn lahs dohs*
It's 3:00, etc.	**Son las tres, etc.**	*sohn lahs trehs*

The number of minutes after the hour is expressed by adding **y** (and) followed by the number of minutes.

It's 4:10.	**Son las cuatro y diez.** *sohn lahs KWAH-troh ee dyehs*
It's 5:20.	**Son las cinco y veinte.** *sohn lahs SEEN-koh ee BAYN-tay.*

A quarter after and half past are expressed by placing **y cuarto** and **y media** after the hour.

It's 6:15.	**Son las seis y cuarto.** *sohn lahs sayss ee KWAHR-toh*
It's 7:30.	**Son las siete y media.** *sohn lahs SYEH-tay ee MEH-dyah*

After passing the half-hour point on the clock, time is expressed in Spanish by *subtracting* the number of minutes from the next hour.

It's 7:35.	**Son las ocho menos veinticinco.** *sohn lahs OH-choh meh-nohs bayn-tee-SEEN-koh*
It's 8:50.	**Son las nueve menos diez.** *sohn lahs NWEH-bay meh-nohs dyehs*
At what time?	**¿A qué hora?** *ah kay OH-rah*
At 1:00.	**A la una.** *ah lah OO-nah*
At 2:00 (3:00, etc.)	**A las dos (tres, etc.)** *ah lahs dohs (trehs)*
A.M.	**de la mañana (in the morning)** *day lah man-YAH-nah*
P.M.	**de la tarde (in the afternoon)** *day lah TAHR-day* **de la noche (at night)** *day lah NOH-chay*
It's noon.	**Es mediodía.** *ehs meh-dee-ohd-EE-ah*
It's midnight.	**Es medianoche.** *ehs MEH-dee-ah-NOH-chay*
It's early (late).	**Es temprano (tarde).** *ehs temp-RAH-noh (TAHR-day)*

Official time is based on the 24-hour clock. You will find train schedules and other such times expressed in terms of a point within a 24-hour sequence.

| The train leaves at 15:30. | **El tren sale a las quince y media.** *ehl trehn SAH-lay ah lahs KEEN-say ee MEH-dee-ah* |
| The time is now 21:15. | **Son las veintiuna y cuarto.** *sohn lahs bayn-tee-OO-nah ee KWAHR-toh* |

DAYS OF THE WEEK

| What day is today? | **¿Qué día es hoy?** *kay DEE-ah ehs oy* |

The days are *not* capitalized in Spanish.

Today is ____.	**Hoy es ____.** *oy ehs*
▨ Monday	**lunes** *LOO-nehs*
▨ Tuesday	**martes** *MAHR-tays*
▨ Wednesday	**miércoles** *MYEHR-kohl-ays*
▨ Thursday	**jueves** *HWEB-ays*
▨ Friday	**viernes** *bee-EHR-nays*
▨ Saturday	**sábado** *SAH-bah-doh*
▨ Sunday	**domingo** *doh-MEEN-goh*
yesterday	**ayer** *ah-YEHR*
the day before yesterday	**anteayer** *ANT-ay-ah-YEHR*
tomorrow	**mañana** *mahn-YAH-nah*
the day after tomorrow	**pasado mañana** *pah-SAH-doh mahn-YAH-nah*
last week	**la semana pasada** *lah seh-MAH-nah pah-SAH-dah*
next week	**la semana próxima** *lah seh-MAH-nah PROHK-see-mah*

tonight	**esta noche**	*EHS-tah noh-chay*
last night	**anoche**	*ahn-OH-chay*

MONTHS OF THE YEAR

The months are *not* capitalized in Spanish.

January	**enero**	*ay-NEHR-oh*
February	**febrero**	*fay-BREH-roh*
March	**marzo**	*MAHR-soh*
April	**abril**	*ah-BREEL*
May	**mayo**	*MAH-yoh*
June	**junio**	*HOO-nee-oh*
July	**julio**	*HOO-lee-oh*
August	**agosto**	*ah-GOHS-toh*
September	**septiembre**	*sep-tee-EHMB-ray*
October	**octubre**	*ohk-TOO-bray*
November	**noviembre**	*noh-bee-EHMB-ray*
December	**diciembre**	*dee-SYEHM-bray*
What's today's date?	**¿Cuál es la fecha de hoy?**	*kwahl ehs lah FAY-chah day oy*

The first of the month is *el primero* (an ordinal number). All other dates are expressed with *cardinal* numbers.

Today is August ____.	**Hoy es ____ de agosto.**	*oy ehs ____ day ah-GOHS-toh*
▪ first	**el primero**	*ehl pree-MEHR-oh*
▪ second	**el dos**	*ehl dohs*
▪ fourth	**el cuatro**	*ehl KWAH-troh*
▪ 25th	**el veinticinco**	*ehl bayn-tee-SEENK-oh*

.

this month	**este mes** *EHS-tay mehs*
last month	**el mes pasado** *ehl mehs pah-SAH-doh*
next month	**el mes próximo** *ehl mehs PROHK-see-moh*
last year	**el año pasado** *ehl AHN-yoh pah-SAH-doh*
next year	**el año que viene** *ehl AHN-yoh kay bee-EN-ay*

THE FOUR SEASONS

spring	**la primavera**	*lah pree-mah-BEHR-ah*
summer	**el verano**	*ehl behr-AH-noh*
fall	**el otoño**	*ehl oh-TOHN-yoh*
winter	**el invierno**	*ehl eem-BYEHR-noh*

THE WEATHER

How is the weather today?	**¿Qué tiempo hace hoy?** *kay tyehm-poh ah-say oy*
It's nice (bad) weather.	**Hace buen (mal) tiempo.** *ah-say bwehn (mahl) tyehm-poh*
It's raining.	**Llueve.** *YWEHB-ay*
It's snowing.	**Nieva.** *NYEHB-ah*
It's ____.	**Hace ____.** *AH-say*
■ hot	**calor** *kah-LOHR*
■ cold	**frío** *FREE-oh*

IMPORTANT SIGNS

Abajo	Down
Abierto	Open
Alto	Stop
Arriba	Up
Ascensor	Elevator
Caballeros	Men's room
Caja	Cashier
Caliente or "C"	Hot
Carretera particular	Private road
Cerrado	Closed
Completo	Filled up
Cuidado	Watch out, caution
Empuje	Push
Entrada	Entrance
Frío or "F"	Cold
Libre	Vacant
No obstruya la entrada	Don't block entrance
No pisar el césped	Keep off the grass
No tocar	Hands off, don't touch
Ocupado	Busy, occupied
¡Pase!	Walk, cross
Peligro	Danger
Prohibido	Forbidden, No ____
____ el paso	No entrance, Keep out
____ escupir	No spitting
____ fumar	No smoking
____ estacionarse	No parking
____ bañarse	No bathing
Reservado	Reserved
Sala de espera	Waiting room
Salida	Exit
Se alquila	For rent
Señoras or Damas	Ladies room
Servicios	Toilets
Se vende	For sale
Tire	Pull
¡Veneno!	Poison!
Venta	Sale

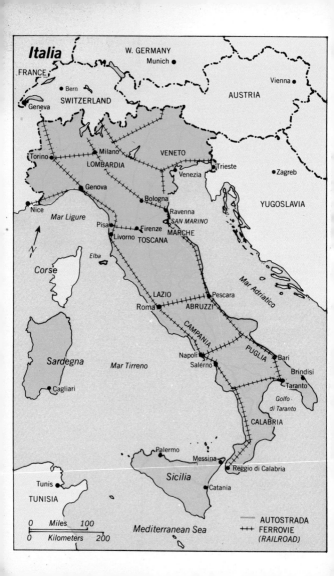